JOURNEY INTO MYSTERY ANNUAL #1

WRITER: STAN LEE
PENCILER: JACK KIRBY
INKER: VINCE COLLETTA
LETTERER: SAM ROSEN

JOURNEY INTO MYSTERY #121

WRITER: STAN LEE
PENCILER: JACK KIRBY
INKER: VINCE COLLETTA
LETTERER: ART SIMEK

JOURNEY INTO MYSTERY #122

WRITER: STAN LEE
PENCILER: JACK KIRBY
INKER: VINCE COLLETTA
LETTERER: ART SIMEK

JOURNEY INTO MYSTERY #123

WRITER: STAN LEE
PENCILER: JACK KIRBY
INKER: VINCE COLLETTA
LETTERER: ART SIMEK

JOURNEY INTO MYSTERY #124

WRITER: STAN LEE
PENCILER: JACK KIRBY
INKER: VINCE COLLETTA
LETTERER: ART SIMEK

JOURNEY INTO MYSTERY #125

WRITER: STAN LEE
PENCILER: JACK KIRBY
INKER: VINCE COLLETTA
LETTERER: ART SIMEK

THE MIGHTY THOR #126

WRITER: STAN LEE
PENCILER: JACK KIRBY
INKER: VINCE COLLETTA
LETTERER: ART SIMEK

THE MIGHTY THOR #127

WRITER: STAN LEE
PENCILER: JACK KIRBY
INKER: VINCE COLLETTA
LETTERERS: SAM ROSEN & ART SIMEK

THE MIGHTY THOR #128

WRITER: STAN LEE
PENCILER: JACK KIRBY
INKER: VINCE COLLETTA
LETTERERS: ART SIMEK & SAM ROSEN

THE MIGHTY THOR #129

WRITER: STAN LEE
PENCILER: JACK KIRBY
INKER: VINCE COLLETTA
LETTERER: ART SIMEK

THE MIGHTY THOR #130

WRITER: STAN LEE
PENCILER: JACK KIRBY
INKER: VINCE COLLETTA
LETTERERS: ART SIMEK & SAM ROSEN

THE MIGHTY THOR #131

WRITER: STAN LEE
PENCILER: JACK KIRBY
INKER: VINCE COLLETTA
LETTERER: ART SIMEK

THE MIGHTY THOR #132

WRITER: STAN LEE
PENCILER: JACK KIRBY
INKER: VINCE COLLETTA
LETTERER: SAM ROSEN

THE MIGHTY THOR #2

KING-SIZE *SPECIAL!*
WRITER: STAN LEE
PENCILER: JACK KIRBY
INKER: VINCE COLLETTA
LETTERER: SAM ROSEN

THE MIGHTY THOR #133

WRITER: **STAN LEE**
PENCILER: **JACK KIRBY**
INKER: **VINCE COLLETTA**
LETTERERS: **ART SIMEK & SAM ROSEN**

THE MIGHTY THOR #134

WRITER: **STAN LEE**
CO-PLOT & PENCILER: **JACK KIRBY**
INKER: **VINCE COLLETTA**
LETTERERS: **SAM ROSEN & ART SIMEK**

THE MIGHTY THOR #135

WRITER: **STAN LEE**
CO-PLOT & PENCILER: **JACK KIRBY**
INKER: **VINCE COLLETTA**
LETTERERS: **ART SIMEK & SAM ROSEN**

THE MIGHTY THOR #136

WRITER: **STAN LEE**
CO-PLOT & PENCILER: **JACK KIRBY**
INKER: VINCE **COLLETTA**
LETTERERS: **ART SIMEK & SAM ROSEN**

REPRINT CREDITS

MARVEL ESSENTIAL DESIGN:
JOHN "JG" ROSHELL OF COMICRAFT
COVER ART:
JACK KIRBY
COVER COLORS:
CHRIS SOTOMAYOR
COLLECTION EDITOR:
MARK D. BEAZLEY
ASSISTANT EDITOR:
JENNIFER GRÜNWALD
SENIOR EDITOR, SPECIAL PROJECTS:
JEFF YOUNGQUIST
DIRECTOR OF SALES:
DAVID GABRIEL
PRODUCTION:
JERRON QUALITY COLOR
BOOK DESIGNER:
TERNARD SOLOMON
CREATIVE DIRECTOR:
TOM MARVELLI
EDITOR IN CHIEF:
JOE QUESADA
PUBLISHER:
DAN BUCKLEY
SPECIAL THANKS TO
RALPH MACCHIO & POND SCUM

JOURNEY INTO MYSTERY
WITH
THE MIGHTY
THOR
APPROVED BY THE COMICS CODE AUTHORITY
MARVEL COMICS GROUP 12¢
113
FEB
MIGHTIER THAN EVER!
AT LAST! THE THUNDER GOD REVEALS HIS TRUE IDENTITY TO JANE
BUT WAIT'LL YOU SEE WHAT HAPPENS WHEN HE DOES!!!

"A WORLD GONE MAD!"
STARRING: THE MIGHTY THOR
WHEN IMPERIOUS ODIN COMMANDS, THOR MUST OBEY! THUS, WE FIND HIM ABOARD A GIANT ASGARD SKY SHIP, LENDING HIS OWN AWESOME MIGHT TO THE BATTLE AGAINST THE DEMON MEN OF JOTUNHEIM! (THIS DOESN'T HAVE TOO MUCH TO DO WITH THE MAIN PART OF OUR STORY, BUT YOU'VE GOT TO ADMIT IT MAKES A SPECTACULAR BEGINNING!)
A TALE TOLD WITH GUSTO BY: STAN LEE
A DRAMA DRAWN WITH GRANDEUR BY: JACK KIRBY
AN IDYLL INKED WITH GALLANTRY BY: CHIC STONE
A LEGEND LETTERED WITH GLEE BY: ARTIE SIMEK
1

WE PROMISED OL' JACK KIRBY THAT WE'D LET HIM GET A FEW OF THESE EYE-OPENING BATTLE SCENES OUT OF HIS SYSTEM, SO HERE THEY ARE! GO AHEAD, ENJOY THEM -- THERE'S NO EXTRA CHARGE!

FEW SIGHTS ON ASGARD OR EARTH CAN BE AS IMPRESSIVE AS THIS BREATH-TAKING CLOSE-UP OF OMNIPOTENT ODIN AND HIS THUNDER-GOD SON FIGHTING SIDE BY SIDE AGAINST A COMMON FOE!

AND NOW, ON TO THE NEXT PAGE, WHERE OUR TALE REALLY BEGINS...

WITH THE BATTLE WON, AND MOPPING-UP OPERATIONS IN EFFECT, THE VICTORIOUS ODIN TURNS TO SPEAK TO HIS SON--TO THE WARRIOR WHO IS THE APPLE OF HIS EYE...
YOU HAVE ACQUITTED YOURSELF WITH HONOR, MY SON! AND, OF ALL THE VIRTUES, HONOR MOST BEFITS THE GOD OF THUNDER!
I THANK THEE, FATHER! BUT, BEING SON OF THINE, I COULD DO NO LESS!
YOU HAVE SPENT MANY LONG MONTHS ON THE PLANET EARTH, VALOROUS ONE! AND NOW, IT IS ODIN'S WISH THAT YOU RETURN TO ASGARD, TO TAKE UP YOUR PRINCELY DUTIES!
NAY, FATHER--I CANNOT! THERE IS MUCH THAT REMAINS TO BE DONE ON THE PLANET OF MORTALS! MY MISSION IS NOT YET FINISHED!
AGAIN YOU DEFY THE WISHES OF ODIN! BUT, I SEE BEHIND YOUR ARROGANT WORDS--IT IS THE GIRL CALLED JANE WHOM YOU DO NOT WISH TO LEAVE!
I CANNOT DENY THAT SHE HAS WON MY HEART, NOBLE FATHER! SO, UNLESS YOU GIVE ME A DIRECT ORDER TO REMAIN HERE--!
NO! I SHALL NOT HUMBLE MYSELF TO KEEP YOU HERE! RETURN TO EARTH! TURN YOUR BACK ON THE CROWN OF ASGARD! I SAY NO MORE! GO!
IN TRUTH, MY SOUL IS SAD! BUT, NEITHER MAN NOR GODLING CAN DO LESS THAN FOLLOW THE URGING OF HIS HEART!
YET, MAYHAP I AM NOT FIT FOR GODHOOD! PERHAPS THE MORE HONORABLE COURSE WOULD BE TO RENOUNCE MY HERITAGE--AND TO BECOME A MORTAL SO THAT I MAY MARRY THE ONE I TRULY LOVE!
3

SO BE IT! MY DECISION IS MADE! EVEN AN IMMORTAL CAN RENOUNCE HIS DESTINY IN THE NAME OF LOVE!

I MUST FIND JANE FOSTER AND TELL HER EVERYTHING! IF SHE IS TO SHARE MY LIFE, THEN SHE MUST HAVE THE RIGHT TO SHARE MY SECRETS!

AND, NEVER HAS A MAN CARRIED SUCH AN AWE-SOME SECRET LOCKED WITHIN HIS BREAST!

MOMENTS LATER...
DR. BLAKE! DON-- I I THOUGHT YOU WERE STILL AT THAT MEDICAL SEMINAR IN CHICAGO!
I DECIDED TO RETURN EARLY, JANE!

IT'S WONDERFUL TO HAVE YOU BACK! I'VE MISSED YOU SO! I'LL TELL YOU ABOUT YOUR PATIENTS AND--
NO! I HAVE SOMETHING TO TELL YOU! SOMETHING THAT CAN WAIT NO LONGER! YOU MUST PREPARE YOURSELF FOR A SHOCK, MY DEAR! DO NOT INTERRUPT UNTIL I HAVE FINISHED!

WHA-WHAT IS IT, DON! I'VE NEVER SEEN YOU LOOK THAT WAY BEFORE-- SO GRIM-- SO DEADLY SERIOUS! IT ALMOST FRIGHTENS ME!
YOU MUST NOT BE FRIGHTENED, MY DARLING! NO MATTER WHAT I SAY...
JUST LISTEN --AND TRY TO UNDERSTAND!

THOUGH YOU KNOW ME AS DR. DON BLAKE, I HAVE ANOTHER IDENTITY AS WELL! ONE WHICH NO OTHER EARTHLY MORTAL WOULD EVER SUSPECT! BUT NOW, MY BELOVED, I MUST TELL YOU--
--I AM THOR, SON OF ODIN, GOD OF THUNDER!

SO STARTLED IS JANE FOSTER THAT IT IS BEYOND OUR POOR MORTAL POWERS TO ADEQUATELY DESCRIBE HER SHOCK! INSTEAD, WE SHALL TEMPORARILY CHANGE OUR SCENE AND VISIT THE ARIFACTS SECTION OF A NEARBY MUSEUM...
THIS STONE STATUE YOU FOUND MUST HAVE BEEN LAYING IN THAT RIVER FOR MONTHS! BUT I'M FINALLY GETTING ALL THE MUD OFF!
IT COULD BE ONE OF THE GREAT DISCOVERIES OF OUR AGE! I'VE NEVER SEEN ANYTHING LIKE IT! BUT HOW DID IT GET TO THE BOTTOM OF THE HUDSON RIVER?
PERHAPS IT WAS CREATED BY A TRIBE OLDER THAN TIME-- WHEN THE RIVER WAS NO MORE THAN A DRY, ARRID PLAIN! DOCTOR! AM I SEEING THINGS! I COULD HAVE SWORN I SAW ITS SHOULDER TWITCH!
IMPOSSIBLE! YOU MUST HAVE IMAGIN-- LOOK! HE IS MOVING! THE STONE IS ALIVE!
NOW I KNOW WHAT IT IS! DON'T YOU REMEMBER, MONTHS AGO...?!!
OF COURSE! THE STRANGE CREATURE CALLED THE GREY GARGOYLE!* HIS VERY TOUCH COULD TURN MEN TO-- MFFFF--!
TO STONE, GENTLEMEN! JUST AS I HAVE TURNED THE TWO OF YOU! WHAT A PITY THE SPELL ONLY LASTS A MERE SIXTY MINUTES!
* YOU MET HIM IN THOR #107, REMEMBER?--STAN.
THEY DESERVE BEING STONE MEN FOR AN HOUR -- THE FOOLS! IF THEY HAD NOT DUG ME UP, I WOULD HAVE REMAINED UNDERNEATH THE RIVER, WHERE THOR DEFEATED ME, FOREVER!
BUT NOW, THE GREY GARGOYLE IS FREE AGAIN! NOW I'M WISER, STRONGER THAN EVER!
SO, ONCE AGAIN I SHALL BATTLE THE THUNDER GOD, UNTIL I TOO POSSESS THE SECRET OF HIS IMMORTALITY!
5

AH, MY ROOM IS EXACTLY AS I HAD LEFT IT! HOW FORTUNATE THAT I PAID MY RENT FOR ONE YEAR IN ADVANCE!
AND NOW, AS THE FANTASTICALLY POWERFUL -- THE SUPREMELY SINISTER GREY GARGOYLE SITS AND PONDERS HIS NEXT MOVE, THIS IS AS GOOD A TIME AS ANY TO REFRESH YOUR MEMORY ABOUT HIS STRANGE ORIGIN...
IT SEEMS LIKE ONLY YESTERDAY THAT IT ALL HAPPENED -- WHEN I WAS ONLY AN UNKNOWN YOUNG CHEMIST IN PARIS...
HOW MUCH LONGER MUST I TAKE ORDERS LIKE A MERE LACKEY? PAUL DUVAL IS MEANT FOR GREATER THINGS!
HMMM, SOMETHING IS WRONG! THE MIXTURE HAS TURNED BLUE INSTEAD OF RED! I MUST HAVE MADE A CARELESS MISTAKE!
I SPILLED SOME ON MY HAND!
IT'S INCREDIBLE! IT FEELS LIKE LIQUID FIRE! IT SEEMS TO HAVE A LIFE OF ITS OWN!
WHAT HAVE I DONE? WHAT'S HAPPENING TO MY HAND??
MY FINGERS -- THEY TURNED TO STONE! IT'S THE STRANGE SUBSTANCE IN THE MIXTURE -- IT GAVE THE LIQUID AN UNBELIEVABLE POWER! BUT -- WHAT WILL HAPPEN TO ME??
OH NO! NO! I TOUCHED MY HAND TO MY FACE, AND NOW--
MY FACE HAS TURNED TO STONE! EVERYTHING I TOUCH BECOMES LIVING STONE! IT -- IT IS MADNESS!
BUT, I SOON LEARNED IT WAS NOT MADNESS! IT WAS A GIFT -- A WONDERFUL, AWESOME GIFT! I COULD ACCOMPLISH ALMOST ANYTHING WITH MY GREAT POWER!
THUS, I SEARCHED FOR THOR -- TO LEARN HIS SECRET OF IMMORTALITY -- FOR THAT IS THE ONLY THING I STILL NEED! ONCE I AM IMMORTAL, THE WORLD WILL BELONG TO THE GREY GARGOYLE!
AND NOW, BEFORE RETURNING TO DON BLAKE, LET US AGAIN VISIT ASGARD, WHERE ODIN IS IN A VIOLENT MOOD SUCH AS ONLY HE CAN ATTAIN!
GO BACK, LOKI! IT IS WORTH YOUR LIFE TO FACE ODIN WHILE HIS FURY RAGES!
YOU CALL THYSELF A CHEF?? OUT OF MY SIGHT, KNAVE! THY FOOD IS BUT FIT FOR SWINE!

SO! THERE IS THE REASON FOR ODIN'S RAGE! I THOUGHT AS MUCH!
MY OWN SON! MY FAVORED ONE! MY RIGHTFUL HEIR! GIVING UP HIS BIRTHRIGHT FOR A MERE MORTAL FEMALE!

AND I AM POWERLESS TO STOP HIM--FOR, NOT EVEN ODIN MAY INTERFERE IN MATTERS INVOLVING THE HEART OF ANOTHER!
IT IS UNTHINKABLE! UNFORGIVABLE! WOULD THAT THE LIFE HAD LEFT MY LIMBS ERE I HAD WITNESSED SO PERNICIOUS A SCENE!
BEGONE, LOKI! I HAVE NO PATIENCE FOR YOU THIS BLACK DAY!

FORGIVE ME, SIRE! I MERELY WISHED TO OFFER MY REGRETS--AND TO TELL YOU THAT I STAND WITH ODIN IN THIS MOMENT OF SHAMEFUL BETRAYAL!
I NOTE AND COMMEND YOUR LOYALTY, MY SECOND SON! THOUGH THOR HAS EVER BEEN MY FAVORED ONE, MAYHAP MY JUDGEMENT WAS FALSE! I SHALL NOT FORGET YOUR PLEDGE, OH, GODLING WHO WALKS ALONE!

AS FOR THE ONE WHO HAS FORSAKEN ME, I WASH MY HANDS OF HIM! FROM THIS MOMENT HENCE, HIS POWER IS GONE! IF HE WOULD REMAIN A MORTAL, THEN SO BE IT! THERE IS NO THUNDER GOD!
THUS, THE ULTIMATE VICTOR IS LOKI--AS I ALWAYS KNEW I WOULD BE!

AND NOW, WE RETURN TO DR. BLAKE...
YOU DON'T BELIEVE ME! I CAN SEE IT IN YOUR EYES! BUT, YOU MUST!
DOCTOR, YOU'VE BEEN WORKING SO HARD! PERHAPS, IF YOU WENT HOME TO BED...
WAIT! WATCH ME! I'LL PROVE THAT I'M THE GOD OF THUNDER!

SEE? ALL I NEED DO IS STAMP MY CANE UPON THE FLOOR, AND-- WHA--? WHAT'S WRONG?
OH, DON, MY DARLING! YOU DON'T HAVE TO TRY TO GLAMORIZE YOURSELF FOR ME! I LOVE YOU JUST AS YOU ARE! I DON'T CARE WHO THOR REALLY IS!
7

IT WAS AT THE OFFICE OF DR. BLAKE THAT I FIRST ENCOUNTERED THOR! I'LL FORCE THE LAME PHYSICIAN TO TELL ME WHERE TO FIND MY ENEMY NOW!
ONLY ODIN HAS THE POWER TO NULLIFY THE ENCHANTMENT OF MY CANE! IT MUST BE HIS DOING!
PLEASE, DON-- YOU MUST RID YOURSELF OF THAT OBSESSION!

BUT, BEFORE ANOTHER WORD CAN BE UTTERED...
CRASH
THE GREY GARGOYLE! HE'S COME BACK!

RUN, JANE! RACE TO SAFETY, MY DARLING! I'LL TRY TO HOLD HIM OFF!
NO! I WON'T LEAVE YOU! I CAN'T LEAVE YOU!
YOU ARE IN NO DANGER --UNLESS YOU REFUSE TO TELL ME WHERE I CAN FIND THOR!

JANE! YOU MUST OBEY ME! RUN TO THE ELEVATOR -- FIND A POLICEMAN! TELL HIM TO SUMMON THE AVENGERS! IT'S OUR ONLY HOPE! I'LL DELAY THE GARGOYLE!

YOU ARE AS BRAINLESS AS YOU ARE FEEBLE, BLAKE! YOU THINK A THROWN BOOK CAN HOLD BACK THE GREY GARGOYLE ??!
SEE HOW IT TURNS TO SOLID STONE, AT THE MERE TOUCH OF MY ROCK-HARD FINGERS!

THUS, IN MY HANDS, IT BECOMES AS DEADLY AS A ROCKET-POWERED PROJECTILE!
THE ELEVATOR IS HERE, DON! HURRY, MY DARLING! BEFORE HE TOUCHES YOU!
HE WON'T! NOT WHILE HE THINKS I'M HIS ONLY LINK TO THOR!
8

AND, THE LAME PHYSICIAN HAS INDEED GUESSED RIGHT! THE GREY GARGOYLE STILL HESITATES, FEARING TO STILL THE TONGUE OF THE ONE HUMAN WHO MIGHT KNOW THOR'S WHEREABOUTS! AND SO...
COME BACK! MY PATIENCE WILL NOT LAST FOREVER!
WE MADE IT! NOW, IF ONLY THE DOORS WILL CLOSE IN TIME!
AND CLOSE THEY DO! BUT, THE ROCK-HARD POWER OF THE GREY GARGOYLE CANNOT BE STOPPED BY MERE METAL DOORS...
I WARN YOU, DO YOU HEAR?? I'LL TURN YOU BOTH TO STONE BEFORE I LET YOU ESCAPE ME!
WHOOOM
BY MERELY TOUCHING THE ELEVATOR CABLES, I MAKE THEM HARD ENOUGH TO SUPPORT MY OWN PONDEROUS WEIGHT!
THERE IS NO PLACE THEY CAN FLEE WHERE I CANNOT FOLLOW!
DON, DO YOU THINK ...?
NO TIME FOR TALK, JANE! KEEP RUNNING!
HE'S SLIDING DOWN THE CABLES AFTER US! WE'RE NOT SAFE YET! WE'VE GOT TO SEPARATE!
NO! I WON'T LEAVE YOU! I'LL NEVER LEAVE YOU!
WHUMP!
A SECOND LATER, A HEAVY FORM LANDS ATOP THE DESERTED ELEVATOR --AS THE SILENT CAR INSTANTLY TURNS INTO-- STONE!
WHILE, BACK IN ASGARD, AN UNUSUAL MEETING OF THOR'S FAITHFUL FRIENDS IS TAKING PLACE...
WE ALL KNOW THAT WITHOUT HIS POWER, THE THUNDER GOD WILL BE FAIR PREY FOR ANY FOE WHO ATTACKS HIM!
IT IS INTOLERABLE! WE MUST GO TO THE AID OF OUR FELLOW IMMORTAL!
ODIN HAS NOT YET FORBAD OUR INTERFERENCE! SO, LET US ACT WHILE WE MAY! ONE OF US SHALL RACE TO EARTH!
9

THOUGH MANY VOLUNTEER, IT IS BALDER, THE BRAVE, WHO IS CHOSEN! BUT, AS THE VALIANT GODLING SPURS HIS MIGHTY STEED...
WITH TRIUMPH ALMOST IN MY GRASP, I SHALL PERMIT NONE TO AID MY ARCH-ENEMY, THE ACCURSED THOR!

THUS DOES SINISTER LOKI, MASTER OF A MULTITUDE OF EVIL SPELLS, MANAGE TO FORESTALL THE COMING OF BALDER...
WHAT OMINOUS QUIRK OF FATE IS THIS? THE SLEEPING SICKNESS HAS STRICKEN MY MOUNT!
I MUST REMAIN AT HIS SIDE, UNTIL THE DREAD SEIZURE HAS PASSED!

THEN, LEARNING WHAT HAS BEFALLEN BALDER, OTHERS PREPARE TO RIDE IN HIS PLACE... UNTIL--
WHERE ARE YOU GOING, WARRIORS?
IT IS OF NO CONCERN TO YOU, LOKI!

YOU ARE WRONG! I HAVE BATTLE ORDERS FOR YOU!
YOU ARE HEREBY DISPATCHED TO PATROL THE EASTERN SECTOR OF OUR REALM UNTIL FURTHER NOTICE!
YOU HAVE NOT THE AUTHORITY, CRAFTY ONE!

NO, BUT ODIN DOES! AND YOU MUST NEVER FORGET, WITH THOR IN DISFAVOR, IT IS LOKI WHO NOW SPEAKS FOR OUR MONARCH!
SO, YOU WILL OBEY MY EVERY COMMAND! AND YOU WILL GIVE UP YOUR USELESS PLAN TO ASSIST THE ONE WHO IS THUNDER GOD NO MORE!
SO BE IT, LOKI!

BUT, WHILE LOKI SMIRKS WITH GLEEFUL SELF-SATISFACTION, ANOTHER IMMORTAL RIDER SECRETLY CROSSES THE LEGENDARY RAINBOW BRIDGE, ON A DRAMATIC MISSION TO THE PLANET EARTH...

THE PLANET EARTH, WHERE--AT THIS VERY INSTANT, WE FIND--
IT'S THE GREY GARGOYLE! HE'S BACK AGAIN!
HAH! YOU HAD FORGOTTEN THAT MY STONE WINGS GIVE ME THE POWER OF LIMITED FLIGHT! YOU CAN NEVER ESCAPE ME!

CALLOUSLY DISREGARDING THOSE HE PASSES, THE SLIGHTEST TOUCH OF THE SINISTER STONE MAN CAUSES HIS UNWITTING VICTIMS TO ASSUME A FORM LIKE HIS--A FORM WHICH WILL BE THEIRS FOR EXACTLY ONE HOUR!
HE'S TURNING EVERYONE HE TOUCHES TO STONE!
HAH! THEY'VE TRAPPED THEMSELVES IN A BLIND ALLEY!

THIS IS YOUR FINAL CHANCE! TELL ME WHERE I MAY FIND THOR--OR YOU'LL NEVER TELL ANYTHING AGAIN!
DO WHAT YOU WILL WITH ME--BUT LET THE GIRL GO!
OH, DON--MY DARLING! IF ONLY YOU REALLY WERE THOR! NONE BUT HE CAN SAVE US NOW!

SO! STILL YOU TRY TO THWART ME! STILL YOU REFUSE TO TELL WHAT I MUST KNOW! FOR THAT, I SHALL GIVE YOU MY SPECIAL TOUCH--AND YOU WILL REMAIN STONE FOREVERMORE!

BUT, SUDDENLY...
TWANNG!

THAT SUDDEN EXPLOSION OF LIGHT! I'M BLINDED! I CANNOT SEE!
11

AND THEN, BY THE TIME THE GARGOYLE'S VISION HAS RETURNED...
THEY'RE GONE! THEY'VE MANAGED TO ESCAPE ME!
BUT HOW?? WHAT CAUSED THAT BLINDING, UNEARTHLY LIGHT? I'VE GOT TO FIND OUT! I'VE GOT TO CATCH THEM AGAIN!

HEARING THE SUDDEN SOUND OF A MOTOR BEING FRANTICALLY STARTED, THE GREY GARGOYLE SPINS AROUND THE CORNER, TO FIND...
HURRY, DON! HE'S AFTER US AGAIN!
DON'T LOSE YOUR NERVE, JANE! WE'LL BEAT HIM SOMEHOW! WE'VE GOT TO!

EVEN IF THEY TOLD ME WHERE TO FIND THOR, I'D STILL DESTROY THEM! IT'S BECOME A MATTER OF PRIDE NOW! I CAN'T LET TWO MERE, PUNY WEAKLINGS CONTINUE TO FRUSTRATE THE GREY GARGOYLE!

I'VE DONE IT! I'M LANDING RIGHT IN FRONT OF THEM! NOTHING CAN SAVE THEM NOW!

THERE! YOUR CAR WILL REMAIN A STONE MASS FOR EXACTLY ONE HOUR!
BUT, ONCE I HAVE CAPTURED YOU, YOUR FATE WILL BE FAR DIFFERENT! I SHALL TURN YOU TO STONE PERMANENTLY! THUS WILL YOU BE REWARDED FOR DARING TO DEFY THE WILL OF THE GREY GARGOYLE!
HE'S MAD, DON! WE'RE BEING MENACED BY A MADMAN!
TRUE, MY DARLING!! BUT HE STILL HAS THE POWER TO CARRY OUT HIS THREAT! I MUSTN'T LET YOU BE HARMED--NO MATTER WHAT!
12

BUT ALAS, THE LAME PHYSICIAN'S LIMBS ARE NOT THE EQUAL OF HIS FIGHTING HEART! IN HIS DESPERATE EFFORT TO BRING HIS LOVED ONE TO SAFETY, HIS WEAKER LEG BUCKLES UNDER HIM, AND...
NOW I'VE GOT YOU!

AT THAT SECOND, A STEEL-SINEWED ARM REACHES OUT, TOUCHING THE FRANTIC DOCTOR WITH A CALM, STEADY SURGE OF ENERGY!
THOR SHALL LIVE AGAIN! YOU HAVE THIRTY SECONDS! MAKE EACH ONE COUNT!

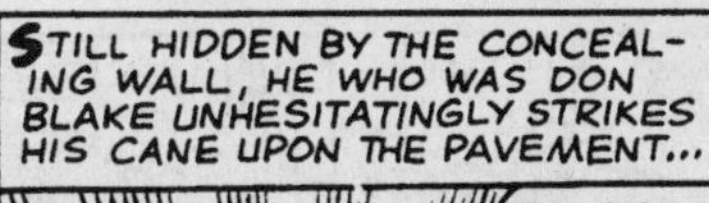
STILL HIDDEN BY THE CONCEALING WALL, HE WHO WAS DON BLAKE UNHESITATINGLY STRIKES HIS CANE UPON THE PAVEMENT...

IF ONLY IT'S NOT TOO LATE!

...AND HE WHO IS GOD OF THUNDER APPEARS ONCE MORE...!

GARGOYLE!! YOU HAVE BEEN SEARCHING FOR THOR--

KKRAKK!
NOW, YOU HAVE FOUND HIM!

ONE MERE HAMMER THRUST CANNOT INJURE MY ROCK-HARD BODY! I DON'T KNOW WHERE YOU CAME FROM, THUNDER GOD, BUT YOU WON'T LEAVE UNTIL I'VE CONQUERED YOU!
WE SHALL SEE WHO IS THE CONQUEROR, AND WHO IS TO BE THE VANQUISHED!

TELL ME-- TELL ME YOUR SECRET OF IMMORTALITY, BEFORE I TURN YOU TO STONE FOREVER!
RRUMM!
THAT IS ONE SECRET YOU CAN NEVER POSSESS --FOR IT IS THE HERITAGE OF BIRTH YOU SEEK!

I MUST LEARN HOW TO BE IMMORTAL! POWER SUCH AS MINE MUST NEVER DIE! NEVER!
MY TIME IS RUNNING OUT! ONLY SCANT SECONDS REMAIN FOR ME TO DEFEAT THAT RAMPAGING MENACE!

TWELVE SECONDS LEFT! CAN I DO IT??
SKAKK!
YOU CAN'T ESCAPE ME NOW!

THE GOD OF THUNDER SEEKS NO SIMPLE ESCAPE! INSTEAD, I SHALL TAP THE MAIN POWER SOURCE OF THIS TRAFFIC LIGHT WITH MY URU HAMMER...

--SENDING A BOLT OF PURE ELECTRICAL POWER, REINFORCED BY THE URU ENERGY OF MY MALLET, INTO YOUR OWN VULNERABLE BODY!
14

I-I CANNOT MOVE MY HANDS OR FEET! WHAT HAVE YOU DONE TO ME?
NO MORE THAN YOU WOULD HAVE DONE TO OTHERS! I HAVE FUSED YOUR STONE MOLECULES SO THEY CANNOT FUNCTION!

THUS WILL HE REMAIN, UNTIL I RETURN! AND NOW, I MUST FIND MY UNKNOWN BENEFACTOR!
BUT, WHY DO MY LIMBS FEEL SO WEAK--? WHY DOES MY HEAD BEGIN TO SPIN....??

I-I HAD FORGOTTEN! MY THIRTY SECONDS HAVE ELAPSED! I CAN REMAIN THOR NO LONGER!

AND, AS THE MIGHTY THUNDER GOD SLUMPS WEARILY TO THE GROUND, A STRANGE, UNNOTICED CLOUD-LIKE FORM SILENTLY RISES FROM THE ALLEY AND SOARS UP INTO THE ENDLESS SKY....!

...UNTIL IT REACHES THE MUCH-VAUNTED REALM OF DISTANT ASGARD, WHERE IT CHANGES INTO ITS NATURAL FORM...
HOW WENT YOUR MISSION? WHERE DO YOU RIDE NOW?
IT WENT WELL! AND NOW I SEEK NOBLE ODIN!

MY LIEGE, HONIR THE HUNTER CRAVES AUDIENCE WITH THEE!
LET HIM ENTER!
I HAVE RETURNED FROM EARTH, MY LORD!

AND SO, ALL COMES BACK TO NORMAL IN A WORLD WHICH SEEMED TO HAVE GONE MAD! TRANQUILITY RETURNS TO ASGARD, AND ONCE AGAIN THE POWER OF THE THUNDER GOD IS LODGED WHERE IT RIGHTLY BELONGS-- WHERE IT MUST EVER REMAIN!

Tales of ASGARD
HOME OF THE MIGHTY NORSE GODS!
ANOTHER MILESTONE IN OUR GREAT BIOGRAPHIES-IN-DEPTH SERIES
"THE BOYHOOD OF LOKI!"
THROUGHOUT THE AGES, THE IMMORTALS OF ASGARD HAVE THRILLED TO ATHLETIC CONTESTS, EVEN AS MORTALS DO TODAY! LET US GO BACK TO THE PAST, WHERE WE FIND TEN-YEAR OLD THOR, AND HIS HALF-BROTHER, LOKI, WATCHING THE TOURNEY!
IS IT NOT EXCITING, LOKI? WHOSOEVER HOOKS THE QUARTERSTAFF FROM THE OTHER WINS THE TOURNAMENT!
NO! IT IS TOO TAME FOR ME, THOR!
A STAN LEE AND JACK KIRBY FABULOUS FEATURETTE!
INKED BY: VINCE COLLETTA
LETTERED BY: ARTIE SIMEK

SEE HOW VERY SKILLFUL ULLER IS! HE IS SURE TO DEFEAT THE MORE CLUMSY VOLSAK!
YOU SEEM TO THINK YOU KNOW EVERY-THING, THOR! I'LL WAGER A GLODEN GLOBULE THAT VOLSAK WILL BE THE VICTOR!

THOR IS RIGHT! ULLER IS THE MORE SKILLFUL!
BUT, I CAN'T BEAR THE WAY THOR IS SO SELDOM WRONG!
A WORTHY BLOW, ULLER! MY FATHER, NOBLE ODIN, HAS INDEED TRAINED YOU WELL!

SEE, LOKI! ULLER IS BUT SECONDS AWAY FROM VICTORY!
AGAIN THOR HAS BEEN PROVEN RIGHT--WHILE LOKI IS WRONG! BUT THERE IS STILL TIME FOR ME TO SAVE THE DAY-- IF I MOVE QUICKLY!

ONE SIMPLE SPELL, TAUGHT TO ME BUT A FEW DAYS AGO BY THE NORN WITCH WOMEN MIGHT CHANGE THE TIDE OF BATTLE!
HOW I LONG FOR THE DAY WHEN I, TOO, SHALL HAVE THE RIGHT TO BRANDISH A WAR CLUB DURING SUCH A JOUST!
2

SUDDENLY...

I DO NOT UNDERSTAND! MY QUARTER-STAFF SIMPLY FELL APART!
IT COULD ONLY HAVE BEEN THE WORK OF A SPELL! AND I SEE THE CULPRITS NOW!
IT MATTERS NOT! VOLSAK IS THE WINNER!

QUICK, THOR! WE MUST FLEE, BEFORE THEY SEIZE US!
NEVER! THE SON OF ODIN RUNS FROM NO ONE!
IT'S THOR-- AND LOKI!
GET THEM!

YOU KNOW THE RULES ABOUT INTERFERING WITH A TOURNAMENT, LOKI!
WHY DO YOU SPEAK ONLY TO MY BROTHER?
WE KNOW THAT YOU WOULD NOT HAVE DONE SO BASE A DEED, YOUNG THOR!

BUT, I WAS AT THE SIDE OF LOKI! IF THERE IS ANY PUNISHMENT TO BE METED OUT, I MUST SHARE IT WITH HIM!

YOU ARE TRULY THE SON OF ODIN! YOUR SOUL IS AS NOBLE AS THE NAME YOU BEAR!
BECAUSE OF YOUR GALLANTRY, YOUNG PRINCE, THERE SHALL BE NO PUNISHMENT! THE INCIDENT IS OVER!

HOW THEY BOW AND SCRAPE BEFORE HIM --GIVING HIM THE DUE THAT SHOULD BE MINE! I CANNOT BEAR THE SIGHT!
ON BEHALF OF LOKI AND MYSELF, I CRAVE YOUR FORGIVENESS, NOBLE LORDS!
GRANTED, YOUNG NOBLEMAN! YOU AND LOKI ARE FREE TO DEPART!

MARK YE WELL MY WORDS! NO GOOD WILL COME OF THE UN-SCRUPULOUS LOKI!
THOUGH HE BE NOT YET FULL-GROWN, THE SEED OF EVIL HAS ALREADY TAKEN ROOT!
BUT, SEE HOW LIKE A KING THE GOLDEN ONE WALKS! BY ASGARD, HE IS DESTINED FOR GREATNESS!!
4

AND SO IT BEGINS--THE DARK, ETERNAL HATRED WHICH *LOKI* FEELS FOR HIS HALF-BROTHER, *THOR!* A HATRED WHICH HAS LIVED THRU THE AGES--AND WHICH CAN NEVER BE DIMMED SO LONG AS THE THUNDER GOD LIVES! ANOTHER CHAPTER IN THIS WIDELY-HERALDED SERIES WILL APPEAR NEXT ISSUE--BUT WE WON'T ENJOY IT UNLESS YOU SHARE IT WITH US!

JOURNEY INTO MYSTERY
WITH
THE MIGHTY
THOR
APPROVED BY THE COMICS CODE AUTHORITY
IND.
MARVEL COMICS GROUP 12¢
THE START OF ANOTHER UNFORGETTABLE SUPER-EPIC!
114 MAR
FOR THE FIRST TIME IN RECORDED HISTORY, THE TITANIC THUNDER GOD BATTLES A DEADLY FOE WHO HAS EVERY BIT OF RAW STRENGTH, EVERY SINGLE SUPER-POWER WHICH THOR HIM-SELF POSSESSES! YOU'LL NEVER FORGET THIS STARTLING SHOCKER!
"THE STRONGER I AM, THE SOONER I DIE!"
THE M.M.M.S. WANTS YOU!

The MIGHTY THOR
"THE STRONGER I AM, THE SOONER I DIE!"
ESCAPE FROM THOR IS INCONCEIVABLE! SURRENDER NOW AND SPARE YOURSELF POSSIBLE INJURY!
Introducing: The ABSORBING MAN, WHOSE SUPER-POWER IS POSSIBLY THE MOST UNBEATABLE OF ANY LIVING MORTAL'S
I KNOW YOU HAVE SWORN NEVER TO TAKE A HUMAN LIFE! I'VE NOTHING TO FEAR! I'LL BEAT YOU YET!
WRITTEN AT WHITE HEAT BY: STAN LEE
DRAWN WITH PURPLE PASSION BY: JACK KIRBY
INKED WITH GOLDEN SERENITY BY: CHIC STONE
LETTERED ON A BLUE MONDAY BY: SAM ROSEN
LET'S BEGIN WITH A BANG, AS THE MIGHTY THUNDER GOD PURSUES AN ENEMY AGENT WHO ATTEMPTS TO FLEE FROM THOR'S AWESOME WRATH IN A SOUPED-UP BUCKET RACING CAR! GOT THE PICTURE? THEN, LET'S GO...!

THEN YOU COMPEL ME TO RESORT TO FORCE? AS MY VENERATED FATHER WOULD SAY, IN HIS AUGUST WISDOM... SO BE IT!
UGHHH!
I MUST KEEP FIGHTING! IF I'M CAPTURED I'LL BE TRIED FOR TREASON... AND THE SENTENCE COULD BE DEATH!

EVEN THOUGH YOU'RE SAID TO BE IMMORTAL, THIS HIGH-POWERED BLASTER CAN STOP ANYTHING THAT LIVES!
PERHAPS! BUT FIRST, IT IS NECESSARY TO HIT YOUR TARGET!

AND, A FAST-MOVING THUNDER GOD IS A FAR MORE ELUSIVE FOE THAN ANY YOU HAVE EVER FACED BEFORE!
THOUGH I AM PLEDGED NEVER TO CAUSE BODILY INJURY TO A HUMAN WITH MY AVENGING HAMMER, STILL IT CAN BE EMPLOYED TO GIVE HIM PAUSE!

AH! IT CAUSED HIM TO FALL PRONE, IN ORDER TO AVOID IT!
WHOOM!

BUT, THOR'S DESPERATE ADVERSARY IS NO AMATEUR IN THE ART OF BATTLE! CALMLY, HE INSERTS A NEW BLAST-CHARGE CLIP INTO HIS POTENT WEAPON...!
I'LL GIVE IT ONE MORE TRY, AND IF IT FAILS, I'LL HAVE TO USE... THE GRENADE!
2.

MEANWHILE, IN FAR-OFF ASGARD, THE MOST EVIL IMMORTAL OF ALL TIME WATCHES THE EARTHLY BATTLE ON A STRANGE, FOUR-DIMENSIONAL, MOLECULE SCREEN ... A SINISTER SCHEME FORMING IN HIS SUPER-HUMAN BRAIN!
THIS IS THE MOMENT I HAVE BEEN WAITING FOR!
NOW, WHILE MY ACCURSED ENEMY IS ENGAGED IN BATTLE, I SHALL WEAKEN HIM... AS ONLY LOKI CAN!

SLOWLY, CAUTIOUSLY, THE MERCILESS GOD OF EVIL POURS A STRANGE POTION INTO A SUBAUTRONIC SPACE DISTORTER!
JUST ONE DROP OF THIS ENCHANTED ELEMENT WILL BE ENOUGH TO SLOW THOR'S REFLEXES, AND MAKE HIM VULNERABLE TO A MORTAL'S ATTACK!

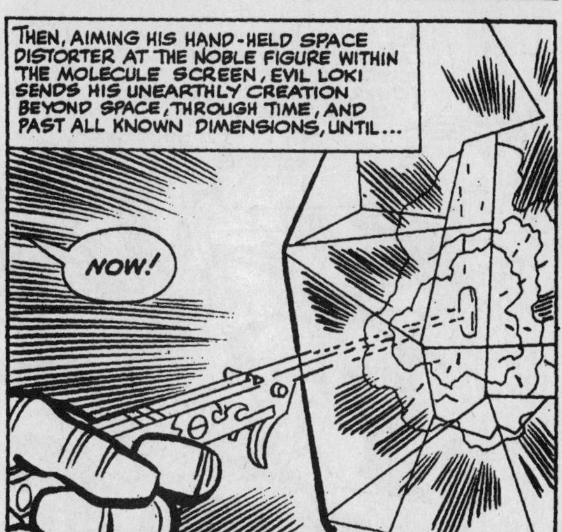
THEN, AIMING HIS HAND-HELD SPACE DISTORTER AT THE NOBLE FIGURE WITHIN THE MOLECULE SCREEN, EVIL LOKI SENDS HIS UNEARTHLY CREATION BEYOND SPACE, THROUGH TIME, AND PAST ALL KNOWN DIMENSIONS, UNTIL...
NOW!

BY A FANTASTIC PROCESS, KNOWN ONLY TO LOKI, A SMALL CAPSULE DROPS TO THE GROUND BEHIND THOR, SPRAYING HIM WITH A THIN, INVISIBLE MIST!
I SENSE DEADLY MENACE NEARBY! BUT, FIRST I MUST COMPLETE THE TASK AT HAND!

AT THAT MOMENT, THE ENEMY AGENT HURLS HIS DEADLY GRENADE...
MY POTION SHOULD SLOW THE THUNDER GOD'S ACTIONS SO THAT THE GRENADE WILL STRIKE HIM! MOREOVER, IT SHOULD WEAKEN HIM ENOUGH SO THAT HE MAY BE DESTROYED!

BUT, CONTRARY TO LOKI'S EXPECTATIONS...
BY MERELY WHIRLING MY HAMMER AT SUPER-SONIC SPEED, I EFFORTLESSLY NULLIFY THE EFFECTS OF ANY EXPLOSIVE!

AND NOW, LET US HAVE DONE WITH THIS CHARADE!
KRAKK!

THIS WILL PIN YOU HELPLESSLY TO THE GROUND UNTIL THE LAW ARRIVES TO DEAL WITH YOU!
CAN'T MOVE! I HAVEN'T GOT A CHANCE! HE'S BEATEN ME!
THWUPP!

WHILE, WITHIN THE DISTANT REALM OF ASGARD...
I FAILED! POWERFUL AS IT WAS, MY POTION HAD NO EFFECT UPON THOR!
I SHOULD HAVE KNOWN... ONLY ODIN CAN STRIP THOR'S POWER FROM HIM!
EVEN I, THE MASTER OF EVIL, THE LORD OF SORCERY, CANNOT DO IT!

BUT, THERE ARE OTHER WAYS! IF I CANNOT CAUSE THOR TO LOSE HIS POWER... I HAVE THE MEANS TO GIVE POWER TO OTHERS! ALREADY, A SCHEME IS FORMING IN MY MIND!

SOME TIME LATER, THE CUNNING, SINISTER LOKI HOLDS A NEW VIAL IN HIS HAND, AS HIS PLAN TAKES SHAPE...
IT IS READY! NOW, ALL I NEED DO IS FIND A LIKELY AGENT ON THE PLANET OF MORTALS...

THERE IS A PERFECT SUBJECT! BRUTAL, SAVAGE, CONSUMED WITH HATRED FOR SOCIETY!
4.

LITTLE DOES HE SUSPECT THAT I HAVE ADDED AN ENCHANTED POTION TO HIS DRINK!

A POTION WHICH WILL MAKE HIM THE MOST DANGEROUS MORTAL ON EARTH WITHIN EXACTLY ONE SECOND! AHHH! HE BEGINS TO FEEL HIS POWER!

NOTHING CAN STOP HIM NOW! ALL I NEED DO IS WATCH... UNTIL HE MEETS THOR... THE ONE HE WILL DESTROY!

WHAT IS THE DREAD POWER WHICH LOKI HAS GIVEN TO THIS CONVICT?? A POWER GREAT ENOUGH TO MENACE THOR!! WE SHALL LEARN IN A MOMENT...
I'M GETTIN' OUT OF HERE! NO JAIL CAN HOLD ME NOW!
HOW ABOUT THAT?! CRUSHER CREEL MUSTA GONE STIR CRAZY!!
24957
DON'T TRY IT, CRUSHER!
LOOK OUT!! HE'S STRONG AS A BULL... AND TWICE AS DANGEROUS!

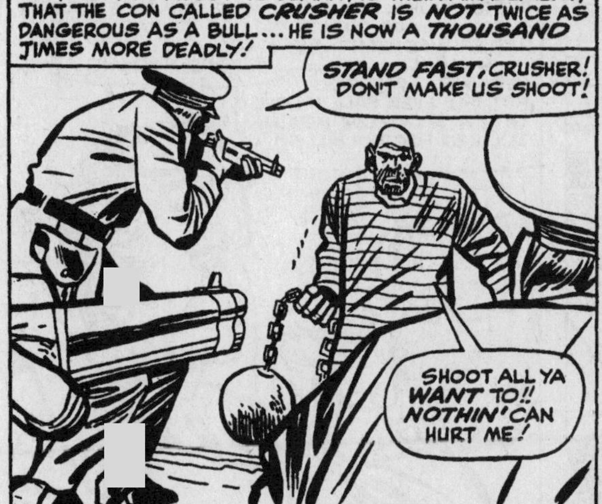
BUT, THEY ARE ABOUT TO LEARN, TO THEIR AMAZEMENT, THAT THE CON CALLED CRUSHER IS NOT TWICE AS DANGEROUS AS A BULL... HE IS NOW A THOUSAND TIMES MORE DEADLY!
STAND FAST, CRUSHER! DON'T MAKE US SHOOT!
SHOOT ALL YA WANT TO!! NOTHIN' CAN HURT ME!

THEN, AS THE MADDENED CON WEILDS HIS BALL AND CHAIN LIKE A DEADLY MALLET, THE GUARDS HAVE NO CHOICE BUT TO FIRE!
LOOK! HIS BODY!! IT... IT'S CHANGED!
IT'S TURNED TO STEEL!! LIKE OUR BULLETS!
THE SHELLS ARE BOUNCING OFF HIM!
5.

NEXT, AS THE DAZED GUARDS CALL FOR MORE POWERFUL WEAPONS, THE MAN KNOWN AS CRUSHER EFFORTLESSLY SMASHES THROUGH THE STONE WALL INTO THE YARD..!
IT'S LIKE BUSTIN' THROUGH A PAPER BAG!! ONE MORE WALL AND I'LL BE FREE!

BEFORE GOING ANY FURTHER, WE WANT TO WARN YOU THAT CRUSHER CREEL'S POWER IS NOT MERELY A STEEL BODY! IT'S SOMETHING FAR FAR MORE! BUT, NOW, LET'S VISIT THE OFFICE OF DR. DON BLAKE..
YOU SAY YOU'RE A REPORTER? HOW DID YOU HURT YOUR ARM THAT WAY, MR. HOBBS?
I SLIPPED ON A BANANA PEEL WHILE RUNNING FOR A TRAIN, DOC! I WAS IN TOO BIG A HURRY!
IT WILL BE ALL RIGHT NOW!

THANKS, DOC! I'VE GOT TO RUSH AND TRY TO CATCH THE NEXT TRAIN NOW!
I'M HOT ON THE TRAIL OF AN ESCAPED CON WITH SUPER-HUMAN POWERS! IF I CAN CHECK IT OUT, IT'LL BE GOOD FOR THE FRONT PAGE!
IS THAT SO?

IF I FIND MY MAN, I'LL DROP YOU A CARD FROM THE BLACK MOUNTAIN SWAMP AREA, WHERE HE'S HIDING!
GOOD LUCK, MR. HOBBS! AND TRY NOT TO STRAIN THAT ARM!
AN ESCAPED CON WITH SUPER POWERS! THAT SOUNDS VERY INTERESTING!

I'M GLAD YOUR LAST PATIENT IS GONE! I'M HUNGRY AS A BEAR!
OH, NO! I FORGOT! I WAS SUPPOSED TO TAKE JANE TO DINNER TONIGHT!

BUTTON NOSE, WOULD YOU MIND GIVING ME A RAIN CHECK ON OUR DINNER DATE? I, EH, HAVE SOME RATHER IMPORTANT RESEARCH TO CARRY OUT BEFORE MORNING!
VERY WELL, DARLING! BUT, IF I EVER FALL IN LOVE WITH A DOCTOR AGAIN, I'LL RUN FOR THE HILLS!
6.

MOMENTS LATER, IN THE SECLUSION OF HIS DESERTED ROOFTOP...
NO POINT IN SUMMONING THE AVENGERS UNTIL I'VE MADE CERTAIN A SUPER-MENACE REALLY DOES EXIST!

AND, ANYWAY, EVEN IF THERE IS AN ESCAPED CON WITH SOME SORT OF STRANGE POWER IN THE BLACK MOUNTAIN SWAMP AREA...

...THE CHANCES ARE THAT THE GOD OF THUNDER WILL BE MORE THAN A MATCH FOR WHOM-EVER IT MAY BE!

BUT, EVEN MIGHTY THOR MIGHT NOT FEEL SO CONFIDENT IF HE KNEW THE FULL EXTENT OF CRUSHER CREEL'S POWER!

I'M PASSING THE TRAIN WHICH HOBBS IS RIDING! LITTLE DOES HE DREAM THAT THOR IS ABOUT TO BEAT HIM TO HIS STORY!

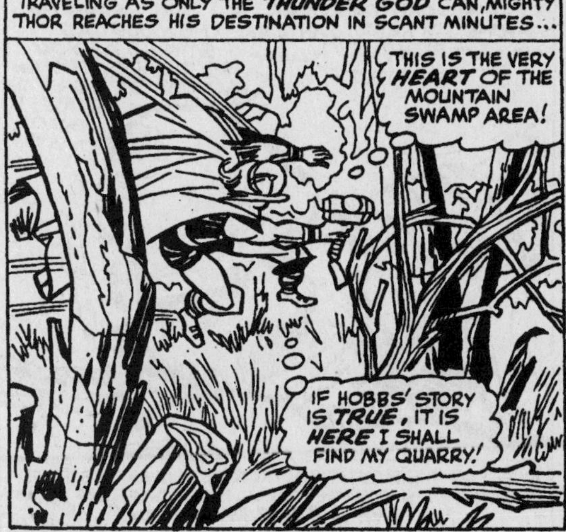
TRAVELING AS ONLY THE THUNDER GOD CAN, MIGHTY THOR REACHES HIS DESTINATION IN SCANT MINUTES...
THIS IS THE VERY HEART OF THE MOUNTAIN SWAMP AREA!
IF HOBBS' STORY IS TRUE, IT IS HERE I SHALL FIND MY QUARRY!

MY ENCHANTED URU HAMMER BEGINS TO TINGLE!
THAT SIGNIFIES THAT A SUPER-NATURAL MENACE IS INDEED NEAR AT HAND!
7

THUS, FOR THE FIRST TIME, THOR REALIZES THE TRUE POWER OF HIS SAVAGE FOE... THE POWER OF THE ABSORBING MAN!

ON AND ON THE BATTLE RAGES, WITH THE ABSORBING MAN DUPLICATING EVERY FANTASTIC FEAT OF THE MIGHTY ADVERSARY HE IS FIGHTING...!
MY STRENGTH HAS BECOME HIS STRENGTH! AND MY HAMMER'S POWER IS MATCHED BY HIS BALL AND CHAIN!
PERHAPS I CAN HURL HIS WEAPON FROM HIM BY CREATING A SUDDEN WHIRLWIND!

BUT, HAVING THE SAME POWER AS THOR, THE ABSORBING MAN MERELY DUPLICATES THE THUNDER GOD'S FEAT!
I'VE FOUND HIM AT LAST!

THEN, AT THAT MOMENT, THE REPORTER, HOBBS, ENTERS THE SCENE...
LUCKY I BROUGHT SOME OF THESE DYNAMITE STICKS WITH ME, IN CASE I NEEDED THEM!
WHAT A SCOOP THIS'LL BE FOR OL' HOBBS!

DROP THAT BALL AND CHAIN, CREEL! SURRENDER, OR I'LL THROW THIS T.N.T.!
THROW IT, YOU FOOL! SEE HOW MUCH GOOD IT'LL DO YA!
GO BACK!! FLEE FOR YOUR LIFE! HE IS MORE DANGEROUS THAN YOU CAN IMAGINE!
9.

IT'S TOO LATE FOR HIM TO ESCAPE ME! FIRST, I'LL KNOCK THAT DYNAMITE OUTTA HIS HANDS, LIKE THIS...!!
CREEL'S SPEED IS THE EQUAL OF MY OWN! HOW CAN I STOP HIM?

NOW, I'LL LIGHT THE FUSE AND LET YA HAVE IT BACK AGAIN!!
ONLY MY OWN ARTIFICIAL WHIRLWIND CAN SAVE YOU NOW!

WHOOOM

FINALLY, AFTER THE SMOKE HAS CLEARED...
THOR! YOU SAVED ME! BUT...HE..HE WAS AS FAST..AS POWERFUL AS YOU!!
HOW CAN THAT BE??!

I DO NOT KNOW! BUT, YOU MUST RETURN TO THE CITY AND WARN THE AUTHORITIES! HE IS TOO DANGEROUS FOR ORDINARY LAW ENFORCEMENT PROCEDURES!
YOU CAN SAY THAT AGAIN! OKAY, THOR... I'M ON MY WAY! AND MANY THANKS!

BUT, WAIT! BEFORE YOU GO...TELL ME...WHERE DID YOU COME FROM? HOW DID YOU MANAGE TO FIND HIM??
NO TIME FOR THAT NOW!
I MUST FIND HIM AGAIN...BEFORE HE GROWS TOO POWERFUL TO EVER BE STOPPED!
10.

A SHORT TIME LATER...
THAT MAN, WALKING DOWN THE HIGHWAY ALONE, WITH A WIDE-EYED LOOK... AS THOUGH HE'S SEEN SOMETHING FRIGHTENING!
YOU! STAY WHERE YOU ARE! I WISH TO SPEAK WITH YOU!
IT LOOKS LIKE... THOR! BUT, HOW CAN I BE SURE!?

AFTER WHAT I JUST SAW, I CAN'T BE SURE OF ANYTHING!! HE WAS STRONG AS THE HULK! THREW ME OUT OF MY OWN CAR, AND DROVE OFF IN IT... LAUGHING LIKE A DEMON!!
WAIT! IT IS HE WHOM I SEEK! YOU MUST TELL ME WHICH WAY HE WENT!

THAT WAY... TOWARDS THE STATE LINE! BUT, I COULD HAVE SWORN I SAW HIS BODY BEGIN TO CHANGE... TO LOOK LIKE IT WAS MADE OF WOOD... THEN STEEL...
YOU MUST TELL ME... AM I GOING MAD?
IF YOU ARE, THEN I AM, TOO! NOW, I MUST GO! HE MUST NOT ESCAPE!

MEANWHILE, AT A SMALL GAS STATION, SOME DISTANCE AWAY...
THAT'LL BE THREE DOLLARS AND FORTY... HEY! WHAT'RE YOU DOIN' WITH THAT BALL AND CHAIN ??!
IT IS TOO BAD YOU NOTICED THAT!!

TOO BAD... FOR YOU!!
HE JUST MISSED ME!! I'VE GOT TO CALL THE POLICE!

I DON'T KNOW HOW IT HAPPENED... AND I DON'T CARE!! BUT, EVER SINCE I GOT THAT FEELIN' OF POWER IN THE PEN, I KNOW I CAN DO ANYTHING!!
I AIN'T JUST CRUSHER CREEL, AN ORDINARY CON ANYMORE! I'M THE ABSORBING MAN... THE MOST DANGEROUS GUY IN THE WORLD!!
11.

I CAN USE MY BALL AND CHAIN JUST LIKE THOR USES HIS HAMMER! IT CAN SMASH THROUGH ANYTHING!

"I'LL BE ABLE TO BREAK IN ANYWHERE I WANT TO... ROB WHAT I PLEASE... I'M TOO STRONG FOR ANYONE TO STOP!"
WHEN I'M NEAR A STEEL FILING CABINET, MY BODY TURNS TO STEEL!

"I'LL EVEN FIND MYSELF A LITTLE COUNTRY SOMEWHERE, AND TAKE IT OVER! IF BULLETS CAN'T HURT ME, I CAN SMASH MY WAY THROUGH A WHOLE ARMY!"
WHEN I'M NEAR ARMORED TANKS, MY BODY BECOMES ARMORED, TOO!

"I'LL BECOME A DICTATOR! AND THEN, IF THAT GETS TOO BORING, I MAY DECIDE TO TAKE OVER THE WHOLE WORLD! I'LL BE THE EMPEROR OF EARTH!"
SILENCE, DOGS! I GOT SOMETHIN' TO SAY!
HAIL TO OUR MIGHTY LEADER!
ALL HAIL THE ABSORBING MAN!

BUT, CRUSHER CREEL'S SAVAGE DAYDREAMS SOON COME TO AN ABRUPT HALT, AS HE SEES...
IT'S THOR!! HE MANAGED TO FIND ME AGAIN!
WELL, THAT'S HIS HARD LUCK! THIS TIME I'LL FINISH 'IM OFF FOR GOOD!
12.

BUT, IT IS THE AVENGING GOD OF THUNDER WHO UNLEASHES THE FIRST BARRAGE, SMASHING THE CAR INTO SHRAPNEL WITH ONE MIGHTY HAMMER BLOW!

THAT WON'T DO YA ANY GOOD! REMEMBER, I CAN ABSORB YOUR POWERS WHEN YOU COME NEAR ME! WHATEVER YOU CAN DO, I CAN DO... AND MAYBE EVEN BETTER!
SO, THE STRONGER YOU ARE, THE SOONER YOU DIE!

WORDS! WORDS! I GROW WEARY OF WORDS!!
THE TIME FOR TALK IS PAST! NOW, MY HAMMER SHALL SPEAK FOR ME... IN A VOICE OF THUNDER!

WHOOOM!
BUT, EVEN THE MOST POWERFUL SINGLE HAMMER BLOW OF ALL TIME CANNOT DO MORE THAN MERELY SHAKE CRUSHER CREEL ... FOR, THE BRUTAL FUGITIVE HAS ABSORBED THE SAME POWER WHICH THOR HIMSELF POSSESSES!
13.

AND THEN, ONE OF THE MOST SPECTACULAR BATTLES IN RECORDED HISTORY BEGINS! NEVER BEFORE HAS A MORTAL BEEN ABLE TO WITHSTAND THE AWESOME POWER OF UNHARNESSED LIGHTNING WHICH A RAMPAGING THOR HURLS AT THE ABSORBING MAN...!
BUT, CRUSHER CREEL DOES MORE THAN MERELY WITHSTAND THE INDESCRIBABLE FURY OF THE LIGHTNING...

HAVING ABSORBED THE SAME POWER WHICH MIGHTY THOR HIMSELF POSSESSES, CREEL WHIPS THE BOLTS OF LIGHTNING BACK AGAIN TO THE IMMORTAL WHO LAUNCHED THEM!
THERE IS NO POWER I CAN EMPLOY WHICH HE CANNOT ALSO USE!
THUS, ONLY ONE COURSE OF ACTION REMAINS FOR ME...!

ENOUGH OF LIGHTNING BOLTS!! I SHALL DISPENSE WITH MY POWERS OVER THE STORM AND THUNDER!

NOW LET US BATTLE... HAND-TO-HAND!!
YOU AIN'T SCARIN' ME, THUNDER GOD!

DON'T FORGET... I ABSORB THE STRENGTH OF ANYONE I FIGHT! SO, NOW I'M AS STRONG AS YOU!!

AND, THE ABSORBING MAN'S BOAST PROVES TO BE TRUE, AS THE IMMORTAL AVENGER AND THE EVIL SUPER-MENACE BATTLE FOR HOUR AFTER HOUR, NEITHER ONE TIRING, NEITHER ONE YIELDING, NEITHER ONE NOTICING THE MYSTERIOUS FOG WHICH SLOWLY BEGINS TO ENVELOP THEM...!
IT IS LIKE FIGHTING MYSELF! HE MATCHES ME BLOW FOR BLOW!
OUR STRENGTH IS EQUAL ...BUT MY HATRED IS GREATER! I CAN'T LOSE!

BUT, THIS IS NO ORDINARY FOG WHICH BLANKETS OUR SCENE! IT IS A MYSTIC, INTRADIMENSIONAL MIST, CREATED BY SOME AWESOME SUPER-NATURAL POWER...!
I SEEM TO FEEL THE RAINBOW BRIDGE, MATERIALIZING BENEATH MY FEET!

SECONDS LATER, THE ENCHANTED FOG FADES AWAY, TO REVEAL...
BALDER! YOU DARED INTERFERE WITH THE THUNDER GOD'S EARTHLY BATTLE?!! BY WHAT AUTHORITY DO YOU...??
IN THE NAME OF OUR FRIENDSHIP, MIGHTY THOR! LOKI HAS CAPTURED YOUR MORTAL LOVED ONE...THE FEMALE KNOWN AS JANE!

IN AN INSTANT, ALL THOUGHT OF THE ABSORBING MAN IS FORGOTTEN BY THE SON OF ODIN...
MY BELOVED IN DANGER!! TO HORSE, THEN! LOKI SHALL RUE THIS DAY!

I HAVE BEEN BLIND! IT MUST BE LOKI WHO MADE THE MORTAL SO STRONG...TO KEEP ME FROM THE ONE I LOVE TILL HE COULD STRIKE!
THOUGH ETERNITY BE ENDLESS, BALDER'S SELFLESS DEED SHALL LIVE IN MY GRATITUDE FOREVER!

MEANWHILE, BACK ON EARTH..!
HE'S VANISHED! HE USED SOME KINDA MAGIC TRICK TO ESCAPE ME!

THAT MEANS I BEAT 'IM! I'M THE FIRST GUY IN THE WORLD EVER TO MAKE THOR RUN FOR COVER LIKE A WHIPPED DOG!
AND, IF I CAN BEAT HIM... NOW I KNOW I CAN BEAT ANYONE!

WHO'S THAT?? IT'S THAT FOOL REPORTER AGAIN! HE MUST BE TIRED OF LIVIN' TO HANG AROUND HERE!
I'LL POLISH 'IM OFF WITHOUT EVEN TAKIN' A BREATH!

NO! SOMEONE MIGHT FIND HIS BODY AND START A SEARCH IN THIS AREA FOR ME! I CAN TAKE CARE OF HIM ANY TIME!
BUT, THE FIRST THING I GOTTA DO IS FIND A PLACE TO SIT DOWN AND MAKE SOME PLANS!

I GOTTA FIGURE OUT EXACTLY WHAT I'M GONNA DO WITH THIS POWER OF MINE! I GOTTA MAKE SURE I DON'T WASTE ANY OF IT!
AND THERE'S JUST WHAT I NEED... A LONELY HOUSE! I'LL MAKE IT MY HANGOUT FOR A WHILE!
I HOPE THERE'S NO ONE LIVIN' INSIDE... FOR THEIR SAKE!
THUS, WE LEAVE THE DEADLY ABSORBING MAN FOR THE TIME BEING... BUT, ONLY FOR THE TIME BEING... AS WE RETURN TO THE MOST DRAMATIC CRUSADER OF ALL TIME, IN FAR-OFF ASGARD...

LET US FIGHT AT YOUR SIDE, THUNDER GOD! FOR YOU GO TO DO BATTLE WITH THE EVIL ONE ON HIS HOME GROUNDS!
NONE CAN DEFEAT LOKI IN HIS OWN STRONGHOLD!
THOR CAN!

TOO LONG HAVE I TARRIED! LOKI HAS FINALLY GONE TOO FAR! WHAT MUST BE DONE NOW, MUST BE DONE BY ME ALONE!

THOUGH HE KNOWS I APPROACH... THOUGH HE SUMMON EVERY EVIL SPELL AT HIS COMMAND... I SHALL RESCUE MY LOVE!
ELSE I AM NOT WORTHY TO CALL MYSELF SON OF ODIN, GOD OF THUNDER, IMMORTAL OF ASGARD!
BY THE ETERNAL RAINBOW BRIDGE, BY THE SPIRES OF THE ENCHANTED KINGDOM, WE VOW THAT MIGHTY THOR WILL THRILL YOU NEXT ISSUE AS NEVER BEFORE, AS HE BATTLES EVIL LOKI AND THE AWESOME ABSORBING MAN! TILL THEN, MAY THE STARS OF ASGARD SHINE EVER FOR THEE!
16.

Tales of ASGARD, HOME OF THE MIGHTY NORSE GODS!
SPECIAL NOTE: WE INTERRUPT OUR "BIOGRAPHIES-IN-DEPTH SERIES" OF THE LIFE OF LOKI TO PRESENT THIS SPECIAL TALE, BASED ON A NEWLY TRANSLATED VERSION OF ONE OF THE WORLD'S MOST ANCIENT LEGENDS! WE THINK YOU WILL RECOGNIZE IT!
"THE GOLDEN APPLES!"
I GIVE THEE GREETINGS, LOVELY GODDESS IDUNA! WHITHER GOEST THOU?
I AM BOUND FOR ASGARD, TO GIVE THE GOLDEN APPLES OF IMMORTALITY TO NOBLE ODIN, SO THAT HE MAY BESTOW THEM UPON THOSE HE DEEMS WORTHY!
THEN GO IN PEACE, IDUNA! AND THE BLESSING OF HAAKUN THE HUNTER BE WITH YOU!
A FABULOUS FEATURETTE BY THE GREATEST NAMES IN COMICDOM... STAN LEE & JACK KIRBY
INKING: VINCE COLETTA • LETTERING: ARTIE SIMEK
1

THUS, RESPLENDANT IN HER CRIMSON CLOAK AND HOOD, THE BEAUTEOUS GODDESS CARRIES HER PRECIOUS BASKET OF GOLDEN APPLES DEEPER INTO THE ENCHANTED FOREST...
MANY ARE THE DANGERS WHICH LURK IN YON FOREST! BUT, NONE WOULD DARE MENACE THE PERSON OF A GODDESS!

BUT, ALAS, IDUNA'S CONFIDENCE IS GREATER THAN HER WISDOM! FOR, THERE IS ONE WITHIN THE DEEP WOODS WHO FEARS NOTHING THAT LIVES-- BEHOLD THE EVIL FENRIS! FENRIS, THE WOLF GOD!
IDUNA APPROACHES! WITH HER PRICELESS GOLDEN APPLES!! THOSE APPLES MUST BE MINE!!

THOUGH IT IS DISTASTEFUL TO ME, I SHALL ASSUME HUMAN FORM IN ORDER TO MAKE THOSE GOLDEN TREASURES MINE! IDUNA WILL SUSPECT NOTHING!

A FRAIL STRANGER-- ALONE UPON THE WINDING TRAIL TO ASGARD! I OFFER YOU MY PROTECTION, HELPLESS ONE!
I NEED NO PROTECTION! KNOW YOU THAT I AM THE GODDESS IDUNA!

AND WHAT DO YOU CARRY IN THAT LITTLE BASKET, MY FAIR IDUNA?
THE GOLDEN APPLES OF IMMORTALITY, WHICH I BRING EACH YEAR TO THE LORDLY ODIN!

AHHH! HOW THEY GLISTEN AND GLEAM! HOW THEY SPARKLE AND GLOW!
STOP! THEY MUST BE TOUCHED BY NONE SAVE ODIN!
WHAT STRANGE HANDS YOU HAVE! SO GRASPING --SO BRUTAL--!!

AND, WHAT AN ODD VOICE YOU HAVE!! LIKE THE GUTTERAL SNARL OF A WILD BEAST!! WHO ARE YOU?? FROM WHENCE DO YOU COME?
I AM BUT A LONELY TRAVELER, ALSO BOUND FOR ASGARD!

BUT YOUR MANNER IS SINISTER-- FRIGHTENING! AND YOUR EYES--THEY BURN WITH HATRED-- WITH PURE SAVAGERY!
YOU SAY TOO MUCH, IDUNA! YOUR WORDS NOW FORCE MY HAND--!
3

ENOUGH THEN OF THIS SENSELESS SHAM!! I AM FENRIS, THE WOLF GOD!
--AND THE GOLDEN APPLES OF IMMORTALITY MUST BE MINE!!
I HAVE NO DEFENSE AGAINST ONE AS EVIL--AS POWERFUL--AS FENRIS!! ALL IS LOST!

BUT, BEFORE THE WOLF GOD CAN SPRING UPON HIS VICTIM...
HAAKUN, THE HUNTER!!
HOLD, EVIL ONE! MY BLADE SHALL FIGHT FOR IDUNA!!

NONE BUT ODIN MAY POSSESS THE ENCHANTED APPLES!!
AND NEITHER GOD NOR MORTAL MAY HARM THE FAIR IDUNA!!

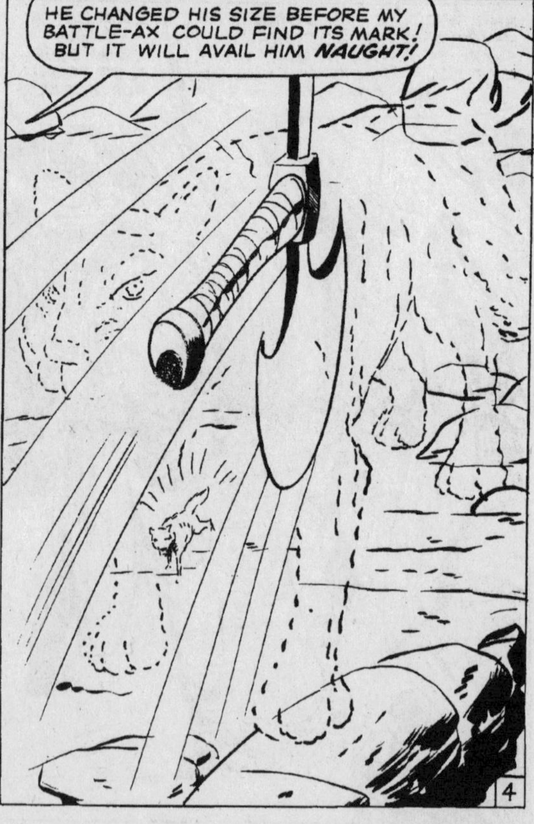
HE CHANGED HIS SIZE BEFORE MY BATTLE-AX COULD FIND ITS MARK! BUT IT WILL AVAIL HIM NAUGHT!

LO, OUR TALE IS DONE! A TALE WHICH HAS BEEN HANDED DOWN THRU THE AGES-- FROM FAR-OFF ASGARD TO THE FERTILE, GREEN HILLS OF EARTH! A TALE WHICH HAS BEEN CHANGED COUNTLESS TIMES IN THE RE-TELLING, UNTIL THE MORTALS OF TODAY LULL THEIR CHILDREN TO SLEEP WITH IT-- CALLING IT THE FAIRY TALE OF *LITTLE RED RIDING HOOD!* THUS, THOUGH THE NAMES AND THE DETAILS MAY CHANGE, THE LEGENDS THEMSELVES CAN NEVER DIE!

WITH
THE MIGHTY THOR
APPROVED BY THE COMICS CODE AUTHORITY
IND.
MARVEL COMICS GROUP 12¢
A NEW EXPERIENCE IN GREATNESS!
115
APR
"THE VENGEANCE OF THE THUNDER GOD!"
THE M.M.M.S. WANTS YOU!

THE MIGHTY THOR!
"the VENGEANCE of the THUNDER GOD"
THE EVIL LOKI HAS CAPTURED JANE FOSTER!! WITH THOSE STAGGERING WORDS RINGING IN HIS EARS, MIGHTY THOR ABANDONS HIS EARTHLY BATTLE WITH THE ABSORBING MAN!* LIKE A LIVING ENGINE OF DESTRUCTION, THE RAGING IMMORTAL RETURNS TO ASGARD, BRAVING THE MENACE OF LOKI'S DEADLY TRAP...!
STORY BY: STAN LEE THE SAGE OF THE MARVEL AGE!
PENCILING BY: JACK KIRBY THE RAGE OF THE MARVEL AGE!
INKING BY: FRANKIE RAY FOR HIS WAGE IN THE MARVEL AGE!
LETTERING BY: ARTIE SIMEK FROM HIS CAGE IN THE MARVEL AGE!
RESPECTFULLY DEDICATED TO YOU, THE GREAT, NEW BREED OF MAGAZINE READER!
*AS PRESENTED IN THOR #114 ... STAN
1

AT LAST, DESPISED HALF-BROTHER, YOU HAVE MADE YOUR MOST FATAL BLUNDER! YOU HAVE STUPIDLY CHOSEN TO BATTLE ME ON MY HOME GROUNDS! NOW YOU SHALL LEARN THAT LOKI IS TRULY YOUR MASTER!
MY ENCHANTED SWORD --- AGAINST YOUR ENCHANTED HAMMER! THOUGH THEIR POWER BE EQUAL, MY CUNNING BRAIN GIVES ME THE ADVANTAGE!
IT'S LIKE SOME MAD NIGHTMARE!! WHY WOULD THE THUNDER GOD RISK EVERYTHING TO RESCUE ME!
HOW DID I BECOME A PAWN IN THIS BATTLE OF TITANS??

YOUR CUNNING SHALL NOT SAVE YOU NOW, EVIL ONE! NAUGHT BUT NAKED POWER CAN STOP THE FIRST-BORN OF ODIN! THIS TIME YOU HAVE SEALED YOUR DOOM!
BAH! YOURS IS THE POWER OF THE BUMBLING OAF!! MINE IS THE POWER OF THE MASTER SCHEMER!

AND REMEMBER -- WHILE YOU STILL CAN -- THOUGH OUR WEAPONS BE EQUAL, LOKI IS PRINCE OF SORCERY!
AND PRINCE OF BRAGGARTS, AS WELL! BUT, WE ARE BOTH PLEDGED NEVER TO HARM A MORTAL BEING, AND YOU HAVE BROKEN THAT PLEDGE BY CAPTURING THE EARTH GIRL!
FOR THAT BETRAYAL, MY HEART CAN HOLD NO FORGIVENESS!

FOOL! I HAVE NOT HARMED HER! SHE WAS MERELY BAIT, TO LURE YOU TO ME!
BUT, NEVER AGAIN SHALL YOU USE SUCH BAIT! NEVER AGAIN SHALL AN UNWITTING HUMAN SERVE YOUR EVIL PURPOSE!

AHHH! I WARNED YOU OF MY SORCERY! YOUR HAMMER CANNOT SHATTER MY SWORD! I MERELY WILL MY BLADE TO ENTER ANOTHER DIMENSION!!
AND NOW, IT IS LOKI'S TURN TO STRIKE --!
2

BUT, WHILE THE AWESOME BATTLE RAGES IN FAR-OFF ASGARD, EVENTS ARE TRANSPIRING ON EARTH WHICH ALSO MERIT OUR SERIOUS ATTENTION...
YOU'RE HARRIS HOBBS, THE REPORTER FOR AFFILIATED PRESS! WHAT ARE YOU DOING OUT HERE, HOBBS?
SAME THING YOU ARE! I'M LOOKING FOR THE ESCAPED CONVICT, CRUSHER CREEL!
WHAT'S ALL THIS ABOUT PEOPLE CALLING HIM THE ABSORBING MAN? WHAT DOES IT MEAN?

UNBELIEVABLE AS IT MAY SOUND, CREEL IS ABLE TO ABSORB THE POWER OF ANYTHING NEAR HIM -- HE ABSORBS IT INTO HIS OWN BODY! IF HE IS NEAR IRON, HIS BODY ITSELF POSSESSES THE POWER OF IRON!
MISTER, YOU SOUND LIKE A NUT TO ME!
LOOK-- THERE ARE MY CREDENTIALS! I'M NO WILD-EYED FANATIC! I SAW CREEL'S BODY CHANGE!

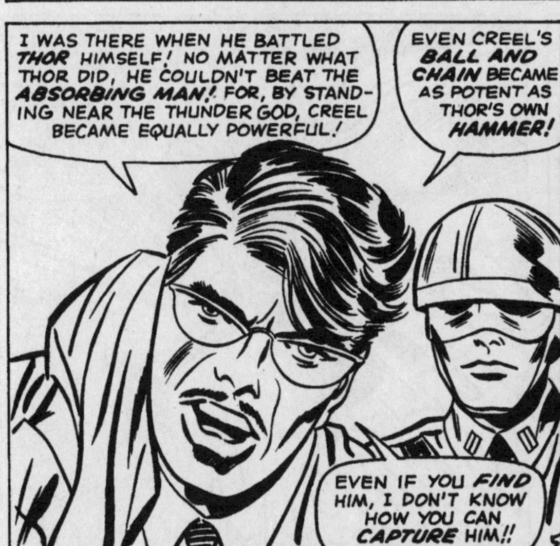
I WAS THERE WHEN HE BATTLED THOR HIMSELF! NO MATTER WHAT THOR DID, HE COULDN'T BEAT THE ABSORBING MAN! FOR, BY STANDING NEAR THE THUNDER GOD, CREEL BECAME EQUALLY POWERFUL!
EVEN CREEL'S BALL AND CHAIN BECAME AS POTENT AS THOR'S OWN HAMMER!
EVEN IF YOU FIND HIM, I DON'T KNOW HOW YOU CAN CAPTURE HIM!!

AND, A FEW MILES TO THE NORTH, HUNGRY AND TIRED, THE ABSORBING MAN COMES UPON A LONELY HOUSE, PEACEFULLY NESTLED AMONGST THE WOODED ACREAGE OF A WEALTHY SUBURBAN COMMUNITY...
THAT'S WHAT I NEED -- A PLACE TO GET SOME GRUB, AND A BED FOR THE NIGHT!

BRAZENLY, THE MERCILESS FUGITIVE MOUNTS THE STEPS, FEARING NOTHING WITH HIS NEW-FOUND POWER--!
IF ANYONE'S AT HOME, IT'LL BE JUST TOO BAD --FOR THEM!

AND, WITHIN THE LUXURIOUSLY-FURNISHED LIVING ROOM, HE SEES...
IT'S GOOD TO BE HOME, ANN! I HAD A TRYING DAY AT THE BANK TODAY!
YOU JUST SIT DOWN AND READ YOUR PAPER, DEAR! I'LL HAVE DINNER READY BEFORE YOU KNOW IT!
3

BETTER PUT ON AN EXTRA PLATE, LADY! YOU'RE GONNA HAVE A GUEST!!
OH!! JOHN-- WHO-- WHO IS THAT??!
I'VE SEEN HIS PICTURE IN THE PAPER! IT'S THE ESCAPED PRISONER-- CRUSHER CREEL! EASY, ANN--EASY! WE MUSTN'T PANIC!
BUT, ONCE AGAIN WE MUST TURN OUR ATTENTION ELSEWHERE--FOR THE BATTLE BETWEEN THOR AND LOKI IS RAPIDLY REACHING ITS INCREDIBLE CLIMAX....!
NOW--BEFORE YOU CAN SWING YOUR ACCURSED HAMMER AGAIN, MY SWORD WILL FREEZE THE MOLECULES IN THE AIR ABOUT YOU!! BY THE POWER OF DEATHLESS SORCERY, LET IT BE SO!
THUS YOU ADMIT YOUR MIGHT IS NO MATCH FOR MINE! NOW YOU RESORT TO MYSTIC SPELLS OF EVIL!
LOKI HAS NO QUALMS! I CARE NOT BY WHAT MEANS I TRIUMPH--SO LONG AS YOU ARE FOREVER DESTROYED!
I'M ENCASED IN A WALL OF ENCHANTED ICE-- STRONGER THAN STEEL ITSELF!
BUT THOR NEEDS NO SPELLS TO SERVE HIS ENDS! THE ENCHANTMENT OF MY HAMMER IS SORCERY ENOUGH FOR THE THUNDER GOD!
WHOOOOM!
THE RAGE IN MY HEART--THE JUSTICE OF MY CAUSE--THE STRENGTH IN MY SINEWS--THESE ARE THE SPELLS WHICH SHALL DEFEAT THE MASTER OF EVIL!!
YIELD, THOU BASE AND HEARTLESS VILLAIN!! YIELD, OR SUFFER THE THUNDER OF MY INVINCIBLE MALLET!
NEVER! VICTORY SHALL YET BE MINE! YOU HAVE NO STOMACH FOR SLAYING A FOE!
4

BUT, AT THAT VERY INSTANT, A DEAFENING EXPLOSION INTERRUPTS THOR'S MOMENT OF FINAL DECISION...!
WHAT NEW MANNER OF SORCERY HAS LOKI EMPLOYED TO DELAY MY RETRIBUTION??
THIS IS NOT MY DOING? WHAT OTHER POWER WOULD DARE INTERRUPT A BATTLE OF GODS??

AND THEN, A SILENT FIGURE APPEARS! STATELY, MOTIONLESS, REGAL -- THE FIGURE OF HIM WHO SPEAKS WHILST GALAXIES OBEY!
NOBLE ODIN -- LORD OF ASGARD!!
YOU SUMMONED HIM, THOR -- TO SAVE YOU FROM DEFEAT!
YOUR WORDS ARE AS FALSE AS YOUR EVIL HEART, HALF-BROTHER!

SO! AGAIN I FIND MY TWO SONS -- ROYAL PRINCELINGS OF ASGARD, ENGAGED IN PRIVATE CONFLICT WHICH HATH NOT THE APPROVAL OF ODIN!
I WISHED TO SPARE YOU, NOBLE LIEGE! KNOWING HOW YOU LOVE THE UNWORTHLY THOR, I COULD NOT BRING MYSELF TO TELL YOU OF HIS TREACHERY!

THE THUNDER GOD HAS COMMITTED THE ULTIMATE BLASPHEMY!! HE HAS BROUGHT THE FORBIDDEN EARTHLING TO ASGARD -- HOPING TO MAKE HER AN IMMORTAL!
I TRIED TO STOP HIM, MY LORD! I WOULD HAVE GIVEN MY LIFE TO SPARE YOU THIS INDIGNITY!
YOU LIE, PRINCE OF SCOUNDRELS--!
JANE!! THE ORDEAL HAS BEEN TOO MUCH! SHE HAS COLLAPSED!
BEHOLD, ALL-WISEST! STILL HE DEFIES THEE! STILL HE FLAUNTS HIS LOVE!

SILENCE! I KNOW TOO WELL THE CUNNING OF THY TONGUE, RUTHLESS LOKI! ODIN SHALL NOT BE DECEIVED!
AND YET, I MUST BELIEVE THE EVIDENCE OF MINE EYES! IT SEEMS THE GOD OF THUNDER HAS FINALLY GONE TOO FAR!
THUS, NAUGHT REMAINS BUT FOR ME TO ORDER -- THE TRIAL OF THE GODS!

ONE BOON, NOBLE FATHER! GRANT ME 48 HOURS TO BRING THE GIRL TO EARTH, AND FINISH A BATTLE WHICH I HAD BEGUN--THEN SHALL I RETURN TO ASGARD TO ENDURE THE TRIAL OF THE GODS!
DENY HIM, SIRE! HE SEEKS TO ESCAPE!
THE THUNDER GOD'S WORD SHALL BE HIS BOND! 48 HOURS-- SO BE IT!

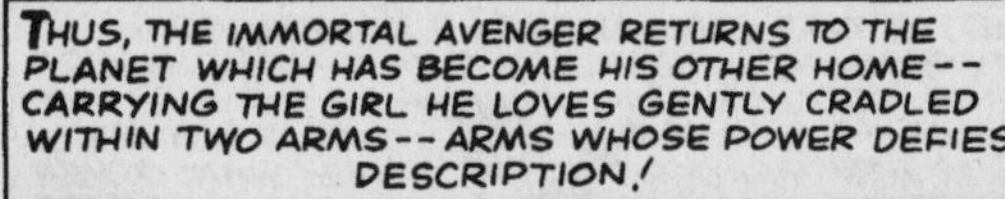
THUS, THE IMMORTAL AVENGER RETURNS TO THE PLANET WHICH HAS BECOME HIS OTHER HOME--CARRYING THE GIRL HE LOVES GENTLY CRADLED WITHIN TWO ARMS--ARMS WHOSE POWER DEFIES DESCRIPTION!

SLEEP, MY BELOVED, FOR YOU ARE SAFE ONCE MORE! NOTHING CAN HARM THEE NOW!

FRAIL MORTAL SENSES WERE NOT MEANT TO COPE WITH THE SIGHTS SHE HAS SEEN, THE THINGS SHE HAS HEARD!

THEREFORE, BY THE POWERS AT MY COMMAND, I GRANT THEE THE GIFT OF--FORGETFULNESS!
UPON AWAKENING, MY LOVED ONE, YOU SHALL REMEMBER NAUGHT THAT HAS TRANSPIRED!

THEN, SATISFIED THAT JANE FOSTER IS SAFE AND SOUND, THE MIGHTY THOR PREPARES ONCE AGAIN TO BATTLE THE UNBEATABLE--!
NO MATTER WHAT THE COST, I MUST AGAIN LOCATE THE ABSORBING MAN!

FOR I HAVE PLEDGED MY VERY LIFE TO THE DEFENSE OF EARTH!
AND, SO LONG AS THAT DEADLY MENACE EXISTS UNCHECKED, ALL MANKIND IS IN THE GRAVEST DANGER!
6

AND, IN ANOTHER SECTION OF THE STATE...
IF YOU THINK YOU CAN BREAK INTO MY HOUSE AND GET AWAY WITH IT, YOU'VE ANOTHER THINK COMING!
NOW, I'LL GIVE YOU FIVE MINUTES TO GET GOING BEFORE I CALL THE POLICE!
IZZAT SO?
MISTER, IT'S TIME I BEGIN YOUR EDUCATION! YOU GOT A LOT TO LEARN ABOUT CRUSHER CREEL!
MAYBE YOU AINT HEARD ABOUT IT YET, BUT I'M THE GUY WHO JUST FOUGHT THOR TO A STAND-STILL AND MADE 'IM GO RUNNIN' OFF WITH HIS TAIL BETWEEN HIS LEGS!
THAT'S IMPOSSIBLE! YOU MUST BE MAD!
TAKE YOUR HANDS OFF MY HUSBAND, YOU HORRIBLE BRUTE!
NO, ANN-- DON'T!! KEEP OUT OF THIS!!
THAT'S OKAY, MISTER! SHE CAN'T BOTHER THE ABSORBING MAN!
WHA-- ?!!
NOW DO YA SEE WHY NOTHIN' CAN STOP ME?? I ABSORB THE POWER OF ANYTHING I'M ATTACKED WITH! GLASS, WOOD, STEEL--- EVEN THOR'S HAMMER!
I-I CAN'T BELIEVE IT! IT MUST BE SOME KIND OF--OF TRICK!
BUT-- LOOK AT HIM!! HE-HE'S MADE OF GLASS!
NOT ANY MORE I AINT! I CAN BECOME RAW SILK, JUST BY TOUCHIN' THIS CURTAIN!
JOHN! THIS IS MADNESS! WHAT WILL WE DO? WHERE WILL IT END?
EASY, DEAR! WE'VE GOT TO SEE IT THRU, SOME HOW!

BUT NO GUY WANTS TO BE MADE OUTTA SILK!
'SPECIALLY WHEN HE CAN TOUCH A STATUE, LIKE THIS -- AND GET HIMSELF THE STRENGTH OF A BODY OF BRONZE!!
STILL THINK I'M JUST SOME KINDA NUT?

AND NOW THAT YOUR EDUCATION'S OVER, I WANTCHA TO HOP WHEN I GIVE AN ORDER, SEE?? THE FIRST THING I WANT NOW IS SOME GRUB! SO, FIX ME A DINNER -- AND BE QUICK ABOUT IT!
DO AS HE SAYS, DEAR! SOONER OR LATER, HELP IS SURE TO REACH US!
I WOULDN'T COUNT ON IT IF I WAS YOU!

AND, DRAWING EVER CLOSER, WE FIND...
WE'RE CLOSING IN, CHIEF! HIS TRAIL IS GETTING CLEARER!
STOP! I MUST TALK TO YOU, HOBBS!
IT'S THOR!
FAN OUT, BOYS! WE'RE GONNA COMB EVERY INCH OF THIS AREA!
WE'VE GOT BAZOOKAS AND FLAME THROWERS! BUT, IF HE CAN ABSORB THEIR POWER--!!!
IF WE FIND HIM, FOLLOW PLAN G!

YOU CAN'T STOP THEM NOW, THOR! THEY'VE ALMOST FOUND HIM!
BUT, HE IS MORE DANGEROUS THAN YOU SUSPECT! YOU MUST LET ME BATTLE HIM FIRST!
THANKS, AVENGER -- BUT WE DON'T NEED ANYBODY TO DO OUR JOB FOR US! YOU CAN JOIN US, IF YOU WANT TO!

I ADMIRE THEIR COURAGE -- BUT I FEAR FOR THEIR SAFETY! I MUST FIND SOME WAY TO REACH THE ABSORBING MAN FIRST!
THERE'S A HOUSE IN THAT CLEARING! THEY'RE GOING TO CHECK IT OUT! THIS COULD BE IT!
8

THIS IS THE PLACE! HIS TRACKS LEAD TO THE BACK DOOR!
SERGEANT, DEPLOY YOUR MEN AROUND THE HOUSE! MOVE!

IT'S CREEL, ALL RIGHT! IT'S A LUCKY THING THEY FOUND HIM!
GO BACK, HOBBS-- AND CONVINCE THE POLICE TO LEAVE, TOO! I'LL DEAL WITH HIM!
WHAT, ME MISS A SCOOP LIKE THIS? NOT A CHANCE!

MEANWHILE, SO CONFIDENT IS THE ABSORBING MAN OF HIS OWN POWER, THAT HE DOESN'T EVEN BOTHER TO INVESTIGATE THE MUFFLED FOOTSTEPS HE HEARS OUTSIDE!
I'M STILL HUNGRY! BRING ME MORE GRUB-- AND BE QUICK ABOUT IT!
MY WRIST--!

YOU'RE NOTHING BUT FLESH AND BLOOD RIGHT NOW! AND, EVEN IF YOU CHANGE TO T.N.T., YOU CAN'T SPEAK TO MY WIFE LIKE THAT!
OH! JOHN, MY DARLING--YOU SHOULDN'T HAVE --THERE'S NO TELLING WHAT HE'LL DO NOW!

TAKEN BY SURPRISE, THE CONVICT IS KNOCKED OFF BALANCE! BUT, REGAINING HIS FEET, HIS HAND TOUCHES HIS IRON BALL AND CHAIN, CAUSING ANOTHER AWESOME CHANGE...
JOHN! LOOK--HE-- HE'S ABSORBED THE POWER OF IRON! WHAT WILL HE DO NEXT??

I AINT GONNA KEEP YOU IN SUSPENSE MUCH LONGER, LADY! I'M GONNA FINISH YOUR HUSBAND'S EDUCATION NOW!
HOLD IT, CREEL! THE HOUSE IS SURROUNDED! YOU HAVEN'T A CHANCE!
THE REPORTER! I WAS HOPIN' I'D SEE YOU AGAIN!
9

I'VE GOT TO TAUNT HIM, LIKE THOR SAID--TO GET HIM OUT OF THE HOUSE!
A PHONY, AM I.?? YOU'LL EAT THOSE WORDS, REPORTER!!
YOU'RE A PHONY, CREEL! THAT POWER OF YOURS IS JUST SOME SORT OF TRICK! NOBODY'S REALLY SCARED OF YOU!

CRASH!
I DID IT! NOW IT'S UP TO THOR!
ANYTHING PHONY ABOUT SMASHIN' MY WAY RIGHT THRU THE WALL OF A HOUSE?

COPS!! OKAY, IT'S JUST AS WELL! I'LL SHOW YA, ONCE AND FOR ALL, THAT NONE OF YA CAN STOP ME!
STAY BACK, CREEL!! DON'T MAKE US FIRE!
WE'RE NOT FOOLING, MISTER! THIS BAZOOKA MEANS BUSINESS!
NO! HOLD YOUR FIRE! IN THE NAME OF THE AVENGERS, I NOW TAKE COMMAND!
THE AVENGERS HAVE A-1 PRIORITY RATINGS! THOR OUT-RANKS US! DON'T FIRE THAT GUN!

CLANNG!
THE THUNDER GOD!
YOU FOOL! BY HITTIN' MY BALL AND CHAIN, YOU MADE ME ABSORB THE STRENGTH OF YOUR HAMMER!

NO MATTER! THOUGH IT COSTS MY VERY LIFE, I MUST FORCE YOU TO DISPLAY THE FULL EXTENT OF YOUR EVIL POWER!
NEVER AGAIN SHALL YOU FIND A VICTIM UNAWARE!
10

THUS, ONE OF THE MOST INCREDIBLE BATTLES OF ALL TIME BEGINS, AS THE NEARBY LAW OFFICERS WATCH IN STUNNED SILENCE-- REALIZING THAT THE MIGHTY THUNDER GOD HAS UNDERTAKEN A SEEMINGLY HOPELESS BATTLE IN ORDER TO GAIN TIME FOR THEM-- TIME TO STUDY THE ENEMY-- TIME TO DEVISE A DEFENSE AGAINST-- THE INDEFENSIBLE!!

I CAN ABSORB WHATEVER I'M HIT WITH!! THE MORE YA USE THAT HAMMER, THE MORE I ABSORB ITS POWER!!

HOW CAN I HOPE TO DEFEAT HIM WHEN MY STRENGTH BECOMES HIS STRENGTH-- MY POWER BECOMES HIS POWER?!!

BUT, ONCE AGAIN THE POWER OF THE ABSORBING MAN IS MORE THAN EQUAL TO ANY CHALLENGE! THE FORCE OF HEAT WHICH THOR HAS HURLED IS INSTANTLY ABSORBED INTO CREEL'S OWN BODY, AS HIS TRIUMPHANT CRY RINGS OUT LIKE A BANSHEE'S WAIL!
NOW I'M STRONGER THAN EVER! I'VE ABSORBED THE POWER OF HEAT!
COME CLOSER, THUNDER GOD--AND I'LL THROW IT RIGHT BACK AT YOU! I CAN DESTROY YOU ANY TIME I WANT!

WE CAN'T STAND IDLY BY THIS WAY!! WE'VE GOT TO HELP THOR--SOMEHOW!! ORDER THE MEN TO STAND BY, COLLINS! I'M GOING TO GIVE HIM A BLAST WITH A RIFLE GRENADE!
YES SIR, CAPTAIN!
HEADS UP, THERE! LOOK ALIVE, MEN --DON'T TAKE YOUR EYES OFF CREEL!

A SPLIT-SECOND LATER...
PWANNG!
A RIFLE-GRENADE!! HAW!! AS IF THAT CAN HURT THE ABSORBING MAN!

THE HEAT OF CREEL'S BODY CAUSED THE MISSILE TO DETONATE ON TARGET! BUT HOW WILL IT AFFECT THE ABSORBING MAN'S POWER??

THE EXPLOSION STUNNED YOU! YOU NO LONGER POSSESS THE POWER OF HEAT!
SO WHAT? I CAN ABSORB ANY POWER I WANT TO--WHENEVER I WANT IT!

HERE, I'LL SHOW YA! BY HOLDIN' ONTO THE GROUND LIKE THIS, I'LL ABSORB EVERY OUNCE OF STRENGTH FROM THE EARTH AROUND ME!

LOOK! LOOK WHAT'S HAPPENING TO HIM!
HE'S GROWING!! AND HE'S ABSORBING ROCK, WOOD, STEEL--EVERY ELEMENT FROM THE EARTH BENEATH!
CREEL--THIS TIME YOU HAVE GONE TOO FAR! HEAR MY WORDS, MORTAL--THIS IS YOUR FINAL CHANCE--!!

YOU'RE DARIN' TO THREATEN ME?? LOOK AT ME! I'M THE STRONGEST THING THERE IS!!
AND I'M GETTIN' STRONGER EVERY MINUTE! STRONG ENOUGH TO FINISH YOU--NOW!
IT IS STILL NOT TOO LATE! TURN BACK--STOP, WHILE YOU CAN! I WARN YOU--DESPITE YOUR STRENGTH, YOU ARE STILL A MORTAL, WHILE I AM--THOR!

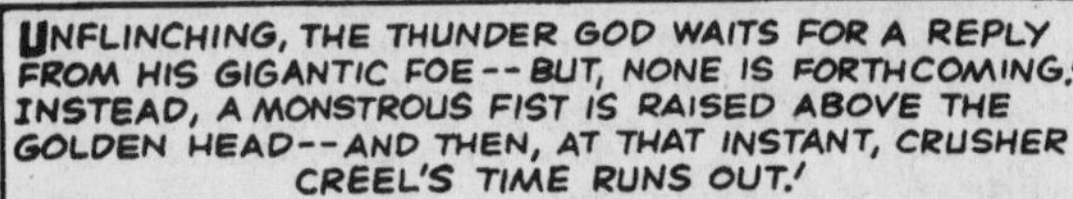
UNFLINCHING, THE THUNDER GOD WAITS FOR A REPLY FROM HIS GIGANTIC FOE -- BUT, NONE IS FORTHCOMING! INSTEAD, A MONSTROUS FIST IS RAISED ABOVE THE GOLDEN HEAD -- AND THEN, AT THAT INSTANT, CRUSHER CREEL'S TIME RUNS OUT!

YOU HAVE MADE YOUR CHOICE! NOW, THERE IS NO TURNING BACK! NEVER AGAIN SHALL THE ABSORBING MAN MENACE HUMANITY!
YOUR HAMMER!! IT'S WHIRLIN' SO FAST-- CAN'T SEE IT!! WHA-- WHAT'S HAPPENIN'??

I TRIED TO WARN YOU! BY SPINNING MY ENCHANTED HAMMER AT CYCLOTRONIC SPEED, I HAVE THE POWER TO TRANSMUTE THE ELEMENTS THEMSELVES!
THUS DO YOU MAKE YOUR NEXT CHANGE-- THE ONE WHICH IS DESTINED TO BE YOUR FINAL CHANGE!

IT WAS LIKE A NUCLEAR EXPLOSION! EVEN THE GROUND IS GLAZED!
BUT, WHAT HAPPENED TO THE ABSORBING MAN?? WHERE DID HE GO??
I SHALL EXPLAIN! BUT YOU MUST PREPARE YOURSELF FOR THE UNBELIEVABLE!

KNOWING THAT HE ABSORBED EVERY POWER, EVERY ELEMENT HE CAME IN CONTACT WITH, I REALIZED MY ONLY HOPE OF BEATING HIM WAS TO CREATE ONE SPECIAL ELEMENT!
WHAT ELEMENT WAS THAT?
HELIUM!! HE ABSORBED THE QUALITY OF HELIUM GAS-- THERE! SEE FOR YOURSELF!
14

HE HAS BECOME LIGHTER THAN AIR, AND IS SWIFTLY BEING DRAWN INTO THE ATMOSPHERE, AS I PLANNED!

"IN THAT GASEOUS STATE, HE CAN SURVIVE INDEFINITELY! I SHALL ALLOW HIM TO DRIFT THRU SPACE UNTIL THE UNEARTHLY POWER HE POSSESSES IS BUT A USELESS, FORGOTTEN MEMORY! THEN, HE SHALL RETURN TO EARTH, ASSUME HIS RIGHTFUL FORM, AND FINISH OUT THE YEARS OF HIS PRISON SENTENCE! THUS, THE ABSORBING MAN WILL BE HEARD OF NO MORE!"

WHEW! I WANTED A SCOOP--BUT NO NEWSPAPER WOULD PRINT A YARN LIKE THIS! I'LL HAVE TO SELL IT TO A SCIENCE-FICTION MAG!
IT WOULD REQUIRE THE WISDOM OF ODIN FOR ANY MORTAL TO SAY WHERE SCIENCE ENDS AND FICTION BEGINS!

KNOW YOU, HARRIS HOBBS, THAT YOU HAVE EARNED THE GRATITUDE OF THOR BY YOUR FEARLESS ASSISTANCE!
I USED TO THINK YOU WERE JUST A CONCEITED, COSTUMED SHOW-OFF! SO, I THANK YOU FOR OPENING MY EYES--FOR SHOWING ME THE BRAVEST, MOST SELF-SACRIFICING CRUSADER I'VE EVER KNOWN!

THEN, WITH THE REPORTER'S WORDS STILL ECHOING AFTER HIM, THE IMMORTAL AVENGER ONCE AGAIN TAKES TO THE AIR, FOR THERE IS STILL MUCH TO BE DONE IN THE FEW HOURS WHICH YET REMAIN--
MY WORK HERE IS FINISHED--
--BUT MANY ARE THE TASKS WHICH STILL AWAIT ME!

HE'S GONE! NOT MANY GUYS WOULD HAVE LEFT BEFORE EVERYONE HAD A CHANCE TO CONGRATULATE THEM AND TELL THEM HOW GREAT THEY ARE!
THOR IS AN AVENGER! THEY'RE A DIFFERENT BREED, MY FRIEND! PRAISE, AND FAME, MEAN NOTHING TO THEM!
YOU'RE JUST AN AVERAGE BUSINESS EXECUTIVE, JOHN DEAR, BUT YOU PROVED TODAY THAT ANYONE CAN BE AN AVENGER IN SPIRIT, AND IN HEART!
I WAS SO PROUD OF YOUR COURAGE, MY DARLING!
15

THUS, THE GOD OF THUNDER STRIDES UNFLINCHINGLY TOWARDS THE SHIMMERING LIGHTS OF ASGARD, TO FACE THE MYSTERIOUS TRIAL OF THE GODS! NEXT ISSUE YOU SHALL BE AMONG THE FIRST MORTALS EVER TO BEHOLD THIS STARTLING SPECTACLE! TILL THEN, MAY THE BLESSINGS OF THE GODS BE SHOWERED UPON THEE! SO BE IT!

Tales of ASGARD HOME OF THE MIGHTY NORSE GODS!
ONCE AGAIN, MORE OF THE EARLY LIFE OF EVIL LOKI!
"A VIPER IN OUR MIDST!"
GHAN, MOST DEADLY OF THE STORM GIANTS, IS ABOUT TO ATTACK ASGARD, AS YOUNG THOR LEADS A TASK FORCE TO BATTLE THE TITANIC INVADER!
I SHOULD BE LEADING THIS PATROL, RATHER THAN MY ACCURSED HALF-BROTHER! I MUST FIND A WAY TO MAKE HIM FAIL!
ANOTHER GREAT LEGEND LIVES AGAIN IN ALL ITS POMP AND PAGEANTRY!
STAND FAST! THE GIANT APPROACHES! NOW WE SHALL PROVE OUR METTLE!
ONCE AGAIN, THE ART OF ILLO-DRAMA REACHES THE PINNACLE OF CLASSIC PERFECTION UNDER THE TALENTED HANDS OF--
STAN LEE, WRITER
JACK KIRBY, ILLUSTRATOR
VINCE COLLETTA, DELINEATOR
ARTIE SIMEK, LETTERER
1

SUPREMELY CONFIDENT, BECAUSE OF HIS GARGANTUAN SIZE, THE RAMPAGING STORM GIANT HURLS A MONSTROUS BOULDER WITH THE FORCE OF A THUNDERCLAP!

DEATH TO THE PUNY LEGIONS OF ODIN!

THE ENCHANTMENT OF MY FLASHING SWORD SHALL UNDO ALL THAT THE THUNDER GOD'S HAMMER CAN HOPE TO ACCOMPLISH!
I SHALL CAST A SPELL TO GIVE GHAN THE FINAL VICTORY-- AND THUS SHALL I CAUSE THE DOWNFALL OF HE WHOM I SO DESPISE!

BUT, BEFORE LOKI'S EVIL SPELL CAN TAKE EFFECT, THE ARROWS OF THE WARRIORS OF ASGARD CAUSE THE LUMBERING STORM GIANT TO HALT HIS DEVASTATING ATTACK--!
SEE HOW THE VILLAINOUS GHAN FEARS TO ADVANCE ANY FURTHER!
LET YOUR CROSSBOWS SING! HE MUST NOW BE DRIVEN BACK!

THEN, SUDDENLY, WITH AN EAR-PIERCING ROAR OF HELPLESS RAGE, THE BRUTAL BEHEMOTH TURNS AND FLEES FROM HIS SMALLER FOES!

HE MUST NOT ESCAPE US! PREPARE TO LET LOOSE THE CATAPULT!
THE SLEEP FUMES WITHIN THIS CONTAINER WILL MAKE HIM LOSE THE WILL TO FIGHT AS SOON AS HE INHALES THEM!

THUS PUZZLED, THE NOBLE THUNDER GOD SCANS THE HORIZON, SEARCHING FOR SOME UNEXPECTED FOE-- BUT, IN VAIN! FOR, NEVER WOULD AN IMMORTAL OF ASGARD SUSPECT THAT ONE OF HIS OWN COULD BE A SCHEMING TRAITOR--!

I'VE DONE IT! I'VE SEIZED VICTORY FROM MY UNWITTING HALF-BROTHER! THIS SHALL BE THE FIRST OF MANY FAILURES FOR THOR!

YOU HAVE BEEN PRIVILEGED TO PEER MANY MANY AGES BACK-- BACK INTO THE EARLY HISTORY OF ASGARD, WHEN THE TRUE MENACE OF LOKI WAS JUST BEGINNING TO MAKE ITSELF KNOWN! SEE HOW THE GOD OF EVIL CONTINUES HIS EFFORT TO MUSTER ADDITIONAL ALLIES IN OUR NEXT GREAT ISSUE, AND IN MANY ISSUES TO COME! SEE ALSO WHY ***TALES OF ASGARD*** HAS WON UNIVERSAL ACCLAIM AS THE MOST ARTISTIC, THE MOST CLASSICAL ENDEAVOR IN THIS, THE MARVEL AGE OF COMICS!

JOURNEY INTO MYSTERY
WITH
THE MIGHTY THOR
APPROVED BY THE COMICS CODE AUTHORITY
IND.
MARVEL COMICS GROUP 12¢
THE TIME HAS COME FOR...
"THE TRIAL OF THE GODS!"
116 MAY

THE MIGHTY THOR!
"THE TRIAL OF THE GODS!"
AT LAST, THOR AND HIS EVIL ARCH-ENEMY LOKI, ARE ABOUT TO UNDERGO THE MOST DANGEROUS TEST OF ALL TIME, TO DETERMINE WHICH OF THEM HAS LIED* TO REGAL ODIN, IMMORTAL MONARCH OF ASGARD!
LET THE TRIAL BEGIN!!
WRITTEN BY IMPERIAL STAN LEE
ILLUSTRATED BY IMPREGNABLE JACK KIRBY
INKED BY IMPLACABLE VINCE COLLETTA
LETTERED BY IMPOSSIBLE ARTIE SIMEK
*AS SHOWN IN THOR #115 -- STAN.
1

A HUSH FALLS OVER THE GREAT CASTLE HALL AS THE COMMANDING VOICE OF ODIN FILLS THE VAST CHAMBER LIKE THE ROAR OF A THOUSAND CANNONS!
I ORDER YOU BOTH TO SKORNHEIM, THE DEADLY LAND BEYOND THE PALE OF ASGARD!
YOU WILL BE UNARMED, SAVE FOR YOUR WITS, AND YOUR OWN NATURAL STRENGTH!

MARK YOU WELL-- EVEN AN IMMORTAL MAY FIND DEATH WITHIN FORBIDDEN SKORNHEIM!
BUT, IF YOU SHOULD SURVIVE, THE FIRST ONE TO RETURN TO ASGARD WILL BE ADJUDGED THE VICTOR! THAT IS ALL!

YIELD YOUR HAMMER, THUNDER GOD! YOU MAY CARRY NO WEAPON!
SO BE IT, NOBLE FATHER!

AND NOW, BY THE POWER OF MY OMNIPOTENCE. I WILL CAUSE YOU BOTH TO BE TRANSPORTED--TO SKORNHEIM!

I HAVE SPOKEN!
2

SKORNHEIM!! LAND OF DARK MYSTERY AND UNDREAMED-OF DANGER! LAND WHERE THE GODS FEAR TO TREAD! SKORNHEIM-- DEADLY ARENA FOR THE MOST SPECTACULAR TRIAL OF ALL TIME!
WE ARE IN THE FURTHEST REACH OF THE DREAD, FORBIDDEN LAND!
I PITY YOU, MY BROTHER! FOR YOU HAVE NAUGHT SAVE THE POWER OF YOUR LIMBS, WHILE I-- I HAVE MY CUNNING AND MY WITS!

WHAT HOLD YOU THERE, EVIL ONE? AN ENCHANTED STONE! DECEIVER! WE WERE ALLOWED NO WEAPONS!
FIE UPON THEE! THIS IS NO WEAPON, DOOMED ONE! MERELY A SIMPLE BAUBLE! BEHOLD HOW IT SPARKLES!

OBSERVE! BY GENTLY TURNING ITS PRISMS, I CAN PROJECT ACTUAL SCENES OF LIFE UPON THE PRIMITIVE PLANET YOU CALL EARTH!

IT IS A TRICK! YOU ARE SHOWING ME THE ONE I LOVE-- THE GIRL JANE FOSTER! YOU PLANNED IT THUS!
OF COURSE, THUNDER GOD! AM I NOT THE MASTER SCHEMER OF ALL TIME?!!

EVEN BEFORE THE TRIAL BEGAN, I WOVE MY WEB OF EVIL! I PERSUADED THE EXECUTIONER, AND THE ENCHANTRESS TO PAY A LITTLE VISIT TO THE FRAIL, MORTAL FEMALE-- AS THEY ARE NOW DOING!

THE VISION HAS FADED! MORE! I MUST SEE MORE! JANE MUST NOT BE HARMED!
CONTROL YOURSELF, THOR! WHO SPEAKS OF HARM?
AH, THE SUN RISES! WE MUST PROCEED TOWARDS OUR GOAL!
3

SAVAGELY, MIGHTY THOR LUNGES AT THE LEERING LOKI! BUT, TENSE AND SHAKEN AT THE PLIGHT OF HIS LOVED ONE, THE IMMORTAL AVENGER MISSES HIS FOOTING, SINKING INTO THE FLUID SOIL BENEATH HIS FEET!
AHH! YOU FORGOT THAT EVERY INCH OF SKORN-HEIM CAN TURN INTO A LETHAL TRAP!

THE HILL TURNS TO QUICKSAND BENEATH THE RAYS OF SKORNHEIM'S BURNING SUN!
NOW, THUNDER GOD, WHILE YOU FLOUNDER, LOKI SHALL ESCAPE WITH EASE!

I KNEW THAT WEAPONS WOULD BE FORBIDDEN, SO I CONCEALED MY ENCHANTED NORN STONES BENEATH MY TUNIC--STONES GREATER THAN ANY WEAPON!
HOW EASILY I CAN TURN THE LAVA INTO A SOLID PATH BY THE SORCERY OF A SHINING STONE!

BUT, THOUGH POSSESSED OF NO SUCH MAGIC AIDS, MIGHTY THOR USES HIS OWN AWESOME STRENGTH TO FREE HIMSELF FROM THE SEA OF LAVA, SECONDS BEFORE IT CAN ENGULF HIM FOREVER!
I DARE NOT FAIL! THERE IS MORE AT STAKE THAN THE LIFE OF A THUNDER GOD!
MY BELOVED IS IN GRAVE PERIL--AND ONLY I AM AWARE OF IT!

LIKE A FLASHING, GOLDEN-HAIRED CYCLONE, THOR SLIDES DOWN THE MOLTEN SLOPE--A RAGING FURY URGING HIM ON--!
ON FOOT, I MAY AGAIN SINK INTO THE DEADLY MIRE! THIS IS THE ONLY WAY!

WHILE, A SHORT DISTANCE AHEAD...
AN IMPENETRABLE FIELD OF SPINY PLANTS--CAPABLE OF TEARING THRU THE STRONGEST ARMOR! BUT THEY MUST NOT STOP ME!
EVEN MY ENCHANTED STONES HAVE NO EFFECT UPON THEM!
4

BUT, MY CUNNING SHALL YET SAVE THE DAY!
THOUGH THE NORN STONES CANNOT AFFECT THE PLANTS, THEY HAVE THE POWER TO TRANSFORM MY OWN BODY'S MOLECULES--!

--ENABLING ME TO BECOME AN UNSOLID, GHOSTLY FIGURE, SLIPPING THRU THE DEADLY BARBS AS EFFORTLESSLY AS THE MIDNIGHT BREEZE!

AND, SECONDS LATER...
AGAIN THE EVIL ONE HAS USED A FORBIDDEN SPELL TO GAIN THE ADVANTAGE!
BUT, BY THE STARS OF ASGARD, I SHALL NOT BE STOPPED!

MY POWER IS IN MY SINEWS--AND THEY SHALL NOT FAIL ME NOW!
IN PLACE OF A MYSTIC STONE, MY OWN HELMET SHALL SERVE ME!

TIGHTER AND TIGHTER I MUST WIND MY FLOWING CAPE! FOR, IF I FALTER, THEN ALL IS SURELY LOST!

BUT, MY MIGHTY LIMBS--MY RAGING HEART --TEMPERED IN A THOUSAND BATTLES, SHALL NOT FAIL ME NOW!
CRUNNCH
RROOOOM

LOKI! PRINCE OF EVIL! NO LONGER WILL YOU MOCK THE POWER OF THE THUNDER GOD!

YOU MADE IT THRU THE PLANTS?!! BUT, HOW--? UNGHHH!!
NO MATTER!! WHAT OF JANE FOSTER?? WHAT FATE HAVE YOU PLANNED FOR HER? SPEAK, MASTER OF INFAMY!

CALL OFF THE EXECUTIONER-- AND THE ENCHANTRESS!! YOU CAN DO IT-- YOU HAVE THE POWER!!
THEY WILL NOT HARM HER! THEIR ORDERS ARE JUST TO MENACE HER-- TO KEEP YOU FROM CONCENTRATING UPON THE BATTLE AT HAND!

SUDDENLY, BEFORE ANOTHER WORD CAN BE UTTERED, AN UNEARTHLY BLAST OF SHEER ENERGY HURLS THE TWO FOES FROM EACH OTHER LIKE TENPINS!

WHO DARES ENTER THE FORBIDDEN REALM OF SKORNHEIM?? ALL WHO ENTER MUST PERISH!!
PREPARE TO MEET YOUR FATE, ASGARDIANS!
FOR, I AM YAGG, INVINCIBLE SLAYER OF ALL WHO INTRUDE!

AT THAT MOMENT, IN FABLED ASGARD...
YOU TRESPASS ON OUR FRIENDSHIP, BALDER! NONE MAY DISTURB ODIN WHILE HE TAKES HIS IMPERIAL BATH!
A THOUSAND PARDONS, NOBLE ONE! BUT, MY BUSINESS IS URGENT! IT CANNOT WAIT! IT CONCERNS THOR AND LOKI!
SPEAK THEN, AND BE QUICK!
QUITE BY ACCIDENT, WHILE VIEWING THE PLANET EARTH, I HAVE LEARNED OF A DARK PLOT ON THE PART OF LOKI!
HE HAS PLACED THE MORTAL GIRL WHOM THOR LOVES IN GRAVE DANGER, SO THAT THE THUNDER GOD WILL BE DISTRACTED BY WORRY AND UNABLE TO FIGHT HIS BEST!
SAY NO MORE!
STAND BACK! I SHALL SEE FOR MYSELF! LET TIME AND SPACE DISSOLVE INTO THE NOTHINGNESS OF THE INFINITE ON MY CELESTIAL SCREEN! THUS SPEAKS ODIN! SO BE IT!
BY THE ETERNAL RAINBOW BRIDGE!! YOU SPEAK THE TRUTH, BRAVE BALDER! THE HEART OF ODIN GROWS COLD WITH RAGE!!
THOUGH I FROWN UPON THOR'S LOVE FOR THAT MORTAL FEMALE, SHE MUST NOT BE USED TO SWAY THE OUTCOME OF THE TRIAL!

MEANWHILE, YAGG, THE SLAYER, PLACES HIS TWO AWESOME ELECTRODES TOGETHER, CAUSING LETHAL BOLTS TO SHOOT AT HIS DARTING VICTIMS!

BY HOLDING AN ENCHANTED NORN STONE AT THE PROPER ANGLE, I CAN LEVITATE MYSELF AND FLY FROM DANGER! BUT, THOR, UNABLE TO LEAVE THE GROUND, WILL SURELY MEET HIS DOOM AT LAST!

THERE IS NO ESCAPE! SOONER OR LATER A DEADLY ENERGY BLAST WILL STRIKE ME, AND ALL WILL BE LOST!

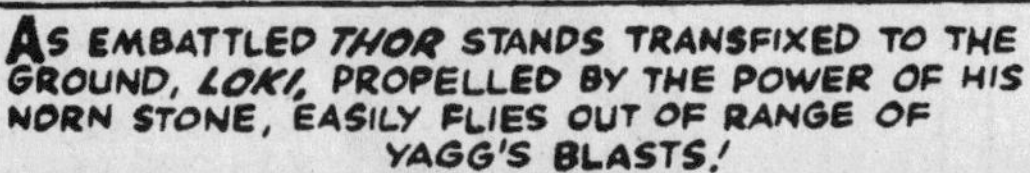
AS EMBATTLED THOR STANDS TRANSFIXED TO THE GROUND, LOKI, PROPELLED BY THE POWER OF HIS NORN STONE, EASILY FLIES OUT OF RANGE OF YAGG'S BLASTS!

HAH! I AM SAFE! BUT MY ACCURSED HALF-BROTHER IS STILL TRAPPED BEHIND ME!

FURIOUS AT HAVING LOST AN INTENDED VICTIM, YAGG SLOWLY TURNS TO THOR, DETERMINED THAT THIS ONE SHALL NOT ESCAPE!
NOW, HELPLESS ONE--YOU DIE!

ONLY THE THUNDER GOD'S STRENGTH, COURAGE, AND WILL TO LIVE ENABLE HIM TO DART AND WEAVE AND DUCK BLAST AFTER BLAST, UNTIL...
HIS ATTACKS ARE ENDLESS! I MUST FIGHT BACK!

THEN, REACHING OUT WITH FINGERS LIKE STEEL VISES, MIGHTY THOR RIPS OFF A FRAGMENT OF PETRIFIED ROCK--

--AND HURLS IT, STRAIGHT AND TRUE, WITH THE FORCE OF A COMET--FELLING THE GIANT YAGG EVEN AS DAVID FELLED GOLIATH MANY AGES BEFORE!
YAGG SHALL SLAY NO MORE!!

I'VE WON! BUT, IS IT TO BE MERELY A HOLLOW VICTORY? LOKI IS NOW FAR AHEAD OF ME! HOW CAN I EVER CATCH HIM--??

YET, I DARE NOT FALTER! SO LONG AS LIFE REMAINS WITHIN ME-- I SHALL GO ON--!

AND, MANY LEAGUES AHEAD, WE FIND LOKI FACING A NEW OBSTACLE-- THE WITHERING HEAT OF THE GLOWING BOULDER-ROAD OF SKORNHEIM...
NEITHER MAN NOR GOD CAN LONG ENDURE THIS UNBEARABLE HEAT!
AGAIN MUST I RESORT TO AN ENCHANTED STONE-- FOR MY TRIAL IS NEARLY ENDED!

BY CREATING A MAGICAL WHIRLWIND ABOUT ME, I CAN EASILY SURVIVE THE OPPRESSIVE HEAT!
HOW TRIUMPHANT SHALL BE MY RETURN TO ASGARD!

BUT, NO SOONER DOES THE PRINCE OF EVIL ENTER A NEW AREA OF SKORNHEIM, THEN HE FINDS...
ANOTHER DANGER! AS GREAT AS THE LAST!
I AM BEING SURROUNDED BY HUNGRY, CARNIVOROUS PLANTS!
10

BUT, VICTORIOUS LOKI SHALL NOT APPEASE THEIR APPETITE-- NOT WHILE MY ENCHANTED NORN STONE CONTAINS A REPELLENT WHICH NO FORM OF PLANT LIFE CAN APPROACH!
AND NOW-- TO ASGARD!
WHILE, BACK ON EARTH, ANOTHER PROBLEM REMAINS UNRESOLVED...
NO NEED FOR HASTE! SHE CANNOT ESCAPE!
HELP ME, SOMEBODY!! HELP!
LOOK AT THE SIZE OF THAT GUY BEHIND THIS GAL!
I'LL TRY TO STOP HIM WHILE SOMEONE GOES FOR THE COPS!
HOLD IT, FELLA! LET GO OF THAT GIRL!
ENCHANTRESS! TAKE HER, WHILE I DEAL WITH THAT RABBLE!
BE QUICK ABOUT IT! THERE IS MUCH YET TO BE DONE!
BEGONE! BEFORE YOU INCUR THE WRATH OF THE EXECUTIONER!
HE--HE'S PUSHING US BACK AS THOUGH WE'RE WEIGHTLESS!
IF ONLY ODIN HAD NOT VOWED CERTAIN DEATH FOR AN IMMORTAL WHO KILLED A HUMAN! IF ONLY I DARED TO DEFY HIS EDICT!
EMPTY WORDS! NEITHER OF US DARE! LOOK-- THEY ARE REGROUPING AGAIN!

C'MON! IF THERE ARE ENOUGH OF US, MAYBE WE CAN STOP HIM!
HE CAN'T RUN ROUGHSHOD OVER US NO MATTER WHO HE IS--NO MATTER WHAT HE CALLS HIM-SELF!
THE FIRST THING WE'VE GOT TO DO IS GET THAT GIRL AWAY FROM THEM!

STAY BACK, EXECUTIONER!
I SHALL HANDLE THIS MY WAY!

ONE SIMPLE SPELL IS ALL THAT I NEED! ONE SPELL TO MAKE THE RABBLE'S EYES HEAVY WITH SLEEP!

BUT, MANY FLOORS ABOVE, AN ALERT MEMBER OF RICK JONES' TEEN BRIGADE HAS OBSERVED THE ENTIRE INCIDENT WITH MOUNTING ALARM....!
THE EXECUTIONER--AND THE ENCHANT-RESS! RIGHT BELOW ME!
THEY STOPPED A CROWD FROM ATTACKING THEM! IT LOOKS SERIOUS!
TEEN BRIGADE
WGLP

I'VE GOT TO CONTACT RICK JONES! IT LOOKS LIKE A RED ALERT CASE COMING UP!
NO ANSWER! WHERE CAN HE BE??!

AT THAT VERY MOMENT, RICK IS ACROSS TOWN, ATTENDING A TOP PRIORITY MEETING OF THE AVENGERS!
I GUESS THAT WRAPS UP THE BUSINESS AT HAND!
WE'D BETTER ADJOURN NOW! THERE'S A LOT TO BE DONE!
TOO BAD WE'VE HAD NO WORD FROM THOR!
I WONDER WHERE HE CAN BE?
12

WE MUST ALL ABIDE BY OUR FOREMOST RULE! EACH AVENGER HAS THE RIGHT TO COMPLETE PRIVACY--THE RIGHT TO ATTEND TO HIS OWN AFFAIRS WITHOUT EXPLAINING TO THE OTHERS!
BUT, OFF THE RECORD, I'M AS WORRIED ABOUT THOR AS THE REST OF YOU ARE!
MAYBE HE'S IN TROUBLE! WHAT IF HE NEEDS HELP?
HE'LL CONTACT US SOMEHOW, RICK!

FINALLY, UNABLE TO REACH RICK, THE TEEN BRIGADER RADIOS AVENGERS' HQ. DIRECTLY--BUT, BY THAT TIME--THE GREAT HALL IS DESERTED...!
BEEP! BEEP!
BEEP!
BEEP!

NOW WHAT DO I DO? THE AVENGERS DON'T ANSWER, EITHER!
SAY! THAT SOUNDS LIKE SOMETHING SLIDING ABOVE THE ROOFTOPS--OUTSIDE MY WINDOW!

IT'S DAREDEVIL! MAYBE HE CAN HELP!
CAN'T STOP TO CHAT WITH FANS NOW! I'VE GOT TO FIND SUB-MARINER!*
DAREDEVIL! WAIT! I WANT TO TALK TO YOU! DAREDEVIL!
*SEE DAREDEVIL # 7--STAN.

HE MUST HAVE THOUGHT I WAS JUST A FAN, WANTING TO GET HIS AUTOGRAPH! WHAT DO I DO NOW? CAN'T LET THE EXECUTIONER AND THE ENCHANTRESS GET AWAY!
I KNOW! I'LL TRY THE BAXTER BUILDING!

THE BAXTER BUILDING! WORLD FAMOUS SKYSCRAPER IN THE HEART OF THE CITY WHICH HOUSES THE FABULOUS FANTASTIC FOUR! BUT, AT THIS MOMENT, THEIR TOWER HEADQUARTERS IS SILENT AND DESERTED--EXCEPT FOR THE STRANGE ANTI-GRAV SHIP WHICH IS ZOOMING TOWARDS IT!
NO ANSWER THERE, EITHER! LOOKS LIKE I STRUCK OUT!

IT SEEMS THAT THE TOP FLOORS OF THE BAXTER BUILDING ARE DESERTED!
YEAH! THE F.F. COULDN'T HAVE LIVED THRU THAT EXPLOSION LAST MONTH!* LET'S TAKE THE PLACE OVER FOR OURSELVES!
IF WE KNEW THEY WERE DEAD, WE WOULDN'T HAVE HAD TO STAY IN HIDING SO BLAMED LONG!
*SEE F.F. #38 --STAN.

HOLD IT! LOOK AT THAT FLAMING STREAK NEAR US IN THE SKY!
IT MUST BE THE TORCH! THEY'RE STILL ALIVE! LET'S GET OUT OF HERE!

AND SO, THE FRIGHTFUL FOUR STREAK FEARFULLY OUT OF SIGHT, LITTLE DREAMING THAT THE FIERY OBJECT THEY HAVE SEEN IN THE SKY IS NOT THE HUMAN TORCH, BUT RATHER...

...THE IMMORTAL FORM OF BALDER THE BRAVE, WHO EVEN NOW RETURNS TO HIS NORMAL SHAPE AFTER A LIGHTNING-FAST JOURNEY FROM THE LEGENDARY KINGDOM OF ASGARD!
YOU SHALL WAIT FOR ME ATOP THIS ROOF, MY NOBLE STEED, UNTIL I RETURN!
I MUST CHANGE TO HUMAN GARB AND FIND THE TWO WHO THREATEN THOR'S LOVED ONE!

THUS, SECONDS LATER, A MAN EMERGES FROM THE LOBBY OF THE BAXTER BUILDING... A MAN WHO SEEMS LIKE ANY OTHER, EXCEPT FOR THE BURNING INTENSITY OF HIS PIERCING EYES--!
I SEE THEM-- JUST ACROSS THE STREET!
SO CONFIDENT ARE THEY OF THEIR UNEARTHLY POWER, THAT THEY DO NOT EVEN BOTHER TO PROCEED WITH HASTE!
BAXTER BUILDING

IT IS USELESS TO STRUGGLE! YOU MUST COME WITH US NOW!
YOU SHALL NOT TAKE HER! TURN, EXECUTIONER-- TURN AND FACE ME!
BALDER HAS FOUND US!
14

BUT NOW, ONCE AGAIN WE RETURN TO MIGHTY THOR, AS HE WEARILY FOLLOWS THE TRAIL OF HIS IMMORTAL ARCH-ENEMY...
I DO NOT KNOW HOW LOKI MADE HIS WAY THRU THIS DEADLY PLAIN OF UNENDING HEAT....!
BUT, BY THE GOLDEN GATES OF ASGARD, WHAT LOKI CAN DO, THOR CAN DO!!

ON AND ON THE VALIANT THUNDER GOD ADVANCES --STAGGERING, STUMBLING, CRAWLING-- MILE BY MILE--YARD BY YARD--INCH BY INCH--HIS MIGHTY HEART ACHING--HIS LUNGS AFLAME-- BUT NEVER FALTERING--NEVER SURRENDERING!
I MUST KEEP GOING--NO MATTER WHAT THE COST!!

AND HE DOES KEEP GOING, UNTIL AT LAST--
MORE KILLER PLANTS! AND, HAVING NO ENCHANTED STONE, AS LOKI DOES, ONLY MY STRENGTH CAN PREVAIL!
YEA, THOUGH MY LIMBS ARE NUMB WITH PAIN, AND FATIGUE--THOUGH MY BODY IS WRACKED BY THIRST--

I SHALL AGAIN OVERCOME!! NOTHING SHALL STOP THOR!!
AND, WHERE THERE ARE PLANTS, TRULY, IN SUCH A PLACE, THERE MUST BE WATER--!!

AND WATER IS WHAT I MOST SORELY NEED!

THEN, HAVING FILLED HIS GREAT LUNGS WITH A GIANT GULP OF AIR, MIGHTY THOR SWIMS FOR MILES BENEATH THE SURFACE, THEREBY AVOIDING THE FOREST OF DEADLY PLANTS WHICH STRETCHES ON AND ON ABOVE HIM....!
THIS IS MY ONLY CHANCE OF CATCHING UP WITH LOKI! BY THE HEAVENS, I PRAY THAT I SUCCEED!

BUT, REACHING THE OTHER SIDE, THE ORDEAL HE HAS BEEN THRU BEGINS TO TELL ON THE EXHAUSTED IMMORTAL! HIS GRIP RELAXES FOR A MOMENT, AND, IN THAT FATAL INSTANT...

YES, LOKI HAS RACED THRU THE FATEFUL DIMENSIONAL BARRIER FIRST! BUT, NEW AND STARTLING SURPRISES AWAIT THE TWO IMMORTALS WHEN THEY REACH THE OTHER SIDE! DON'T MISS NEXT ISSUE! WE HAVE SPOKEN!

Tales of ASGARD
HOME OF THE MIGHTY NORSE GODS!
ON THOR #63, WE SAW HOW LOKI WON HIMSELF AN ALLY IN PREPARATION FOR HIS EVENTUAL BATTLE WITH THE THUNDER GOD! NOW, HERE WITH HIS HALF-BROTHER ON A DIPLOMATIC MISSION TO KING HYMIR, HE TRIES TO MAKE A SECOND ALLY...
"The CHALLENGE!"
THEN IT IS AGREED, KING HYMIR?
YES! SHOW ME A WAY TO MAKE A SLAVE OF THOR, AND I SHALL BE YOUR WILLING ALLY!
SEE HOW HE SPEAKS TO MY SISTER, PRINCESS RINDA! THE FOOL SUSPECTS NOTHING!
STORY: STAN LEE
PENCILLING: JACK KIRBY
INKING: VINCE COLLETTA
LETTERING: ARTIE SIMEK
1

WE ARE HERE ON A DIPLOMATIC MISSION, TO GAIN YOUR FRIENDSHIP FOR ASGARD!
THEREFORE, THOR IS HONOR-BOUND TO ACCEPT ANY CHALLENGE YOU GIVE HIM! AND YOU ARE FAMOUS FOR YOUR EVIL CHALLENGES!
OF COURSE! IF HE REFUSES, HE LOSES HONOR! AND, IF HE FAILS ---HE LOSES ALL!! IT SHALL BE DONE!

THUS, SCANT MINUTES LATER...
FROM HIS MAJESTY, KING HYMIR!
A CHALLENGE!! TO PROVE THAT I'M WORTHY OF VISITING HIM AT COURT!
OH NO!! YOU MUST NOT ACCEPT! I BEG THEE!

SEE THE FATE THAT BEFALLS THOSE WHO ACCEPT HYMIR'S CHALLENGES--AND WHO LOSE!
A LIFE OF SLAVERY!
YET, I AM THOR, SON OF ODIN! I MUST ABIDE BY THE CUSTOMS OF OTHER SOVREIGNS! MY HONOR IS AT STAKE!

AND SO IT COMES TO PASS THAT THE YOUTHFUL THUNDER GOD ACCEPTS THE FIRST OF HYMIR'S CHALLENGES--TO BRING BACK ONE FISH FROM THE DREADED SEA OF ETERNAL DARKNESS!
THIS IS THE PLACE! NOW WE MUST LEAVE YOU! WE MAY NOT VENTURE BEYOND THIS SPOT!
CATCHING ONE FISH SEEMS A SIMPLE ENOUGH TASK!
AHH, BUT YOU HAVE NOT YET SEEN THE FISH WHO ABOUND HERE!
2

MOMENTS LATER, THOR REALIZES WHAT WAS MEANT BY THAT CRYPTIC REMARK...
THESE ARE NOT MERE FISH-- BUT UNDERSEA MONSTERS! NO FISHING LINE COULD CAPTURE SUCH A CREATURE!

BUT THE MIGHTY HAMMER OF THOR CAN!

AND SO...
THE DEED IS DONE, KING HYMIR!
DO NOT GLOAT YET! YOUR FIRST CHALLENGE WAS A SIMPLE ONE -- TO TEST YOUR METTLE! BUT NOW--!
YOU ARE BOUND TO ACCEPT THE MAIN CHALLENGE! A TASK WHICH WILL RESIST EVEN YOUR MATCHLESS POWER!

WITHIN TWO MINUTES FROM THIS VERY SECOND, I ORDER YOU TO BREAK THIS DRINKING GOBLET! IF YOU SHOULD FAIL, YOU BECOME MY SLAVE!
BREAK A SIMPLE DRINKING GOBLET? CAN THE KING BE MAD??
3

NO NEED TO RUSH, BROTHER! IT IS SURELY A SIMPLE TASK!
LOKI TRIES TO DELAY ME! THERE IS MORE TO THIS THAN MEETS THE EYE!
I MUST ACT NOW!

WITHOUT ANOTHER WORD, MIGHTY THOR HURLS THE INNOCENT-LOOKING GOBLET AT A HUGE STONE PILLAR NEARBY, ONLY TO FIND...
THE PILLAR ITSELF IS SMASHED! IT IS AS I FEARED--
THE GOBLET IS ENCHANTED!!

EVEN MY HAMMER, WHICH CAN TOPPLE A MOUNTAIN, HAS NO EFFECT UPON IT!!
YET, FOR EVERY SPELL THERE IS A COUNTER-SPELL!!
BUT, HOW CAN I FIND IT, IN THE SECONDS WHICH REMAIN??

THERE MUST BE SOME ELEMENT WHICH WILL SHATTER THIS GOBLET! AND, IT IS BOUND TO BE THAT WHICH I WOULD LEAST SUSPECT! BUT, MY TIME IS ALMOST GONE!
ONLY ONE HOPE REMAINS! IF KING HYMIR IS SLAIN, THEN I WHO ACCEPTED THE CHALLENGE NEED NOT PAY THE PRICE!
YET-- IT MIGHT BREAK THE HEART OF FAIR PRINCESS RINDA!
NAY, GOOD THOR! IT IS NOT SO! DO WHAT YOU MUST! FOR HE HAS TRULY DECEIVED YOU!
4

MANY ARE THE SINISTER SCHEMES OF LOKI-- AND MANY ARE THE SPECTACULAR TALES WHICH AWAIT YOU ON THESE PAGES IN THE MONTHS TO COME! SO, TILL WE ARE ONCE AGAIN SUMMONED TO THE IMPERIAL REALM, MAY THE EYES OF ASGARD BE EVER UPON THEE!

JOURNEY INTO MYSTERY
WITH
THE MIGHTY
THOR
APPROVED BY THE COMICS CODE AUTHORITY
IND.
MARVEL COMICS GROUP 12¢
117
JUNE
THE MOST POWERFUL AVENGER OF ALL TIME THUNDERS...
"INTO THE BLAZE OF BATTLE!"
MIGHTIER THAN EVER BEFORE!

THE MIGHTY THOR
"INTO THE BLAZE OF BATTLE!"
BY SHEER TRICKERY, THE EVIL LOKI HAS MANAGED TO RETURN TO ASGARD, SECONDS AHEAD OF THOR, THUS WINNING THE AWESOME "TRIAL OF THE GODS"...
BEHOLD! MIGHTY THOR HAS BEEN BESTED! LOKI WAS THE FIRST TO APPEAR THRU THE DIMENSION BARRIER!
LOKI IS THE VICTOR!
REGALLY WRITTEN BY: STAN LEE
DAZZLINGLY DRAWN BY: JACK KIRBY
INVINCIBLY INKED BY: VINCE COLLETTA
LONESOMELY LETTERED BY: ARTIE SIMEK
*AS WE SHOWED YOU IN THOR #116-- STAN.
1

LOKI! YOUR VICTORY IS A FRAUD! THOSE ENCHANTED STONES YOU CARRY WON THE TRIAL FOR YOU!
YOU KNOW IT, THOR-- AND SO DO I! BUT NO ONE ELSE SHALL EVER KNOW!

JUST WAIT! ALL OF ASGARD SHALL KNOW WHEN I SHOW THEM YOUR BAG!
THEY'LL SEE THAT YOU WON BY DEFYING THE RULES OF THE TRIAL!
WHAT ARE YOU DOING? WHAT ARE THOSE MYSTIC GESTURES YOU MAKE?

CAN'T YOU GUESS? I'M MERELY SEEING TO IT THAT YOU CAN NEVER TELL I CHEATED DURING THE TRIAL! I'M SENDING THE EVIDENCE FAR OUT OF YOUR REACH!
THERE! IT IS DONE!

SO! YOU REMAIN A FOE WITHOUT HONOR TILL THE VERY END!
UHHH! -- CALL ME WHAT YOU WILL-- THE VICTORY IS MINE!

NOT YET! I CAN STILL CRUSH YOU! I CAN STILL RID THE UNIVERSE OF YOUR EVIL BEFORE ODIN'S GUARD CAN STOP ME!
AND, DO IT I SHALL-- UNLESS YOU TELL ME WHERE YOU HAVE HIDDEN YOUR ENCHANTED STONES!
STAY YOUR HAND! THEY ARE ON EARTH-- WHERE YOU CAN NEVER FIND THEM!

THEN, AT THAT VERY MOMENT...
BY OUR SOVEREIGN'S COMMAND! WE COME TO BRING YOU TO THE GREAT HALL OF VALHALLA!*
THE IMPERIAL GUARD OF ODIN!
*VALHALLA! THE CEREMONIAL CHAMBER OF ODIN! --STAN.

MOMENTS LATER, IN THE PALACE OF ODIN, THE ALL-WISE, THE ALL-POWERFUL--!
THOR LIES, MOST NOBLE ODIN! I POSSESSED NO SUCH MAGIC STONES! THE VICTORY IS RIGHTFULLY MINE!
SILENCE, CRAFTY ONE! I ALONE SHALL DECIDE WHOSE LIPS HAVE MOUTHED A FALSEHOOD!
SEND ME TO EARTH, HONORED FATHER! LET ME BRING THEE BACK PROOF OF LOKI'S DARK DECEIT!

YOU HAVE EARNED THAT BOON, MY SON-- BY YOUR PROWESS IN BATTLE, BY YOUR COUNTLESS VALIANT DEEDS, BY YOUR HEROISM AND UNSWERVING LOYALTY!
THEREFORE, GO THEE TO EARTH! BRING ME LOKI'S BAG OF STONES, IF SUCH THERE BE! YOU HAVE TWENTY-FOUR HOURS BEFORE I PASS FINAL SENTENCE!

SO BE IT!

MEANWHILE, AN IMMEASURABLE DISTANCE AWAY, BALDER THE BRAVE BATTLES WITH THE SINISTER EXECUTIONER TO SAFEGUARD THE LIFE OF JANE FOSTER, THE GIRL THOR LOVES!
OF WHAT CONCERN IS THE SAFETY OF ONE EARTH MORTAL TO YOU, BALDER?
SHE IS THE BELOVED OF MY FRIEND! THAT IS REASON ENOUGH, VILLAINOUS ONE!

THE ENCHANTRESS CANNOT STAND IDLY BY WITHOUT AIDING HER PARTNER IN PERFIDY! ONE SIMPLE SPELL MAY YET DEFEAT BALDER!
EVIL DEMONS, HEAR MY CALL! CAUSE THAT SIGN TO QUICKLY FALL!
JUST WHAT I NEEDED-- AN INTERRUPTION, TO ALLOW ME TO DEVISE A NEW PLAN OF ATTACK UPON BALDER!
THIS IS YOUR CHANCE, EXECUTIONER! DEFEAT HIM NOW, WHILST THE CITY STILL LIES BENEATH MY SPELL OF SLUMBER!
BUT SUDDENLY, A STIRRING BATTLE CRY RINGS OUT, AS A FLASHING, FLYING FORM HURTLES TOWARD THE SCENE OF BATTLE--!
THOR!!
BALDER, MY FRIEND! NO LONGER NEED YOU FIGHT THE THUNDER GOD'S FIGHT ALONE, AND UNAIDED!
HOW DID HE GET HERE? DID LOKI LOSE THE TRIAL??
AFTER MENACING HIS LOVED ONE, I DARE NOT FACE HIS WRATH! I MUST INSURE THAT HE NEVER REACHES ME!
THERE! BY SMASHING THAT WATER TRUCK, I'LL BE ABLE TO SLOW HIS ADVANCE--IF I MANAGED TO HIT IT AT JUST THE RIGHT ANGLE!
WHOOSH
A POWERFUL GEYSER OF WATER-- SHOOTING UP IN FRONT OF ME--OBSCURING MY VISION-- BUT, IT WON'T STOP ME!

ENCHANTRESS! RELEASE THE FEMALE! THE ODDS ARE TOO GREAT--WE MUST ESCAPE!
WE SHOULD NEVER HAVE TRUSTED LOKI! HE PROMISED THOR WOULD BE DESTROYED!

THERE! YOU CAN HAVE THE MORTAL GIRL! SHE IS NO LONGER OF ANY USE TO US!

BALDER! IS SHE--IS SHE ALL RIGHT?
SHE IS UNHARMED, MY FRIEND! I HAVE GRANTED HER THE GIFT OF FORGETFULNESS! SHE WILL REMEMBER NOTHING WHEN SHE AWAKENS--AND NEITHER WILL THE OTHER MORTALS WHO RESIDE IN THIS VAST CITY!

FOR ALL THE YEARS TO COME I SHALL REMEMBER THY DEVOTION, BRAVE BALDER! I SHALL REMEMBER HOW YOU TOOK THE GUISE OF A MORTAL AND SPED TO EARTH, HERE TO SAFEGUARD MY BELOVED WHILST I DID BATTLE IN SKORNHEIM WITH EVIL LOKI! KNOW YOU FOREVER THAT THOR IS GRATEFUL!
AND NOW, THERE IS STILL A TASK I MUST COMPLETE!

COMPLETE IT, THEN! I SHALL SEE THE FEMALE SAFELY HOME--AND, MAY THE EYES OF ASGARD FOLLOW THEE, MIGHTY THOR!
IF I SUCCEED, ALL WILL BE AS BEFORE! BUT, IF I FAIL--YOU ARE LOOKING YOUR LAST AT THE GOD OF THUNDER!

NOW I MUST SOAR HIGH ABOUT THE PLANET! I MUST FIND A VANTAGE POINT WHERE ALL OF EARTH ROLLS BY BELOW ME! AND THEN...

THE URU POWERS OF MY HAMMER SHALL BE ATTRACTED TO THE ENCHANTMENT OF LOKI'S MYSTIC STONE!

TRUE TO THE THUNDER GOD'S PREDICTION, THE MAGIC MALLET SOON CHANGES DIRECTION, PULLING THE GOLDEN AVENGER THRU THE SKY, ATTRACTED BY THE INVISIBLE FIELD OF ENERGY RADIATING FROM LOKI'S BEWITCHED BAG OF STONES!
I AM BEING DRAWN TO THE CONTINENT OF ASIA!
BUT, THOUGH IT LEADS ME PAST THE VERY EDGE OF ETERNITY, I SHALL NEVER ABANDON MY QUEST!

FINALLY, AT A COMMUNIST LOOKOUT POINT IN THE VIET CONG AREA OF VIET NAM...
UNIDENTIFIED OBJECT FLYING OVER OUR LINES!
ALL ANTI-AIRCRAFT BATTERIES-- OPEN FIRE!!

WHAT TYPE OF MISSILE IS IT, COMRADE?
IT LOOKS MORE LIKE A-A-NO! IT CANNOT BE!!
BRAKK
NO MATTER WHAT IT IS, OUR SHELLS SHALL BRING IT DOWN!

AN ARTILLERY BARRAGE!! I HAVE ENTERED THE VIET NAM WAR ZONE!
ALTHOUGH MY LIFE SPAN IS ENDLESS UNDER NORMAL CONDITIONS, I CAN STILL BE SLAIN BY WEAPONS OR OTHER ARTIFICIAL MEANS!
YET, I DARE NOT STOP NOW! I MUST FIND THE MYSTIC STONES I SEEK!

SURROUNDED ON ALL SIDES BY DEADLY ACK-ACK, THOR SUDDENLY CHANGES DIRECTION, HURTLING TO EARTH BEFORE ANY OF THE HIGH-IMPACT SHELLS CAN FIND THEIR MARK!
I'M SAFE FOR THE MOMENT, BUT--
--I HEAR THE SOUND OF MEN RACING THRU THE UNDERBRUSH--CHARGING FROM ALL SIDES!

THEY'RE ATTACKING! THERE IS NO WAY TO AVOID BATTLING WITH THEM! SO BE IT!

WITH ONE MIGHTY SWING OF HIS HAMMER, THE MAJESTIC SON OF ODIN CUTS A SWATH THRU THE DENSE UNDERBRUSH, CLEARING THE WAY FOR HIS NEXT THRUST AS HIS AWESOME BATTLE CRY RINGS FORTH--!
FORWARD--FOR ASGAAAAARD!

BUT, AS THE STARTLED VIET CONG INFANTRYMEN FALL BACK BEFORE THE IRRESISTIBLE POWER OF THOR'S MALLET, A GIGANTIC MORTAR SHELL, FIRED FROM A NEARBY HILL, SCORES A NEAR HIT ON THE UNPROTECTED THUNDER GOD--!

THOUGH SUCH A SAVAGE BLAST COULD REDUCE A STONE WALL TO RUBBLE--COULD RIP A STEEL TANK TO SHREDS--COULD TEAR A GAPING HOLE INTO THE SIDE OF A BATTLE CRUISER--IT DOES NOT BRING DESTRUCTION TO THE MIGHTY THOR!!
BUT, IT DOES CAUSE THE THUNDER GOD TO PLUNGE INTO THE DARK ABYSS OF UNCONSCIOUSNESS--

--UNTIL A SHORT TIME LATER, WHEN HE AWAKENS TO FIND...
I AM IN A HUT! THERE ARE NO SOLDIERS--NONE BUT A VIETNAMESE FAMILY...

BEHOLD, MOTHER! THE MESSENGER OF BUDDHA AWAKENS!
THEY BROUGHT ME HERE! THEY THINK OF ME AS AN OMEN FROM THEIR GOD!
WHAT HAPPENED TO THE TROOPS WHO ATTACKED ME?
THE EVIL ONES DEPARTED, THINKING YOU WERE DEAD! THEN WE CAME BY-- WE HEARD YOU BREATHING, AND BROUGHT YOU TO OUR HUMBLE HOME!
BUDDHA HAS ANSWERED OUR PRAYERS! HE SENT THEE TO DESTROY THE GUERRILLAS!

I MUST NOT PAUSE IN MY SEARCH FOR THE ENCHANTED STONES! AND YET, I SEE TRAGEDY AND FEAR ON THESE FACES--!
I AM CALLED CHO! I HELP PROTECT OUR FARMERS AS THEY WORK IN THE FIELDS!
I AM KIM! I, TOO, LABOR IN THE FIELDS, THAT OUR PEOPLE MAY EAT!
BUT THE GUERRILLAS ARE EVERYWHERE! THERE IS NO SAFETY-- NO PEACE!

THEY SPEAK THE TRUTH! THOUGH THE FIELDS ARE FERTILE, THERE IS LITTLE FOOD! THE RED GUERRILLAS HAVE BROUGHT FAMINE TO THE LAND!
HERE, IN THIS REMOTE VILLAGE, FEAR AND HUNGER ARE ETCHED ON EVERY FACE!

I SEE HELICOPTERS ON PATROL --SEARCHING FOR THE HIDDEN GUERRILLAS! BUT, THEY ARE SO FEW, AND THE COMMUNIST FOE IS SO MANY--AND SO CUNNING!

THEN, BEFORE THOR CAN DECIDE UPON HIS NEXT MOVE, FATE ITSELF POINTS THE WAY--!
MY URU HAMMER TINGLES IN MY HAND! THE STONES I SEEK ARE SOMEWHERE NEAR!

UNHESITATINGLY, THE GOLDEN AVENGER FOLLOWS THE TINGLING OF HIS HAMMER, UNTIL HE LEAVES THE TINY VILLAGE BEHIND HIM...
ONCE THE STONES ARE MINE, I SHALL RETURN TO AID THOSE WHO FIGHT THE TYRANTS!

BUT, AS THE TRAIL LEADS DEEPER AND DEEPER INTO THE DENSE JUNGLE...
THE UNDERBRUSH IS TOO THICK! MY COSTUME SLOWS ME DOWN!

THUS, ACTING UPON A SUDDEN IMPULSE, THE IMMORTAL FROM ASGARD POUNDS HIS HAMMER UPON THE SOIL BENEATH HIS FEET...

AND, A SPLIT-SECOND LATER, IN PLACE OF MIGHTY THOR, THE SLIM FORM OF DR. DON BLAKE MAKES HIS WAY THRU THE JUNGLE, UNIMPEDED BY HIS TRAILING CLOAK...
AT A TIME LIKE THIS, A MERE MORTAL CAN WEAVE HIS WAY THRU THE FOLIAGE FASTER THAN THE BROAD-SHOULDERED, COSTUMED THOR!
I KNOW THE STONES ARE SOMEWHERE STRAIGHT AHEAD! EVERY FEW MINUTES I'LL CHANGE BACK TO THOR AND RECHECK MY POSITION!

BUT, UNKNOWN TO THE LAME DOCTOR, ANOTHER IS AGAIN ABOUT TO TAKE A HAND IN THE GRIM GAME BEING PLAYED UPON THE CHESSBOARD OF FATE!
LOKI! AS QUEEN OF THE NORNS, I HAVE COME TO RECLAIM MY MAGIC STONES!
SOON, MY LOVELY ONE, SOON! I AM USING THEM AS BAIT TO DESTROY THE ONE I DESPISE!

YOU HAVE TRIED EVERY WILE AT YOUR COMMAND, AND STILL MIGHTY THOR LIVES ON! I WARN YOU, LOKI-- IF ODIN EVER LEARNS OF YOUR BASE DECEIT--!
ODIN? DO NOT MENTION THAT NAME AGAIN TO ME! ONCE I HAVE DISPOSED OF THOR, I SHALL FIND A WAY TO USURP THE THRONE OF ODIN HIMSELF! FOR, SUCH IS MY DESTINY!

WAIT! WHY DO YOU VANISH SO QUICKLY? WHY DO YOU LEAVE ME?
EVEN I, WHO HAVE NO LOVE FOR ODIN--I, WHO DABBLE IN EVIL CHARMS-- EVEN I RECOIL IN HORROR AT THE SHEER VILLAINY WITHIN YOUR HEART!

BEGONE THEN, WEAKLING! WHAT CAN YOU KNOW OF THE AMBITIONS OF LOKI?? HOW CAN YOU UNDERSTAND THE HATRED I HAVE NURTURED FOR LO, THESE MANY YEARS?

I, WHO WAS BORN THE SON OF A KING-- I, WHOSE FATHER WAS SLAIN BY THE HAND OF ODIN-- I WAS MEANT TO RULE!!
ALL THE POWERS OF EVIL ARE AT MY COMMAND! I HAVE BUT TO USE THEM WISELY, AND THEY SHALL BRING ME TRIUMPH!

AND, WHERE ODIN IS KIND, LOKI SHALL BE CRUEL! WHERE ODIN IS MERCIFUL, LOKI SHALL BE DEADLY! WHERE ODIN IS GOOD, LOKI SHALL BE THE TRUE EMBODIMENT OF ALL THAT IS EVIL!

THRU THE AGES, THE ACCURSED THOR HAS BEEN MY GREATEST STUMBLING BLOCK! BUT NOW, HE SHALL STAND IN MY WAY NO LONGER!

I HAVE WAITED TOO LONG, PLANNED TOO WELL! AT LAST, MY TRAP IS SET! THE TIMING IS PERFECT!
EVERYTHING PROCEEDS EXACTLY AS I WILLED IT TO!

THE THUNDER GOD TRANSFORMED HIMSELF TO HIS MORTAL FORM JUST WHEN I WANTED HIM TO! HE CANNOT KNOW THAT A DETACHMENT OF ENEMY TROOPS ARE POISED TO STRIKE!
AND, I HAVE ARRANGED THE FINAL IRONY! HE SHALL KEEP HIS ENCHANTED CANE-- BUT, HE WILL NOT BE ABLE TO USE IT!
NOW, MY WITLESS PAWNS-- STRIKE AT THOR! THE TIME IS NOW!

AT THAT SPLIT-SECOND, BEFORE THE STARTLED DR. BLAKE CAN AGAIN POUND HIS ENCHANTED WALKING STICK, HE IS OVERWHELMINGLY ATTACKED AND CAPTURED BY A BAND OF GUERRILLAS WHO POUR FORTH FROM SECRET UNDER-GROUND TUNNELS!
IT IS A YANKEE! SEIZE HIM!
UHHH--!
IT IS A PUZZLEMENT! THERE ARE NO OTHERS! HE IS ALONE!

TAKE HIM TO THE COMRADE COMMANDER! HE WILL KNOW WHAT TO DO WITH THE YANKEE DOG!
THEY'RE BINDING MY ARMS WITH MY CANE! AT LEAST THEY HAVEN'T TAKEN IT FROM ME!

BUT, WHAT USE IS IT TO ME IF I CAN'T POUND IT! UNLESS I CAN CHANGE BACK TO THOR QUICKLY, MY LIFE ISN'T WORTH A NICKEL HERE!
AN UNDERGROUND AMMO DUMP AND HIDING PLACE! SO THIS IS WHY THE HELICOPTERS COULD NEVER FIND THE MAIN FORCE OF GUERRILLAS!
THE COMRADE COMMANDER AWAITS!

SO! YOU HAVE CAPTURED A YANKEE SPY! GOOD WORK, MINH CHU!
NOW LEAVE US! I SHALL ENJOY TOYING WITH THE DOOMED AMERICAN DOG!

YOU CAN BE CERTAIN THAT YOU WILL BE PUT TO DEATH AS A SPY! BUT, IF YOU TELL ME EVERY-THING I WANT TO KNOW, YOUR DEATH MAY BE A QUICK ONE!
NOW SPEAK, YANKEE SWINE! WHO SENT YOU? WHAT IS YOUR MISSION?
I-I'M A DOCTOR! I WANT ONLY TO HELP THE SUFFERING VILLAGERS!
HIS EYES ARE MERCILESS! --COLD AS ICE!

OBSERVE THIS PICTURE! IT WAS TAKEN BY OUR AUTOMATIC SPY CAMERA BATTERY!
HAVE YOU EVER SEEN SUCH A PERSONAGE? OR, IS IT MERELY A YANKEE TRICK? SPEAK!
EVEN IF I KNEW, I'D NEVER TELL YOU!

BAH! MY PATIENCE IS AT AN END! NOW I'LL MAKE YOU TALK! IT IS KNOWN HOW SOFT-HEARTED YOU YANKEE FOOLS ARE--!
BRING IN THE HOSTAGES! IF THE AMERICAN DOES NOT TALK--THEY WILL DIE!

HERE ARE THE LATEST BATCH OF HOSTAGES, COMRADE! IT WAS KNOWN THAT THEY SHELTERED THE UNKNOWN FLYING MAN!
THE FAMILY THAT HELPED ME WHEN I WAS THOR! I CAN'T LET HARM COME TO THEM!
SO!

THEY ARE ALL THAT IS LEFT OF ONE OF THE PEASANT FAMILIES FROM THE HILLS, COMRADE! THE MOTHER CLAIMS TO HAVE ONE OTHER SON, BUT SAYS HE HAS BEEN MISSING FOR YEARS!
SILENCE! DO NOT BORE ME WITH UNIMPORTANT DETAILS! LEAVE ME ALONE WITH THEM! BEGONE!

BUT, AS SOON AS THE OTHER TROOPS HAVE LEFT...
SO! IT HAS COME TO THIS! MY OWN FAMILY, DEFYING THE MIGHT OF THE COMMUNIST VIET CONG!
HU SAK, MY BROTHER! IS THIS WHY YOU LEFT US--TO SERVE THE MERCILESS RED TYRANTS?
MY HEART IS GRATEFUL THAT YOUR FATHER NO LONGER LIVES TO WITNESS YOUR SHAME!
I'VE GOT TO MAKE A RUN FOR IT! IT'S NOW OR NEVER!

SURPRISE WAS ON MY SIDE! THEY DIDN'T EXPECT ME TO TRY A DASH FOR FREEDOM!
NOW, IF I CAN JUST FIND A WAY TO STRIKE MY CANE AGAINST THE GROUND BEFORE THEY CATCH ME--!
AFTER HIM! YOU'LL ANSWER TO ME IF THE YANKEE ESCAPES!

THEN, WITH ONLY SECONDS TO ACT, DON BLAKE DOES THE ONLY THING POSSIBLE--!
I'VE GOT TO THROW MYSELF TO THE GROUND, FALLING SO THE CANE STRIKES FIRST!
I DID IT!

EXACTLY ONE HEARTBEAT LATER, THE MIGHTY THUNDER GOD HURLS HIS INCREDULOUS PURSUERS ASIDE AS THOUGH THEY'RE MADE OF STRAW...!
BACK! BACK! FLEE, WHILE STILL YOU MAY!
NOTHING SHALL BAR THE PATH OF THOR, SON OF ODIN!

MY HAMMER! IT ALL BUT LEAPS FROM MY HAND! LOKI'S ENCHANTED STONES MUST BE RIGHT WITHIN REACH!
I SEE THEM--WITHIN THAT CAVE AHEAD!

THE PACKET RESTS ATOP THAT CACHÉ OF ARTILLERY SHELLS!
THIS IS NO MERE COINCIDENCE! EVIL LOKI PLANNED IT THIS WAY! HE MEANT FOR ME TO ENTER FIGHTING --FOR, IF THOSE SHELLS WERE TO EXPLODE ALL AT ONCE, EVEN MY GREAT STRENGTH MIGHT NOT SAVE ME FROM ANNIHILATION!

MEANWHILE...
YOU ARE NO LONGER MY BROTHER! YOU HAVE BETRAYED YOUR FAMILY, YOUR PEOPLE, BY SERVING THE RED TERRORISTS!
I HAVE POWER OF LIFE AND DEATH HERE! YOU DARE SPEAK SO TO ME?!! WATCH YOUR TONGUE, YOUNG FOOL!
HIS WORDS ARE TRUE, HU SAK! YOU HAVE BROUGHT GREAT SHAME TO US ALL!

NO! NO! I AM COMMANDER HERE! YOU DO NOT MATTER! NOBODY MATTERS! ONLY THE COMMUNIST CAUSE IS IMPORTANT! PEOPLE MEAN NOTHING! HUMAN LIVES MEAN NOTHING!
DON'T YOU UNDERSTAND?? YOU'RE WRONG! WRONG! WRONG!

AND THEN, THE CHAMBER IS STILL! UNTIL, AN ANGUISHED CRY RINGS OUT--!
CHO! MY BROTHER! WHAT HAVE I DONE??
I DID NOT MEAN IT TO END LIKE THIS! I ONLY MEANT TO-- TO-- MOTHER!! OH-- NO!

SHE THREW HERSELF IN THE PATH OF THE BULLETS! SHE WANTED TO SAVE CHO! BUT NOW-- BOTH OF THEM--!!
MOTHER-- SPEAK TO ME! MOTHER--!!
IT IS--HOPELESS!! I SHALL NEVER HEAR HER VOICE AGAIN!

KIM-- MY SISTER-- COME BACK!! KIM--!
HELP! HELP! HE IS A MURDERER! MY OWN BROTHER! HELP--!

THAT CRY! FROM WITHIN THE TUNNEL! IT IS THE GIRL--KIM! I MUST GO TO HER! IF SHE IS IN DANGER HERE, ONLY THOR CAN SAVE HER!

THEN, WITH THE FURY OF A THOUSAND STORMS, WITH THE RAGE THAT ONLY A THUNDER GOD CAN FEEL, THE MIGHTY THOR BATTERS HIS WAY THRU THE ONRUSHING GUERRILLAS--!

SWINGING HIS SHATTERING HAMMER WITH THE CRUSHING, SMASHING FORCE OF A NUCLEAR HOLOCAUST, HIS EYES BLAZING LIKE A THOUSAND SUNS-- THE STEEL CORDS OF HIS MIGHTY MUSCLES RIPPLING ALONG HIS GREAT ARMS--THOR ADVANCES RELENTLESSLY AS AN AVALANCHE!

--UNTIL, SCANT SECONDS LATER, THE VALIANT IMMORTAL EMERGES TRIUMPHANT, AS-- NEVER SLACKENING HIS PACE-- HE RACES TOWARDS THE GIRL WHOSE CRY HAD SUMMONED HIM--!

THE EPIC TALE YOU HAVE JUST READ IS BUT A PRELUDE TO THE STILL GREATER ONE WHICH AWAITS YOU NEXT ISSUE! SO, TILL WE MEET AGAIN, MAY THE STARS OF ASGARD SHINE ON THEE!

Tales of Asgard
HOME OF THE MIGHTY NORSE GODS!
"the SWORD in the SCABBARD!"
BEGINNING: ONE OF THE GREATEST SAGAS OF ALL TIME!! BY:
STAN LEE + JACK KIRBY
INKING: VINCE COLLETTA
LETTERING: ARTIE SIMEK
ASGARD HAS BEEN AT PEACE TOO LONG! HAVING NO NATURAL ENEMIES TO BATTLE, THE BORED, HOT-BLOODED WARRIORS OF ODIN SOON BEGIN TO BRAWL WITH EACH OTHER!
1

The Lord Odin has spoken!

We can do naught but obey!

Where are my sons? Where are Thor and Loki!??

You will find them in the east chamber, Supremacy!

They were eager to battle in the jousting room!

AND, ENTERING THE BARREN CHAMBER, ODIN SEES...
IT IS **YOU** EVIL LOKI, WHO SOWS THE SEEDS OF **DISCONTENT** AMONGST OUR WARRIORS! BUT THIS TIME YOU HAVE GONE **TOO FAR!**
YOUR **HAMMER** HOLDS NO TERROR FOR **ME,** THUNDER GOD! NOT WHILE I POSSESS MY BE-WITCHED **BLADE!**

IMPERIAL ONE, THE FAULT WAS NOT MINE! IT WAS THOR WHO STARTED IT!
YOU LIE, PRINCE OF VILLAINS!!
SILENCE! I BID YOU BOTH COME WITH ME!
I AM FACED WITH A GRAVE PROBLEM IN MY PALACE! IN ORDER TO SOLVE IT, YOU TWO MAY SOON BE FIGHTING SIDE-BY-SIDE!
WHAT IS THE PROBLEM, SIRE?
YOU SHALL SEE IN GOOD TIME--!
FOLLOW ME!
NOBLE FATHER! I PRAY IT DOES NOT CONCERN THE AWESOME OVERSWORD OF ASGARD!!*
SIRE!! THINK WHAT YOU DO! YOU MUST NEVER DRAW THE BLADE!
I DRAW IT NOT!
FOR, IF EVER THIS MIGHTY SWORD BE UNSHEATHED, THE PLANETS THEMSELVES WOULD TREMBLE WITH FEAR!
*SOMETIMES, REFERRED TO AS ODINSWORD! ACCORDING TO LEGEND, IF EVER IT LEAVES ITS SHEATH, THE END OF THE UNIVERSE WILL BE AT HAND! -- STAN.

FATHER! THE BLADE-- IT HAS A CRACK IN IT!
OF COURSE! THIS IS THE WORK OF SOME POWERFUL EVIL FORCE!
WHO COULD HAVE DAMAGED THE GREAT OVERSWORD--AND WHY?
A FORCE SO STRANGE, SO TOTALLY ALIEN, THAT EVEN I CANNOT COMPREHEND ITS POWER OR PURPOSE!

BUT, SIRE--THE LARGER THE CRACK IN THE BLADE BECOMES, THE CLOSER WE COME TO ANNIHILATION!!
AYE! UNLESS I CAN LEARN WHO MY HIDDEN FOE IS--AND THEN DESTROY HIM!

WHOMEVER HE MAY BE--WHETHER HUMAN OR IMMORTAL--WHETHER GODLIKE OR BESTIAL--NO MATTER WHAT HIS POWER--HE MUST BE FOUND, AND--HE MUST BE UTTERLY, TOTALLY CRUSHED!! --SO BE IT!!
5

THUS, I ORDER THE TWO OF YOU ON AN EXPEDITION--FIND OUR UNKNOWN ENEMY, AND THEN--DESTROY HIM!
YOU DARE NOT FAIL, FOR--IF YOU DO, THE CRACK IN THE OVERSWORD MAY GROW LARGER, AND A UNIVERSE WILL PERISH!!
THE END
NEXT ISSUE, YOU WILL WITNESS THE SPELLBINDING "START OF THE QUEST"! FOR ADVENTURE-FANTASY AT ITS GREATEST, DON'T MISS THOR# 118--AND, FOR THE LOVE OF ASGARD, KEEP YOUR OVERSWORD SHEATHED!

Journey into Mystery
with
The Mighty Thor
Approved by the Comics Code Authority
IND.
Marvel Comics Group 12¢
118
July
"To Kill a Thunder God!"
Introducing: The Indestructible Destroyer!

HE, WHO BEARS THE NAME: DESTROYER, POSSESSES THE POWER
"TO KILL A THUNDER GOD!"
REMEMBER LAST ISH? WE SAW MIGHTY THOR REGAIN LOKI'S ENCHANTED STONES ON A VIETNAMESE BATTLEFIELD! NOW, ALL THAT REMAINS IS TO CARRY THE GIRL, KIM, TO SAFETY, AND THEN RETURN TO ASGARD! BUT FATE--AND THE DESTROYER--HAVE OTHER PLANS!
ON YOUR TOES, CHARLIE! ENEMY AIR-CRAFT ZEROING IN AT SIX O'CLOCK!
NO! WAIT! IT'S NOT A PLANE! IT'S--IT'S--CHARLIE! LOOK FOR YOURSELF!
I'VE HEARD ABOUT HIM--READ ABOUT HIM--BUT, TO SEE HIM THIS WAY--NOW!
A STORY STEEPED IN SPLENDOR BY... STAN LEE
ARTWORK BATHED IN BEAUTY BY.... JACK KIRBY
INKING DIPPED IN DRAMA BY........ VINCE COLLETTA
LETTERING COUCHED IN CLICHÉS BY.. ARTIE SIMEK
1

HE--HE LEFT THE GIRL WITH US, AND TOOK OFF AGAIN WITHOUT A WORD!
THEN, WE'RE NOT SEEIN' THINGS! IT REALLY IS THOR HIMSELF!
IT IS TRULY THOR--THE ONE WHO SAVED MY LIFE!
THE GIRL WILL BE BROUGHT TO SAFETY NOW!
AND SO, I NEED TARRY NO LONGER ABOVE THIS DESOLATE BATTLEFIELD!

FOR, I MUST BRING THE ENCHANTED STONES TO ASGARD, TO PROVE TO NOBLE ODIN THAT MY EVIL HALF-BROTHER HAD CHEATED DURING THE "TRIAL OF THE GODS"! *
*IF YOU MISSED THAT CLASSIC, IN THOR #116, YOU'VE ONLY YOURSELF TO BLAME! --STAN.

BUT FIRST, I SHALL PAUSE A MOMENT TO MAKE CERTAIN MY PRIZE IS STILL INTACT!

I SHALL INSPECT LOKI'S POUCH ONCE AGAIN, COUNTING EACH STONE WITH CARE!
FOR, WOE UNTO MANKIND IF ANY HUMAN SHOULD UNWITTINGLY FIND ONE OF THE ACCURSED GEMS!

BUT, EVEN AS THE THUNDER GOD EXAMINES THE NORN STONES, LOKI'S HATE-FILLED EYES FOLLOW HIS EVERY MOVE FROM FAR-OFF ASGARD--!
IF THOR IS TO BE STOPPED, IT MUST BE NOW!
2

ONCE HE REACHES ASGARD, IT WILL BE TOO LATE FOR ME! THOR WILL HAVE WON!
I MUST FIND A WAY TO DEFEAT HIM BEFORE HE LEAVES EARTH! AND FIND IT I SHALL!

EVEN NOW MY BRAIN FORMS A SCHEME--SO CUNNING, SO CLEVER, THAT ONLY LOKI COULD HAVE CONCEIVED IT!
NOT FAR FROM THOR IS A RENEGADE HUNTER! HIS HEART IS FILLED WITH GREED--HE IS MY MAN!

HE DOES NOT SUSPECT THAT HE STANDS NEAR THE TEMPLE OF--THE DESTROYER!! BUT, I SHALL REVEAL IT TO HIM--IN MY OWN WAY!
FIRST, I MUST MAKE CERTAIN THAT HE SEES THE THUNDER GOD, WHO EVEN NOW PREPARES TO FLY TO ASGARD--!
WHO'S THAT--AHEAD OF ME??!

THOR!! THE GREATEST PRIZE OF ALL TO ANY HUNTER!
I WOULDN'T DARE RISK A MERE BULLET ON SUCH A TARGET--BUT, THIS ANESTHETIC SHELL, WHICH CAN INSTANTLY STOP A HERD OF ELEPHANTS, MAY PUT HIM TO SLEEP!

AND SO, THE MIGHTY THOR IS TEMPORARILY FELLED BY THE ONE WEAPON WHICH HIS INDESCRIBABLE STRENGTH IS USELESS AGAINST--A SIMPLE, FAST-ACTING SLEEPING-GAS SHELL!
I DID IT! I'VE BAGGED THE GREATEST GAME OF ALL--HE'S MY CAPTIVE!

THERE MUST BE THOSE WHO WILL PAY ME A KING'S RANSOM FOR SUCH A CAPTIVE! INTERNATIONAL CRIME LORDS--SUPER-POWERED FOES WHOM HE HAS DEFEATED--HEADS OF ENEMY STATES!! I MUST THINK--THINK!!

BUT LOKI, WATCHING EVERY MOVE FROM HIS CHAMBER IN ASGARD, DRIVES THAT THOUGHT FROM THE HUNTER'S MIND! FOR, THE GOD OF EVIL HAS OTHER PLANS FOR HIM--FAR, FAR MORE FANTASTIC ONES--!
LEAVE THOR SECURELY TIED! BEFORE DEALING WITH HIM, I MUST EXAMINE THESE ANCIENT TREASURES WHICH I HAVE FOUND HIDDEN IN THE NEARBY HILLS!
THEY MUST BE CENTURIES OLD--FROM THE DAYS OF THE VIKINGS--OF THE NORSE GODS!
BUT, HOW DID THEY GET HERE? WHAT DOES IT MEAN?
LITTLE DOES THE CONNIVING HUNTER DREAM THAT IT IS ALL PART OF LOKI'S MASTER PLAN--AND THAT HE IS NO MORE THAN A PAWN IN THE GREAT CHESS GAME OF THE IMMORTALS!

I'VE BEEN A FOOL TO HUNT FOR MERE GAME, WHEN TREASURES SUCH AS THIS ARE HIDDEN IN THE JUNGLE!
BUT, MASTER--THOSE OBJECTS WERE NOT THERE EARLIER TODAY! WE KNOW, FOR WE HAVE SEARCHED THESE HILLS!
HOLD YOUR TONGUES!

ARE YOU TRYING TO TELL ME THERE IS SOME MAGIC INVOLVED?? SOME SUPERSTITIOUS MUMBO-JUMBO? THEY CAME FROM NOWHERE??
YOUR PARDON, MASTER--WE DO NOT KNOW THE ANSWER! BUT THESE OBJECTS REEK OF EVIL--OF DANGER--!

YOU COWARD!!
BACK TO YOUR DUTIES! SO LONG AS I PAY YOU, YOU'LL SERVE ME AND NEVER QUESTION!

AND NOW, I HAVE A FEELING THAT THE GREATEST TREASURE OF ALL IS NEARBY! I MUST FIND IT!
I HAVE CHOSEN MY CAT'S-PAW WELL!
HOW EASY IT IS FOR ME TO CONTROL THE THOUGHTS AND ACTIONS OF A MORTAL, IF HE HAS SUFFICIENT EVIL IN HIS HEART!
4

AND, WHEN THE SMOKE CLEARS-- WHEN THE RUBBLE IS STILLED--THE DAZZLED EYES OF THE STILL UNSUSPECTING HUNTER GAZE UPON--

A MONSTROUS TEMPLE--FROM SOME BYGONE AGE!!

IT MUST HAVE STOOD HERE-- HIDDEN BENEATH THE CONCEALING PLATEAU--SINCE TIME IMMEMORIAL!! BUT--*WHY???*

MEANWHILE, THE SLEEPING GAS HAVING FINALLY WORN OFF, THE MIGHTY THOR AWAKENS!!

WHAT IS THIS?? THE SON OF ODIN, BOUND AND FETTERED LIKE A HEAD OF CATTLE!!

WITH THE MEREST SHRUG OF HIS POWER-PACKED MUSCLES, THE GOLDEN HAIRED IMMORTAL SEVERS HIS BONDS, AND THEN...
NOW TO LEARN WHO IS RESPONSIBLE FOR THIS MONUMENTAL INDIGNITY!

DO NOT SLAY US, MAN WITH LIMBS OF STEEL! IT WAS THE HUNTER WHO BADE US SHACKLE YOU!
HE HAS RUN OFF, TOWARDS THE PLATEAU OF SILENCE!
THEN THOR SHALL FOLLOW!
FEAR NOT! NO HARM SHALL COME TO THE INNOCENT!

REACHING THE SITE IN SECONDS, THOR GASPS IN SHOCK AS HE REALIZES...
IT IS THE TEMPLE OF DARKNESS-- BUILT BY ODIN, UNTOLD AGES AGO, TO HOUSE THE DESTROYER!!
WHAT SINISTER FORCE HAS EXPOSED IT NOW--BEFORE THE APPOINTED TIME???

THE DESTROYER IS THE MOST DANGEROUS, THE MOST DEADLY SINGLE ENTITY EVER CREATED!
IF THE HUMAN REACHES IT BEFORE I DO, HIS BRAIN WILL UNDERGO THE MYSTIC TRANSFER--ENTERING THE DESTROYER'S BODY, AND BRINGING THE MONSTER TO LIFE!

BY THE STARS OF ASGARD--I'VE ARRIVED TOO LATE!
HIS BODY STANDS RIGID! HIS BRAIN HAS ALREADY ACTIVATED THE DESTROYER!!

BACK, THUNDER GOD!! DO NOT APPROACH WHAT WAS ONCE MY MORTAL BODY!
YOU LIVE!!!

I DO MORE THAN LIVE! I DO WHAT I WAS CREATED FOR!! I DESTROY!!
NO!! BY THE GOLDEN GATE OF ASGARD-- IT MUST NOT BE!!
THE ALL-WISE ODIN PLACED YOU HERE AGES AGO-- TO FIGHT FOR EARTH SHOULD DANGER THREATEN!! THE TIME HAS NOT YET COME!!

YOU HAVE AWAKENED TOO SOON!! YOU MUST RETURN TO THE ENDLESS SLEEP! YOU MUST BE STOPPED, BEFORE IT IS TOO LATE!!

IT IS ALREADY TOO LATE! EVEN THE POWER OF YOUR HAMMER CANNOT STEM THE FURY OF ODIN'S OWN CREATION!

HE SPEAKS THE TRUTH! OF ALL WHO LIVE-- ONLY THE DESTROYER CAN ALSO LIFT THOR'S HAMMER --FOR ODIN HAS MADE HIM ALL-POWERFUL!

IF I AM DEFEATED, ALL OF EARTH WILL BE HELP-LESS BEFORE HIM!! YET, HOW CAN I TRIUMPH OVER HE WHOM ODIN MADE UNBEATABLE??!
8

HE WAS CREATED TO DESTROY THE FIRST THING HE SAW, AFTER BEING BROUGHT TO LIFE!
FOR, ONLY SOME DREAD MENACE TO EARTH COULD HAVE FOUND HIM, AND AWAKENED HIM!

BUT, THAT UNWITTING HUNTER HAS AWAKENED HIM TOO SOON--I AM THE FIRST ONE HE HAS SEEN!! HE WILL NEVER REST UNTIL I AM VANQUISHED...
AND, BY DECREE OF IMPERIAL ODIN, HE HAS THE POWER TO SLAY ME!

MEANWHILE, THE SAME CHILLING THOUGHT STRIKES LOKI...!
EVEN I DID NOT SUSPECT THE FULL POWER OF THE DESTROYER! IF HE IS NOT STOPPED, THE THUNDER GOD WILL DIE!

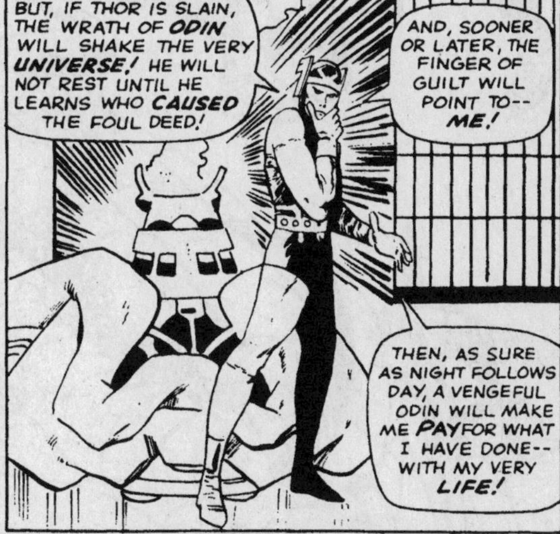
BUT, IF THOR IS SLAIN, THE WRATH OF ODIN WILL SHAKE THE VERY UNIVERSE! HE WILL NOT REST UNTIL HE LEARNS WHO CAUSED THE FOUL DEED!
AND, SOONER OR LATER, THE FINGER OF GUILT WILL POINT TO--ME!
THEN, AS SURE AS NIGHT FOLLOWS DAY, A VENGEFUL ODIN WILL MAKE ME PAY FOR WHAT I HAVE DONE--WITH MY VERY LIFE!

I MEANT ONLY TO STOP THOR--NOT TO CAUSE HIS DEATH! I ONLY WISHED TO HAVE HIM LOSE MY ENCHANTED STONES!
BUT, FOR THE FIRST TIME, I HAVE OUT-SMARTED MYSELF! I MUST SAVE THOR, IF I VALUE MY OWN LIFE!
ONLY ODIN HIMSELF HAS THE POWER TO STOP THE DESTROYER! I MUST WARN HIM--BEFORE IT IS TOO LATE!

GUARDS! STAND ASIDE! I MUST HAVE IMMEDIATE AUDIENCE WITH REGAL ODIN!
IT IS FORBIDDEN! NONE MAY ENTER!
9

UNHAND ME! YOU SPEAK TO LOKI, SON OF ODIN, BROTHER OF THOR! I CLAIM MY IMPERIAL PRIVILEGE!
EVEN YOU HAVE NOT THE RIGHT! OUR MONARCH SLEEPS THE SLEEP OF LIFE-- THE RITUAL HE MUST ENDURE FOR ONE FULL DAY EACH YEAR, IN ORDER TO PRESERVE HIS IMMORTALITY!
NONE MAY AWAKEN HIM! THOUGH THE HEAVENS THEMSELVES MAY TREMBLE, ODIN SHALL SLEEP THIS DAY!
REMOVE THE PRINCE OF EVIL--OR PAY WITH YOUR LIVES!
10

BACK, YOU UNTHINKING CLODS! THERE IS MORE AT STAKE THAN THE SLEEP OF LIFE! ODIN MUST BE TOLD OF THE DANGER THAT THREATENS--!
GUARDS! TO MY SIDE-- IN THE NAME OF ODIN!

YOU WITLESS FOOLS! THE LIFE OF THE THUNDER GOD IS AT STAKE!
STOP HIM!

RELEASE ME!! OR THE DEATH OF THOR SHALL BE UPON YOUR HANDS!!
YOU LIE, MASTER OF TRICKERY!
THOR IS YOUR ENEMY-- AS ALL OF ASGARD KNOWS!

YOU WOULD NEVER DARE AWAKEN ODIN TO SAVE THE ONE YOU HATE!
WE KNOW NOT WHAT VILE SCHEME YOU PLAN, BUT WE'LL HAVE NO PART OF IT!
WAIT! STOP! YOU DON'T UNDERSTAND!

WE UNDERSTAND THAT ONLY KNAVES WOULD HEED THE WORD OF EVIL LOKI!
COME BACK! LISTEN TO ME --YOU MUST LISTEN--!
YOU SHALL REMAIN IN THE DUNGEON OF NO-ESCAPE UNTIL ODIN AWAKENS! WE SHALL HEAR NO MORE!

MEANWHILE, A WORLD AWAY, THE INCREDIBLE BATTLE CONTINUES TO RAGE...
NEVER BEFORE HAVE I FACED THE DEADLY ONSLAUGHT OF MY OWN HAMMER!

BUT, LUCKILY, THE AIM OF THE DESTROYER IS NOT YET THE EQUAL OF THOR'S!
I MUST REGAIN MY MALLET BEFORE HE STRIKES AGAIN!

IT IS MINE AGAIN!! BUT-- HOLD--!!
THE VERY GROUND SHAKES BENEATH MY FEET! WHAT NEW ATTACK DOES THE INVINCIBLE ONE LAUNCH?

A BOLT OF LIMITLESS FORCE-- BLAZING FROM HIS DEADLY FINGERS!

AND THEN, FOR THE FIRST TIME WITHIN MEMORY OF MAN OR IMMORTAL, THE IMPOSSIBLE-- THE INCREDIBLE-- THE UNBELIEVABLE BECOMES A STAGGERING REALITY--!
MY HAMMER!! HE SLICED IT IN TWO!!

IF FATE DECREES THAT I DO BATTLE WITH NO WEAPON-- THEN SO BE IT! BUT, THOUGH ONLY DEATH CAN BE THE OUTCOME, I SHALL FIGHT WHILE A SINGLE BREATH REMAINS WITHIN ME!
12

BUT WAIT! I AM NOT WEAPONLESS! I HAVE THE STONES OF LOKI!

AND WITH THESE ENCHANTED STONES, THE POWER OF LEVITATION IS MINE!
FLOATING OUT OF REACH CANNOT SAVE YOU FROM THE DESTROYER! FOR I POSSESS EVERY FORCE IN THE UNIVERSE!

HE SPEAKS TRUE! ODIN DESIGNED HIM TO BE UNBEATABLE!
A SIMPLE MAGNETIC FORCE WILL BRING YOU TO ME WITHIN SECONDS!

AND NOW, I'LL MAKE CERTAIN YOU CANNOT EVADE ME AGAIN!
IS THIS TRULY TO BE THE END OF THE THUNDER GOD? NO! SUCH A GRIM MOCKERY OF FATE CANNOT BE! IT MUST NOT BE!

ANOTHER FORCE BEAM IS LIQUIFYING THE VERY ELEMENTS OF THE CHAMBER FLOOR!!
ZZZTT!

AND NOW HE MAKES THE MOLECULES DIAMOND-HARD-- TRAPPING ME BEFORE HIM!

AND, AT THAT VERY MOMENT, IN A DUNGEON IN FABLED ASGARD...
I MUST SAVE THOR--I MUST! FOR, IF HE SHOULD PERISH, THEN MY LIFE WILL SURELY BE FORFEIT!!

BUT, EVEN MY POWERS OF ENCHANTMENT CANNOT MELT THE WALLS OF ODIN'S DUNGEON OF NO ESCAPE!
YET, EVERY CHAIN HAS ITS WEAKEST LINK--AND THIS CELL IS NO EXCEPTION!

THOUGH THE VERY WALLS ARE ESCAPE-PROOF, I SHALL STRIKE BY CONTROLLING THE WEAKEST LINK--ONE OF THE GUARDS!
DO NOT LOOK AWAY FROM YON DUNGEON! LOKI IS THE MASTER OF CUNNING!
BAH! EVEN HE COULD NEVER--WAIT!
WHAT IS THAT--THAT STRANGE, SHIMMERING LIGHT??

IT IS A TRICK!! AVERT YOUR EYES! DO NOT LOOK AT IT!!
TOO LATE! IT DAZZLES MY SENSES! MY MIND GROWS BLANK--!

NONE BUT LOKI COULD HAVE CONCEIVED SUCH A PLAN!
I--MUST--FREE--THE--PRISONER!

BUT, EVEN THE GOD OF EVIL CAN FAIL! HIS HYPNOTIC LIGHT ONLY TRAPPED THE ONE OF US--I WAS ABLE TO RESIST--AND STRIKE BACK!
UNHHHH--!

NOW BACK, THOU PRINCE OF KNAVES!!
FOOL THAT I AM!! I WAS UNFORGIVEABLY CARELESS! THERE WERE TWO OF THEM!
YOU SHALL REMAIN SHACKLED HERE TILL ODIN DOTH AWAKE!
BUT--THAT WILL BE TOO LATE--!! CAN'T YOU SEE--??

IT'S USELESS! THERE IS NO MORE I CAN DO! THESE SHACKLES WERE FORGED BY COMMAND OF ODIN HIMSELF!
I CANNOT ESCAPE TO AWAKEN THE ALL-WISE ONE! THUS, THE THUNDER GOD WILL SURELY MEET HIS DOOM AT THE HANDS OF THE INVINCIBLE DESTROYER!

AND, THE SLAYING OF THOR IS CERTAIN TO SOUND MY OWN DEATH KNELL! FOR THE FIRST TIME, LOKI HAS ENTRAPPED HIMSELF!
NOTHING CAN SAVE THE SONS OF ODIN! THE TWO OF US ARE --DOOMED!

BUT, MIGHTY THOR IS MADE OF STERNER STUFF THAN HIS WICKED HALF-BROTHER! FOR, THE INDOMITABLE FIGHTING SPIRIT OF THE THUNDER GOD CAN NEVER BE CRUSHED--NOT WHILST THE SLIMMEST SHRED OF LIFE REMAINS...!
YOU STRUGGLE IN VAIN! NO POWER IN THE UNIVERSE CAN LOOSEN THOSE MOLECULES ONCE THEY HAVE BEEN HONED TO THE HARDNESS OF ASGARDIAN DIAMONDS!
NO STRUGGLE IS EVER IN VAIN!! IT IS ONLY BASE SURRENDER WHICH LEADS DOWN THE PATH OF FAILURE AND DESPAIR!
15

BUT, THOUGH WE HAVE REACHED THE FINISH OF THIS MONTH'S TITANIC TALE, THERE IS **MORE** TO COME!! BY THE HALLOWED GATES OF ASGARD, YOU MUST JOIN US NEXT ISSUE SO THAT WE MAY SHARE TOGETHER THE WONDERMENT THAT AWAITS US!

Tales of ASGARD
HOME OF THE MIGHTY NORSE GODS!
"THE CRIMSON HAND!"
NOW BEGINNING
THE START OF ONE OF THE GREATEST QUESTS OF ALL TIME!
I AM ALMOST FINISHED WITH YOUR MAP, THUNDER GOD!
IT IS NO EASY TASK TO PLOT THE COURSE FOR A JOURNEY THAT WILL TAKE YOU INTO THE UNKNOWN... BEYOND ASGARD!
BUT, IF ANY-ONE CAN CHART SUCH A COURSE, IT IS YOU, WISE MORDUK!
STORY BY: STAN LEE The LEGEND TELLER!
ART BY: JACK KIRBY The LEGEND MAKER!
INKING BY: VINCE COLLETTA The LEGEND PORTRAYER!
LETTERING BY: SAM ROSEN The LETTERER!

YOUR MISSION MUST NOT FAIL, MIGHTY THOR! FOR, IF YOU DO NOT LEARN WHO HAS CRACKED THE GREAT OVERSWORD OF ASGARD,* THE UNIVERSE WILL NEVER AGAIN BE SAFE!
I THINK NOT OF FAILURE, WISE MORDUK! AND MY HALF-BROTHER, LOKI, SHALL BE WITH ME, TO LEND ME HIS CUNNING AND HIS GUILE!
*AS DRAMATICALLY SHOWN IN THOR # 117... STAN.

AYE, NOBLE GODLING! AND IT IS FOR THAT REASON THAT YOU SHALL NEED YET ANOTHER WEAPON ... ONE OF THE MOST MYSTICAL OF ALL! I SHALL GIVE YOU ... THE CRIMSON HAND!
THE CRIMSON HAND? WHAT MANNER OF WEAPON IS THAT, TRUSTED SAGE?

YOU SHALL SEE FOR YOURSELF, MIGHTY ONE! LONG HAS IT LAIN HIDDEN, HERE WITHIN A SECRET CRYPT, UNTIL SUCH TIME AS NOW... WHEN IT WILL BE MOST SORELY NEEDED!
IT IS BUT A GLOVE! A WARRIOR'S CRIMSON GLOVE!
NAY, 'TIS FAR MORE THAN SO SIMPLE AN OBJECT!

WHEN THE ENCHANTED DISCS ON YON GLOVE'S PALM MAKE CONTACT WITH ANOTHER'S HAND, NEITHER YOU NOR HE CAN MOUTH ANY WORDS UNLESS THEY BE THE SOLEMN TRUTH!
A MYSTIC HAND OF TRUTH! I THANK THEE, MORDUK!

YOU TARRY TOO LONG, BROTHER! I AM EAGER TO BEGIN OUR QUEST!
LOKI! I TOO AM READY! BUT, WHO STANDS AT YOUR SIDE?
HIS NAME IS BRAGGI! I HAVE SELECTED HIM TO BE OVERSEER OF OUR VESSEL'S CREW!

WHILST YOU HAVE DALLIED HERE WITH AGED MORDUK, I HAVE CHOSEN THOSE WHO WILL SERVE US ON OUR GREAT JOURNEY!
I PRAY YOU HAVE CHOSEN WISELY! I GREET THEE, BRAGGI, AND WISH THEE WELL!

BUT, NO SOONER DOES THE CRIMSON GLOVE TOUCH BRAGGI'S NAKED HAND, WHEN...
AND I WISH THEE NAUGHT BUT HARM, UNSUSPECTING ONE!
ONCE WE HAVE SET SAIL, I SHALL SMITE THEE FROM BEHIND AND SLAY THEE!
WHA... WHAT HAVE I SAID??!
THE TRUTH, THOU BASE ASSASSIN!

THEN BE THAT AS IT MAY! YOU HAVE FORCED MY HAND! I SHALL STRIKE NOW INSTEAD OF LATER!
NONE WOULD DARE RAISE SWORD TO THOR... UNLESS THEY BE MAD... OR UNDER THE SPELL OF ANOTHER!

AND MADNESS DOES NOT SHOW IN YOUR EYES!! I SEE NAUGHT BUT EVIL THERE!

YET, YOU ARE BUT A TOOL! IT IS THE ONE WHO HIRED YOU... THE ONE WHO GAVE YOU YOUR DEADLY COMMAND WHO IS MY TRUE ENEMY! YOU ARE LIKE UNTO A SWORD, POSSESSING NO WILL SAVE THE WILL OF HE WHO USES YOU!

NOW BEGONE! THE AWESOME WRATH OF THOR IS NOT TO BE WASTED ON ONE AS LOWLY AS THEE!
IT IS FORTUNATE YOU LEARNED OF HIS DUPLICITY, BROTHER! YET, I CANNOT UNDERSTAND HOW YOU ACCOMPLISHED SUCH A FEAT!
WE SHALL SPEAK OF THAT ANOTHER TIME! THERE IS MUCH TO DO NOW!

WE SHALL PROBABLY NEVER LEARN WHO BRIBED THE ASSASSIN, BRAGGI!
THAT GLOVE! THAT CRIMSON HAND! NOW I KNOW! AFTER ALL THESE AGES...!
PERHAPS NOT! BUT LET US CLASP HANDS, MY BROTHER LOKI, AND THEN BEGIN OUR QUEST!
4.

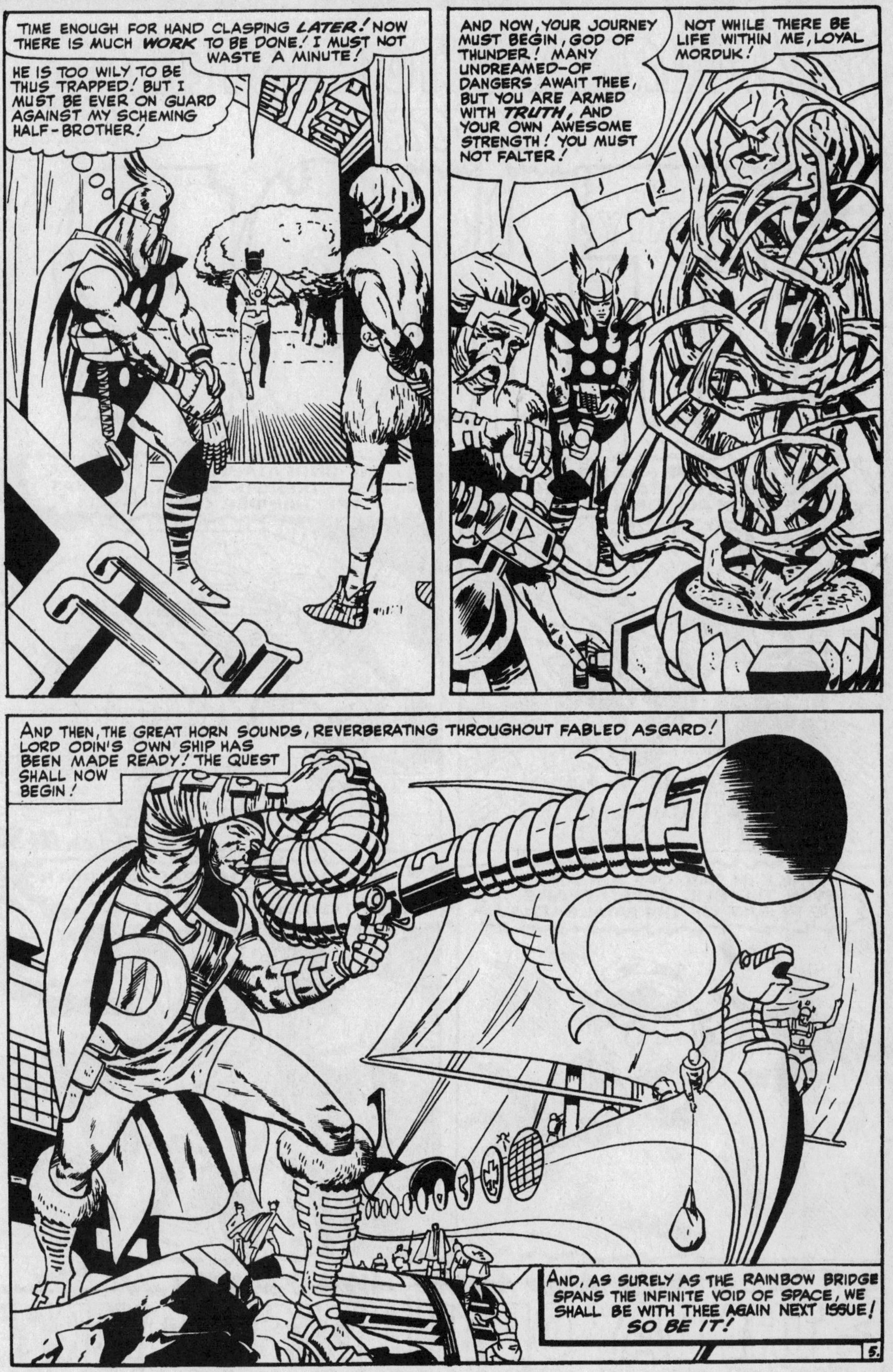

AND THEN, THE GREAT HORN SOUNDS, REVERBERATING THROUGHOUT FABLED ASGARD! LORD ODIN'S OWN SHIP HAS BEEN MADE READY! THE QUEST SHALL NOW BEGIN!

AND, AS SURELY AS THE RAINBOW BRIDGE SPANS THE INFINITE VOID OF SPACE, WE SHALL BE WITH THEE AGAIN NEXT ISSUE! *SO BE IT!*

JOURNEY INTO MYSTERY
WITH
THE MIGHTY
THOR
APPROVED BY THE COMICS CODE AUTHORITY
IND.
MARVEL POP ART PRODUCTIONS 12¢
119
AUG
MIGHTY THOR HAS NO CHOICE BUT TO FACE THE MOST POWERFUL FOE OF ALL TIME...
...THE UNBEATABLE DESTROYER, WHOSE STRENGTH SURPASSES THAT OF THE THUNDER GOD HIMSELF!
WHILE IN FAR-OFF ASGARD, EVEN THE EVIL LOKI FEARS THE RESULT OF THE FATAL BATTLE!
FOR ONLY ODIN HAS THE POWER TO STOP THE DESTROYER..ODIN WHO IS FORBIDDEN TO INTERFERE!
ALL THIS AND MORE AWAITS YOU IN
"THE DAY OF THE DESTROYER!"

"THE DAY OF THE DESTROYER!"
THE DESTROYER! THE MIND-STAGGERING MENACE CREATED COUNTLESS AGES AGO BY ODIN HIMSELF! HIS PURPOSE: TO SAVE MANKIND FROM SOME FUTURE FOE--IF NEEDED! BUT, ACCIDENTALLY, THE DESTROYER IS BROUGHT TO LIFE TOO SOON, AND THE FOE HE FACES IS--THE MIGHTY THOR!
ONCE HIS BLINDING BOLT OF ELEMENTAL POWER TOUCHES ME, I'LL BE TRANSFORMED INTO ANOTHER ELEMENT!! BUT--WAIT!! I AM CHANGING ALREADY!
WHO BUT STAN LEE COULD HAVE WRITTEN THIS TALE?
WHO BUT JACK KIRBY COULD HAVE DRAWN IT?
WHO BUT VINCE COLLETTA COULD HAVE INKED IT?
WHO BUT ARTIE SIMEK COULD BE CALLED ARTIE SIMEK?
1

SOME MIRACULOUS POWER HAS SAVED ME BEFORE I COULD BE TRANSFORMED!
MY ENTIRE MOLECULAR STRUCTURE HAS BEEN CHANGED SO THAT I AM NOW UNSOLID! THUS, I CANNOT BE HARMED!

SO, I AM SAFE FROM ATTACK!! BUT-- FOR HOW LONG?
ODIN CREATED THE DESTROYER TO DEFEAT ANYTHING THAT LIVES!
SOONER OR LATER HE WILL DEVISE A MEANS TO SLAY ME!

THE DENSITY OF YOUR MOLECULES HAS CHANGED! THEREFORE, ALL I NEED DO IS CHANGE THE DENSITY OF MY FORCE BOLT--
AND NOW, THUNDER GOD, ONCE AGAIN YOU ARE DOOMED!

HE WAS A FOOL TO ANNOUNCE HIS INTENTION! I STILL HAVE SECONDS IN WHICH TO ESCAPE!

BEING NOW UNSOLID, I CAN EFFORTLESSLY SINK THRU THE STONE FLOOR AND ENTER THE PASSAGEWAY BELOW!

BUT, WHAT STRANGE ENCHANTMENT IS THIS??
NO SOONER DO I LAND BELOW, THAN MY BODY RETURNS TO NORMAL AGAIN! ONCE MORE I AM A THING OF FLESH, AND BLOOD, AND SINEWS!

SUCH SORCERY CAN COME ONLY FROM FABLED ASGARD!! BUT, WHO--WHO AMONG THE IMMORTALS HAS TAKEN A HAND IN THIS DEADLY GAME??

BUT, THOUGH THE THUNDER GOD HIMSELF CANNOT REACH THE GOLDEN GATES TO LEARN THE ANSWER, WE ARE MORE FORTUNATE, AS WE TRAVEL THE RAINBOW BRIDGE TO THE HOME OF THE GODS--!

--AND WE TURN OUR ATTENTION TO THE DUNGEON OF NO-ESCAPE WHICH HOLDS THE PRISONER LOKI!
THE PRISONER HAS BEEN TOO SILENT OF LATE! LOOK YOU IN UPON HIM!
INDEED! FOR HE IS SLY BEYOND ALL MEN!

WHAT TRICK IS THIS? HE LIES PROSTRATE UPON YON FLOOR!
IT IS NO TRICK! 'TIS THE RESULT OF A MYSTIC TRANCE--OF WHICH HE IS THE MASTER!

I KNOW WELL THE SYMPTOMS! HE HATH SENT A FORCE OF THOUGHT TO EARTH, AND THE EFFORT THEREOF HATH RENDERED HIM UNCONSCIOUS!

CAREFUL! HE AWAKES!
I DID IT! I SAVED THOR! I MADE HIS FORM UNSOLID!

CAN IT BE THE MADNESS IS UPON HIM?
NO MATTER! IT IS NO CONCERN OF OURS!
BUT, THE STRAIN WAS TOO GREAT! MY TRANCE IS ENDED! NOTHING CAN SAVE HIM NOW-- EXCEPT THE POWER OF ODIN, HIMSELF!

BUT, ODIN SLEEPS THE SLEEP OF LIFE-- AND NONE MAY AWAKEN HIM, UNDER PAIN OF DEATH!
BUT WAIT! THERE IS ONE WHO MIGHT SUCCEED WHERE I HAVE FAILED-- THE MISTRESS OF MAGIC --THE NORN QUEEN!

THOR MUST BE SAVED, FOR, IF HE DIES, ODIN WILL KNOW T'WAS MY DOING--!
ONLY THE NORN QUEEN CAN HELP-- I MUST SEND HER A MENTAL WAVE IMAGE--!!

LIKE A LIVING THING, THE FORCE OF PURE MENTAL ENERGY CROSSES THE BARREN NETHER LANDS OF ASGARD ON ITS WAY TO THE MYSTIC KINGDOM OF THE NORNS...!

WHILE, BACK ON EARTH--!
AND STILL THE DESTROYER PURSUES ME!
HOW MY LIMBS ACHE TO STRIKE OUT-- TO SMASH AND PUMMEL HIM-- TO FIGHT WITH ALL THE AWESOME POWER AT MY COMMAND! AND YET, IT WOULD BE TO NO AVAIL!
ODIN CREATED HIM TO BE STRONGER THAN ANY LIVING BEING-- GOD OR MORTAL! BUT SOMEHOW, HE MUST BE STOPPED!!

THEN, REALIZING THAT THOR'S FORM IS **SOLID** ONCE AGAIN, THE TIRELESS DESTROYER HURLS A BOLT OF **MOLTEN FORCE** WHICH RAKES THE WALLS AND CEILING, TURNING THE VERY GROUND INTO A FLAMING, DEADLY RIVER OF LAVA!!

BUT, ONCE AGAIN, THE SPEED AND COURAGE OF THE GOD OF THUNDER WHISK HIM OUT OF HARM'S WAY, WHILE HIS FIGHTING HEART SEETHES WITHIN HIS BREAST--!

ENOUGH OF THIS SENSELESS **FLEEING!!** I AM NO SCARED RABBIT, TO RUN FROM DANGER AT EVERY TURN! THOUGH DEATH ITSELF BE MY REWARD, I AM **THOR**, SON OF ODIN!! I SHALL STAND AND **FIGHT!!**

STAND YOUR GROUND, DESTROYER! THE GOD OF THUNDER RUNS NO FURTHER!!

THOUGH YOUR **STRENGTH** BE VIRTUALLY BEYOND MEASURE, YOU SHALL SEE WHAT THE STRENGTH OF **THOR** CAN ACCOMPLISH!

HE STANDS DIRECTLY BELOW-- NOT KNOWING WHAT MY PLAN MAY BE!

THIS THEN IS MY MOMENT TO STRIKE! **THIS** IS WHEN THE MIGHT OF A **THUNDER GOD** SHALL YET WREST **VICTORY** FROM THE DREGS OF DEFEAT!

KRAKK!

THERE, IN THAT LONELY, LONG-LOST TEMPLE, A FEAT OF STRENGTH IS PERFORMED--THE LIKE OF WHICH HAS NEVER BEEN WITNESSED BY LIVING EYES, AS MIGHTY THOR, USING THE POWER OF HIS IMMORTAL LIMBS ALONE, WRENCHES LOOSE A MILLION-TON ARCH OF SOLID ROCK, SENDING IT CRASHING DOWN UPON THE STUNNED FIGURE BELOW--!
THIS CANNOT SLAY THE DESTROYER, FOR HE IS TRULY INDESTRUCTIBLE!! YET, PERHAPS IT WILL STUN HIM--SLOW HIM DOWN LONG ENOUGH FOR ME TO LAUNCH A NEW ATTACK!
BUT, THE DESTROYER WAS CREATED BY ODIN! ODIN, THE ALL-WISE! ODIN, THE ALL-POWERFUL! ODIN, THE OMNIPOTENT! STANDING HIS GROUND BENEATH THE TORRENT OF ROCK, HE DOES NOT EVEN LOSE HIS FOOTING AS THE HOLOCAUST TAKES PLACE AROUND HIM!!
IT'S USELESS! FORCE ALONE CANNOT DEFEAT HIM! AND YET, THERE MUST BE A WAY! FOR, IF I FAIL TO STOP HIM, HIS NEXT TARGET WILL BE THE HUMAN RACE, ITSELF!!
6

THERE IS ONE OTHER AVENUE YET OPEN TO ME!!
IT WAS AN UNSUSPECTING HUNTER WHO FIRST FOUND THE DESTROYER, AND THEREBY BROUGHT HIM TO LIFE!
IT IS THE HUNTER'S BRAIN WHICH GUIDES THE DESTROYER, WHILE HIS OWN MORTAL BODY STANDS LIFELESS!

PERHAPS THAT VERY BODY IS THE WEAPON I NEED TO STOP THE DESTROYER! IF I CAN BUT REACH IT IN TIME!

THERE IT IS-- HIS OWN FRAIL, HUMAN FIGURE!
YOU ARE TOO LATE, DESTROYER! I SHALL REACH IT FIRST!

COME NO CLOSER! IF YOU STRIKE AT ME, YOU WILL DESTROY YOUR OWN MORTAL BODY!
YOU WILL BE TRAPPED IN THE GROTESQUE FORM OF THE DESTROYER FOR ALL ETERNITY!

HAVE YOU FORGOTTEN MY MISSION, THUNDER GOD! I MUST DESTROY-- NO MATTER WHAT THE COST! WHEN I LOWER THIS VISOR, MY GREATEST POWER SHALL BE UNLEASHED-- THE POWER OF COMPLETE DISINTEGRATION!
7

YOU HAVE PLEDGED NEVER TO TAKE A MORTAL LIFE! THEREFORE, YOU MUST RELEASE THAT BODY-- YOU DARE NOT LET IT BE DISINTEGRATED ALONG WITH YOU!
HE SPEAKS THE TRUTH! MY LAST HOPE IS GONE! EVEN NOW, HIS DESTRUCTIVE FORCE BUILDS UP-- HE MAKES READY TO STRIKE--!

MEANWHILE, LOKI'S MENTAL WAVE IMAGE HAS FINALLY REACHED THE FORBIDDING NORN QUEEN--!
WE HAVE BEEN ALLIES IN THE PAST, WE TWO!
YOU MUST DO THIS SERVICE FOR ME NOW!!

YOU MUST CAUSE ODIN TO AWAKEN, THAT THOR BE SAVED! FOR, IF HE PERISHES-- MY LIFE, TOO, IS LOST!
GO, CONSORT OF EVIL! IT SHALL BE DONE!

POWERS OF DARKNESS FROM THE SEA AND THE LAND, COME FORTH TO SERVE ME, HEED YOUR NORN QUEEN'S COMMAND!*
* THIS IS ACTUALLY A VERY LOOSE TRANSLATION, AS WE FEEL THAT VERY FEW OF OUR READERS WOULD FULLY UNDERSTAND THIS CHANT IF RECITED IN THE ORIGINAL NORN DIALECT! --STAN.

SECONDS LATER, IN THE GREAT CHAMBER WHERE ODIN DOTH SLEEP--!
MY LORD, AWAKEN! GREAT IS THE DANGER THAT THREATENS THE SON OF THY HEART!

THEN, WITH A SUDDEN START, THE REGAL HEAD BEGINS TO LIFT--AS THE IMPERIAL EYELIDS SNAP OPEN WITH THE FORCE AND MAJESTY OF A THUNDERCLAP, AS ONE WORD ISSUES FORTH FROM THE ROYAL LIPS--!
THOR!
8

WARRIORS OF THE REALM, STAND ASIDE! I HAVE HEARD A MESSAGE IN A DREAM! THE GOD OF THUNDER IS IN DANGER! WOE TO ANY WHO MAY BE RESPONSIBLE FOR SUCH DIRE TIDINGS!!

LET THE HEAVENS PART!! LET THE DARKNESS VANISH! LET THE SON OF ODIN BE VISIBLE TO MINE EYES! I HAVE SPOKEN!

WHAT MONUMENTAL DISASTER IS THIS! WHO HATH WAKENED THE DESTROYER?? EVEN MIGHTY THOR POSSESSES NOT THE STRENGTH TO COPE WITH MY OWN DREAD CREATION!!

MY SON! STAND AWAY WHILST YOU CAN! ONLY I HAVE THE POWER TO HALT THE ATTACK OF THE INVINCIBLE DESTROYER!
THE VOICE OF LORD ODIN! HE KNOWS!
NAY, MY FATHER! STAY THY HAND! THE GOD OF THUNDER MUST WAGE HIS OWN BATTLE, NO MATTER WHAT THE COST!
NOW, DESTROYER-- DO YOUR WORST!

SLOWLY, FALTERINGLY, THE DESTROYER LIFTS HIS INVINCIBLE HAND TO HIS VISOR, AS THE EXPLOSIVE FORCE WITHIN HIM BEGINS TO SUBSIDE...
I CANNOT DO IT! I CANNOT DESTROY MY OWN MORTAL FORM!
THIS ROUND IS YOURS, SON OF ODIN!

BUT, THE NEXT-- THE LAST-- SHALL BE MINE!
YOUR LIFE ESSENCE-- IT IS RETURNING TO YOUR MORTAL BODY--I CAN SENSE IT!!

TRUE, FOR I SUDDENLY REMEMBERED--YOU ARE PLEDGED NEVER TO HARM A HUMAN!

THEREFORE, YOU CANNOT STRIKE AT ME--FOR, WITH YOUR GOD-LIKE POWER, THE SLIGHTEST BLOW WOULD BRING DEATH TO MY FRAIL, HUMAN BODY!
HE PLANS A TRICK! I MUST BE VIGILANT!
10

THEN, SUDDENLY, HIS FOE'S SINISTER SCHEME BECOMES CLEAR TO MIGHTY THOR--!
YOU PLAN TO REACH THE DESTROYER BEFORE ME--ENTER HIS BODY AGAIN--AND HAVE HIM PROTECT YOUR MORTAL FORM BEFORE I CAN REACH YOU!
AND YOU'RE TOO LATE TO STOP ME!

UNGHHH!
THE GOD OF THUNDER-- TOO LATE??? NEVER, WHILE MY LIFE ENDURES!
WHOOM!

YOU'RE DEMOLISHING THE TEMPLE--BEFORE I HAD TIME TO RETURN TO THE BODY OF THE DESTROYER!
WITHOUT MY LIFE FORCE GUIDING HIM, HE CANNOT MOVE! HE CAN'T SAVE ME!
I'LL BE KILLED!
CEASE YOUR WHIMPERING, MORTAL! IT ILL BECOMES ONE WHO WISHED TO MASTER A WORLD!

BUT NOW, MY WORK IS DONE! THE DESTROYER CANNOT LIVE AGAIN UNLESS ANOTHER HUMAN STANDS WITHIN ARM'S LENGTH OF HIM!

AND THAT SHALL NEVER BE-- AT LEAST, NOT WITHIN THE SPACE OF A HUNDRED LIFETIMES!!
11

FOR, THE TEMPLE OF DARKNESS, WHICH WAS BUILT TO HOUSE THE MOST DESTRUCTIVE LIVING FORCE ON EARTH, SHALL NOW BURY IT BEYOND THE POWER OF ANY MORTAL EVER TO UNEARTH AGAIN!
12

SOMEHOW, A VICTORY HAS MORE MEANING WHEN IT IS WON BY THE FORCE OF YOUR OWN ARMS, THE INGENUITY OF YOUR OWN BRAIN! THIS BATTLE I SHALL REMEMBER FOR MANY YEARS TO COME!

WHAT--WHAT WILL YOU DO TO ME NOW--?
DO TO YOU, MORTAL? NOTHING!
YOU WERE BUT A HELPLESS PAWN, BUFFETED ABOUT BY FORCES YOU COULD NEVER HOPE TO COMPREHEND!!

I MUST HAVE BEEN MAD TO THINK THAT I COULD EVER PREVAIL IN A BATTLE WITH-- YOU!
ALAS, IT IS A MADNESS WHICH ALL MORTALS ARE HEIR TO--THE CRAVING FOR SUPERHUMAN STRENGTH--THE LUST FOR LIMITLESS POWER--AS IF THOSE CAN EVER REPLACE JUSTICE, AND TRUTH!

MY FATHER, THE BATTLE IS ENDED--THE VICTORY WON! I THANK THEE FOR REMAINING ALOOF--FOR STAYING THY HAND!
MY HEART SWELLS WITH PRIDE AT THY GALLANTRY, MY SON! I HAVE SEEN ENOUGH! SO BE IT!
13

MOMENTS LATER...
ONLY CUNNING LOKI COULD HAVE ARRANGED FOR THE DESTROYER TO LIVE AGAIN!
WE BRING THEE THE PRISONER, LOKI, AS COMMANDED, SIRE!

ON YOUR KNEES, MASTER OF TREACHERY!!
NOTHING SHALL SAVE YOU FROM MY ROYAL WRATH THIS DAY!
BY YOUR LEAVE, SIRE --THE PRISONER DID TRY TO AID THE THUNDER GOD!
HE BEGGED TO WAKEN YOU, BUT WAS REFUSED!

INDEED! CRAFTY TO THE END, ART THOU NOT? YOU KNEW THAT THE DEATH OF THOR WOULD MEAN YOUR OWN EXECUTION!
AND YET, I DO CALL THEE SON! I CANNOT FIND IT IN MY HEART TO BE MERCI-LESS TO THEE!

ATTEND MY WORDS! THIS SENTENCE DO I NOW PRONOUNCE--
I BIND THEE IN SERVITUDE TO ULARIC, MY ROYAL WARLOCK!* YOU SHALL LABOR FOR HIM TILL IT PLEASES ME TO RELEASE YOU!
NOW, GO THOU--!
*FOR THOSE FEW OF YOU WHO'VE NEVER BEEN TO ASGARD, WE HASTEN TO EXPLAIN THAT A WARLOCK IS ANOTHER NAME FOR WIZARD, OR SORCERER!--HELPFUL STAN.

I AM FORTUNATE TO HAVE ESCAPED WITH MY LIFE! AND YET, I AM NO HUMBLE PEASANT, TO BE APPRENTICED TO THE ROYAL WARLOCK! I AM LOKI, PRINCE OF EVIL!

WHILE I LIVE, I SHALL PLAN-- I SHALL SCHEME-- I SHALL CONSPIRE!
BUT, THOR STILL POSSESSES MY MYSTIC NORN STONES! THEY ARE EVIDENCE OF MY PAST TREACHERY! HE MUST NEVER BE ALLOWED TO BRING THEM TO ODIN!!

AND, EVEN AS WILY LOKI PLANS A MONUMENTAL NEW DECEPTION, WHAT OF THE MIGHTY GOD OF THUNDER--?
YOU MEAN I'M FREE? YOU'LL LET ME GO??
NO MAN IS EVER TRULY FREE! NOT WHILE CONSCIENCE AND MEMORY REMAIN! BUT I AM DONE WITH YOU!

MY HAMMER! I HAD ALL BUT FORGOTTEN! IT WAS SORELY DAMAGED IN THE BATTLE WITH THE DESTROYER!

I MUST SEE WHETHER IT CAN STILL SERVE ME-- WHETHER IT WILL STILL ALLOW ME THE FREEDOM OF THE SKIES!

IN TRUTH, IT DOES HURL ME INTO THE AIR, BUT I AM UNABLE TO CONTROL ITS FLIGHT!! IT VEERS CRAZILY, LIKE A BIRD WITH BUT ONE WING!!

UNABLE TO GUIDE HIS ENCHANTED MALLET ACCURATELY, THE GOLDEN-HAIRED IMMORTAL SOON PLUMMETS BACK TO EARTH, LIKE A WOUNDED EAGLE!
BY THE STARS! HOW UNSEEMLY A LANDING FOR THE GOD OF THUNDER!!

MY MIGHTY HAMMER!! LONG HAVE YOU SERVED ME--AND WELL! AND STILL SHALL YOU SERVE ME! FOR I SHALL REPAIR THEE!

MIRACLES SHALL PASS BEFORE YOUR EYES IN THE ISSUES THAT FOLLOW! YOU MUST NOT MISS A SINGLE ONE! THE RAINBOW BRIDGE BECKONS! WE HAVE SPOKEN!

Tales of ASGARD
HOME OF THE MIGHTY NORSE GODS!
"GATHER, WARRIORS!"
WRITTEN WITH GALLANTRY BY STAN LEE
DRAWN WITH GREATNESS BY JACK KIRBY
INKED WITH GRANDEUR BY VINCE COLLETTA
LETTERED WITH A STRAIGHT FACE BY ARTIE SIMEK
THE MISSION OF MISSIONS IS ABOUT TO BEGIN!! WITH AN ARMY OF PICKED WARRIORS, MIGHTY THOR PREPARES TO SAIL INTO THE UNKNOWN, TO LEARN WHAT DREAD POWER HAS CAUSED A CRACK IN ODIN'S ENCHANTED OVERSWORD OF ASGARD! FOR, IF THE CRACK SHOULD GROW ANY LARGER, THE ENTIRE UNIVERSE MAY BE DESTROYED!
1

WHEN WILL WE BE READY TO SAIL, BALDER? MY LIMBS ACHE FOR ACTION!
SOON, MY FRIEND-- SOON!
THERE ARE STILL MORE WARRIORS TO BE ACCOUNTED FOR!

I SEE SOME NEW VOLUNTEERS APPROACHING EVEN NOW!
YES! I SHALL ENTER THEIR NAMES TO THE LIST! I BELIEVE THEY HAVE BEEN RECRUITED BY YOUR CO-CAPTAIN, LOKI!

MAKE WAY FOR HOGUN, THE GRIM! I COME TO JOIN THE GREAT MISSION!
HOGUN-- THE SILENT, SINISTER, MYSTERY WARRIOR! NONE CAN PROBE HIS INNERMOST THOUGHTS!

AND I SEE FANDRAL, THE DASHING, JOINING OUR RANKS!
AYE! AS WELL AS KRODA, THE DUELLIST, AND MAGRAT, THE SCHEMER! I TRUST THEM NOT, MIGHTY THOR!
2

AHH, I MIGHT HAVE GUESSED!

IT IS VOLSTAGG, THE ENORMOUS! VOLSTAGG, THE BLUSTERING, BOASTING GIANT OF A WARRIOR!

HAVE AT YOU, PUNY SCOUNDRELS! STAND ASIDE FOR VOLSTAGG! BY MY SWORD, THERE SHALL BE MANY A FLATTENED HEAD THIS DAY!!

BACK!! BY THE GOLDEN GATES OF ASGARD--BACK, YOU KNAVES!! THE PATIENCE OF THOR IS NOT WITHOUT LIMIT!

'TIS THE UNKNOWN ENEMY WHO HAS CRACKED THE GREAT OVERSWORD WE MUST FIGHT--NOT EACH OTHER!!

HOW SAY YOU, VOLSTAGG?? DO YOU ACCEPT THE THUNDER GOD'S COMMAND??
AYE, SON OF ODIN! MY PLACE IS AT THY SIDE! BUT, KNOW YOU THIS--A MOMENT MORE AND I WOULD HAVE CRUSHED YON RUFFIANS!

MY BODY BEARS A THOUSAND WOUNDS GAINED IN ODIN'S SERVICE! ALWAYS HAVE I BEEN IN THE FORE OF EVERY BATTLE FOR ASGARD!
'TIS TRUE, GOOD VOLSTAGG--BUT THOU HAST EATEN TOO WELL SINCE THEN--!
4

RAGNAROK, THE DAY OF THE LAST GREAT BATTLE--THE DAY IN WHICH IT HAS BEEN WRITTEN THE GODS THEMSELVES WILL PERISH! RAGNAROK, THE ONLY MOMENT THAT ODIN HIMSELF AWAITS WITH FEAR AND DREAD! IS RAGNAROK TRULY UPON US?? BY THE BRISTLING BEARD OF ODIN, WE SHALL LEARN MORE NEXT ISSUE! SO BE IT!

JOURNEY INTO MYSTERY
WITH
THE MIGHTY
THOR
APPROVED BY THE COMICS CODE AUTHORITY
MARVEL POP ART PRODUCTIONS 12¢
120
SEPT
"IN MY HAND ...THIS HAMMER!"

THE MIGHTY THOR!
"WITH MY HAMMER IN HAND....!"
I KNEW THAT HERE IN THE GREAT BLAST FURNACES OF PITTSBURGH, I WOULD FIND A GIANT FORGE TO MEND MY HAMMER!
THOR DID IN AN HOUR WHAT WOULD HAVE TAKEN US A MONTH!
WHEW I CAN ALMOST BELIEVE HE IS THE GOD OF THUNDER!
WRITTEN IN THE FIRE OF INSPIRATION BY.... STAN LEE
DRAWN IN THE FLAME OF DEDICATION BY.... JACK KIRBY
INKED IN THE HEAT OF DEVOTION BY...... VINCE COLLETTA
LETTERED IN THE OTHER ROOM BY.......... ARTIE SIMEK
1

THERE! IT IS DONE! MY HAMMER CAN STRIKE ONCE MORE!
I'D SURE LIKE TO SEE HIM TOSS THAT THING!
HOW ABOUT IT, THOR?

I MUST PUT MY URU MALLET TO THE TEST--SO BEHOLD!
THAT CYLINDER OF SOLID STEEL IS WAITING TO BE MELTED INTO ORE --PERHAPS THIS MAY HELP SPEED THE TASK!
KWUNNG!

AND NOW, MY ENCHANTED HAMMER RETURNS TO ME-- AS IT HAS EVER DONE--AS IT SHALL EVER DO... FOR ODIN HAS SO ORDAINED!
MAN! THE METS WOULD TRADE THEIR WHOLE FIRST TEAM FOR A GUY WHO CAN DO THAT!
WHERE DO THEY SELL THAT URU STUFF? I WANNA BUY ME SOME!

MINUTES LATER...
HEY, MIKE! DON'T SQUEEZE TOO HARD --YA MIGHT HURT 'IM!!
FAT CHANCE! HIS FINGERS ARE LIKE STEEL BANDS!
REMEMBER--WHENE'ER MY HAMMER STRIKES FOR JUSTICE, YOU WILL HAVE HELPED!
HOW ABOUT THAT!

AND NOW FOR THE FINAL TEST-- WILL MY MALLET HURL ME UNERRINGLY INTO THE SKY?

SWIFT AS AN EAGLE--TRUE AS AN ARROW--THE GOLDEN-HAIRED IMMORTAL ZOOMS INTO THE AIR AS ONLY A VIKING IMMORTAL CAN...
PRAISE TO IMPERIAL ODIN! MY POWERS ARE INTACT! I AM TRULY GOD OF THUNDER ONCE MORE!

BUT NOW SHALL I DESCEND AND PLAN MY FUTURE COURSE OF ACTION!
I MUST INSPECT THE NORN STONES WHICH I HAVE REGAINED FROM LOKI --I MUST BE CERTAIN THAT THEY ARE INTACT!

THEN, ONLY BY SHOWING THOSE ENCHANTED GEMS TO ODIN CAN I PROVE THAT EVIL LOKI CHEATED DURING THE "TRIAL OF THE GODS"!
FOR, HE USED THE STONES AS WEAPONS, WHILST I ENDURED THE TRIAL WITH NAUGHT SAVE MY OWN NATURAL STRENGTH AND WITS! *
*OUR MORE FORGETFUL FANS MAY REFRESH THEIR MEMORIES BY RE-READING THOR #'S 116, 117, AND 118 --HELPFUL STAN.

BUT, MY HALF-BROTHER'S TIME OF RECKONING IS NEAR AT HAND--!
HE SHALL LEARN HOW INEVITABLE IS THE VENGEANCE OF THOR!
3

THUS, THERE IN THE HALCYON FOREST, THE THUNDER GOD REMOVES THE FATEFUL GEMS FROM THEIR LEATHER POUCH...!
HOW LOVELY THEY ARE! HOW BEAUTIFULLY THEY SPARKLE IN THE MIDDAY SUN!

AND YET, THESE SELFSAME STONES-- UPON WHICH A LITTLE ROBIN PEACEFULLY STANDS--COULD POSE THE GREATEST THREAT TO MANKIND IF THEY SHOULD FALL INTO THE WRONG HANDS!

BUT, I HAVE DALLIED LONG ENOUGH!
IT IS TIME TO RETURN TO ASGARD!

ALAS, AS THE SON OF ODIN SOARS SKYWARD, HE CANNOT KNOW THAT ONE NORN STONE HAS FALLEN FROM THE ANCIENT POUCH...

...ONE STONE OF STRANGE, UNEARTHLY ENCHANTMENT... WHICH NOW LIES SILENTLY WAITING-- IN A LONELY, PRIMEVAL FOREST--WAITING FOR DESTINY TO UNLEASH ITS HIDDEN POWER...!

WHILE, SOMEWHERE IN A FAR DISTANT WORLD...
HOW MY HEA EVER THRILLS-- MY SOUL EVER SINGS--AT THE GLORY AND GRANDEUR OF THE RAINBOW BRIDGE!

AND SO IT COMES TO PASS THAT THE GOD OF THUNDER STANDS IN THE PRESENCE OF ODIN ONCE AGAIN, AND PROVES THAT THE WORD OF THOR IS A BADGE OF HONOR--AND THE DEFEAT HE HAD SUFFERED WAS IN TRUTH--A VICTORY!
THE HEART WITHIN ME SWELLS WITH PRIDE, MY SON! YOU HAVE PROVED THAT LOKI'S VICTORY WAS TRULY A HOLLOW ONE--FOR HE RESORTED TO FORBIDDEN POWER IN ORDER TO ACHIEVE IT!
WHILEST YOU, THE GREATEST WARRIOR OF ALL, WITHOUT WEAPONS--WITHOUT DEFENSES--STILL CAME WITHIN A HAIRSBREADTH OF DEFEATING HIM WHO IS NOT WORTHY TO BE CALLED THY BROTHER!

REVERED FATHER--ALL-WISE ODIN--NOW THAT MINE HONOR HAS BEEN VINDICATED, I BEG TO PLEAD FOR LOKI! HE CANNOT HELP THE EVIL HE PERPETRATES... SO, BE NOT TOO AWESOME IN THY WRATH!
BY THE STARS! THAT THOU--WHOM LOKI MOST HATH WRONGED, SHOULD BE THE ONE TO PLEAD HIS SUIT!
ONLY THY STRENGTH CAN EQUAL THY MATCHLESS NOBILITY!

MEANWHILE, IN THE CASTLE OF ULARIC, THE AGED WARLOCK OF ASGARD, WHOM LOKI IS ALREADY SENTENCED TO SERVE IN BONDAGE...
FETCH ME YON CYLINDER OF ELIXIR, LOKI--AND HAVE A CARE NOT TO SPILL A DROP!
HOARY FOOL! NOT MUCH LONGER SHALL YOU BARK ORDERS TO THE GOD OF EVIL!

THOUGH IT MEANS DEFYING THE SENTENCE OF ODIN HIMSELF, I CAN ENDURE THIS HUMILIATION NO LONGER! AM I NOT THE EQUAL OF THOR IN LINEAGE--IN TITLE--IN CUNNING--AND YEA, EVEN IN POWER--FOR MINE IS THE ULTIMATE POWER OF SORCERY!
WHY SO SILENT, EVIL ONE?

AMONG MY ENEMIES, ULARIC, THERE IS A SAYING--"WHEN THE VOICE OF LOKI IS STILL, LOOK TO YOUR WEAPONS--FOR SURELY THERE IS MENACE IN THE AIR!"
WHAT KNAVERY IS THIS? DO YOU DARE THREATEN ULARIC??
THE GOD OF EVIL WASTES NO TIME WITH MERE IDLE THREATS!
BY USING YOUR OWN POTIONS, UNKNOWN TO YOU, I HAVE CREATED A SUSPENDED ANIMATION MIST-- AND SO DOES LOKI GAIN HIS FREEDOM!
FOOL! WHEN ODIN LEARNS WHAT YOU-- -UHHH-!
BY THEN IT SHALL BE TOO LATE!

THE DIE IS CAST! NOW, THERE CAN BE NO TURNING BACK!
ULARIC SHALL REMAIN WITHIN THIS SPHERE TILL THE POTION WEARS OFF--BUT FIRST, I MUST CONCEAL THE SPHERE ITSELF--

THERE! HE SHALL REMAIN HIDDEN FROM OTHER EYES WITHIN HIS OWN TIME VAULT!

WHILE LOKI NOW IS MASTER OF THE WARLOCK'S ENCHANTMENTS--AS WELL AS MY OWN!
THUS, I SHALL STRIKE AT THE VERY RULE OF ODIN HIMSELF--AND NONE SHALL SUSPECT ME--FOR, IS LOKI NOT THE HELPLESS PRISONER OF ULARIC?!!

AND, THERE SEEMS TO BE TRUTH IN LOKI'S PREDICTION, FOR NOT EVEN THE THUNDER GOD SUSPECTS THE DANGER BEING BREWED...
I CANNOT EXACT VENGEANCE UPON MY HALF-BROTHER WHEN HE IS ALREADY UNDER SENTENCE BY LORD ODIN!
AND NOW, THE DAYS SEEM EMPTY AND ENDLESS HERE IN TRANQUIL ASGARD!
THERE IS BUT ONE THING LEFT TO DO...!
6

WHY HATH THE SON OF MY HEART PETITIONED AN AUDIENCE THIS EARLY IN THE DAY?
HONORED FATHER-- THE TIME HANGS TOO HEAVY UPON ME!
AS THOU WELL KNOWEST, I AM BORN TO ACT, TO FIGHT, TO DARE!! THE VERY FIBERS OF MY BEING REVOLT AT THE THOUGHT OF QUIETUDE, AT THE MINUTES WHICH DRAG TORMENTINGLY ON WITHOUT THE CHALLENGE OF BATTLE!!
SO, I BESEECH THEE, MOST NOBLE FATHER-- GRANT THY PERMISSION THAT I MAY RETURN TO EARTH!

WELL DO I KNOW THAT IT IS THERE WHERE THY HEART TRULY DWELLS! AND THOU HAST EARNED THE RIGHT TO WALK AMONG MORTALS ONCE MORE!
ODIN HATH SPOKEN!!

SO BE IT!

AT LAST-- I AM FREE TO SEE THE ONE WHO HOLDS MY HEART!
NONE CAN KNOW HOW I HAVE MISSED JANE FOSTER THESE MANY LONG WEEKS!

THIS IS MOST PASSING STRANGE! NEVER HAVE THE WINDOWS OF DR. BLAKE'S OFFICE BEEN LOCKED BEFORE!
I DARE NOT FORCE THEM OPEN, FOR SOME WOULD WONDER WHO COULD HAVE DONE IT!
BUT WHY IS ALL SO QUIET? WHY DO I HAVE A PREMONITION OF GRAVE DANGER?
7

'TIS THE VERY MIDDLE OF DAY --WHEN THE OFFICE OF DR. BLAKE SHOULD BE FILLED WITH WAITING PATIENTS!!
YES, IT IS STRANGELY BARE-- UNCOMMONLY DESERTED!

AND, I SEE NO TRACE OF JANE-- THE LOVELY, LOYAL JANE, WHO, EVEN NOW, SHOULD BE EXCUSING MY ABSENCE TO THOSE WHO CALL!
WHAT CAN IT MEAN? WHERE CAN SHE BE?

THEN, WITH A FEELING OF GRIM FOREBODING, THOR EFFORTLESSLY REACHES THE ROOF...
THOUGH I DARE NOT FORCE MY WAY INSIDE WHILST I AM STILL THE GOD OF THUNDER, THERE IS A BETTER WAY...

THE TIME HAS COME FOR THOR TO VANISH...

--WHILE THE MORTAL DR. DONALD BLAKE INSTANTLY TAKES HIS PLACE!

THE FRONT DOOR IS ALSO LOCKED! WHY?
DON BLAKE M.D.
SAY, IT'S DR. BLAKE! WE ALL WONDERED WHERE YOU'VE BEEN, DOCTOR?
8

THEN, AFTER THE JANITOR HAS UNLOCKED THE DOOR WITH HIS PASSKEY--
JANE WAS SUPPOSED TO HAVE GENERAL HOSPITAL SEND ANOTHER DOCTOR TO LOOK AFTER MY PATIENTS WHILE I WAS GONE!
BUT, THE APPOINTMENT BOOK IS BLANK--AND MY OFFICE A SHAMBLES!

THE MEMO PADS ARE JUST EMPTY SHEETS! JANE WOULD NEVER HAVE LEFT WITHOUT LEAVING A NOTE! THERE'S ONLY ONE POSSIBLE ANSWER...
DR. BLAKE! I'VE BEEN WANTING TO SEE YOU! YOUR RENT BILL IS MONTHS OVERDUE, AND YOUR NURSE HASN'T BEEN HERE TO PAY IT FOR YOU!
THAT CINCHES IT! JANE WOULD NEVER FORGET TO PAY MY BILLS FOR ME! SOMETHING HAS HAPPENED TO HER!

NOW THEN, DOCTOR-- IF YOU WOULD BE GOOD ENOUGH TO LET ME HAVE A CHECK FOR THE PAST DUE AMOUNT --?
HOW CAN YOU SPEAK OF MONEY AT A TIME LIKE THIS?!! JANE FOSTER IS MISSING-- VANISHED WITHOUT A TRACE-- WITHOUT THE SLIGHTEST POSSIBLE CLUE!

BUT, DR. BLAKE--!
YOU'LL GET YOUR RENT! BUT FIRST I'VE GOT TO LEARN WHAT HAPPENED TO JANE!
HERE COMES NORMA THAXTON, ONE OF MY PATIENTS! I CAN'T STOP TO SEE HER NOW!

MISS THAXTON, SOMETHING IMPORTANT HAS JUST COME UP! IF YOU CAN WAIT TILL TOMORROW--
DON'T RUSH ON MY ACCOUNT, DR. BLAKE! I'VE BEEN USING THE CHARMING NEW DOCTOR ACROSS THE HALL DURING YOUR ABSENCE!
AND I INTEND TO CONTINUE USING HIM! GOOD DAY!

SHE'S ANGRY-- AND I DON'T BLAME HER! HOW MANY MORE PATIENTS HAVE I LOST BECAUSE MY OFFICE HAS BEEN DESERTED?
NOW LOOK, DOCTOR-- I'VE GOT TO HAVE MY RENT BY THE END OF THE WEEK!
IT'S LIKE TALKING TO A WALL! HE DOESN'T EVEN HEAR ME!

SHAKEN BY DOUBT AND WORRY, DON BLAKE ACCIDENTALLY STRIKES HIS ENCHANTED CANE AS HE TURNS A CORNER OF THE HALL--
I'VE GOT COUNTLESS ENEMIES-- CRIMINALS OF EVERY TYPE WHOM I'VE FOUGHT IN THE PAST!
ANY ONE OF THEM COULD BE RESPONSIBLE-- STRIKING AT ME-- THRU JANE!
THACK!
AND, BY THE TIME THE STARTLED LANDLORD REACHES THE SPOT...
THOR! BUT-- WHERE--?
IF YOU'RE LOOKING FOR A MAN WITH A CANE, HE JUST TOOK THE ELEVATOR DOWN!
THAT WAS TOO CLOSE FOR COMFORT! MY ANXIETY MADE ME DANGEROUSLY CARELESS!
HEY! LOOK WHO IT IS!
WOW! SOMETHIN' MUST BE UP!
IF ONLY I HAD MY CAMERA!
BUT, AT THIS MOMENT, THE THUNDER GOD IS IN NO MOOD FOR THE ATTENTION OF CURIOUS ONLOOKERS...
BACK! STAND BACK-- ALL OF YOU!
I'VE GOT TO GO SOMEWHERE AND THINK! EVEN THOR CANNOT FIND ONE GIRL FROM AMONG THE TWO BILLION HUMANS WHO INHABIT THIS PLANET!
AT A TIME SUCH AS THIS, THE GOD OF THUNDER NEEDS THE ASSISTANCE OF OTHERS-- I MUST ENLIST THE AID OF MY FELLOW AVENGERS!
HEY, MOVE IT, MISTER! YOU'RE HOLDIN' UP TRAFFIC!
OOGA OOGA!! OOGA
DO YOU SEE WHAT I SEE, HARRIET?
YES! BUT-- I ALWAYS THOUGHT HE WAS THE FIGMENT OF SOME SILLY IMAGINATION!
BACK UP, DEAR! PERHAPS WE CAN GET HIS AUTO-GRAPH!
H3514

BUT, REACHING THE EAST SIDE MANSION WHICH HOUSES THE MIGHTY AVENGERS, THOR IS ASTONISHED TO FIND...
QUICKSILVER!! THE SCARLET WITCH! AND--HAWKEYE!
YOU OCCUPY THIS ROOM AS IF YOU BELONG HERE--!
WE DO BELONG! WE'RE THE REPLACEMENTS FOR IRON MAN, GIANT-MAN-- AND, WE THOUGHT--FOR YOU!
GO TO THE HEAD OF THE CLASS, CURLY! YOU GOT ALL THE NAMES RIGHT!
OF THE ORIGINAL AVENGERS, ONLY CAPTAIN AMERICA REMAINS! BUT, HE IS ON AN ERRAND NOW!

THEN, MINUTES LATER, AFTER EXPLANATIONS HAVE BEEN MADE ALL AROUND...
WE'RE DOIN' PRETTY GOOD BY OURSELVES! WE DON'T NEED ANY OLD-TIMERS COMING BACK AND TRYIN' TO STEAL THE SHOW!
I AM NOT INTERESTED IN STEALING THE LIMELIGHT FROM YOU! I HAD COME HERE FOR ANOTHER REASON!
WHAT IS IT, THOR?
WHY DO YOU NOT WAIT TILL CAPTAIN AMERICA RETURNS?
WE DON'T NEED THAT SHIELD SLINGER! WHAT NEEDS DOIN', PAL? WE'LL DO IT!

IT IS NOTHING! YOU CANNOT HELP ME! I SHALL BE ON MY WAY AGAIN!
THROUGH MANY BATTLES HAVE I FOUGHT SHOULDER-TO-SHOULDER WITH THE OLD AVENGERS! BUT--THESE NEW, BRASH, ARROGANT YOUNGSTERS --I CANNOT BRING MYSELF TO REQUEST THE AID OF SUCH AS THEY!

WAIT! WHAT SHALL WE TELL CAPTAIN AMERICA?
TELL HIM AN OLD BATTLE COMPANION DROPPED BY--TO WISH HIM WELL!

THEN, FOR HOURS ON END, THOR SEARCHES IN VAIN--UNTIL--
TIS NO USE! SHE COULD BE ANYWHERE--OR--NOWHERE!

I MUST PAUSE, AND CONSIDER THE MATTER WITH CARE! SOMEWHERE A CLUE MAY BE HIDDEN!
JANE WOULD NEVER HAVE DESERTED DR. BLAKE OF HER OWN FREE WILL--OR--WOULD SHE? HOW CAN I BE CERTAIN?

WHILE, AT THAT VERY MOMENT, IN ANOTHER PART OF THE CITY, THE GIRL IN QUESTION STARES SILENTLY, TENSELY, OUT OF AN OPEN WINDOW...
WILL I EVER SEE DON BLAKE AGAIN? OR, WILL THE LOVE IN MY HEART TURN TO ASHES--FOREVER!

SUDDENLY, A FIRM, COLD HAND GRIPS HER SHOULDER ...AS A DEEP, EXPRESSIONLESS VOICE MUTTERS...
YOU MUST FORGET HIM! YOU MUST PUT HIM OUT OF YOUR LIFE! YOU HAVE NO OTHER CHOICE!

WHILE, AN INDESCRIBABLE DISTANCE AWAY, GREAT COSMIC "BULLETS" STREAK ACROSS THE FATHOMLESS VOID OF SPACE...

FOR, IN HALLOWED ASGARD, THE PRINCE OF VILLAINS--EVIL LOKI, SENDS HIS MACRO-MESON PARTICLES OF LIMITLESS ENERGY INTO THE INFINITE--PROBING SPACE FOR ONE CERTAIN OBJECT--SEARCHING--SCANNING--SCHEMING--!
BEFORE I BEGIN MY MOST SINISTER--MY MOST AMBITIOUS PROJECT--THE DETHRONING OF ODIN HIMSELF, I MUST FIRST BE SURE THAT THOR WILL BE UNABLE TO COME TO THE AID OF THE BEARDED ONE!
THUS, I MUST FIND THE ONE CREATURE IN ALL THE UNIVERSE WHO CAN DESTROY THE THUNDER GOD--!

AH! I HAVE LOCATED HIM AT LAST!
HE ALMOST SUCCEEDED IN SLAYING MY ACCURSED HALF-BROTHER THE LAST TIME THEY FOUGHT--BUT WAS OUT-SMARTED BY THOR AT THE MOMENT OF DECISION!
BUT, THIS TIME HE WILL BE ON GUARD--HE WILL NOT BE TRICKED AGAIN!

ONLY MY EYES--THE CUNNING EYES OF THE PRINCE OF EVIL--COULD HAVE DETECTED THAT DRIFTING CLOUD OF HELIUM VAPOR--THE CLOUD WHICH WAS ONCE A MAN!

UNERRINGLY, THE MACRO-MESON "BULLET" SHATTERS THE HELIUM CLOUD, BOMBARDING IT WITH COUNTLESS PARTICLES OF LIVING ENERGY!

SLOWLY, NEW ELEMENTS BEGIN TO EMERGE--AND, AMIDST THE AWESOME RESHAPING OF DORMANT MATTER, THE CLOUD STARTS TO ASSUME A HUMAN FORM...
13

EVERYTHING PROCEEDS PERFECTLY! NOW, ALL I NEED DO IS FIRE A TRANSLUCENT SPHEROID TO ENCLOSE HIM, AND TO PROTECT HIM ON HIS JOURNEY TO EARTH!

IT IS DONE! I HAVE SET IN MOTION FORCES WHICH NO ONE CAN HALT! THE STAGE IS SET--THE PLAYERS ARE READY--THE TRAGEDY IS ABOUT TO BEGIN!!

WHILE, BACK ON EARTH, THOR NOTICES A FOREIGN FILM STAR BEING INTERVIEWED FOR TV COVERAGE...
WOULD YOU CARE TO TELL US ABOUT YOUR NEWEST FILM, MADEMOISELLE?
MAIS OUI, MON CHER! I THOUGHT YOU WOULD NEVAIRE ASK!
TELEVISION CAMERAS! THAT'S THE ANSWER I NEED!

WHEREVER JANE IS, SHE MUST BE WITHIN SIGHT OR SOUND OF A T.V. SET! I'LL USE TELEVISION TO LOCATE HER!
I'LL BROADCAST A MESSAGE TO HER--UNTIL I RECEIVE A RESPONSE!

THE NETWORKS ARE CERTAIN TO COOPERATE! THEY HAVE OFFERED ME A FORTUNE TO FACE THE CAMERAS IN THE PAST!
IT IS THE ONLY WAY!

BUT, ON HIS WAY TO THE NETWORK STUDIO, THE MIGHTY-MUSCLED IMMORTAL SEES--
A SMOKING, SPEEDING **SPHEROID**--HURTLING FROM THE HEAVENS TO THE CITY STREETS BELOW!

WITH THE SPEED OF THOUGHT, THE THUNDER GOD CHANGES COURSE--
TRULY, NO **HUMAN** POWER CAN BE RESPONSIBLE FOR **THAT!**

I CANNOT HELP BUT FEEL THAT MY SIGHTING YON OBJECT WAS **NO ACCIDENT!** IT WAS **INTENDED** THAT I SEE IT--THAT I **FOLLOW** IT--
BUT--**WHY??**

MY ANSWER WILL NOT BE LONG IN COMING! IT HAS LANDED--AND SEEMS TO BE **WAITING**--WAITING--FOR **ME!**

THEN, AS THE SON OF ODIN SLOWLY APPROACHES THE MYSTERIOUS OBJECT--
IT **MOVES!!** IT CHANGES SHAPE--!
IT IS AS THOUGH SOMETHING INSIDE IS STRUGGLING--TO **BREAK OUT!**
15

CRASH!
WHATEVER WAS WITHIN HAS SMASHED THE SPHEROID! IT'S FREE!
BUT--THAT BALL AND CHAIN!! IT CAN ONLY BELONG TO--
CRUSHER CREEL--THE ABSORBING MAN!
YOU THOUGHT YOU GOT RID OF ME WHEN YOU SENT ME OFF INTO SPACE, HUH?* WELL, I'M BACK AGAIN--AND STRONGER THAN EVER!
*WE MET CRUSHER IN THOR #114 AND SAW HIM DEFEATED IN #115--REMEMBER? --STAN.
BUT, I INTENDED YOU TO REMAIN IN SPACE TILL YOU LOST YOUR POWER! ONLY ANOTHER IMMORTAL COULD HAVE FREED YOU--!
NEVER MIND ABOUT THAT!! I'M FREE NOW--AND YOU WON'T GET A CHANCE TO OUTSMART ME AGAIN! THIS TIME I FIGHT UNTIL YOU'RE FINISHED!!
AND, USING HIS INCREDIBLE POWER OF ABSORPTION, THE CREATURE WHO HAD ONCE BEEN CONVICT CRUSHER CREEL, ABSORBS THE POWER OF THE NEARBY BRICK WALL, AS HE ADVANCES TOWARD HIS INTENDED VICTIM!
NEXT ISSUE WE SHALL PRESENT A BATTLE SUCH AS NEVER WITNESSED BEFORE--ON EARTH, OR ASGARD! WE'D BE DEEPLY HONORED IF YOU'D JOIN US! WE HAVE SPOKEN!
16

TALES OF ASGARD, HOME OF THE MIGHTY NORSE GODS
"SET SAIL!"
THE CREW HAS BEEN GATHERED... AND, UNDER THE WATCHFUL EYE OF LORDLY ODIN, THE STRANGEST VOYAGE OF ALL TIME IS ABOUT TO BEGIN!
TRULY A MARVEL MASTERWORK!
TOLD BY: STAN LEE
DRAWN BY: JACK KIRBY
INKED BY: VINCE COLLETTA
LETTERED BY: ARTIE SIMEK
THE EYES OF ODIN SHALL BE EVER ON THEE!
1

THUS, THE GREAT SHIP--SUCH AS NO MORTAL EYES HAVE EVER BEHELD--TAKES TO THE AIR-- GUIDED BY THE ENDLESS CURRENTS OF SPACE--!!

SAIL ON! WE SHALL NE'ER RETURN TILL WE HAVE FOUND, AND BESTED THE FORCES OF EVIL! SAIL ON-- IN THE NAME OF ODIN, THE ALL-WISE!!

AND, AS THE NOBLEST, THE BRAVEST, AND THE MOST BELOVED WARRIORS OF ASGARD SAIL INTO THE UNKNOWN, THERE IS SADNESS IN THE HEARTS OF THOSE WHO ARE LEFT BEHIND...
THE FORCES OF EVIL HAVE GREAT POWER--PERHAPS AS MUCH AS ODIN HIMSELF! WHAT IF OUR LOVED ONES SHOULD BE DEFEATED IN BATTLE?
WITH MIGHTY THOR IN COMMAND?? IT IS UNTHINKABLE! THE VICTORY MUST BE OURS!
HOW HANDSOME THEY LOOK!! AND, HOW MAGNIFICENTLY FEARLESS!
BEHOLD! VOLSTAGG, THE ENORMOUS, IS SHOUTING A LAST FAREWELL!
BE OF GOOD CHEER, FAIREST FLOWERS IN ALL OF ASGARD! WE SHALL RETURN!
WE SHALL BRING THEE GIFTS, AND RARE TREASURES FROM THE FURTHEST REACHES OF THE UNIVERSE!
YEA, VOLSTAGG SHALL BE THE GREATEST HERO OF ALL--AND I SHALL EMBRACE EACH OF THEE IN THY TURN, FOR MY HEART IS FILLED WITH LOVE!
BUT THEN, THE BLUSTERING, BOISTEROUS GIANT SEES A SIGHT THAT MAKES HIS VERY BLOOD RUN COLD--!!
BACK!! LET ME BACK, THOU CRAVEN SCOUNDRELS!!
WHAT MADNESS IS THIS, VOLSTAGG!!? I THOUGHT THOU FEARED NEITHER MAN NOR BEAST!!
IN TRUTH, I DO NOT--!!
BUT THAT IS NEITHER MAN NOR BEAST-- IT IS--MY WIFE!!
WELL MIGHT YOU HIDE, TREMBLING ONE! HER FACE HATH THE FURY OF A THOUSAND STORMS!
A DAMSEL GOOD AND TRUE IS SHE --BUT SHE UNDERSTANDS NOT A WARRIOR'S YEARNING FOR ADVENTURE!

BUT THEN, IN THE MIDST OF THE FRIENDLY BANTERING, A STERN VOICE RINGS OUT, AND THE COLD, CRUEL PRESENCE OF LOKI IS MADE KNOWN!
TO WORK, THOU ANCIENT USELESS ONE! THIS IS NO PLACE FOR FOOLS OR BUFFOONS!!
BEND THY KNEE WHEN YOU ARE ADDRESSED BY LOKI!!

ENOUGH, HALF-BROTHER!! NO CREWMAN OF MINE WILL BE TREATED THUS WHILE THOR IS IN COMMAND!! THEY ARE OUR FELLOW WARRIORS --NOT SERFS UPON WHOM YOU MAY VENT YOUR WRATH!
YOU DARE TO SIDE WITH HIM AGAINST ME BEFORE THE ENTIRE CREW??! YOU SHALL LIVE TO REGRET THIS INDIGNITY, THUNDER GOD!

AND, EVEN AS THE TWO IMMORTALS SPEAK, MAGRAT, THE SCHEMER WHISPERS A SINISTER SUGGESTION TO KRODA, THE DUELLIST--!
NOW IS YOUR CHANCE, KRODA! LOKI WILL PAY HANDSOMELY FOR SUCH A DEED!
LOKI DOES AS LOKI WISHES! I MAKE NO PROMISES!
OUR JOURNEY WILL BE LONG, AND FRAUGHT WITH DANGER! WE MUST FIGHT TOGETHER IF WE WOULD ENDURE!

BUT, NO SOONER DOES MERCILESS KRODA DRAW HIS BLADE FROM ITS SCABBARD, THEN ANOTHER STEEL SHAFT BURIES ITSELF IN THE MAST BEFORE HIM!!
STAY THY HAND, BASE ASSASSIN!!
WHO DARES--??

I DARE!
HOGUN, THE GRIM!! THE SILENT WARRIOR WHO HAS NEVER LOST A BATTLE--WHOSE HEART IS SAID TO BE COLDER THAN THE STEEL OF HIS BLADE!
HE SAYS NO MORE! HE MERELY RETRIEVES HIS WEAPON--SLOWLY --SILENTLY--!

THE MOMENT HAS BEEN LOST! I SHALL FIND ANOTHER TIME TO STRIKE--AND TO REPAY HOGUN FOR THIS INSOLENCE, AS WELL!
HAVE A CARE, KRODA!! THERE IS MORE TO THAT ONE THAN MEETS THE EYE! NEVER HAVE I BEHELD A FACE SO MERCILESS!

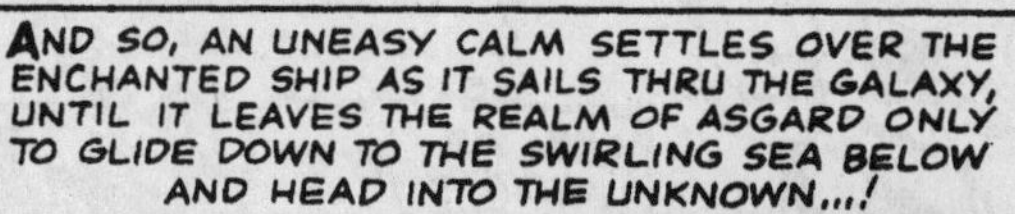
AND SO, AN UNEASY CALM SETTLES OVER THE ENCHANTED SHIP AS IT SAILS THRU THE GALAXY, UNTIL IT LEAVES THE REALM OF ASGARD ONLY TO GLIDE DOWN TO THE SWIRLING SEA BELOW AND HEAD INTO THE UNKNOWN...!

LET EACH MAN SEARCH HIS SOUL FOR COURAGE--FOR WE ENTER A WORLD WE HAVE NEVER KNOWN BEFORE!
5

WHILE, BACK IN THE FABLED CITY, EVEN A KING CAN FEEL THE FEARFUL PANGS OF DARK UNCERTAINTY...
HOW THINK YOU, MASTER OF PROPHECY? WAS MY DECISION A WISE ONE?
MORE THAN THAT, SIRE! IT WAS THE ONLY ONE THOU COULDST MAKE!
WHAT DECISION DOES NOBLE ODIN REFER TO? WHAT SHADOWY SECRETS ARE HIDDEN BENEATH THE SURFACE OF ODIN'S GREAT VOYAGE? WE SWEAR BY ASGARD'S GOLDEN SPIRES THAT THE QUEST WILL CONTINUE NEXT ISSUE--AND WE'LL FACE IT TOGETHER! SO BE IT!

THOR ANNUAL
72 BIG PAGES
MARVEL COMICS GROUP 25¢
SPECIAL KING SIZE ANNUAL!
APPROVED BY THE COMICS CODE AUTHORITY
JOURNEY INTO MYSTERY WITH
THE MIGHTY
THOR
#1 1965
SEE THE CLASH OF TITANS!
ALL-NEW "THOR VS. HERCULES"
PLUS... THE MOST REQUESTED FIRST APPEARANCES OF THOR'S MOST DEADLY FOES...!
LOKI, THE EMBODIMENT OF EVIL!
THE MYSTERIOUS RADIO-ACTIVE MAN!
THE DEMON DUPLICATORS!
THE LAVA-MAN!

MONTH AFTER MONTH, WE HAVE RECEIVED AN AVALANCHE OF MAIL DEMANDING THAT WE PIT THE MIGHTIEST IMMORTALS OF ALL TIME IN HAND-TO-HAND COMBAT! THOUGH NEITHER HISTORY NOR LEGEND RECORD SUCH A BATTLE, IF EVER THE SON OF ODIN HAD FOUGHT THE SON OF ZEUS, THE MATCHLESS IMAGINATIONS OF LEE AND KIRBY VISUALIZE A BATTLE TO STAGGER THE SENSES AND DAZZLE THE EYES! A BATTLE WHICH MIGHT HAVE BEEN FOUGHT, THEN SWEPT AWAY IN THE WHIRLPOOL OF TIME! A BATTLE SUCH AS THIS...!!
"WHEN TITANS CLASH!"
THOR vs. HERCULES!
Mighty story by: STAN LEE
Majestic art by: JACK KIRBY
Masterful inking by: VINCE COLLETTA
Mostly lettered by: SAM ROSEN

EVER EAGER FOR ADVENTURE, MIGHTY THOR ENTERS THE FORBIDDEN LAND OF JOTUNHEIM, WITH HIS HALF-BROTHER LOKI AT HIS SIDE! JOTUNHEIM... WHERE THE STORM GIANTS DWELL! JOTUNHEIM... WHERE THE POWERFUL ENEMIES OF ASGARD ASSEMBLE!
WE ARE FOOLS TO COME HERE! EVEN OUR LIVES CAN BE LOST IN THIS BARREN LAND!
HE WHO NEVER VENTURES, NEVER WINS! WE ARE SONS OF ODIN! WE RIDE WHERE WE PLEASE!

ALL HE SEEKS IS NEW GLORY TO WIN FOR ASGARD! BUT THIS TIME HE'LL FIND NAUGHT BUT DEATH!
LOKI! THERE ARE TWO STORM GIANTS AHEAD! THE FATES HAVE SMILED UPON US!
THEY SEEK THE ENTRANCE TO THE LOST PASSAGE! THE PASSAGE WHICH LEADS TO OLYMPUS!

THE LEGENDS TELL US THAT THE STORM GIANTS WERE HURLED OUT OF OLYMPUS AGES AGO! THUS, IT IS MY DUTY TO PREVENT THEM FROM EVER RETURNING!
AT LAST WE HAVE FOUND THE HIDDEN ENTRANCE!!
AFTER ALL THESE CENTURIES WE SHALL RETURN... TO MENACE OLYMPUS ANEW!

NOT WHILE THOR LIVES!! I STRIKE FOR ODIN AND VICTORY!
THE GOD OF THUNDER! YOU DARE COME HERE??!
ONE BLOW OF MY MIGHTY SPEAR WILL SMASH YOU LIKE A WORM!

NEVER DID A WORM POSSESS A URU HAMMER... SUCH AS THOR'S!

LOKI!! TO MY SIDE!
NO ANSWER! THE FAITH-LESS ONE HAS FLED!!

SO BE IT! THEN THOR SHALL BATTLE ALONE!
BEGONE, EVIL ONES! YOU ARE NO MATCH FOR THE SON OF ODIN!

IF OLYMPUS TRULY EXISTS, THE LIKES OF YOU SHALL NEVER THREATEN IT!

BACK, I SAY!! GET YOU BACK!!
NONE CAN FACE THE FLASHING FURY OF THOR!

BUT, EVEN AS THE GALLANT THUNDER GOD'S POUNDING ATTACK DRIVES HIS TWO GIGANTIC FOES INTO FULL RETREAT, THE UNIMAGINABLE FORCE OF THOR'S HAMMER BLOWS CAUSES THE VERY GROUND BENEATH HIS FEET TO CRUMBLE IN A SUDDEN ROCK SLIDE...!
I HAVE CAUSED AN AVALANCHE! THE GROUND IS SHATTERED BELOW ME!
3.

THUS, THE THUNDER GOD FALLS.. FOR TIME WITHOUT END..THROUGH A VAST VOID OF HEAVY NOTHING-NESS...OF SHIMMERING ENERGY BARRIERS AND MYSTIC SPACE DIS-RUPTERS... UNTIL HE REALIZES...
THIS IS NO ORDINARY FALL! I HAVE UNWITTINGLY CRASHED THROUGH THE HIDDEN ENTRANCE TO... OLYMPUS!

FINALLY, HIS SPEED IS SLACKENED AS THE STRANGE, SUPERNATURAL JOURNEY REACHES ITS CONCLUSION, AND THOR FINDS HIMSELF WITHIN...
A SHADOWY CHAMBER... LIKE NOTHING I HAVE EVER SEEN IN ASGARD!

THEN, FOLLOWING A TWISTING, WINDING CORRIDOR, THE SON OF ODIN EMERGES ON THE OUTSKIRTS OF...
OLYMPUS! IT CAN BE NO OTHER PLACE!
THIS IS THE LAND HINTED AT BY OUR ANCIENT LEGENDS! THE LAND WHERE OTHER IMMORTALS DWELL!

IT IS SO DIFFERENT FROM THE HOME I HAVE KNOWN, AND YET... IN MANY WAYS... IT BEARS GREAT RESEMBLANCE TO FABLED ASGARD!
4.

BUT, I MUST SEEK A WAY BACK TO THE GOLDEN CITY! I SHALL CROSS THAT CRUDE BRIDGE AND SEEK INFORMATION FROM THE ONE WHO STANDS THUS BOLDLY!
HOLD! COME NO FURTHER! YOU MAY CROSS YON BRIDGE ONLY AFTER HERCULES HAS DONE SO!

IF THERE BE ROOM FOR ONLY ONE TO CROSS AT A TIME, THAT ONE SHALL BE THOR, WHO BACKS OFF TO NO MAN!
THE MADNESS MUST BE UPON THEE ... TO DARE DEFY THE WILL OF HERCULES!

AND THEN, BEFORE ANOTHER WORD CAN BE UTTERED...
HE UPROOTED THE BRIDGE WITH ONE SIMPLE MOTION!! THIS IS NO POWERLESS BUMPKIN I FACE!
BE THUS WARNED! MY STRENGTH IS THE EQUAL OF MY TEMPER!

YOU SPEAK OF STRENGTH... YOU SPEAK OF TEMPER.. TO THOR, GOD OF THUNDER??! WERE YOU MY EQUAL, I'D CRUSH THEE LIKE A FLEA!
HE SEEMS NOT TO HEAR ME! HE CALMLY LIFTS A BOULDER THAT MIGHT EVEN BALK A STORM GIANT!

HE ATTEMPTS TO CREATE A NEW BRIDGE... USING MONSTROUS BOULDERS AS STEPPING STONES!
MOVE ASIDE, COSTUMED CLOD! I SHALL TOSS THIS GIGANTIC ROCK WHERE YOU STAND!

IF YOU SEEK TO IMPRESS ME WITH YOUR POWER, HERCULES, YOU WASTE YOUR EFFORT!
BEGONE, BRASH ONE! THY RANTING BEGINS TO BORE ME!
5.

I SHALL BORE THEE NO MORE, INSOLENT ONE! MY HAMMER SHALL NOW SPEAK FOR ME!
HE WITNESSES MY STRENGTH, YET STILL HE PROVOKES ME!
WHAT MANNER OF FOOL CAN HE BE??

AS EASILY AS YOU CAN LIFT THAT BOULDER, MIGHTY THOR CAN SHATTER IT TO BITS!
BY ZEUS, ARROGANT ONE! THOU HAST TRULY GONE TOO FAR!

THY HAMMER POSSESSES POWER INDEED... BUT THE GOLDEN MACE OF HERCULES SHALL PROVE MORE THAN THY MATCH!
GUARD THYSELF, THEN! FOR I SHALL TEACH THEE A LESSON IN MANNERS THAT SHALL NEVER BE FORGOTTEN!

FIRST, I CATCH YOUR WRIST ON MY HAMMER'S THONG, HURLING YOU OFF-BALANCE AS EASILY AS I MIGHT SNAP A TWIG!

YET, BY THE TIME THE ENCHANTED MALLET REACHES THE GROUND...
NOTHING CAN KEEP HERCULES OFF-BALANCE! MY MATCHLESS STRENGTH MAKES ME THE MASTER OF EVERY SITUATION!

BUT, NO SOONER DOES THE HAMMER RETURN TO EARTH, THAN IT AGAIN TOPPLES HERCULES AS IT WRENCHES ITSELF OFF HIS WRIST AND HURTLES BACK TO THOR!
BY JUPITER!! THE MALLET SEEMS TO BE ALIVE!

BUT NOW, ENOUGH OF HAMMER AND MACE! I SHALL THRASH YOU ROUNDLY, AS YOU WELL DESERVE, WITH MY BARE FISTS!
AGREED! I, TOO, SHALL FIGHT WITHOUT WEAPON!!

BEFORE THE THUNDER GOD CAN RELEASE HIS HAMMER, THE MOST POWERFUL BLOW HE HAS EVER FELT SLAMS HIM TO THE GROUND...
NONE CAN RESIST THE SMASHING ATTACK OF HERCULES!

WHAT??! YOU GAIN YOUR FEET SO QUICKLY?! WHAT MANNER OF WARRIOR ART THOU??!
I AM THOR! THE ONE WHO SHALL PUMMEL THEE TO THY KNEES!

AND THEN, WITH ONE SINGLE, SMASHING BLOW, THE THUNDER GOD DOES WHAT NO LIVING BEING HAS EVER DONE BEFORE... HE BATTERS HERCULES OFF HIS FEET!!
WHHOP!

BUT, NOW IT IS THOR'S TURN TO BE AMAZED...!
YOU RECOVER WITHIN SECONDS! I HAVE NEVER SEEN THE LIKE!
NOR SHALL YOU SEE IT EVER AGAIN!

BY THE GOLDEN SPIRES, YOU FIGHT LIKE A SON OF ODIN!
WHILST THY STRENGTH IS WORTHY OF ZEUS HIMSELF!! BUT, STILL SHALL HERCULES PREVAIL!

SEE HOW I WHIP THEE AWAY FROM ME WITH AN ARM WHICH CAN FELL THE TALLEST TREE!

BUT, SEE HOW I FORCE BACK THAT ARM, AND HURL THEE BACKWARDS TO THE GROUND!
8.

YIELD, HERCULES!! YIELD TO THOR, GOD OF THUNDER... PRINCE OF VIKINGS... SON OF ODIN!
NEVER!!

YOUR MOST SAVAGE ATTACK FAILED TO BEST ME! MY POWER IS TOO GREAT!

AND NOW, IT IS MY TURN! NOW SHALL THOR FACE THE FURY OF HERCULES' ATTACK!

I SHALL NOT SLAY ONE SO VALIANT! INSTEAD, I SHALL BIND THEE AND MAKE THEE MY CAPTIVE!
9.

NONE BUT HERCULES CAN BEND THE ENCHANTED POLE OF HEROES! IT SHALL MAKE THEE MY PRISONER!
FIE!! YOU UTTER THE MOUTHINGS OF A JESTER!

YOUR WORDS ARE BOLD, GOLDEN STRANGER, BUT THE STRENGTH OF HERCULES HAS INDEED DEFEATED THEE!

BUT THEN, IN A SAVAGE PAROXYSM OF ANGER, THOR'S IRON MUSCLES BEGIN TO TENSE AND SWELL AS HIS FIGHTING HEART RAGES WITHIN HIM, UNTIL...
THOR... DEFEATED BY HERCULES..???

NEVER!!!

BY THE BEARD OF MY FATHER!! NEVER HAVE I BATTLED ONE SUCH AS THEE! DOST THOU NOT KNOW THE MEANING OF FEAR?!!
IF NOT, I SHALL TEACH THEE NOW!!

I SHALL STRIKE ONE SPOT OVER AND OVER AGAIN, UNTIL YOU BEG FOR RESPITE! ONLY THEN SHALL THIS BATTLE END!
10

AGAIN AND AGAIN, HERCULES STRIKES THE THUNDER GOD UPON THE SAME SPOT... EACH BLOW STRONGER THAN THE ONE BEFORE!!
ANY OTHER WOULD HAVE CRUMBLED LONG AGO! NEVER DID I THINK I'D BATTLE ONE WHOSE STRENGTH COULD MATCH MY OWN!

THEN, SUDDENLY...
NOW HE FALLS!! BUT, DID MY ATTACK TOPPLE HIM? OR DID HE LOSE HIS FOOTING ON THE DEW-COVERED GRASS?

BUT, IN THE NEXT SECOND, THE COMMANDING VOICE OF THOR AGAIN HURLS A CHALLENGE AT HIS FOE!
YOU HAVE DONE YOUR UTMOST! NOW, YOU SHALL FEEL THE POWER OF THE THUNDER GOD ONCE MORE...!

SEIZING THE VERY GROUND WHICH LIES BENEATH THEM, MIGHTY THOR'S STEEL-LIKE FINGERS PEEL OFF AN ENTIRE SECTION OF SOD, CRACKING IT LIKE A GIGANTIC BULL-WHIP!

AND NOW TO BRING THIS TO AN END! THOSE ROCKS CANNOT STOP THOR!
IN THE HANDS OF HERCULES THEY ARE MORE THAN ROCKS..!
WITH THOSE WORDS, THE TITANIC SON OF ZEUS CLAPS HIS HANDS TOGETHER WITH THE POWER OF COLLIDING COMETS...!

HE HAS REDUCED THE ROCKS TO THE FINEST POWDER...!!
IT FILLS MY EYES! I CANNOT SEE!!

I'LL HAVE TO LEAP FORWARD... KEEP SWINGING BLINDLY... HOLD HIM AT BAY, UNTIL MY EYES CLEAR!!
IF I AM EVER TO GAIN FINAL VICTORY, IT MUST BE NOW!

AT THAT SPLIT-SECOND, THOR RECEIVES THE MOST POWERFUL BLOW EVER INFLICTED UPON MAN OR IMMORTAL...

...BUT, BY A SUPREME EFFORT, MANAGES TO STAY ON HIS FEET AND DELIVER AN EQUALLY STRONG COUNTER-BLOW...!!
12.

THEN, BEFORE EITHER COMBATANT CAN MAKE ANOTHER MOVE, A SUDDEN CATACLYSMIC GROUND-SWELL HURLS THEM BOTH INTO THE AIR ...!

AND, WHEN THE UPHEAVAL SUBSIDES, THEY SEE...
LET THE FIGHTING CEASE!!

IT IS MY FATHER... THE VENERATED ZEUS!! HAIL, SUPREME ONE
ZEUS! THE MONARCH OF OLYMPUS, EVEN AS ODIN IS LORD OF ASGARD!
I HAVE WITNESSED YOUR BATTLE AND FOUND IT HONORABLE! IN TRUTH, YOU ARE EACH DESERVING OF VICTORY!

RISE, VALOROUS STRANGER! THY COURAGE AND THY RESPECT DO THEE CREDIT, AND REFLECT HONOR UPON THY LIEGE!
YOUR WORDS HAVE THE WISDOM OF MINE OWN FATHER, WHO IS ALSO A SOVEREIGN, MY LORD!
13.

NOW CLASP YOU EACH OTHER'S HAND, FOR TRULY HAVE YOU THE POWER AND NOBILITY OF PRINCELY IMMORTALS!
THE FRIENDSHIP OF HERCULES IS THINE!
SO TOO DOES THOR CALL HERCULES FRIEND!

BUT NOW, I MUST TO MY OWN KINGDOM RETURN, FOR MANY ARE THE TASKS THAT AWAIT ME!
THEN RETURN YOU SHALL ... FOR THE WILL OF ZEUS IS SUPREME IN IMPERIAL OLYMPUS!

TO THINE OWN WORLD I DISPATCH THEE, BY THE POWERS AT MY COMMAND!
THEN 'TIS HAIL AND FAREWELL...!

THOR! YOU RETURN! BUT, FROM WHERE??
IT MATTERS NOT! ALREADY, THE MEMORY GROWS DIM WITHIN ME...!

I HAD THOUGHT THAT YOU WERE DEAD!
AND THE THOUGHT IS OFTEN INSPIRED BY THE WISH, IS IT NOT, LOKI?

BUT, WHAT OF YOU, BROTHER? YOU RAN OFF WHILST I FOUGHT THE STORM GIANTS!
HOW YOU WRONG ME, THOR! I MERELY FLED TO SEARCH FOR HELP!
14.

THEN, SUDDENLY...
BACK, LOKI! SOME INCALCULABLE POWER IS AT WORK HERE!
BOULDERS! BEING HURLED FROM THE PIT BELOW!

IT IS THE WORK OF THE STORM GIANTS! WE SHOULD NEVER HAVE COME TO THIS ACCURSED LAND!
NO STORM GIANTS LIVE WHO COULD ACCOMPLISH SUCH A FEAT WITH SUCH BLINDING SPEED!

ONLY A POWER EQUAL TO THAT OF ODIN'S COULD BE RESPONSIBLE FOR THE STAGGER-ING SIGHT BEFORE US!
BUT, WHO CAN IT BE... AND FOR WHAT PURPOSE?

IT IS BEST THAT LOKI NEVER KNOWS! FOR, HE WOULD SURELY USE THE KNOWLEDGE OF OLYMPUS TO SERVE HIS OWN EVIL ENDS!

ZEUS HAS CREATED A MOUNTAIN TO FOREVER SEAL OFF THE HIDDEN ENTRANCE TO HIS REALM!

BUT, SOMEDAY I SHALL LEARN MORE OF THAT LAND WHERE IMMORTALS DWELL... SOMEDAY I SHALL AGAIN MEET... HERCULES!

FOR TIME IS ENDLESS, AND MY TRUE DESTINY HAS YET TO BE FULFILLED!
THUS, THE GOD OF THUNDER KEEPS HIS SECRET LOCKED WITHIN HIM! BUT, ONE DAY THAT SECRET WILL BE EXPOSED, AND WHEN IT IS, WE SHALL ALL SHARE THE THRILLS TOGETHER!
FINIS
15.

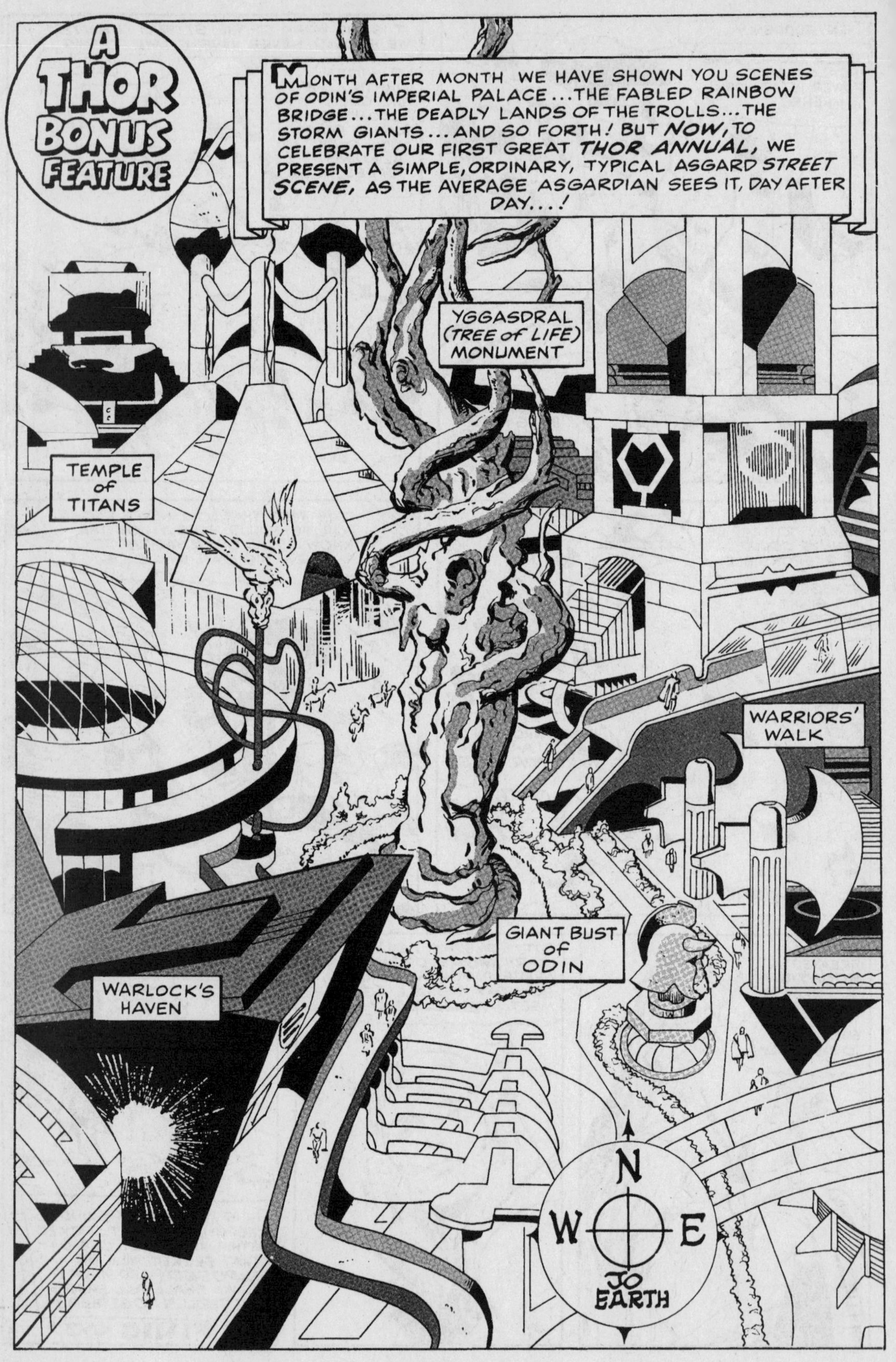
A THOR BONUS FEATURE
MONTH AFTER MONTH WE HAVE SHOWN YOU SCENES OF ODIN'S IMPERIAL PALACE... THE FABLED RAINBOW BRIDGE... THE DEADLY LANDS OF THE TROLLS... THE STORM GIANTS... AND SO FORTH! BUT NOW, TO CELEBRATE OUR FIRST GREAT THOR ANNUAL, WE PRESENT A SIMPLE, ORDINARY, TYPICAL ASGARD STREET SCENE, AS THE AVERAGE ASGARDIAN SEES IT, DAY AFTER DAY...!
YGGASDRAL (TREE of LIFE) MONUMENT
TEMPLE of TITANS
WARRIORS' WALK
GIANT BUST of ODIN
WARLOCK'S HAVEN
N
W
E
TO EARTH

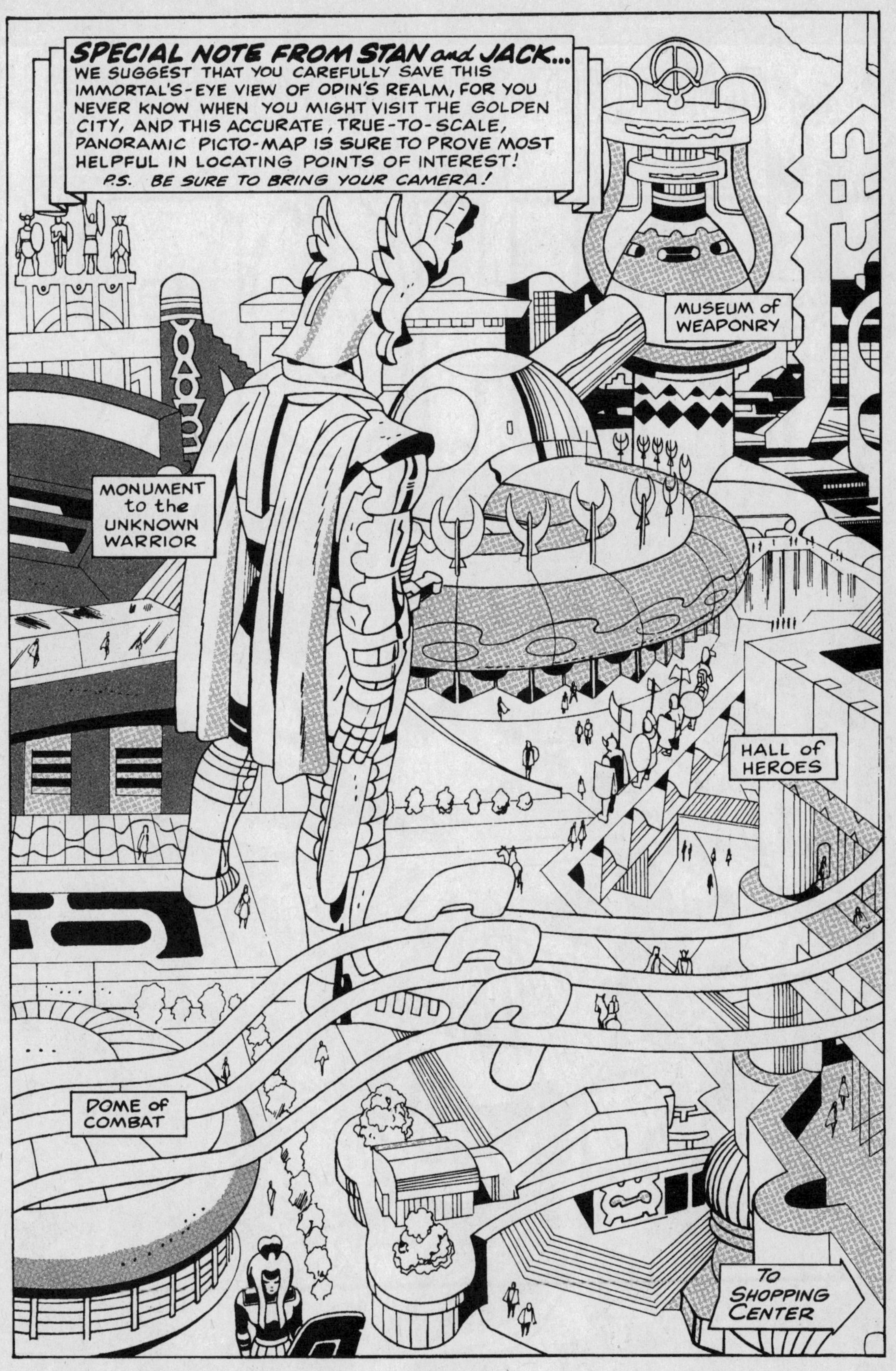
SPECIAL NOTE FROM STAN and JACK...
WE SUGGEST THAT YOU CAREFULLY SAVE THIS IMMORTAL'S-EYE VIEW OF ODIN'S REALM, FOR YOU NEVER KNOW WHEN YOU MIGHT VISIT THE GOLDEN CITY, AND THIS ACCURATE, TRUE-TO-SCALE, PANORAMIC PICTO-MAP IS SURE TO PROVE MOST HELPFUL IN LOCATING POINTS OF INTEREST!
P.S. BE SURE TO BRING YOUR CAMERA!
MUSEUM of WEAPONRY
MONUMENT to the UNKNOWN WARRIOR
HALL of HEROES
DOME of COMBAT
TO SHOPPING CENTER

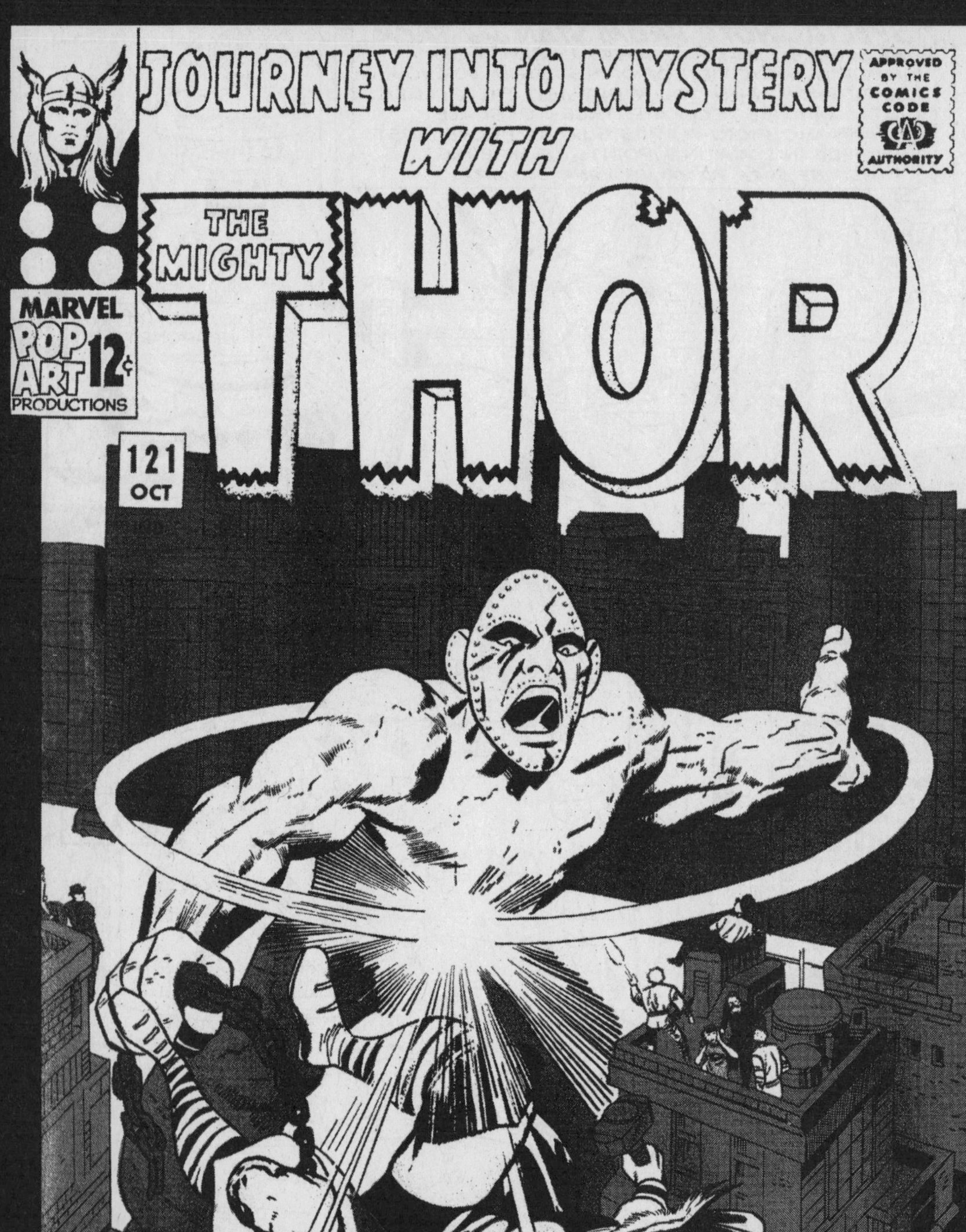

JOURNEY INTO MYSTERY
WITH
THE MIGHTY
THOR
APPROVED BY THE COMICS CODE AUTHORITY
MARVEL POP ART PRODUCTIONS
12¢
121
OCT

THE MIGHTY THOR!
"The POWER! The PASSION! The PRIDE!"
OF ALL THE FOES HE HAS EVER BATTLED, NONE CAME CLOSER TO DEFEATING THE MIGHTY THUNDER GOD THAN HE WHO IS CALLED THE ABSORBING MAN!
AND NOW, ON HIS RETURN TO NEW YORK, THOR FINDS HIMSELF MENACED ONCE AGAIN BY THE ONE DEADLY ENEMY WHOSE POWER CAN MATCH HIS VERY OWN...
ONLY LOKI COULD HAVE BROUGHT YOU BACK TO CHALLENGE ME AGAIN!
YEAH? SO WHAT? YOU WON'T BE AROUND LONG ENOUGH TO WORRY ABOUT IT!
ANOTHER TOWERING TRIUMPH FOR STAN LEE, WRITER! ANOTHER FABULOUS FEAT FOR JACK KIRBY, ILLUSTRATOR! ANOTHER AMAZING ACHIEVEMENT FOR VINCE COLLETTA, DELINEATOR! ANOTHER DAY, ANOTHER DOLLAR, FOR ARTIE SIMEK, LETTERER!
EXPECT TO SEE A MARVEL MASTERWORK! YOU'LL STILL BE PLEASANTLY SURPRISED!
1

REMEMBER, THUNDER GOD, NO MATTER HOW STRONG YOU ARE, YOU CAN'T HURT ME!
I ABSORB THE POWER OF ANYTHING I TOUCH-- SO YOUR STRENGTH BECOMES MINE!
NO MATTER! I BESTED YOU ONCE--AND, BY THE GOLDEN SPIRES OF ASGARD, I SHALL DO IT AGAIN!

MY HAMMER!
DON'T COUNT ON IT!

I WAS CARELESS! I FORGOT THAT HIS BALL AND CHAIN CAN ALSO ABSORB THE POWER OF MY ENCHANTED MALLET!
HAH! I'M THE ONLY ONE ON EARTH WHO CAN YANK YOUR HAMMER AWAY FROM YOU--LIKE THIS!

AND, BY HOLDING IT, ITS URU POWER BECOMES MY URU POWER! FACE IT, THOR--THERE'S NO WAY YOU CAN BEAT ME!

YOU TRICKED ME LAST TIME! BUT NOW I'M TOO SMART TO-- HEY!
WHAT'S GOIN' ON? WHAT'S HAPPENIN' TO THIS NUTTY HAMMER--?
DESPITE ALL YOUR STRENGTH, MY MALLET MUST ALWAYS RETURN TO ME! IT IS SO ORDAINED!
2

THAT SUITS ME FINE!
I'LL EVEN HELP IT ALONG! I GOT NO USE FOR THE CRUMMY THING!
THIS'LL SHOW YA HOW IT FEELS TO BE ON THE RECEIVING END FOR A CHANGE!
BY THROWING IT WITH YOUR STRENGTH, I'LL SMASH YOU WITH YOUR OWN WEAPON!

BUT, THE THUNDER GOD IS TOO SWIFT-- TOO AGILE--AND...
IT IS LIKE BATTLING MYSELF! I MUST FORGET ALL THE OLD RULES! I MUST BE READY FOR ANYTHING!

EVEN I NEVER FULLY REALIZED WHAT A DEVASTATING, AWESOME MENACE MY MALLET CAN BE, WHEN THROWN WITH MAXIMUM FORCE!

YOU HAVE REVERTED BACK TO MERE FLESH AND BLOOD AGAIN...!
MEBBE SO-- BUT THAT STILL DOESN'T MEAN THAT YOU CAN STOP ME!

EASILY DUCKING UNDER THE EX-CONVICT'S FLAYING BALL-AND-CHAIN, THOR LANDS A POUNDING BLOW, BUT--
AS SOON AS YOU TOUCH ME, YOUR STRENGTH BECOMES MINE, SO I CAN SHRUG OFF YOUR PUNCH!
3

HE'S RIGHT! IT'S AS THOUGH I AM AGAIN BATTLING HERCULES*
BEING EVENLY MATCHED, NEITHER OF US CAN FULLY DEFEAT THE OTHER!
*AS SEEN IN THE UNFORGETTABLE THOR ANNUAL #1, NOW ON SALE! -- STAN.

BUT, THOUGH OUR POWER BE EQUAL, THE GOD OF THUNDER WAS BORN FOR BATTLE! WHILE YOU MAY MATCH MY STRENGTH, YOU CAN NEVER MATCH MY SKILL!
HE'S WEARIN' ME DOWN! HE MOVES TOO FAST--HE'S OUT-FIGHTING ME--!

MEANWHILE, ALMOST FORGOTTEN IN THE FRAY, THOR'S ENCHANTED HAMMER INEXORABLY FREES ITSELF FROM THE WALL OF BRICK AND MORTAR IN WHICH IT HAD BEEN IMBEDDED...
FOR, ODIN HAS DECREED THAT IT MUST ALWAYS RETURN TO ITS RIGHTFUL OWNER, DESPITE THE OBSTACLES-- THOUGH GALAXIES TOTTER!

KRUNNTCH!
THUS, EXERTING A FORCE THAT NO POWER ON EARTH COULD HOPE TO RESTRAIN, THE BEWITCHED HAMMER DISLODGES ITSELF, PULLING A SECTION OF WALL ALONG WITH IT...!
4

BUT, ITS UNEXPECTED RETURN TO THE BATTLING IMMORTAL, ACCOMPANIED BY FLYING PARTICLES OF SHATTERED BRICK, TEMPORARILY BLIND THE GOLDEN-HAIRED AVENGER, GIVING THE ABSORBING MAN PRECIOUS SECONDS TO BACK AWAY AND REGAIN HIS FADING STRENGTH!
GOTTA GET AWAY FROM HIM-- TILL I CAN GET MY BREATH BACK--!

COME BACK, MORTAL! COME BACK AND LEARN THAT EQUAL POWER ALONE CAN NEVER WIN A VICTORY --CAN NEVER STAY THE WRATH OF THOR!
HE IS CERTAIN TO BE MORE CAUTIOUS NOW--MAKING MY TASK DOUBLY DIFFICULT!

MEANWHILE, FROM THE OLYMPIAN HEIGHTS OF ASGARD, THE SLYEST, MOST MERCILESS, MOST SINISTER EYES OF ALL WATCH THE EPIC BATTLE WITH GROWING CONCERN...!
THE ABSORBING MAN MUST DEFEAT MY ACCURSED HALF-BROTHER! EVERYTHING DEPENDS UPON IT!
ONLY WITH THOR'S COMPLETE DESTRUCTION WILL I BE FREE TO CHALLENGE THE RULE OF ODIN HIMSELF!

A SUDDEN SOUND! SOMEONE APPROACHES!
NONE MUST SUSPECT THAT LOKI HAS FREED HIMSELF FROM THE BONDAGE OF ULARIC, THE WARLOCK--AND THAT EVEN NOW ULARIC IS MY PRISONER!

BALDER, THE BRAVE! WHY COMES A FRIEND OF THOR TO THE PLACE WHERE LOKI IS CONFINED?
IT IS BECAUSE OF MY FRIENDSHIP FOR THE GOLDEN-HAIRED ONE THAT I COME TO MAKE SURE YOU CAN DO HIM NO FURTHER HARM!

WHERE IS ULARIC, THE ONE YOU HAVE BEEN SENTENCED TO SERVE?
HE IS OFF ON AN ERRAND FOR ODIN! I HAVE BEEN ORDERED TO REMAIN HERE AND REPLENISH HIS SORCERER'S POTIONS TILL HE RETURNS!
SO TRUSTING IS THE INNOCENT BALDER, HE WILL NEVER THINK TO DOUBT MY WORD!
5

WHERE GO YOU NOW, THOU WITLESS MILKSOP!
ANY PLACE WHERE THE VERY AIR ITSELF IS NOT HEAVILY-LADEN WITH THE AURA OF LOKI'S EVIL!
THE VERY SIGHT OF THEE IS OFFENSIVE TO MINE EYES!

HOW DIFFERENT BALDER'S TUNE SHALL BE--IF HE IS STILL ALIVE-- WHEN LOKI IS LORD OF ASGARD!
AND, WITH THE CRUSHING DEFEAT OF THOR, THAT GREAT MOMENT WILL SOON BE HERE!

MEANWHILE, EVEN AS LOKI SCHEMES...
THE ABSORBING MAN IS CAUSING PANIC IN THE STREETS!
EVEN THE PRESENCE OF THOR SEEMS NOT TO REASSURE THE MILLING THRONGS!

OUR BULLETS ARE USELESS AGAINST HIM! HE SEEMS TO ABSORB THEIR STEEL AS THEY TOUCH HIM!
WEAPONS ALONE CANNOT TURN HIM BACK!
YOU MUST HOLD BACK THE CROWDS! THE POWER OF THOR IS NEEDED HERE!

HE HAS BECOME MORE DANGEROUS THAN EVER!
AND YET, I DARE NOT FAIL! THE FATE OF A WORLD MAY BE AT STAKE!
6

YOU COULD NOT DEFEAT ME BEFORE--SO NOW YOU SEEK VICTORY BY ABSORBING THE CONCRETE AND STEEL OF THE BUILDINGS AROUND YOU--BY TRANSFORMING YOURSELF INTO A VERITABLE COLOSSUS OF STONE AND IRON!
CALL IT WHAT YOU WANT TO, THUNDER GOD--!
YOU JUST MADE YOUR BIGGEST MISTAKE, ATTACKIN' ME NOW--YOUR LAST MISTAKE!
7

HIS FIST IS BLUDGEONING OUT TOWARDS ME-- THIS IS MY CHANCE-- ONE SHATTERING HAMMER BLOW, NO MATTER WHAT HIS STRENGTH MAY BE!

ROARING IN PAIN FROM THE INDESCRIBABLY POWERFUL HAMMER BLOW, THE ENRAGED GIANT HURLS THOR FROM HIM AS A MASTIFF WOULD SHAKE A FLEA...!
I HURT HIM... BUT, NOT ENOUGH TO VANQUISH HIM!

USING HIS INVINCIBLE HAMMER LIKE A GRAPPLING HOOK, THE HURTLING THUNDER GOD STOPS HIS FANTASTIC FLIGHT BY ANCHORING HIMSELF TO A NEARBY ROOF...
I MUST RETURN TO CARRY ON THE BATTLE! HE MUST HAVE NO TIME TO MAKE NEW PLANS--TO ABSORB NEW STRENGTH--!

AND, AS THE VALIANT POLICE CONTINUE TO EVACUATE ALL RESIDENTS FROM THE ENTIRE AREA, THE ABSORBING MAN CONTINUES TO BELLOW IN RAGE, LIKE SOME NIGHTMARISH BEAST AT BAY!
YOU WON'T GET A CHANCE TO HURT ME AGAIN, DO YA HEAR??
JUST WAIT!! I'LL SLAP YA DOWN LIKE AN INSECT!

THEN, GRABBING THE SKELETON OF A CONDEMNED BUILDING, IN THE PROCESS OF BEING DEMOLISHED, HE WHO HAD ONCE BEEN CRUSHER CREEL COMPLETES THE JOB IN AN INSTANT!
THE MORE STEEL I ABSORB, THE STRONGER I BECOME! NOTHIN' CAN HURT ME NOW!

HIS STRENGTH INCREASES WITH EACH PASSING SECOND! NEVER HAS MAN OR IMMORTAL FOUGHT SUCH A FOE!

BUT, NO MATTER HOW AWESOME THE ODDS MAY BE, I AM SON OF ODIN, PRINCE OF ASGARD! I WOULD EVER CHOOSE THE ETERNAL SLEEP, RATHER THAN A MOMENT'S COWARDICE!

THEN, SEEING THE FLIGHT OF THE GOLDEN-HAIRED GOD, THE TOWERING TITAN HURLS A BALL OF TWISTED STEEL GIRDERS DIRECTLY IN THOR'S PATH--!
THIS WILL FINISH YOU FOR GOOD!

NOT WHILST THESE TWO ARMS CAN STILL WIELD THE HAMMER OF THOR...!

HE SHATTERED IT-- WITH ONLY ONE BLOW OF THAT BLASTED HAMMER OF HIS!!
AND NOW I CAN'T SEE! HAVE TO KEEP MY EYES SHUT --BECAUSE OF THE FLYING STEEL SLIVERS!

CAN'T TAKE A CHANCE OF HIM HITTING ME WHILE MY EYES ARE CLOSED! I CAN ONLY ESCAPE THE FLYING SLIVERS BY BECOMING MAN-SIZED AGAIN...!
WITH MY ABSORBING POWER, I SHOULD BE ABLE TO DEFEAT ANYONE! BUT THERE'S SOMETHING ABOUT THOR-- IT'S LIKE FIGHTING A WHIRLWIND!

HE'S ATTACKING AGAIN!
THERE'LL BE NO RESPITE FOR YOU, MORTAL-- NO MERCY-- TILL YOU SURRENDER!

NO! EVERY TIME YOU HIT ME, I ABSORB MORE OF YOUR POWER! I'LL SMASH YOU YET!
NEVER! NOT WHILE LIFE ENDURES!

NO?? LOOK AT THIS! MY BALL AND CHAIN ARE AGAIN AS STRONG AS YOUR HAMMER --AND MY LIMBS ARE THE EQUAL OF YOURS!
SEE HOW EASILY I CAN THROW YOU FROM ME--!

REMEMBER-- NOT ONLY CAN I ABSORB THE SAME AMOUNT OF STRENGTH WHICH YOU POSSESS, BUT I ALSO KEEP MY OWN NORMAL POWER-- WHICH HAS TO GIVE ME THE EDGE!
AND, ONCE I'VE FINISHED YOU, THE WHOLE WORLD'LL BE AT MY FEET!
THAT MUST NEVER BE!
YOUR BRUTAL WORDS HAVE REINFORCED MY WILL TO WIN!

AND, AS THE GRIM BATTLE CONTINUES TO RAGE, THE UNTIRING POLICE RESPOND TO THE CRISIS WITH SPEED AND VALOR...
SORRY, FOLKS! THIS AREA IS OFF-LIMITS! TAKE SHELTER IN THE ARMORY ON 34TH STREET...!
SO FAR, SO GOOD! AT LEAST NO BYSTANDERS HAVE BEEN INJURED!

WHILE A SAD-EYED GIRL RUSHES TO A BULLET-PROOF WINDOW, NOT FAR FROM THE SCENE OF BATTLE...
EVEN THOR COULD NOT HELP ME NOW! NOT WHILE HE'S FIGHTING FOR HIS LIFE AGAINST A DEADLY, ALL-POWERFUL ENEMY!
STAND AWAY FROM THE WINDOW, JANE FOSTER! YOU ARE NOT TO BE SEEN, BY ANYONE!

BUT WHY NOT? WHEN ARE YOU GOING TO EXPLAIN ALL THIS TO ME??
WHEN THE TIME IS RIPE! TILL THEN, MY LIPS MUST BE SEALED!

YOU HAVE BEEN TREATED WELL, HAVE YOU NOT? YOU HAVE NOT BEEN HARMED--YOUR PRIVACY HAS BEEN RESPECTED--AND YOU HAVE BEEN GRANTED EVERY COMFORT AND CONVENIENCE!
THAT'S TRUE! BUT I STILL DON'T KNOW WHY I WAS BROUGHT TO THIS PLACE--WHY I'M NOT PERMITTED TO LEAVE?
I CAN ONLY REPEAT THAT IT IS FOR YOUR OWN GOOD! I CAN SAY NO MORE!

SO LONG AS THAT BATTLE CONTINUES OUTSIDE, YOU MUST REMAIN HERE! THAT IS ALL YOU MAY BE TOLD!

WAIT! AT LEAST TELL ME WHO YOU ARE--WHY YOU WEAR THAT DREADFUL HOOD??
NOT YET!
IT'S NO USE! HIS VOICE SOUNDS VAGUELY FAMILIAR, BUT I CAN'T IDENTIFY IT! I SIMPLY CAN'T!

BUT, MANY ARE THE EVENTS WHICH DEPEND UPON THE OUTCOME OF THOR'S DESPERATE BATTLE! IN FAR OFF ASGARD, LOKI USES A VISI-PROBE TO SEE BENEATH THE COLD STONE FLOOR...
NOW THAT I AM ALONE ONCE MORE, IT IS SAFE TO CONTINUE MY OWN SECRET ENDEAVERS...
I MUST BE CERTAIN THAT ULARIC, THE WARLOCK, STILL SLEEPS IN CAPTIVITY BELOW!

GOOD! HE STILL LIES HELPLESSLY WITHIN THE TIME CAPSULE, OBLIVIOUS TO ALL THAT TRANSPIRES!

WHILST THE SICKENINGLY NOBLE BALDER BEGINS A ROUTINE PATROL OF ASGARD'S BORDERS... HENCE, I NEED NO LONGER CONCERN MYSELF WITH HIM!

EVEN OMNIPOTENT ODIN, BELIEVING ALL TO BE TRANQUIL IN ASGARD, CONCERNS HIMSELF WITH SPORT AND GAMES, LITTLE DREAMING THAT LOKI IS FREE ONCE AGAIN!

THUS, THE STAGE IS SET FOR MY GREATEST FEAT OF EVIL--ONE SO DARING, SO SUBLIME IN ITS VILLAINY, THAT IT WILL ROCK THE VERY STONES OF ASGARD THEMSELVES!

AND, AS AN INSCRUTIBLE FATE FORGES HER CHAIN OF EVENTS, ONE VITAL LINK IS ALL BUT UNNOTICED BY ALL CONCERNED! HIDDEN DEEP WITHIN A PRIMEVAL FOREST, LIES THE ENCHANTED NORN STONE WHICH THOR HAD DROPPED SOME DAYS BEFORE--A STONE WHOSE STRANGE POWER WE CAN ONLY GUESS AT FOR THE TIME BEING...!
*AS WITNESSED BY ALL WHO HAD THE GOOD FORTUNE AND FORESIGHT TO READ THOR #120--STAN.

MEANWHILE, BACK TO THE BEDLAM ON BROADWAY...
I'LL CONQUER YOU YET, FOR TIME IS ON MY SIDE! YOU MUST GROW WEARY SOONER OR LATER...
...WHILE I ABSORB MORE AND MORE POWER EACH TIME I STRIKE YOU!
HIS WORDS ARE TRUE! EACH PASSING MINUTE BRINGS ME FURTHER FROM VICTORY!

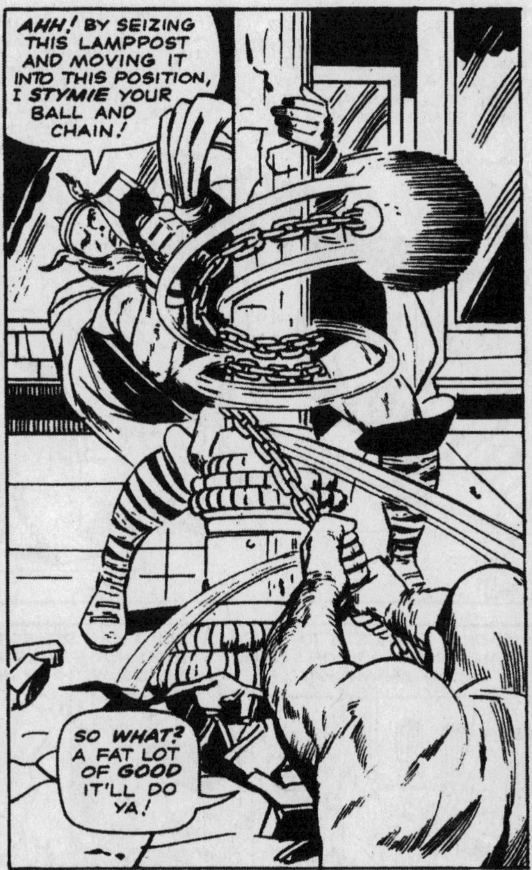
AHH! BY SEIZING THIS LAMPPOST AND MOVING IT INTO THIS POSITION, I STYMIE YOUR BALL AND CHAIN!
SO WHAT? A FAT LOT OF GOOD IT'LL DO YA!

IT WILL INDEED! BY SIMPLY PULLING ON THE CHAIN, I YANK YOU OFF YOUR FEET! AND NOW, THE INITIATIVE IS MINE!
THAT'S WHAT YOU THINK! ALL I GOTTA DO IS TOUCH ANOTHER PIECE OF STEEL, OR CONCRETE...!

OF COURSE! THAT IS WHY I HURLED YOU WHERE A GLASS WINDOW WOULD BE THE FIRST THING YOUR HAND WOULD CONTACT!
HE TRICKED ME! I TURNED INTO GLASS! I-I'M VULNERABLE TO HIM NOW!

BY THE BRISTLING BEARD OF ODIN! SOMETHING STAYED MY HAND! I COULD NOT DELIVER A LETHAL BLOW! I AM STILL MINDFUL OF MY OATH TO NEVER SLAY A MORTAL HUMAN!
I--I DON'T GET IT! HE MISSED ME!
BLAST IT! SOON AS I TOUCHED MY BALL AND CHAIN, THEY TURNED TO GLASS, ALSO!
MY ONLY CHANCE IS TO TOUCH SOMETHING MADE OF STEEL-- LIKE A BANK VAULT!
ALL I CAN DO IS PURSUE HIM! I CANNOT STRIKE A MAN OF GLASS WITH MY URU HAMMER!
HAH! I DID IT! I TURNED TO STEEL AGAIN! NOW I'LL LOCK MYSELF INSIDE THIS VAULT, TO GIVE ME TIME TO THINK!
DO NOT WASTE YOUR SHOTS! MERE BULLETS CANNOT HARM HIM NOW!
KRAK!
HE TRAPPED HIMSELF FOR SURE THIS TIME! I'LL GET SOME EQUIPMENT TO TRY TO OPEN THAT DOOR! IT'S FITTED WITH AN UNBREAKABLE TIME LOCK!
THERE IS NO TIME FOR THAT! I HAVE A FASTER WAY--!
RUN INTO THE STREET-- QUICKLY! THE SUDDEN CONCUSSION IN HERE MIGHT PROVE FATAL TO A HUMAN!
YOU DON'T HAVETA TELL ME TWICE, MISTER!

THEN, APPLYING THE FORCE AND POWER OF HIS OWN MUSCLES--PULLING WITH A PRESSURE WHICH IS IMPOSSIBLE TO DESCRIBE IN OUR OWN INADEQUATE HUMAN LANGUAGE, THE MIGHTY THUNDER GOD ACHIEVES HIS INCREDIBLE OBJECTIVE...!
NO PLACE ON EARTH CAN FURNISH A HAVEN FROM THOR!

AND NOW, EVIL ONE--THE TIME FOR A RECKONING IS COME!

I HAVE YOUR STRENGTH--PLUS MY OWN! WHY CAN'T I BEAT YOU? WHY??
THINK, HUMAN!! CAN YOU EVER HOPE TO POSSESS THE FIGHTING HEART OF --AN IMMORTAL!

BACK! GET BACK!! THEY'RE CRASHING THRU!

LOOK! THE BATTLE IS STILL RAGING!
NEITHER OF THEM CAN BE HURT--THEY BOTH POSSESS SUPER POWERS! HOW CAN IT EVER END?

IT MUST END WITH THOR TRIUMPHANT! FOR, IF HE LOSES--!
BUT, HE CAN'T DEFEAT SOMEONE WHO CAN ABSORB HIS OWN POWER!! LOOK--!
WHATEVER YOU CAN DO--
--I CAN DO --IN SPADES!
15

AS SURELY AS FAITHFUL HEIMDALL GUARDS THE RAINBOW BRIDGE, YOU SHALL THRILL TO THE CLIMAX! OF THIS IMMORTAL SAGA NEXT MONTH! YOU ARE NOT TO MISS IT! WE HAVE SPOKEN!

TALES OF ASGARD, HOME OF THE MIGHTY NORSE GODS
"MAELSTROM!"
HOPING TO POSTPONE THE DAY OF RAGNAROK (THE END OF THE WORLD, WHEN EVEN THE GODS SHALL PERISH), THOR LEADS HIS MIGHTY CREW OF ARGONAUTS INTO THE DREAD SEA OF FEAR, SEARCHING FOR THE HIDDEN FORCES OF EVIL WHO THREATEN IMMORTAL ASGARD...
BEWARE! WE APPROACH THE DEADLY PILLARS OF UTGARD!
TO SAIL BETWEEN THEM MEANS INSTANT DESTRUCTION!
A SAGA STEEPED IN GRANDEUR BY:
STAN LEE + JACK KIRBY
WRITER ILLUSTRATOR
DELINEATED BY: VINCE COLLETTA
LETTERED BY: ARTIE SIMEK
1

FALLING UNDER THE DEADLY ENCHANTMENT OF THE SEA OF FEAR, THE CREW GROWS NUMB WITH DREAD, AS THEY SHOUT TO THEIR CAPTAIN...
MIGHTY THOR, LET US TURN BACK WHILE STILL THERE IS TIME!!
NO MERE SHIP CAN BRAVE A MAELSTROM SUCH AS THIS!!
REMAIN AT YOUR POSTS!! SO LONG AS I AM MASTER HERE--WE SAIL EVER ONWARD!
WHY IS LOKI NOT IN COMMAND?? SURELY HE WOULD HAVE SET SAIL FOR HOME BY NOW!
I HAVE HEARD WHISPERED MURMERINGS OF MUTINY! PERHAPS THE GOLDEN-HAIRED ONE WILL NOT BE MASTER MUCH LONGER!
HEED NOT THE WORDS OF COWARDS, THUNDER GOD! WE SHALL TRIUMPH OVER THIS STORM--AND OVER MANY MORE LIKE IT!
BUT WHAT IF THE WINDS FORCE US BETWEEN THE PILLARS OF UTGARD? WE WILL BE DOOMED!
2

THOR, THIS IS MADNESS!! IF YOU HAVE NOT THE WIT TO ORDER OUR RETURN TO ASGARD, GIVE ME COMMAND OF THE SHIP!
NEVER, PRINCE OF EVIL!! WE PLEDGED NOBLE ODIN TO JOURNEY ON UNTIL WE FOUND THE FORCES OF EVIL-- AND WE SHALL KEEP THAT PLEDGE!

THINK YOU NOT THAT I AM AFRAID! LOKI FEARS NOTHING! BUT LOOK AT YOUR CREW, GOD OF THUNDER!
TURN BACK, THOR! TURN BACK!
NOTHING CAN SURVIVE THIS MAELSTROM!! HERE, ON THE FIRST LAP OF OUR VOYAGE, THOR HAS BROUGHT US TO THE EDGE OF DOOM!
THE WINDS ARE TOO STRONG! WE CANNOT GUIDE THE SHIP!

WITH EACH PASSING SECOND, THE VALIANT ODINSHIP, NOW VIRTUALLY OUT OF CONTROL, APPROACHES CLOSER AND CLOSER TO THE PILLARS OF UTGARD--!
GIVE ME THAT TILLER!! I SHALL PUT MY OWN SHOULDER TO IT!!
NAY, THUNDER GOD--EVEN YOUR MATCHLESS STRENGTH CANNOT PREVAIL! THE TILLER IS BROKEN! WE ARE AT THE MERCY OF THE STORM!!

ACCORDING TO THE LEGENDS, THE PILLARS ARE MERELY THE FEET OF THE UTGARD DRAGON! BENEATH THE WAVES HIS JAWS LIE OPEN, WAITING FOR EVERY SHIP THAT PASSES!
CEASE YOUR ENDLESS PRATTLE, BOY! EVEN DEATH CAN BE GLORIOUS IN THE SERVICE OF ONE SUCH AS THOR!

TIS TRULY HOPELESS! OF WHAT USE ARE OARS AGAINST THE FURY OF THE STORM??

TO YOUR POSTS, QUICKLY! LET NO MAN DESPAIR! MAY ODIN STEADY THY HANDS!

Like demons possessed, the Argonauts take to their oars, as the blades bite into the water like living things, spurred on by the courage and inspiration of *Thor...*

Faster!! Harder! Row, Asgardians-- row as never before-- in the name of *Odin!!*

Meanwhile, unnoticed by the others, a lone figure attempts the dangerous climb atop the ship's figurehead in the buffeting wind and storm...

I must make it! I *must!*

As the daring immortal turns, we see that it is *Balder!!* Balder the brave! Balder the loyal-- the bold! Desperately, he drags a great *horn* to his precarious perch-- for a reason that *none* of us will know, till next issue!

WITH
THE MIGHTY
THOR
APPROVED BY THE COMICS CODE AUTHORITY
MARVEL
POP ART
12¢
PRODUCTIONS
122
NOV
"WHERE MORTALS FEAR TO TREAD!"

THE MIGHTY THOR!
"WHERE MORTALS FEAR TO TREAD!"
LAST ISSUE, WHILE BATTLING THE DREADED ABSORBING MAN, MIGHTY THOR TURNED TO AID A HELPLESS CHILD! AS HE DID SO, HIS FOE STRUCK HIM FROM BEHIND, DOWNING HIM! AND NOW...
A NEW MARVEL MASTERWORK, STEEPED IN SPECTACLE, FRAUGHT WITH FANTASY!
I'VE BEATEN THOR AT LAST! NOW, NOTHIN' ON EARTH CAN STAND UP TO THE ABSORBING MAN!
DOES HE THINK THE GOD OF THUNDER CAN BE SO EASILY DISPATCHED? DID HE NOT SUSPECT I WAS MERELY STUNNED?
WRITTEN WITH COMPASSION BY: STAN LEE
DRAWN WITH COMPREHENSION BY: JACK KIRBY
INKED WITH COMPETENCE BY: VINCE COLLETTA
LETTERED FOR COMPENSATION BY: ARTIE SIMEK
1

SUDDENLY, FINGERS WITH THE STRENGTH OF IRON VISES GRIP THE POWERFUL SHOULDER OF THE ESCAPED CONVICT WHO HAD ONCE BEEN KNOWN AS CRUSHER CREEL...
YOU PRESUME TOO MUCH, EVIL ONE! THE SON OF ODIN DOES NOT YIELD WHILE A BREATH OF LIFE REMAINS!
YOU!!

THE BLOW WITH WHICH YOU FELLED ME WAS DELIVERED WHILEST MY HEAD WAS TURNED! BUT, THOR HAS NO NEED FOR TACTICS SO FOUL!
NO! IT WON'T DO YOU ANY GOOD! REMEMBER-- I ABSORB THE POWER OF ANYTHING THAT TOUCHES ME!

I HAVE NOT FORGOTTEN!
BUT, MY TOUCH SHALL BE TOO FLEETING-- TOO SWIFT-- LIKE A SUDDEN THUNDERCLAP!!

WHAT SAY YOU NOW, MORTAL ??
EVEN BY ABSORBIN' HIS OWN STRENGTH, I CAN'T TAKE MANY MORE BLOWS LIKE THAT! NOBODY COULD!!

BUT, WHAT AM I SCARED OF? I'M AS STRONG AS HE IS NOW!
ALL I GOTTA DO IS LAND A PUNCH OF MY OWN-- AND IT'LL HURT HIM JUST AS MUCH!
STAY RIGHT THERE, THUNDER GOD! NOW IT'S YOUR TURN!
2

CLANGG!
BLAST IT!! HE WAS TOO FAST FOR ME! I MISSED 'IM!
HAVE I NOT WARNED YOU IN THE PAST--? BRUTE STRENGTH ALONE CAN NEVER BE ENOUGH!

IT MUST BE COUPLED WITH SPEED--AND WITH SKILL--LIKE THIS!
UHHHH--!
WHIIITTTT

YOU PRESUMED TO THINK YOURSELF THE EQUAL OF THOR??!
SUCH BASE INSOLENCE MUST NOT GO UNPUNISHED!
HOW CAN I FIGHT 'IM? HE'S EVERYWHERE AT ONCE!!

YIELD, MORTAL!!
FOR, TILL YOU DO, THE FIGHT GOES ON--THUS SPEAKS THOR!

MEANWHILE, FROM A VANTAGE POINT IN LEGENDARY ASGARD, THE SINISTER IMMORTAL WHO HAD GIVEN THE ABSORBING MAN HIS DREADED POWER WATCHES THE BATTLE WITH HATE-FILLED EYES--!
I GAVE HIM STRENGTH TO CHALLENGE A GOD--BUT EVEN LOKI COULD NOT GIVE HIM VALOR TO MATCH THAT OF THOR!
BUT, THIS IS MERELY A MINOR SETBACK! THOR YET SHALL TASTE DEFEAT!

UNTIL THIS MOMENT, MY MASTER PLAN HAS WORKED TO PERFECTION!
ULARIC, THE SORCERER, LIES IN SUSPENDED ANIMATION IN THE DUNGEON BENEATH MY FEET! ULARIC, WHO WAS SUPPOSED TO BE MY CAPTOR! BUT NONE CAN HOLD LOKI PRISONER!

AND, WITH EACH PASSING HOUR, MORE AND MORE OF ODIN'S PICKED WARRIORS GO FORTH FROM ASGARD, ON ROUTINE PATROLS!
SO UNSUSPECTING IS ODIN OF THE DANGER THAT THREATENS, THAT HE PERMITS A MERE SKELETON FORCE TO REMAIN WITHIN THE GOLDEN CITY!
AND, WITH THOR HIMSELF STILL ON EARTH, THE MOMENT FOR ME TO STRIKE HAS FINALLY ARRIVED!

BUT, I MUST USE EVERY WEAPON--EMPLOY EVERY BIT OF CUNNING, OF VILLAINY THAT I AM MASTER OF!
AND, AT THIS FATEFUL MOMENT, I SHALL RALLY THE POWER OF THE ABSORBING MAN TO MY SIDE!
ALL I NEED DO IS DIRECT THIS ATTRACTOR BEAM TO EARTH--!

THUS, I SHALL SAVE MY HUMAN PUPPET FROM DEFEAT--WHILE HIS POWER WILL INSURE MY OWN COMPLETE VICTORY!
4

AND, AT THAT VERY MOMENT...
YIELD, I COMMAND YOU.!!
CAN'T TAKE MUCH MORE OF THIS--!

IT AINT FAIR!! WHAT GOOD'S MY STRENGTH-- MY POWER-- IF I CAN'T LAND A BLOW?!! I DIDN'T KNOW IT WAS GONNA BE LIKE THIS!!
DROP YOUR IRON BALL AND CHAIN AND SAY NO MORE! YOUR VERY VOICE IS OFFENSIVE TO MY EARS!

BUT THEN, SEEMINGLY FROM EVERYWHERE AT ONCE--FROM NOWHERE--FROM SPACE BEYOND SPACE, TIME BEYOND TIME--THE ATTRACTOR BEAM AIMED BY EVIL LOKI, ENVELOPS THE DUMBFOUNDED MORTAL--!
NO! NO! WHA- WHAT'S HAPPENIN' TO ME??!

HE'S GONE!
VANISHED--BEFORE MY VERY EYES!

THAT DAZZLING BOLT OF LIGHT DID IT!
I HAVE SEEN SUCH A PHENOMENON BEFORE!! IT IS THE ATTRACTOR BEAM OF ULARIC!
THAT MEANS I MUST SEEK MY FOE--IN ASGARD!!!

BUT, BEFORE THE IMMORTAL AVENGER CAN MAKE ANOTHER MOVE...
AN EXPLOSION!! FROM THE BUILDING ABOVE!!

AND, MANY STORIES ABOVE -- THE IMPRISONED JANE FOSTER, WHO HAD DARINGLY CAUSED A GAS EXPLOSION IN ORDER TO SHATTER HER BULLET-PROOF WINDOW GLASS, SCREAMS AS ONLY A DESPERATE FEMALE CAN--!
HE'S LOOKING UP! HE'S GOT TO NOTICE ME! HE'S GOT TO!!
THOR!! THOR!! HELP ME! PLEASE-- HELP ME!
HE HEARD ME! THANK HEAVEN-- HE'LL FIND A WAY TO FREE ME!
GET BACK FROM THE WINDOW-- WHILE MY HAMMER STRIKES!
HER FACE!! CAN IT REALLY BE--?? NO! IT IS TOO MUCH TO HOPE FOR!!
EVER SINCE SHE VANISHED, I SEEM TO SEE JANE FOSTER'S LOVELY FEATURES EVERYWHERE I LOOK--!!
I AM JUST IN TIME! SHE HAS BEEN OVERCOME BY THE SMOKE FROM THE EXPLOSION!
BUT, WHO IS SHE? WHY WAS SHE HELD PRISONER HERE-- AND BY WHOM??
BUT THEN, AS HE TENDERLY TURNS THE UNCONSCIOUS GIRL TO FACE HIM, THOR SEES...
ODIN BE PRAISED!! IT IS SHE! THE GIRL I LOVE! BUT-- WHAT HAS BEFALLEN HER?
IF SHE IS INJURED, THEN DR. BLAKE CAN AID HER MORE THAN THE GOD OF THUNDER!
WITH THOSE GRIM WORDS, THE MIGHTY THOR POUNDS HIS ENCHANTED MALLET UPON THE FLOOR, AS THE VERY HEAVENS SEEM TO TREMBLE...!
6

BUT, NO SOONER DOES THE LAME DOCTOR--WHO NOW STANDS WHERE AN IMMORTAL HAD STOOD --LIFTS THE LIMP GIRL IN HIS ARMS, THEN--!
AT LAST-- MY LONG WAIT HAS BEEN REWARDED!
A CAMERA FLASH GUN!!

WHOEVER HE IS, HE MUST HAVE SEEN ME CHANGE FROM THOR TO MY MORTAL FORM!
WHO ARE YOU?? WHY HAVE YOU BEEN HOLDING THIS GIRL CAPTIVE??
I MEANT HER NO HARM! SHE WAS MERELY THE BAIT WHICH I NEEDED TO CATCH YOU!

I'D HAVE RISKED ANYTHING--EVEN MY LIFE-- --IN ORDER TO GET THAT ONE PICTURE!
IF YOU'VE LEARNED WHAT I SUSPECT YOU'VE LEARNED --YOU SHOULD KNOW I CAN'T ALLOW YOU TO KEEP THAT KNOWLEDGE!
I ALSO KNOW THERE'S NOTHING YOU CAN DO ABOUT IT!

AND THEN, SLOWLY, DRAMATICALLY, THE MASKED MAN REMOVES HIS IDENTITY-CONCEALING HOOD, ONLY TO STAND REVEALED AS--
HARRIS HOBBS!! THE AFFILIATED PRESS REPORTER! WE MET THE FIRST TIME THOR FOUGHT THE ABSORBING MAN--MONTHS AGO!*
YOU MEAN-- THE FIRST TIME YOU FOUGHT HIM, DON'T YOU, DOCTOR BLAKE? I KNOW YOUR SECRET NOW!!
*WILL YOU EVER FORGET THAT THRILLING MOMENT IN THOR #114? --STAN.

AND, EVEN AS THE STUNNING IMPACT OF HOBBS' WORDS SINKS INTO DON BLAKE'S CONSCIOUSNESS, NEW AND STARTLING EVENTS ARE TAKING SHAPE IN ASGARD...
WHAT HAPPENED?? WHERE AM I?
TURN, MORTAL! TURN AND FACE YOUR MASTER --LOKI!!

I DUNNO WHERE I AM, OR WHO YOU ARE, BUT YOU GOT ONE THING WRONG...
...NOBODY CAN CALL HIMSELF THE MASTER OF THE ABSORBING MAN!
AND, IN CASE YA WANT A LITTLE PROOF...
FOOL! IT WAS I WHO GAVE YOU YOUR POWER--AND ONLY I KNOW HOW TO NULLIFY IT!

I AINT BUYIN', MISTER! LET'S SEE YA NULLIFY THIS!

BUT, BEFORE THE AWESOMELY DESTRUCTIVE IRON BALL CAN STRIKE ITS TARGET...
I MUST BE LOSIN' MY MARBLES! ALL OF A SUDDEN, I'M--SOMEWHERE ELSE!
CAN'T SEE NOTHIN' BUT ICE--AN' SNOW--IT'S FREEZIN' HERE!

I-I'M ABSORBIN' ALL THE COLD--TURNIN' INTO A LIVIN' SNOW MAN!
BUT HOW LONG CAN I TAKE IT?? IT'S TOO COLD TO BEAR--I NEED HELP--BEFORE I FREEZE TO DEATH--
IT WAS THE GUY I SWUNG AT--HE MUSTA DONE THIS! HE'S GOTTA BRING ME BACK--HE'S GOTTA!!

AND THEN, FASTER THAN THE BRAIN CAN COMPREHEND...
YOU ARE SAFE NOW, MORTAL!
BUT, REMEMBER THIS WELL--I CAN SEND YOU BACK TO THE DEADLY COLD --ANYTIME!
I--AINT ABOUT TO FORGET--A THING LIKE THAT!
8

NOW, HEED MY WORDS! IF YOU SERVE ME FAITHFULLY, WITHOUT QUESTION, YOU AND I CAN SHARE DOMINION OF THE UNIVERSE! BUT, IF YOU DEFY ME, YOUR PUNISHMENT WILL BE SWIFT AND MERCILESS!
I GET THE PICTURE! SO, OKAY --I'M YOUR BOY!

A SHORT TIME LATER, WARRIORS STANDING IN THE HALLOWED HALLS OF ODIN'S IMPERIAL PALACE, ARE STARTLED TO SEE...
DO MY EYES DECEIVE ME?? CAN THAT BE LOKI--THE PRINCE OF EVIL??
THERE IS TREACHERY MOST FOUL HERE! LOKI IS UNDER SENTENCE TO SERVE ULARIC!
KEEP WALKING! WITH LOKI AT YOUR SIDE, YOU NEED FEAR NOTHING THAT LIVES!
HE CALLED THIS PLACE ASGARD! BUT--WHERE IS IT? WHY WON'T HE TELL ME?

STAND FAST! BY WHAT RIGHT DO YOU COME HERE? ON WHOSE AUTHORITY HAS YOUR SERVITUDE TO ULARIC THE WARLOCK BEEN ENDED?
AND, THAT CREATURE WITH YOU-- IF HE BE A MORTAL, YOU HAVE COMMITTED THE GRAVEST CRIME BY BRINGING HIM TO ASGARD!

SPEAK NOT TO LOKI OF CRIME! WITHIN THE HOUR, MY EVERY WISH SHALL BE THE IMPERIAL LAW! FOR THIS MORTAL IS MORE THAN HE SEEMS--HE IS THE WEAPON WITH WHICH I SHALL DETHRONE ODIN HIMSELF!
YEAH! YOU SQUARES DON'T CUT NO ICE WITH ME! I CAN LICK THE WHOLE BUNCH OF YA! WHAT LOKI SAYS GOES!
NOW, ATTACK!

AND THEN, WITHOUT WARNING, LOKI'S MOST DANGEROUS CREATION STRIKES...!
THE MORE OF YA I FIGHT, THE MORE POWER I ABSORB! I BECOME AS STRONG AS ANYONE I TOUCH!
THE ALARM! SOUND THE ALARM!
THIS IS MADNESS! NEVER HAS REGAL ODIN BEEN SO THREATENED!!

THEN, LIKE A HUMAN BATTERING RAM, THE ABSORBING MAN CHARGES THRU THE EVER-GROWING ARMY OF WARRIORS, GAINING INCREASED POWER WITH EACH PASSING SECOND...!

NO POWER, SAVE THAT OF **THOR**--OR **ODIN**, CAN STOP HIM!

AND YET, HE MUST HAVE A PLAN TO OVERCOME ODIN **HIMSELF**--OR HE'D NOT HAVE DARED SUCH AN ATTACK!

HE SPOKE THE **TRUTH!** HIS STRENGTH IS THE EQUAL OF ALL OUR **COMBINED** POWER!

ONLY ONE **OTHER** MIGHT CONQUER HIM--**LOKI**, WITH HIS MIRACULOUS **MAGIC**, MIGHT BE HIS MASTER!

YET, THE EVIL ONE FIGHTS **WITH** OUR FOE--**AGAINST ODIN!**

MEANWHILE, BACK ON EARTH, IN A CHEERY HOSPITAL ROOM...
YOU'LL BE ALL RIGHT, JANE! YOU JUST NEED SOME REST AFTER YOUR STRANGE ORDEAL!
BUT-- HOW DID YOU FIND ME, DON?? AND--WHO WAS THAT MYSTERIOUS HOODED MAN WHO HELD ME PRISONER??
AND, WHY WAS I HELD CAPTIVE?? I FELT LIKE A PAWN-- IN A MUCH BIGGER, MORE DANGEROUS GAME!

NO NEED TO WORRY ABOUT THAT NOW, DEAR! I'LL EXPLAIN IT ALL TO YOU LATER, WHEN YOU'RE A BIT STRONGER! RIGHT NOW, JUST REST UP, AND REMEMBER--YOU'RE PERFECTLY SAFE!
I ALWAYS FEEL SAFE WHEN YOU'RE NEAR, DON! PROMISE YOU'LL NEVER DISAPPEAR FOR SUCH A LONG TIME AGAIN!
HOW I WISH I COULD MAKE SUCH A PROMISE--!

EXCUSE ME, DOCTOR! THERE IS A PHONE CALL FOR YOU!
HOBBS! I PROMISED I'D MEET HIM SECRETLY THIS AFTERNOON!
VERY WELL! I'LL BE RIGHT THERE, NURSE!

DON! THAT STRANGE LOOK IN YOUR EYE! DOES THE CALL HAVE ANYTHING TO DO WITH THE HOODED MAN?? ARE--ARE YOU GOING TO LEAVE ME AGAIN--?
YOU JUST REST, HONEY! DON'T WORRY ABOUT A THING! I'LL BE GONE NO LONGER THAN NECESSARY--I PROMISE!

MINUTES AFTER TAKING THE CALL, ON THE HOSPITAL ROOF...
I WAS RIGHT! HE WANTS TO MEET ME--NOW! PROBABLY EXPECTING TO BLACKMAIL ME WITH THE PICTURE HE TOOK!

AND, MEET HIM I SHALL...

...AS THOR--GOD OF THUNDER!

THE SECRET OF MY DUAL IDENTITY MUST NEVER BE REVEALED TO THE WORLD! AND IT SHALL NOT BE!
HARRIS HOBBS IS ABOUT TO LEARN THAT THE PICTURE HE RISKED SO MUCH TO OBTAIN MAY WELL BE THE MOST DANGEROUS OBJECT ANY MORTAL EVER POSSESSED!
SECONDS LATER, AT A LONELY, PREARRANGED MEETING PLACE...
I KNEW HE'D BE HERE! HE WOULDN'T DARE FAIL TO SHOW UP SO LONG AS I HAVE THE PICTORIAL PROOF THAT HE IS ALSO DR. DON BLAKE!
I AM NOT HERE TO DISCUSS TERMS, MORTAL! YOU HAVE THE PHOTO! I WANT IT! THERE IS NOTHING MORE TO BE SAID!
HOLD IT, THOR! DON'T TRY ANY STRONG-ARM STUFF ON ME! I DON'T HAVE THE PICTURE WITH ME! IT'S HIDDEN IN A SAFE PLACE!
YOU'VE GOT TO DEAL WITH ME! I HOLD ALL THE CARDS!
I'M NOT TRYING TO CAUSE ANY TROUBLE, THOR-- BUT, AS A REPORTER, I'VE A JOB TO DO--
AND, IF YOU'D GIVE ME THE WHOLE STORY BEYOND YOUR DOUBLE IDENTITY, IT WOULD BE THE SCOOP OF THE CENTURY!
BY THE BRISTLING BEARD OF ODIN, YOU PRESUME TOO MUCH! THE GOD OF THUNDER IS NO GRIST FOR A NEWSMAN'S MILL!
YOU POSSESS THAT WHICH NO MORTAL HAS THE RIGHT TO POSSESS! YOU MAY NOT KEEP IT!
RAGE ALL YOU WANT-- I'M NOT AFRAID! I KNOW YOU'RE PLEDGED NEVER TO HARM A HUMAN!
WHOOOM!
12

I DO NOT NEED TO CAUSE BODILY INJURY --THERE ARE OTHER MEANS!
HE'S CREATING SOME SORT OF WIND VORTEX WITH HIS HAMMER-- RIGHT BEFORE MY EYES!
YOUR HAMMER! THAT SPINNING CURRENT OF WIND! WHA-WHAT ARE YOU DOING--??!

I AM ABOUT TO SHOW HOW FOOLHARDY IT IS TO INCUR THE WRATH OF THOR!
NO! NO!

DO NOT FEAR-- YOU SHALL NOT BE HARMED!
NO! DON'T TAKE ME IN THERE! THIS IS MORE THAN I BARGAINED FOR--! DON'T--!

THERE IS NO TURNING BACK NOW! YOU ARE ABOUT TO TAKE A JOURNEY SUCH AS NO MORTAL HAS EVER TAKEN BEFORE!
A JOURNEY BEYOND THE VERY BOUNDS OF TIME AND SPACE....

OPEN YOUR EYES, HOBBS! YOU CAN SEE THRU THE VORTEX! LOOK ABOUT YOU--!
THAT WORLD BELOW! IT-- IT CAN'T BE--!

TO THE GOD OF THUNDER, ANYTHING IS POSSIBLE!
I COULD DEPOSIT YOU SAFELY BELOW AND ABANDON YOU! I WOULD BE TRUE TO MY OATH NOT TO HARM A MORTAL!
WHAT HAPPENS TO YOU AFTER I LEAVE WOULD BE NO CONCERN OF MINE!

NO! NO! YOU CAN'T-- YOU MUSTN'T--!
VERY WELL, THEN-- PERHAPS YOU WOULD PREFER ANOTHER AGE?

INSTANTLY, THE INCREDIBLE VORTEX STREAKS LIKE A METEOR THRU THE ETHEREAL VEIL OF INFINITY, UNTIL IT REACHES...

THE FUTURE! YOU ARE LOOKING AT THE WORLD, MILLIONS OF YEARS FROM YOUR OWN TWENTIETH CENTURY!
EARTH IS ABOUT TO COLLIDE WITH ANOTHER DYING PLANET --AND THE HUMAN RACE HAS LONG SINCE EMIGRATED TO THE BECKONING STARS! YOU MIGHT NOT BE TOO LONELY HERE-- FOR A NEW RACE IS EVOLVING, AS YOU CAN SEE!
TAKE ME BACK-- PLEASE--TAKE ME BACK!

SO BE IT!!!

I SALUTE YOUR COURAGE, MORTAL! YOUR EXPERIENCE HAS SHAKEN YOU--BUT IT HAS NOT BROKEN YOUR RESOLVE! YET, I CANNOT PERMIT YOU TO KEEP THAT FATEFUL PICTURE!

I AM GRATEFUL TO YOU, THOR! YOU HAVE BEEN GENEROUS! YOU PROVED YOUR POWER--WITHOUT ACTUALLY HARMING ME!

IF I VOW TO DESTROY THE EVIDENCE OF YOUR DUAL IDENTITY, WILL YOU GRANT ME ONE FAVOR--ONE LAST BOON?

IF IT BE WITHIN REASON!

TAKE ME TO ASGARD! LET ME SEE THE FABLED CITY--THE LEGENDARY GLORY--JUST ONCE!

I'LL SWEAR NEVER TO REVEAL WHAT I SEE! YOU CAN EVEN ERASE IT FROM MY MEMORY--!

THEN WHAT IS YOUR MOTIVE--?

REMEMBER, I AM A REPORTER! IT WOULD BE THE GREATEST STORY OF ALL! EVEN IF I NEVER WRITE IT--EVEN IF I MUST ONE DAY FORGET IT--STILL, I WOULD HAVE DONE WHAT NO NEWSMAN BEFORE ME HAS EVER DONE! I'D HAVE SEEN THE HOME OF THE GODS!

HE IS A BRAVE MAN--A DEDICATED MAN! I MUST VISIT ASGARD NOW MYSELF! I SHALL DO IT!

VERY WELL, MORTAL! YOUR WISH IS GRANTED! PREPARE TO BEHOLD WONDERS SUCH AS MEN HAVE ONLY DREAMED OF BEFORE!

BUT, EVEN MIGHTY THOR DOES NOT SUSPECT THE INCREDIBLE EVENTS THAT AWAIT HIM IN THE GOLDEN REALM...

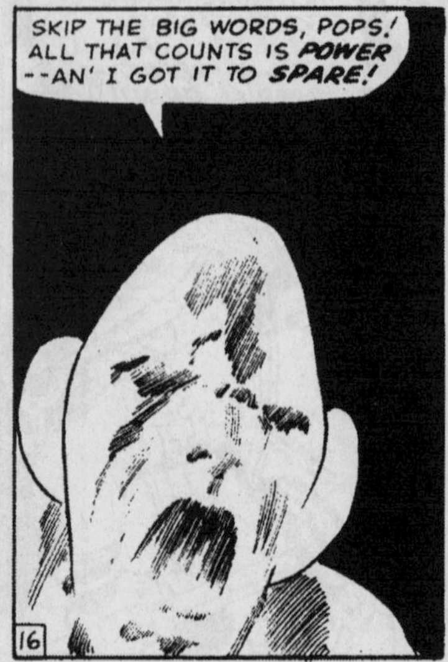

SPECTACLE BEYOND WORDS! WONDERS BEYOND DESCRIPTION! SURPRISES BEYOND ANY MERE MORTAL EXPECTATION! ALL THESE AND MORE SHALL BE YOURS NEXT ISSUE! DON'T DARE MISS IT! WE HAVE SPOKEN!

TALES OF ASGARD, HOME OF THE MIGHTY NORSE GODS
"THE GRIM SPECTER OF MUTINY!"
DRIVEN BY YOUR MAD VANITY, YOU ARE LEADING US TO OUR DOOM! BUT WE SHALL SAIL NO FURTHER, THUNDER GOD!
SAILING INTO THE MYSTERIOUS SEA OF FEAR, THOR'S MIGHTY CREW OF ARGONAUTS SEES THAT THE DREADED PILLARS OF UTGARD LOOM AHEAD... THE PILLARS WHICH BRING INSTANT DEATH TO ANY VESSEL WHICH SAILS BETWEEN THEM! AND THEN, AS THE SHIP ENTERS THE MAELSTROM, THE PANIC BEGINS...!
WE STAND WITH LOKI!
GIVE THE COMMAND, THOR! WE MUST TURN BACK!
A STAN LEE STORY SPECTACULAR!
A JACK KIRBY PENCILLING PANORAMA!
A VINCE COLLETTA DELINEATION DRAMA!
AN ARTIE SI EK LETTERING LAND ARK!
1

SILENCE, YOU SPINELESS DOLTS!! I'LL HEAR NO MORE!
WE SAIL TO SAVE ETERNAL ASGARD! IN THE NAME OF ODIN, THERE SHALL BE NO TURNING BACK!
THOR HAS SPOKEN!
THEN LOKI CLAIMS COMMAND OF THIS SHIP! TO MY SIDE, WARRIORS!
PUT THE THUNDER GOD IN CHAINS!
YOU DARE TO MUTINY??! MY HAMMER SHALL ANSWER FOR ME!
CLANG!
FIGHT ON! FOR THOR-- AND ASGARD!
STRIKE!! IN THE NAME OF LOKI!
2

THOUGH SOME THERE ARE WHO SUPPORT THE EVIL LOKI, THE VALIANT GOLDEN-HAIRED IMMORTAL IS NOT WITHOUT HIS SUPPORTERS, TOO! SUPPORTERS SUCH AS--
MAKE WAY, THOU BASE AND LOWLY VARLETS! MAKE WAY FOR FANDRAL, THE DASHING!!
FANDRAL, THE DASHING--BAH! LONG HAVE I WAITED TO LET THEE TASTE THE COLD STEEL OF MY--URKK-!
LONGER YET WILT THOU HAVE TO WAIT, BUMPKIN!
WITH THE DAZZLING STYLE OF A MASTER, AND THE GAY ABANDON OF A CAREFREE YOUTH, FANDRAL FIGHTS LIKE A TRUE ALLY OF THOR!
WHAT? ONLY A DOZEN BLADES AGAINST ME? FIE UPON THEE, KNAVES!
AND, YET ANOTHER THERE IS WHOSE PROWESS IS BROUGHT INTO PLAY ON THE SIDE OF MIGHTY THOR! BUT, HOGUN THE GRIM, FIGHTS WITH A DIFFERENT STYLE--RUTHLESS, SAVAGE, AND UNYIELDING--!
BACK, THOU DASTARDLY MUTINEER--BACK, I SAY!
WHANG!
NOW SHALL YOU LEARN THAT HOGUN'S WRATH IS MORE TO BE FEARED THAN THE PILLARS OF UTGARD! THY FATE IS SEALED, MUTINEER!
NO, HOGUN--NO! IT WAS LOKI'S FAULT--I KNEW NOT WHAT I DID!
-UNNNNN-!
MUTINY! THE VERY WORD MAKES THE HACKLES OF HOGUN RISE!!!

WHILE, TOWERING ABOVE ALL OTHERS, THE AGED, BUT STILL POWERFUL FIGURE OF GIGANTIC VOLSTAGG LOOMS MENACINGLY, AS HIS STENTORIAN VOICE BOOMS OUT--
FEAR NOT, THUNDER GOD! THOU HAST THE SUPPORT OF INVINCIBLE VOLSTAGG!
THE MERE SIGHT OF MY NOBLE SELF MAKES STRONG MEN TREMBLE!!
A FEW STOUT BLOWS FROM THY HAND WOULD NOT BE AMISS EITHER, ENORMOUS ONE!

OF COURSE, SON OF ODIN! I WAS MERELY AWAITING THE PROPER MOMENT TO STRIKE!
THIS WILL STILL THY BOASTFUL TONGUE!
AND NOW, WHO SHALL BE THE FIRST TO FEEL THE WRATH OF VOLSTAGG!

BWANNG!
TO YOUR HEELS, BRAVE COMPANIONS!!
A JACKAL HATH FELLED THE LION OF ASGARD!

HE ACCOMPLISHED MORE IN DEFEAT THAN HE COULD HAVE IN VICTORY!
HIS VERY FALL TOPPLED HALF OF THE MUTINEERS!!
WHOOOMF!

BUT THEN, A MOUNTAINOUS WAVE SWEEPS O'ER THE SHIP, REVIVING THE FALLEN VOLSTAGG...
I AM DROWNED! THE MIGHTY SEA HAS DONE WHAT ALL MY ENEMIES' SWORDS COULD NEVER DO--!
CLOSE YOUR MOUTH, VOLSTAGG! IF YOU DO DROWN, IT WILL BE YOUR OWN FAULT!
THEN, SUDDENLY, THE FIGHTING COMES TO A SWIFT HALT, AS THE ALMOST DEAFENING BLAST OF A GREAT HORN RINGS OUT--!
WHOOOOO
LOOK! ABOVE US--THAT FIGURE! WHO CAN IT BE??
I RECOGNIZE HIS VISAGE! IN TRUTH, I WOULD KNOW HIM ANY-WHERE!
'TIS BALDER THE BRAVE, LASHED TO THE SHIP'S FIGUREHEAD! HE CONTINUES TO BLOW HIS HORN, AS THOUGH SERENADING THE DREADED PILLARS OF UTGARD WHICH LIE DIRECTLY AHEAD!
WHAT MADNESS IS THAT??
IF THIS DOES NOT SAVE THE SHIP, THEN TRULY ARE WE DOOMED!
BALDER! COME DOWN! IT IS TOO LATE! WE CANNOT ESCAPE THE MAELSTROM!
5
EVEN NOW WE ARE ENTERING THE ZONE OF DEATH, BETWEEN THE TWO AWESOME PILLARS!
THERE CAN BE NO TURNING BACK!! WE MUST ACCEPT WHATEVER BEFALLS!
NEXT ISSUE, SAIL WITH THOR AND HIS IMMORTAL CREW AS THEY HEAD DIRECTLY INTO THE DRAGON'S JAWS! FORSOOTH, THOU MUST NOT MISS IT!

JOURNEY INTO MYSTERY
WITH
THE MIGHTY
THOR
APPROVED BY THE COMICS CODE AUTHORITY
IND.
MARVEL COMICS GROUP 12¢
123 DEC
"WHILE A UNIVERSE TREMBLES!"

THE MIGHTY THOR!
"WHILE A UNIVERSE TREMBLES!"
PREPARE FOR WONDERS WITHOUT END, MORTAL!! FOR I TAKE YOU NOW, TO-- ASGARD!
WE SWEAR BY THE URU HAMMER THAT THESE WORDS HAVE THE RING OF TRUTH...
AGAINST HIS BETTER JUDGEMENT, MIGHTY THOR HAS PROMISED TO TAKE THE DETERMINED REPORTER, HARRIS HOBBS, TO ASGARD--LITTLE DREAMING THAT THE ABSORBING MAN, SPURRED ON BY EVIL LOKI, IS NOW DARING TO BATTLE ODIN HIMSELF WITHIN THE GOLDEN REALM!!
WRITTEN BY STAN LEE
ILLUSTRATED BY JACK KIRBY
EMBELLISHED BY VINCE COLLETTA
LETTERED BY ARTIE SIMEK
1

REMEMBER, IN RETURN FOR THIS BOON, YOU MAY NEVER REVEAL WHAT YOU HAVE LEARNED ABOUT MY TRUE IDENTITY!
THAT'S A ***PROMISE,*** THOR! ALL I WANT NOW ARE SOME PRICELESS ***PICTURES*** OF OUR JOURNEY TO ASGARD!
THAT WHICH NOW TRANSPIRES CAN BE SEEN BY ***NO*** MORTAL EYES!
FOR THE VERY ***SIGHT*** WOULD BE MORE THAN HUMAN MIND COULD ENDURE!
H-HOW LONG WILL IT ***TAKE...??***
TIME HAS NO ***MEANING*** IN A VORTEX! EVEN AS THE MIST ENCLOSES US-- WE HAVE ***ARRIVED!***

ALAS, I FEAR THAT ***CANNOT*** BE!
WE TRAVEL BY MEANS OF A ***VORTEX,*** CREATED BY MY ENCHANTED MALLET!

THE VORTEX IS ***FADING!*** ***NOW*** I CAN GET MY PICTURES ***--NOW!***

BUT, SO INDESCRIBABLY AWESOME IS THE SIGHT WHICH STUNS THE MORTAL'S EYES, THAT HE CANNOT ***MOVE!***
SUCH BEAUTY! SUCH SPECTACLE! SUCH MAGIC--!

IT-- IT'S LIKE BEING IN THE CENTER OF THE ***UNIVERSE!*** LIKE BEING PART OF-- ***ETERNITY!***
WE STAND ON ***BIFROST,*** KNOWN TO THE WORLD AS THE GLEAMING ***RAINBOW BRIDGE!***
2

AS THE AWESTRICKEN HUMAN FEELS HIS SENSES REELING BEFORE THE MONUMENTAL GRANDEUR OF WHAT HE BEHOLDS, THERE IS--THERE CAN BE--**NO THOUGHT** OF PICTURE-TAKING--NO THOUGHT OF ANYTHING SAVE THE NUMBING WONDERMENT WHICH FILLS HIS SOUL...

WALK YOU NOW AT MY SIDE, MORTAL--WITH SLOW AND MEASURED TREAD!

THEN, AT LAST, THOR ENCOUNTERS THE REMNANTS OF ODIN'S GUARD! HAVING BEEN HURLED BACK BY THE ATTACKING ABSORBING MAN, THEY NOW REGROUP, MUSTERING THEIR FORCE FOR ANOTHER CHARGE...

MIGHTY THOR! TRULY, THE FATES HAVE SENT THEE IN THIS HOUR OF GRAVEST NEED!

A STRANGE, MORTAL BEING, ABLE TO ABSORB OUR OWN POWER AND REPEL US WITH IT, IS EVEN NOW INVADING THE THRONE ROOM ITSELF!

THE ABSORBING MAN! ONLY LOKI COULD HAVE BROUGHT HIM HERE!

YEA, VERILY! THY TRAITOROUS HALF-BROTHER HATH PROCLAIMED THE MORTAL INVADER TO BE HIS ALLY!

THEY STRIVE TO TOPPLE ODIN FROM HIS THRONE! LISTEN! THE BATTLE HATH BEGUN WITHIN THE IMPERIAL PALACE!

THEN STAND YOU BACK! THIS MOMENT BELONGS TO THOR!

WHOOM

FOR ODIN, AND ASGARD!

HE'S FORGOTTEN ABOUT ME! BUT, I'VE GOT TO SEE THIS THRU!

AND, AS THE MIGHTY THUNDER GOD AGAIN RUSHES FORWARD...
HERE'S YOUR OWN CRUMMY BOLT RIGHT BACK ATCHA, WHISKERS! LET'S SEE HOW YOU CAN TAKE IT!

ODIN CANNOT BE THREATENED WITH HIS OWN POWERS!
MY IMPERIAL SCEPTER OF SUPREMACY SWALLOWS THE COSMIC FURY, EVEN AS THE FIBERS OF MY BEING QUIVER WITH MOST REGAL RAGE!

RAGE ALL YA WANT TO, BIG MAN! I CAN LICK ANYTHING THAT LIVES-- AND THAT GOES FOR WHITE-HAIRED SQUARES WHO TRY TO IMPRESS ME BY GARGLIN' A LOTTA FIVE-DOLLAR WORDS!

THE LORD OF ASGARD FIGHTS WITH FAR MORE THAN WORDS, INSOLENT ONE!
WITH A SINGLE GESTURE OF MY SCEPTER, I SUBJECT THEE TO THE FORCE OF A MOLECULAR CYCLONE!
STOP, FATHER-- YOU KNOW NOT WHAT YOU DO!
TOO LATE! THE DEED IS DONE!
5

YA SHOULDA LISTENED TO GOLDILOCKS, POPS! ALL YA DID WAS HAND THAT CYCLONE POWER OF YOURS OVER TO ME!
FATHER! BE WARNED! WHATSOEVER HE TOUCHES, THAT VERY THING DOES HE BECOME-- THAT VERY STRENGTH DOES HE TAKE UNTO HIMSELF!
SUCH IS THE FEARSOME POWER OF THE ABSORBING MAN!

THEN, STAY YOU BACK, MY SON--FOR THE FORCE OF MY MOLECULAR CYCLONE CAN STAGGER EVEN THEE!

BUT, ODIN'S WARNING COMES TOO LATE...
WHOOOM!!

AT THIS POINT, IT IS NECESSARY TO INTERRUPT OUR SAGA IN ORDER TO PRESENT A NEW, EQUALLY STARTLING CHAIN OF EVENTS--EVENTS WHICH SHALL SOON HAVE A VITAL, FANTASTIC BEARING UPON THE LIFE OF THOR! AND SO, WE TURN OUR ATTENTION TO AN ASIAN JUNGLE, WHERE WE FIND...
UNTIL WE HAVE SLAIN THEIR WITCH DOCTOR, OUR RULE OVER THE LOCAL TRIBE WILL NEVER BE COMPLETE!
SO, FAN OUT! COMB EVERY INCH OF THIS ACCURSED JUNGLE!
THE COMMUNIST TAKE-OVER IN THIS AREA MUST NOT BE FOILED BY AN IGNORANT, PAINTED SAVAGE!

WHY DO THE GODS NOT AID ME? WHY DO THEY NOT SHOW THEIR POWER, TO HELP RID OUR LAND OF THE INVADERS?
IF THEY WOULD BUT SEND ME A SIGN-- A TOKEN OF THEIR SUPPORT!

THEN, INCREDIBLY, A STRANGE, BRIGHTLY GLOWING OBJECT SEEMS TO FALL FROM THE HEAVENS ABOVE...!
MY PRAYERS HAVE BEEN ANSWERED! THE GODS HAVE NOT FORESAKEN ME!
THIP!
THE GRATEFUL WITCH DOCTOR HAS NO WAY OF KNOWING THAT HE IS GAZING UPON THE MISSING NORN STONE WHICH THOR HAD ACCIDENTALLY DROPPED SOME WEEKS BEFORE! (ISH#120!)
--THE ENCHANTED STONE WHICH CAN NEVER REMAIN FOR LONG IN ANY ONE PLACE, BUT LEVITATES ITSELF AT RANDOM--AS IT HAS JUST NOW DONE--TRAVELLING THOUSANDS OF EARTH MILES IN ONE SINGLE, MYSTIC JOURNEY...
AND, THE MOMENT THE HUNTED MAN GRASPS THE BEWITCHED BAUBLE, A FANTASTIC CHANGE COMES OVER HIM--
THE GODS HAVE GRANTED ME POWER! POWER ENOUGH TO SHAKE THE WORLD!
LOOK! THERE HE IS!
THE FOOL! HE HAD NOT BRAINS ENOUGH TO REMAIN HIDDEN! BY RISING, HE HAS SEALED HIS DOOM! FIRE!
IT IS PASSING STRANGE! THERE IS NO TRACE OF FEAR IN HIS DEMEANOR!
THOOM!
KRAK!
BEGONE, EVIL ONES! YOUR TYRANNY IS ENDED!
7

YOUR THUNDER STICKS CANNOT HARM ME NOW!
WHAT MADNESS IS THIS? HE HAS BECOME A DEMON!

YOU CAUGHT OUR SHELLS-- IN YOUR TWO HANDS!
THE SPIRITS THEMSELVES HAVE RISEN AGAINST US! WE MUST FLEE!

AND, AS THE ETERNALLY-GLOWING NORN STONE SPARKLES AGAINST HIS WAIST, THE ONCE-HOUNDED WITCH DOCTOR STRIKES BACK LIKE A MAN POSSESSED...!

NEVERMORE SHALL YOU SUBJUGATE OUR PEOPLE-- ENSLAVE OUR LAND--!

NOT WHILE THE GODS HAVE GIVEN ME THE GIFT OF MATCHLESS POWER!

BANISHING YOU IS BUT CHILD'S PLAY TO ME NOW! I AM DESTINED FOR FAR GREATER FEATS--FOR A FAR GREATER DESTINY!

HE WHO HOLDS THIS STONE CAN RULE THE WORLD! NOT FOR NOTHING HAVE THE GODS BEQUEATHED IT TO ME! I AM MEANT TO CONQUER--AND I SHALL NOT FAIL!
8

BUT, THE TIME HAS COME TO LEAVE EARTH ONCE AGAIN, AND RETURN TO THE STAGGERING SPECTACLE WHICH AWAITS US IN ASGARD...
NOTHIN' CAN GET NEAR ME WHILE I'VE GOT YOUR CYCLONE POWER-- BUT THAT AINT GOOD ENOUGH FOR ME....!
I'VE GOTTA ABSORB SOME NEW POWER, SO I CAN FINISH YA OFF-- FOR GOOD!
I BESEECH THEE, MY FATHER! TAKE THY LEAVE SO THAT I MAY FIGHT THE GOOD FIGHT FOR THEE!
NAY, GOD OF THUNDER! STILL AM I ODIN, THE ALL-POWERFUL! STILL AM I SUPREME!
YOU JUST DON'T DIG THE MESSAGE, POPS! THIS IS YOUR SWAN SONG!
I'M GONNA ABSORB ENOUGH STRENGTH FROM THIS MARBLE TO GROW AND GROW, TILL I CAN CRUSH YA LIKE A FLEA!
AND, IF YOU'RE STILL DUMB ENOUGH TO THROW ANY MORE GIZMOS AT ME, I'LL ABSORB THEM, TOO! YOU'VE HAD IT, WHISKERS!
"THEN, IN CASE YOU'RE INTERESTED, AFTER YOU'RE DONE FOR, I'LL ABSORB EVERY HUNK OF STRENGTH IN ALL OF ASGARD!! BEFORE I'M DONE, I'LL RULE THE WHOLE BLAMED UNIVERSE!"

HE SPEAKS THE TRUTH! WHATEVER I HURL AT HIM--MY MOST POTENT, MOST DESTRUCTIVE DEVICES, ALL BECOME PART OF HIS OWN EVER-GROWING POWER!
STAY THY HAND, MY FATHER! WHATEVER ELSE YOU DO, LET IT BE DONE WITH THOR STANDING FIRM AT THY SIDE!

EXTRICATING HIMSELF WITH ARMS FAR STRONGER THAN ALL THE BULLDOZERS OF EARTH, THE THUNDER GOD HASTENS TO STAND WITH HIS LIEGE....!
ATTA BOY, GOLDILOCKS! YOU MAKE SCENE, TOO! I'M JUST ITCHIN' TO FLATTEN YOU AS WELL AS OL' WHITEY THERE!

HOLD THY TONGUE! FOR EACH NEW INSOLENCE, YOU YET SHALL PAY A THOUSANDFOLD!

MISTER, YOU JUST THREATENED YOUR LAST THREAT! BUT, IF YOU WANNA GO OUT YAKKIN', THAT'S YOUR BUSINESS!
FATHER, SAY THE WORD! LET ME HUMBLE HIM FOREVER!
NOT YET, MY SON!
FINISH THE DEED, MORTAL! EVEN IN DEFEAT, ODIN IS NOT ONE TO TRIFLE WITH!

LOKI! ARE YOU THEN SO SURE OF YOURSELF THAT YOU DARE FLAUNT YOUR TREASON BEFORE MY VERY EYES??!
YOUR TIME HAS COME, STEP-FATHER! YOU HAVE RULED LONG ENOUGH! IT IS TIME YOU TOOK--YOUR REST!
ONLY THE STRONGEST MAY POSSESS THE SUPREME SCEPTER! LET IT NOW BE MINE!

IT WAS I WHO GAVE THE ABSORBING MAN HIS POWER! ONLY I CAN CONTROL HIM! AT LAST MY DESTINY HAS BEEN FULFILLED! LOKI IS TRIUMPHANT!
MINE ANGUISHED EARS CAN BEAR NO MORE!
HOLD, MIGHTY THOR! LET THE DRAMA BE PLAYED OUT....!
10

I HAVE NO WISH TO SEE MY KINGDOM DESTROYED! ALWAYS HAST THOU LUSTED FOR MY SCEPTER, EVIL ONE! THEN TAKE IT! LET IT BE THINE!
I KNEW YOU'D SURRENDER, RATHER THAN RISK A BATTLE WHICH COULD DESTROY YOUR BELOVED ASGARD!
I HAVE WON! THE UNIVERSE IS MINE TO COMMAND!
OH, MOST SHAMEFUL MOMENT! MOST PERFIDIOUS SIGHT!
THAT THE GLORY WHICH WAS ASGARD, SHOULD COME TO-- THIS!
I NOW PROCLAIM THE REIGN OF LOKI, THE CUNNING!
MORTAL, RETURN YOU TO NORMAL SIZE! HENCEFORTH, NONE SHALL TOWER OVER LOKI! ALL THAT LIVE MUST GROVEL BEFORE ME!
YOU BEEN LIVIN' IN A FOOL'S PARADISE, CHUM! I HAD TIME TO LEARN HOW POWERFUL I REALLY AM! THAT SCEPTER BELONGS TO ME!
WHAT?!! YOU DARE SULLY IT WITH MORTAL HAND??! HAVE YOU FORGOTTEN IT WAS I WHO CREATED THE ABSORBING MAN??
AND, IT IS I ALONE WHO HAVE THE POWER TO DESTROY YOU!
I MEAN NO DIS-RESPECT, SIRE, BUT THERE WAS NO REASON FOR ABJECT SURRENDER! I STILL CAN REGAIN YON SCEPTER IF THOU BUT SAY THE WORD!
ANOTHER MOMENT'S PATIENCE, VALIANT ONE! THE PLAY IS NOT YET ENDED!
11

THE SCEPTER SHALL NEVER BE TORN FROM LOKI'S GRASP!
BUNK! NOTHIN'S GONNA MAKE ME LET GO!
THERE IS MUCH TRUTH IN WHAT YOU SAY! FOR NEITHER OF YOU CAN RELINQUISH YOUR HOLD!

HEY! HE'S RIGHT! HE FOUND A WAY TO MAKE US STICK TO THE BLAMED THING!
BUT NOTHIN' CAN HOLD ME FOR LONG! I'LL ABSORB THE SCEPTER'S OWN POWER, AND FINISH OFF ASGARD ITSELF, ONCE 'N FOR ALL!
NO! YOU CANNOT STEAL MY VICTORY! YOU CANNOT!!!

VICTORY? AND THOU PRESUMED TO CALL THYSELF CUNNING! DIDST THOU TRULY THINK ODIN COULD SO EASILY BE BESTED??
SEE HOW I RENDER THEE BOTH WEIGHTLESS WITH A SINGLE GESTURE!

DIDST THOU NEVER ONCE SUSPECT?? MY POWER RESTS NOT IN ANY CEREMONIAL SCEPTER, BUT DEEP WITHIN MYSELF!
I PERMITTED THY BASE CHARADE TO CONTINUE, FOR I DESIRED TO SEE THE EXTENT OF THINE AMBITION-- OF THINE EVIL PURPOSE! AND NOW, ODIN HATH WITNESSED ENOUGH!

TAKE THE WORTHLESS SCEPTER--AND BEGONE! THY PUNISHMENT IS POETICALLY JUST, GOD OF EVIL--!
WE'RE FLYIN' OUT-- INTO NOWHERE! ODIN FOOLED US--HE WAS JUST TOYIN' WITH US! HE COULDA DONE THIS TO US ANY TIME!
THOU HAST WHAT THOU WANTED! THE BESTIAL MORTAL TO SERVE THEE--AND FREEDOM FROM MY RULE--AS ENDLESS SPACE BECKONS THEE!
12

THY JOURNEY THRU THE VOID SHALL CONTINUE FOR SO LONG AS IT DOTH PLEASE ME!

NEITHER THE BURNING HEAT, NOR FREEZING COLD OF SPACE SHALL STOP THEE!
I HAVE SPOKEN!

THE HEART OF ODIN IS PROUD OF ASGARD'S WARRIORS! YOUR SOVEREIGN SALUTES THEE, ONE AND ALL!
HAIL ODIN

AND THOU, MY SON, PROVED MOST COURAGEOUS OF ALL!
I, FATHER??

INDEED! IT IS FAR MORE DIFFICULT TO STAY THY ARM WHEN THY VERY SOUL CRIES OUT FOR COMBAT! BUT, THOU DIDST OBEY THY FATHER, AND HE IS MIGHTILY PLEASED!
NOBLE FATHER! I JUST REMEMBERED --THE MORTAL!
MORTAL??
WHA- WHAT HAPPENED ??

YOU WERE RENDERED UNCONSCIOUS BY THE FORCE OF THE ABSORBING MAN'S CYCLONIC BOLT!
YOU MEAN-- IT'S ALL OVER?? I MISSED THE WHOLE THING?
YOU'D BE A GREAT GUY, IF YOU'D ONLY LEARN TO SPEAK LIKE A PERSON!
ANOTHER MORTAL, IN FORBIDDEN ASGARD?!! BE CAREFUL YOU DO NOT TURN MY GRATITUDE TO KINGLY WRATH, MY SON!
I CAN EXPLAIN, MY LIEGE! WE HAD ENTERED INTO A COMPACT!
THAT'S ODIN! IN THE FLESH! ODIN HIMSELF!
MY CAMERA!! I-I'VE GOTTA GET A PICTURE!
OH NO! NO! IT--IT WAS SMASHED, DURING ALL THE EXCITEMENT!
THE CHANCE OF A LIFETIME-- AND-- I'VE FLUBBED IT! FLUBBED IT FOR GOOD!
THE RANTINGS OF A HUMAN ARE NO CONCERN OF MINE! LET HIM BE REMOVED FROM MY SIGHT--AND FROM MY REALM! SO BE IT!
HOW DOES A GUY BECOME THAT HAUGHTY IN ONLY ONE LIFETIME?
YOU COULD NOT COMPREHEND HOW LONG HIS LIFETIME REALLY IS!
LOOK, THOR--COULDN'T I STAY AROUND JUST LONG ENOUGH TO MAKE SOME PENCIL SKETCHES, SO IT WON'T BE A COMPLETE WASTE?
ODIN HAS SPOKEN! THERE IS NOTHING MORE TO BE SAID!
BUT, IF I ONLY HAD SOME PICTURES TO SHOW-- EVEN ROUGH SKETCHES-- MAYBE SOMEONE WOULD BELIEVE--!
YOUR LABORS WOULD BE FOR NAUGHT, MORTAL! ALL THESE LONG CENTURIES, MEN HAVE TOLD OF ASGARD --STORIES HAVE BEEN WRITTEN--SONGS HAVE BEEN SUNG--AND STILL MANKIND CALLS IT---LEGEND!
14

STOP! STAY WHERE YOU ARE! YOU MUST NOT FEAR ME!

THE GODS HAVE GIVEN ME A MISSION-- AND YOU SHALL HELP ME CARRY IT OUT!

A DEMON YOU HAVE CALLED ME--AND A DEMON SHALL I BE! BOW DOWN, BEFORE THE MAJESTY OF YOUR LEADER--BEFORE THE POWER OF--THE DEMON!

YOU ARE BUT THE FIRST--THE FIRST OF AN ARMY OF MILLIONS WHICH I SHALL RECRUIT, TO OVERRUN THE WORLD! A WORLD WHICH WILL SOON BOW IN HOMAGE TO THE DEMON, EVEN AS YOU DO, NOW!

THUS, WITH THE ENCHANTED NORN STONE STILL IN HIS GRASP, THE MASKED MAN FALLS DEEPER AND DEEPER UNDER ITS SPELL, AS THE GLINT OF DEMONIACAL MADNESS GLEAMS BRIGHTER IN HIS FANATICAL EYES...!

...EYES THAT ARE SOON DESTINED TO GAZE AT THOR WITH THE SAME POWER, THE SAME HATRED AS NOW SEEM TO NOURISH HE WHOM FATE HAS NAMED--THE DEMON!

WHILE, IN A LONELY WOODED AREA IN THE SUBURBS OF NEW YORK, A SWIRLING VORTEX TAKES SHAPE OUT OF THE NOTHINGNESS SURROUNDING IT...!

TALES OF ASGARD, HOME OF THE MIGHTY NORSE GODS
"THE JAWS OF THE DRAGON!"
EVEN AS THOR'S MUTINOUS CREW OF ARGONAUTS HEADS INTO THE DREADED PILLARS OF UTGARD ON THE UNCHARTED SEA OF FEAR... BACK IN ASGARD, REGAL ODIN, ATOP THE TALLEST PEAK IN THE UNIVERSE, SEES A TERRIFYING SIGHT...!
ON THE FAR HORIZON... A SIGHT TO STAGGER THE SENSES OF A GOD!
AN EXPERIENCE IN MATCHLESS SPECTACLE, AS ONLY STAN LEE, WRITER, JACK KIRBY, PENCILLER, VINCE COLLETTA, INKER, ARTIE SIMEK, LETTERER, COULD CREATE IT!
MOST NOBLE LORD... BEHOLD! I SEE OMINOUS SIGNS AND PORTENTS AHEAD... OMENS OF THE COMING OF RAGNAROK!*
*RAGNAROK: THE END OF THE WORLD! THE DAY ON WHICH EVEN THE GODS SHALL PERISH!
1

THIS IS THE SIGHT OMNIPOTENT ODIN SEES--! A GIGANTIC DARK CLOUD, WRITHING AND SEETHING WITH COUNTLESS FIGURES OF SHADOWY WARRIORS, LOCKED IN ENDLESS, TITANIC COMBAT!!
EVEN MY BRAVEST FOLLOWERS FLINCH AT THE AWESOME SIGHT, FOR THEY BELIEVE THAT IT SURELY PREDICTS-- THE BEGINNING OF THE END!!
BUT, FINALLY--AFTER LONG, ANGUISHED MINUTES...
THE SHADOWS HAVE FADED--FOR NOW! BUT, WHAT OF THOR, ON HIS GREAT JOURNEY?
CAN HE HAVE SEEN THE OMEN, TOO? OR, IS HE NOW OCCUPIED WITH OTHER MATTERS?

THE LEGENDS ARE TRUE!! IT IS THE DRAGON'S HEAD! HE IS AWAKENED!

MAY ODIN PRESERVE US!! WE SAIL DIRECTLY INTO THE GAPING JAWS!!

GOD OF THUNDER-- SAVE US! FOR TRULY, YOU ALONE ARE OUR ONLY HOPE!
WHAT FLESH AND BLOOD CAN ACHIEVE, I SHALL DO! THIS DO I PLEDGE TO ALL!
WHATE'ER BEFALLS, I SHALL NOT FLINCH! STRIKE, THOU CREATURE OF DARKNESS --THOR STANDS READY!
BUT SUDDENLY, THE MAST BENEATH HIS FEET SPLINTERS AND CRUMBLES, HURLING THE MIGHTY IMMORTAL OFF-BALANCE!
KRAKK!
AND, AS THE SEEMINGLY-DOOMED SHIP APPROACHES THE DRAGON'S JAWS, ONLY THE STRANGE NOTES FROM BALDER'S HORN CAN BE HEARD OVER THE SHRIEKING OF THE CATACLYSMIC STORM--!
4

AND THEN, JUST AS THE MONSTROUS STONE JAWS SEEM READY TO CLAMP DOWN UPON THE HELPLESS VESSEL...

BALDER GIVES ONE FINAL, EAR-PIERCING NERVE-SHATTERING BLAST--!

...A BLAST WHICH CAUSES THE DESCENDING JAWS TO TREMBLE, QUIVER, AND THEN-- VIOLENTLY *EXPLODE*, HURTLING STONE METEORS TO THE FARTHEST ENDS OF THE UNIVERSE!!
THE SHIP IS *SAVED!* BALDER HAS VANQUISHED THE UTGARD DRAGON!
NEXT, A NEW AND AWESOME RACE WILL BE MET BY THE ARGONAUTS-- AND *YOU!!* STAN AND JACK HAVE *SPOKEN!*
5
THE END

JOURNEY INTO MYSTERY
WITH
THE MIGHTY
THOR
MARVEL COMICS GROUP
124
JAN
12¢
APPROVED BY THE COMICS CODE AUTHORITY
IND.
ENTER HERCULES!
"THE GLORY AND THE GRANDEUR!"

THE MIGHTY THOR!
"THE GRANDEUR AND THE GLORY!"
ANYBODY CAN STOP TO READ A NEWSPAPER ON THE STREETS OF NEW YORK! BUT, WHEN THE TALL, IMPOSING FIGURE OF THE GOD OF THUNDER DOES IT, PEOPLE HAVE A WAY OF NOTICING...!
BACK PAGE SPECIAL!!
UNKNOWN "DEMON" UNLEASHES PLUNDERING JUNGLE HORDES
REPORTS
STORY BY: STAN (THE MAN) LEE
PENCILLING BY: JACK (KING) KIRBY
DELINEATION BY: VINCE (THE PRINCE) COLLETTA
LETTERING BY: ARTIE (SUGAR LIPS) SIMEK
1

HESITANT AT FIRST--UNABLE TO BELIEVE THEY ARE REALLY IN THE PRESENCE OF MIGHTY *THOR*-- THE CROWD SLOWLY DRAWS CLOSER! THEN, REALIZING IT TRULY *IS* THE IMMORTAL AVENGER, THEY SPEAK--!

YOU WERE READING ABOUT THAT *DEMON* CHARACTER! IS *HE* THE ONE YOU'LL TACKLE NEXT?

SOMEBODY HAS TO STOP HIM BEFORE IT'S TOO *LATE!*

THIS IS THE FIRST I HAVE *HEARD* OF THE *DEMON!* I MUST LEARN MORE--!

THOSE SHOULDERS! THAT VOICE! SIGH!

IF HE COULD *SING,* HE'D BE A *SMASH* WITH THAT CRRRAZY HAIR!

MY DADDY WAS WOUNDED IN VIET NAM! HE'S BIG AND STRONG AND NICE--JUST LIKE *YOU,* MR. THOR! HAVE *YOU* EVER BEEN IN VIET NAM?

SALLY! A LITTLE GIRL MUSTN'T BOTHER AN IMPORTANT PERSON LIKE *THOR!*

I ASSURE YOU, MADAM, IT IS NO BOTHER!

LET'S SEE YOUR LICENSE TO GIVE A PUBLIC DEMONSTRATION IN THE STREET!
LICENSE?? I HAVE NO LICENSE! I AM THOR!
I DON'T CARE IF YOU'RE MOTHER HUBBARD! YOU'RE NOT GONNA DO ANY HAMMER-SWINGIN' ON MY BEAT, MISTER!

PERHAPS YOU ARE RIGHT! THERE IS ALWAYS A CHANCE OF ONE BEING INJURED DUE TO THE SURGING AIR CURRENTS MY MALLET CREATES!
IT WILL BE A SIMPLE MATTER TO LAUNCH MYSELF FROM A HIGH ROOF-TOP, INSTEAD!
MOVE ALONG! MOVE ALONG! AINTCHA EVER SEEN A THUNDER GOD BEFORE?!!

THE EXPRESS ELEVATOR WILL HAVE ME UPSTAIRS IN SECONDS!
MY AD FOR A BANK GUARD APPEARED IN THIS MORNING'S PAPER! I WONDER IF HE--?
OH NO! I-I HOPE NOT! I'M SURE WE COULD NEVER AFFORD HIM!

ALWAYS MORTAL HEADS TURN TO STARE WHEN I APPEAR IN PUBLIC! BUT, I MUST REMAIN ALOOF-- AS BEFITS THE SON OF ODIN!

I'VE SEEN CHARACTERS PARADING AROUND TOWN SHAVED LIKE MR. CLEAN... AND TEENAGERS WHO LOOK LIKE THE BEATLES... BUT THAT GUY TAKES THE CAKE!
S-STEP TO THE R-REAR OF THE CAR--IF Y-YOU DON'T MIND--THAT IS--!
THAT REMINDS ME--I'M DUE FOR A PERMANENT AT NOON!

AND THEN, AFTER HASTILY LEAVING THE ELEVATOR...
AT LAST I HAVE AMPLE ROOM TO SAFELY SWING MY HAMMER! NOW, NO DESTINATION IN THE WORLD CAN BE DENIED ME!
3

NOW LET ME TRAVEL AS A THUNDER GOD SHOULD! PROPELLED BY THE POWER OF MY ENCHANTED MALLET-- GUIDED BY THE STRENGTH OF MY OWN RIGHT ARM!
4

SECONDS LATER, THE FABULOUS FLYING FIGURE OF MIGHTY THOR LANDS ATOP A WIDE WINDOW LEDGE ON AN UPPER STORY OF ONE OF MANHATTAN'S MANY MODERN HOSPITAL BUILDINGS--!
BEFORE REACHING MY ULTIMATE DESTINATION, I MUST VISIT THE GIRL I LOVE!
SHE SHOULD BE ALMOST READY TO LEAVE THE HOSPITAL BY NOW!*
*AS EVERY LOYAL MARVELITE KNOWS, LOVELY JANE FOSTER HAD SUFFERED FROM SMOKE INHALATION AS SHOWN IN THOR #122--STAN.

WHAT IS THIS ?!!
THE DOCTORS VIEW HER WITH CONCERN! SHE SEEMS SO PALE--SO WEAK--!
SHE SHOULD HAVE RECOVERED BY NOW! I DON'T UNDERSTAND!
IF ANYTHING-- SHE'S GROWN WORSE!

WHAT COULD HAVE HAPPENED TO HER DURING MY ABSENCE??
I MUST LEARN THE ANSWER--AT ONCE!

AND, AT THAT VERY MOMENT, ON THE OTHER SIDE OF THE WORLD, THE DEMON'S SAVAGE ARMY ATTACKS A FORTIFIED OUTPOST...
KEEP FIRING! WE'LL NOT SURRENDER TO ANY HORDE OF MARAUDERS!

SUDDENLY, THE ATTACKERS MAKE WAY FOR THEIR LEADER TO STORM THRU THEIR RANKS! WEARING THE MYSTERIOUS NORN STONE TIED SECURELY AROUND HIS NECK*, THE MASKED DEMON STRIDES FEARLESSLY TOWARDS THE FORTRESS....!
MIGHTY IS THE DEMON!!
SURRENDER, OR PERISH!
NONE CAN STOP THE DEMON!
*ONLY BY THE POWER OF THE MAGICAL NORN STONE, WHICH THOR HAD LOST, DID THE ONCE HUMBLE WITCH DOCTOR BECOME THE AWESOME DEMON!--STAN.
5

LAY DOWN YOUR ARMS, AND PLEDGE YOURSELVES TO SERVE ME! YOU HAVE NO OTHER CHOICE!
YOU CANNOT RESIST THE POWER OF THE DEMON!
YOUR ANSWER-- I DEMAND IT NOW!

YOU SHALL HAVE IT, MADMAN!! THIS IS OUR ANSWER! WE SHALL FIGHT TILL THE LAST MAN!

THOUGH THE DEADLY GRENADE HURTLES TOWARDS HIM, THE FIGURE OF THE DEMON REMAINS MOTIONLESS--CONFIDENT--SEEMINGLY INVULNERABLE!

THEN, AFTER THE SHATTERING IMPACT HAS SPENT ITSELF--
NOTHING CAN HARM ME, SO LONG AS I WEAR THE MYSTIC STONE I FOUND!!
FATE HAS SENT IT TO ME! FOR, I AM DESTINED TO CONQUER ALL!
HE COMES CLOSER! PREPARE THE BOULDER!

NOW!

IT IS GOOD THEY DO THIS! ONCE I DISPLAY MY POWER ANEW, THEY WILL BE MINE TO COMMAND!

THOOM
CRAK

NOW FORWARD, MY WARRIORS!! ATTACK-- IN THE NAME OF THE DEMON!
THERE IS NO NEED FOR HASTE! THEY RUN LIKE FRIGHTENED JACKALS! SEE THEM THROW DOWN THEIR ARMS IN SURRENDER!

THUS, MOMENTS LATER, THE MARCH OF CONQUEST CONTINUES--!
EACH DEFEATED FOE JOINS MY OWN TRIUMPHANT ARMY! SOON, NO POWER ON EARTH WILL BE ABLE TO STAND AGAINST THE DEMON--AND HIS GLEAMING STONE!

MEANWHILE, BACK AT THE HOSPITAL, A MYSTIFIED THOR HAS CHANGED TO HIS MORTAL IDENTITY OF DR. DON BLAKE...
I MUST LEARN WHAT IS WRONG WITH MY BELOVED--!
JANE! MY DARLING --DO YOU HEAR ME?

JANE!
HIS VOICE! I HEAR IT AGAIN! BUT--THIS TIME I'M AWAKE! DOES IT MEAN --I'M LOSING MY MIND?
I'M GOING MAD!! I KNOW IT!

DON'T BE FRIGHTENED, MY DEAREST! IT IS ME! I'VE RETURNED TO YOU! I'M BACK!
I-I'M AFRAID TO LOOK! BUT, I MUST-- I MUST--!

IT'S YOU!! THEN--I DIDN'T IMAGINE IT! IT WAS YOUR VOICE I HEARD--!

OF COURSE, DEAR! YOU KNEW I'D RETURN--!
NO! I DIDN'T KNOW! I NEVER KNOW--I'M NEVER SURE! ONE MOMENT YOU'RE BESIDE ME--AND THEN --YOU'VE VANISHED!

I CAN'T BEAR IT ANY MORE! NEVER KNOWING WHERE YOU ARE--WHEN YOU'LL COME BACK AGAIN---OR IF YOU'LL COME BACK!
THEN THIS IS WHAT WAS WRONG! SHE'S SUFFERING A FIT OF DEPRESSION-- AND I'M THE CAUSE OF IT!

YOU'VE TOLD ME YOU LOVE ME-- BUT I KNOW YOU'RE KEEPING SOME TERRIBLE SECRET FROM ME-- SOME SECRET YOU'VE NEVER ALLOWED ME TO SHARE!
IT'S TRUE, MY DARLING! BUT, IT HAS NEVER AFFECTED MY LOVE FOR YOU--!
HOW CAN I BELIEVE THAT-- WHEN YOU DESERT ME FOR DAYS-- WEEKS AT A TIME--
I NEVER KNOW WHERE YOU ARE-- WHAT YOU'RE DOING! I ONLY KNOW-- YOU'RE GONE!!

I WANT TO SHARE MY SECRET WITH YOU--SO DESPERATELY, MY BELOVED! I WANT TO MARRY YOU--MAKE YOU MINE--
BUT ODIN-- MY FATHER--FORBIDS IT!
GET OUT--OUT-- DO YOU HEAR ME--??

I CAN'T GO ON THIS WAY! I-I NEVER WANT TO SEE YOU AGAIN! YOU DON'T LOVE ME! YOU'VE NEVER LOVED ME--!
SHE'S ON THE VERGE OF HYSTERIA! SHE'S LOSING HER WILL TO LIVE! I MUST CONVINCE HER-- SOMEHOW--!
DON'T CRY, DEAREST-- YOU'RE TOO WEAK--!
JANE-- LISTEN! YOU MUST BELIEVE ME!
8

NO! I'LL LISTEN TO NO MORE LIES! NOTHING MATTERS ANY MORE! I JUST WANT TO BE LEFT ALONE! I WANT YOU TO GO--TO LEAVE ME--FOREVER--!
HER HEART IS BREAKING!! AND I'M THE CAUSE OF IT! I CAN'T BEAR TO SEE HER LIKE THIS! I CAN'T--!
JANE! MY DARLING! I'LL PROVE MY LOVE--!

LOOK AT ME, JANE FOSTER!
I COMMAND YOU TO LOOK!

THOOOM!
FORGIVE ME, MY FATHER--

--THIS IS THE ONLY WAY!

KNOW YOU, NOW AND FOREVER, THAT I AM THOR, SON OF ODIN, GOD OF THUNDER!!
'TIS AN IMMORTAL OF ASGARD WHOM YOU LOVE, JANE FOSTER--
--AND WHO TRULY LOVES YOU, AS WELL!

THOR!! DON BLAKE!! BOTH--THE SAME MAN! AND YET--IN MY HEART--I SOMEHOW SUSPECTED!
THUS HAS IT EVER BEEN!

NOW YOU SHARE MY SECRET--AS YOU SHARE MY HEART! THE DEED IS DONE! THERE IS NO TURNING BACK!
YOU MUST PROMISE--PROMISE THAT YOU'LL NEVER LEAVE ME AGAIN!!
FOR, AFTER THIS--HOW COULD I BEAR TO LOSE YOU--??

AS HONOR IS MY MANSION--AS FAITH IS MY SHIELD--I SWEAR TO THEE--
HOLD!! SOMEONE APPROACHES--!

NO OTHERS MUST LEARN THAT WHICH WE NOW SHARE--!

SORRY, DR. BLAKE! IT'S TIME FOR HER DINNER NOW!
DON'T FAIL ME, DON! I'LL BE WAITING FOR YOU! REMEMBER, MY DARLING--I'LL BE WAITING!
I'LL RETURN TOMORROW!

BUT, AT THAT MOMENT, IN HALLOWED ASGARD--
MY SON HATH BETRAYED HIS HERITAGE!
10

BY THE GOLDEN GATES OF ASGARD--!!!
--TO THINK THAT I SHOULD EVER WITNESS SO SORDID A SIGHT!!
MY OWN SON--HEIR TO THE PROUDEST THRONE IN ALL THE UNIVERSE--HATH DIVULGED HIS IMMORTAL IDENTITY TO A FEMALE OF EARTH!
'TIS A WONDER THE HEAVENS THEMSELVES DO NOT QUIVER AND QUAKE IN CELESTIAL INDIGNATION!!
THOUGH I BE ODIN, THE ALL-POWERFUL, STILL HAVE I A FATHER'S HEART! AND VERILY, IT LONGS TO BURST WITH PARENTAL RAGE!
THOUGH THOR BE BLOOD OF MY BLOOD, FLESH OF MY FLESH--THOUGH HE BE FAVORED OVER ALL WHO LIVE--HE HATH BROKEN MY LAW!
MY CHOICE IS CLEAR! THERE MUST BE A RECKONING!
WHILE, ON THE PLANET EARTH, IN THE OFFICE OF DR. DON BLAKE...
YOUR ARM IS HEALING NICELY, MR. WILKENS! THE CAST CAN COME OFF TOMORROW!
I'M NOT COMPLAININ', DOC! I'M A LOT BETTER OFF THAN THOSE POOR NATIVES IN ASIA BEING THREATENED BY THE DEMON!
THE DEMON AGAIN! EVERYONE IS TALKING ABOUT HIM!

BEFORE I GO, IT'S JUST TIME FOR THE HOURLY NEWS SUMMARY--!
--NEW REPORTS FROM OVERSEAS INDICATE THAT THE DEMON'S ARMY CAN NOW BE NUMBERED IN THE THOUSANDS, AND IS GROWING WITH EACH NEW CONQUEST!

NOT SINCE THE HORDES OF GENGHIS KHAN SACKED AND PILLAGED THE FAR EAST, HAS ANYONE CAUSED SUCH A MASS EXODUS OF REFUGEES FROM VILLAGES AND TOWNS...
WITH ALL THE TROUBLE IN VIET NAM, AND OTHER PARTS OF THE WORLD, NO GOVERNMENT CAN AFFORD TO WORRY ABOUT THE DEMON YET! BUT, IF HE ISN'T STOPPED SOON-- IT MAY BE TOO LATE!

ALONE IN HIS OFFICE ONCE MORE, DON BLAKE SEEMS TO SEE THE SAVAGERY, THE MENACE OF THE DEMON IN HIS MIND'S EYE--!
I CAN ALMOST HEAR THE CRIES OF THE WOUNDED, THE WEAK, AND THE OPPRESSED!

THE DEMON MUST POSSESS SOME FANTASTIC, SUPERNATURAL POWER--SOME SECRET WEAPON WHICH MAKES HIM UNSTOPPABLE!
I CAN'T STILL THE SOUNDS OF GUNFIRE IN MY BRAIN-- THEY GROW LOUDER--LOUDER--

YET, THEY MUST BE STILLED-- FOR EACH DAY, THE DEMON GROWS STRONGER! BUT, WHATEVER HIS POWER-- SURELY THOR CAN CRUSH HIM!
NO! WHAT AM I THINKING?? WHAT AM I SAYING? I PROMISED JANE I'D LEAVE HER NO MORE! AND YET--!
WHERE DOES DUTY REALLY LIE--WHETHER ONE BE MAN-- OR GODLING?
12

NO!! I CAN'T STAND IDLY BY WHEN I'M NEEDED!! NOT WHEN I HAVE THE MEANS--THE POWER--TO ACT!
FORGIVE ME, JANE! NO MATTER WHAT MY HEART DICTATES--THE CALL OF DUTY SPEAKS LOUDER STILL!

WHATEVER IS TO BE DONE, THOR WILL DO AS QUICKLY AS POSSIBLE-- AND THEN, RETURN!

FASTER!! FASTER!! I MUST BE THERE AND BACK BEFORE THE ONE I LOVE CAN MISS ME!!

TRAVELING AS ONLY THE GOD OF THUNDER CAN, THE MIGHTY THOR, PROPELLED BY HIS AWESOME ENCHANTED MALLET, BREAKS THE SOUND BARRIER AS HE SOARS ACROSS THE VAST ATLANTIC...!
CRACK!

CRACK!
BUT, ON A MAJESTICALLY TOWERING MOUNTAIN, WHOSE PEAK BRUSHES AGAINST THE VERY STARS THEMSELVES, THAT SAME EAR-SHATTERING SOUND IS HEARD--!

AND THERE, ATOP MYSTICAL MOUNT OLYMPUS, THE LORDLY ZEUS, MONARCH OF ALL HE SURVEYS, RISES TO HIS FEET--!
THE TIME HAS COME! WE MUST TURN OUR ATTENTION EARTHWARD--TO THE PLANET OF MORTALS!
ZEUS HAS SPOKEN!
13

WITH SLOW AND MEASURED TREAD, THE MASTER OF THE ENDLESS REALM APPROACHES THE JOUSTING AREA--AND THEN RAISES HIS IMPERIAL VOICE--!
HOLD!! STAY YOUR ARMS!! HERCULES! ATLAS! THUS SPEAKS ZEUS!!

BEHOLD! AN IMAGE HAVE I CREATED--OF THE PLANET EARTH! IT IS THERE YOU MUST GO--AFTER ALL THESE AGES.!!
I HEAR AND OBEY, VENERABLE LORD!
ALL THESE LONG CENTURIES--WE THOUGHT ZEUS HAD FORGOTTEN EARTH! YET NOW, HE DISPATCHES HERCULES THERE!
HOW THE LEGENDS, IN AGES TO COME, SHALL SING OF THIS GLORIOUS MOMENT!

DOWN FROM OLYMPUS, AT LAST!! BUT, WHAT SHALL I FIND--WHAT NEW CHALLENGES AWAIT ME BELOW??
--SURELY NOTHING AGAINST WHICH MY MATCHLESS STRENGTH CANNOT PREVAIL!

WHILE, ON THE TEEMING, TEMPESTUOUS PLANET OF SHORT-LIVED MORTALS...
ONCE WE CRUSH YONDER FINAL FORTRESS, NOTHING CAN STOP US TILL WE REACH THE SEA!
FIRE--IN THE NAME OF THE DEMON!!!

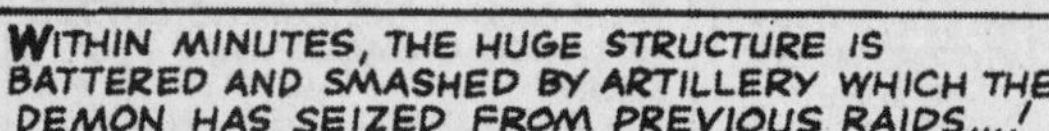
WITHIN MINUTES, THE HUGE STRUCTURE IS BATTERED AND SMASHED BY ARTILLERY WHICH THE DEMON HAS SEIZED FROM PREVIOUS RAIDS...!

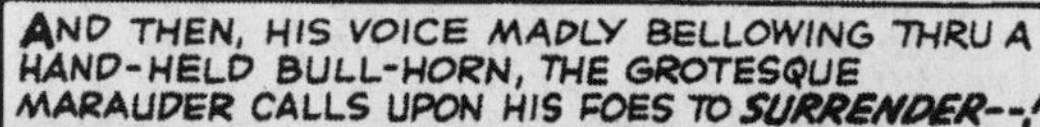
AND THEN, HIS VOICE MADLY BELLOWING THRU A HAND-HELD BULL-HORN, THE GROTESQUE MARAUDER CALLS UPON HIS FOES TO SURRENDER--!

FLING OPEN YOUR GATES!! THROW DOWN YOUR ARMS!! THE DEMON COMMANDS!

BUT, FROM WITHIN THE BESEIGED FORTRESS, COMES A DRAMATIC, UNEXPECTED ANSWER--!
SURRENDER?? TO A TYRANT??
KLANNG!
NEVER!
'TIS YOU WHO SHALL LAY DOWN YOUR ARMS--OR FACE THE FURY OF THOR!!
NOTHING THAT LIVES CAN DEFY THE POWER OF MY MAGIC STONE! THEREFORE--PREPARE TO PERISH!
THAT BAUBLE WORN 'ROUND HIS NECK!! I WOULD KNOW IT ANYWHERE! IT IS A BEWITCHED NORN STONE!
NO WONDER HE HAS MADE A CONTINENT TREMBLE!
I KNOW NOT WHO YOU ARE--BUT I SHALL CRUSH YOU WITH MY BARE HANDS!
16
I AM THOR, OF ASGARD!! LET IT BE HAND-TO-HAND, THEN!
SO LONG AS I POSSESS MY MYSTIC STONE, VICTORY MUST BE MINE!
THUS BEGINS THE TITANIC BATTLE BETWEEN THUNDER GOD AND DEMON-- WITH THE FATE OF A WORLD IN THE BALANCE!!
NEXT ISSUE: "THE COMING OF HERCULES!"

TALES OF ASGARD, HOME OF THE MIGHTY NORSE GODS
"CLOSER COMES THE SWARM!"
FROM THE GIANT STONE HIVE OF THRYHEIM, TO THE NOBLE ODINSHIP OF THOR, IS A LONG AND DANGEROUS DISTANCE... BUT NOT TO THE FLYING TROLLS OF QUEEN ULA, AS SHE SENDS HER LIMITLESS LEGIONS TO ATTACK THE LONELY SHIP WHICH HER WINGED SCOUTS HAVE SIGHTED...
HOW GALLANT, THIS SCRIPT BY: STAN LEE
HOW GLORIOUS, THIS ARTWORK BY: JACK KIRBY
HOW GRACIOUS, THIS INKING BY: VINCE COLLETTA
HOW COME? THIS LETTERING BY: ARTIE SIMEK
1

FASTER! FASTER! WE HAVE NOT FOUND SO RICH A PRIZE SINCE OUR LAST INCUBATION!

BUT, ETERNAL QUEEN, THEY ARE UNDER THE PROTECTION OF ODIN HIMSELF!

WHAT MATTER?!! ULA AND HER SAVAGE SWARM HERE REIGN SUPREME!

AND SO, THE ENDLESS STREAM OF FANATICAL FLYING TROLLS CONTINUES TO ISSUE FORTH-- FROM OUT OF THE GIGANTIC, ALMOST-LEGENDARY STONE NEST OF THRYHEIM....!

WHILE, ON THE MAJESTIC ODINSHIP, BRAVE BALDER LIES LIMP AND HELPLESS AFTER DEFEATING THE UTGARD DRAGON--*

*HE DID IT BY TOOTING HIS ENCHANTED HORN LAST ISSUE, REMEMBER?--STAN.

VOLSTAGG! CATCH YOU THE HORN OF BALDER, WHICH HAS FALLEN FROM HIS LIMP FINGERS!
LET THE OTHERS OF YOU MAKE WAY! SUMMON HOGUN THE GRIM--FOR HE POSSESSES THE ELIXER OF RECOVERY!
NONE BUT VOLSTAGG THE ENORMOUS COULD BE TRUSTED WITH SO VITAL A TASK!

SPEAK, BRAVE BALDER! LET FANDRAL, THY BROTHER-AT-ARMS, HEAR THY WELCOME VOICE ONCE MORE!
SPEAK HE SHALL, DASHING ONE! FOR HOGUN APPROACHES EVEN NOW!

MAKE WAY, ALL! NO HARM SHALL COME TO BALDER WHILST HOGUN LIVES!
IS IT NOT PASSING STRANGE THAT THE GRIM ONE-- THE TAKER OF COUNTLESS LIVES IN BATTLE-- SHOULD BE SO EAGER TO PROTECT THE SINGLE LIFE OF BALDER?
YEA! YET, NONE DARE QUESTION HOGUN!

BUT, A SUBTLE SOFTENING OF HOGUN'S GRIM EXPRESSION DENOTES THE HIGH REGARD HE PLACES ON THE LIVES OF ANY WHO ARE BRAVE!
DRINK, BALDER-- AND, ONCE AGAIN THINE EYES SHALL OPEN...!
3

BEHOLD! THE ELIXIR HATH DONE ITS WORK WELL! BALDER RECOVERS!
THE UTGARD DRAGON!! IS-- IS IT--?
IT IS DESTROYED! THANKS TO THY COURAGE, BRAVE ONE!

IN THE NAME OF ODIN-- HAIL, BALDER! LONG SHALL THY DEED LIVE WITHIN THE HEARTS OF ALL!
HOGUN DEPARTS! BUT, NO MATTER! NOT FOR HIM IS THE JOY OF CELEBRATION! HE EVER CHOOSES TO WALK ALONE!

AND, NOT FOR LOKI AND HIS BLACK-HEARTED COHORTS EITHER IS THE JOY OF CELEBRATION--!
AGAIN THE SHIP IS SAVED! AGAIN THOR HOLDS COMMAND!
DESPAIR NOT, LOKI! I SHALL YET DEVISE A PLAN TO DESTROY HIM! MAGRAT THE SCHEMER SHALL NOT FAIL THEE!
SCHEMES, BAH! THE BLADE OF KRODA IS FAR MORE SURE!
I SHALL GO FORTH AND SPY ON THOR! MAYHAP IT WILL PROVE FRUITFUL!

OUR JOURNEY IS STILL NOT ENDED! MUCH CAN HAPPEN BEFORE WE REACH OUR GOAL! AM I FULLY UNDERSTOOD?
FULLY INDEED, MASTER OF EVIL! IT IS OUR TASK TO SEE THAT THE THUNDER GOD COMPLETES NOT THE VOYAGE!
4

MEANWHILE, LED BY THE GARGANTUAN, IRREPRESSIBLE VOLSTAGG, THE CHEERING FOR THE IMMORTAL WHO HAS SAVED THE ODINSHIP CONTINUES, UNTIL--
SILENCE!! I AM ABOUT TO PERFORM A MOST PRODIGIOUS FEAT...!
IN HONOR OF OUR DELIVERANCE, IT IS ONLY FITTING THAT THE MIGHTY LUNGS OF VOLSTAGG BLOW THE ENCHANTED HORN ONCE MORE--!
THIS I DO BECAUSE MY GREAT HEART IS FULL OF LOVE FOR BALDER-- WHO IS STILL WEAK!
ODD!! THOUGH I BLOW WITH MY USUAL EXTRAORDINARY FORCE AND POWER, ALL I HEAR IS A DULL HUM--
CAN THIS BE PART OF THE HORN'S ENCHANTMENT?? THE SOUND SEEMS TO COME FROM BEHIND MY HEROIC FIGURE--GROWING EVER LOUDER!
MIGHTY THOR!! OBSERVE! OVER THE HORIZON--!
WEAPONS IN HAND!! FOR ODIN! FOR ASGARD!
STOP!! SHEATH THY WEAPONS!! SURELY, I DID NOT PLAY THE HORN SO BADLY!!
'TIS NOT YOUR PLAYING WE TAKE ARMS AGAINST, O MOUNTAINOUS ONE!!
TURN, VOLSTAGG!! TURN AND BEHOLD-- THE FLYING TROLLS OF THRYHEIM!!
5
NO MATTER WHAT THE PROVOCATION, YOU SHALL NOT MISS THE NEXT ISSUE! WE HAVE SPOKEN!

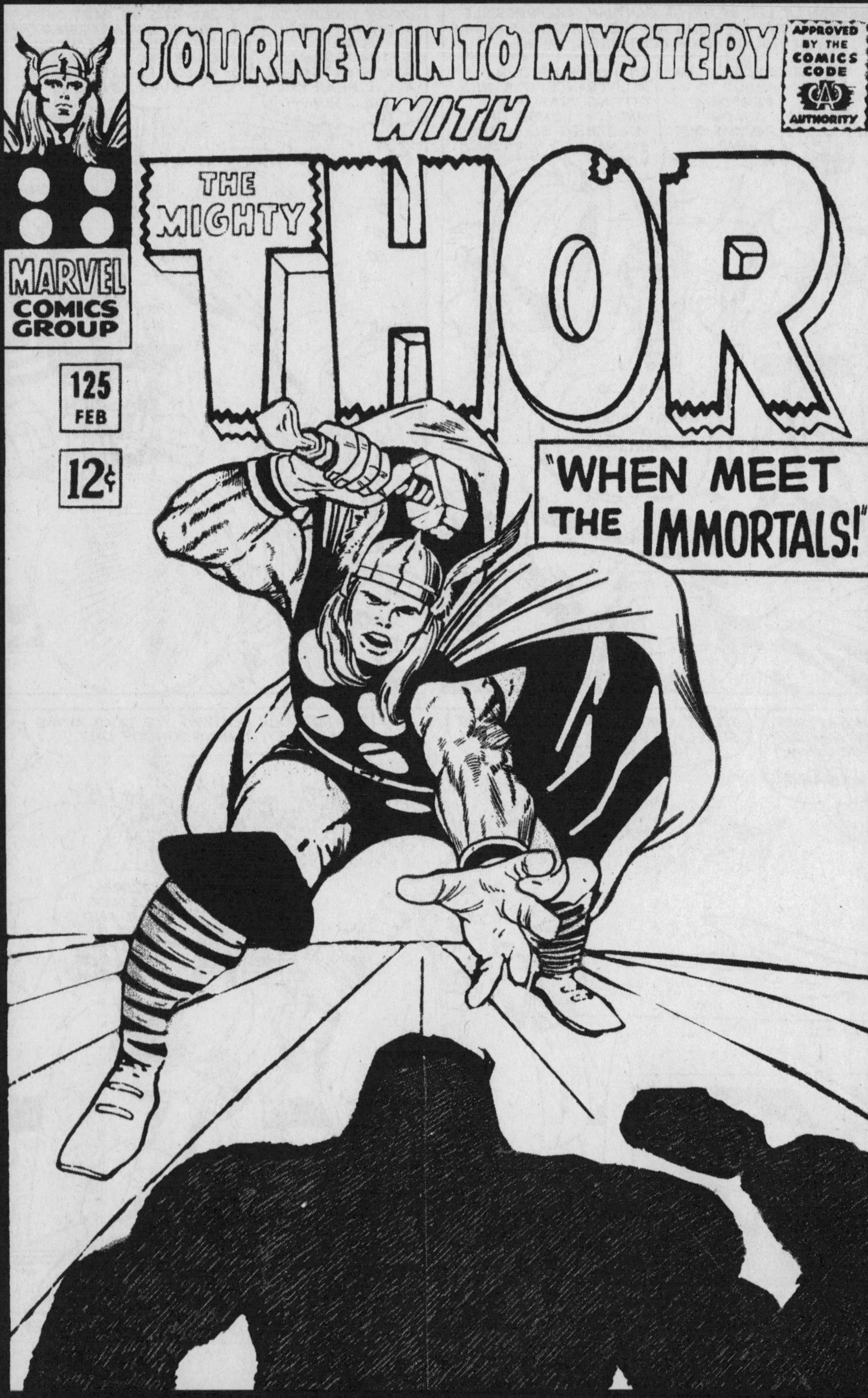
JOURNEY INTO MYSTERY
WITH
THE MIGHTY
THOR
APPROVED BY THE COMICS CODE AUTHORITY
MARVEL COMICS GROUP
125
FEB
12¢
"WHEN MEET THE IMMORTALS!"

THE MIGHTY THOR!
"WHEN MEET THE IMMORTALS!"
FEATURING: THE COMING OF HERCULES!
DID YOU EVER SAMPLE AN INSTANT SYNOPSIS? TRY THIS--!
A WITCH DOCTOR FOUND ONE OF THOR'S LOST NORN STONES!
ITS POWER CHANGED HIM INTO THE DREADED DEMON! (THE WITCH DOCTOR, NOT THOR!)
THOR HAS TO DEFEAT HIM AND REGAIN THE ENCHANTED STONE!
THERE! HOWZAT?
BOMBASTICALLY WRITTEN BY STAN LEE
BRILLIANTLY DRAWN BY JACK KIRBY
BEAUTIFULLY INKED BY VINCE COLLETTA
BASHFULLY LETTERED BY ARTIE SIMEK
1

BACK, YOU RAMPAGING SAVAGE! BACK BEFORE THE IMPERIAL FURY OF MIGHTY THOR!
THOOOM!
IT CANNOT BE!
SEE! THE DEMON FALLS!

AROUND YOUR NECK HANGS AN ENCHANTED NORN STONE! ITS PLACE IS IN ASGARD-- NOT HERE!
RETURN IT TO ME, AND MAYHAP I SHALL LIGHTEN THE WEIGHT OF MY THUNDEROUS ANGER!
NEVER! THIS STONE HAS GIVEN ME 'POWER! POWER SUCH AS NO MAN HAS EVER KNOWN! IT WILL ALWAYS BE MINE!

NO MATTER WHO YOU ARE--NO MATTER WHAT YOU CALL YOURSELF--NO MAN'S STRENGTH CAN EQUAL THE DEMON'S!
SKRUNCH!

THEN STILL YOU DO NOT FULLY COMPREHEND!
'TIS NO MERE MAN YOU ATTACK--!
--'TIS THE SON OF ODIN-- THE GOD OF THUNDER--AN IMMORTAL OF ASGARD!!
BAH! EMPTY WORDS CANNOT SAP THE STRENGTH OF THE DEMON!
2

INDEED--EMPTY WORDS CAN ACCOMPLISH ***NAUGHT!***

BUT, A ***WORLD*** CAN BE TORN ASUNDER BY THE HAMMER, AND THE ARM OF ***THOR!***

KRAKOOOM!

BUT, EVEN AS THOR SWINGS HIS ENCHANTED MALLET, HALF-WAY 'ROUND THE WORLD, ON A GRASSY FIELD IN AMERICA, A STRANGELY-GARBED, POWERFUL FIGURE TAKES HIS EASE ON A SILENT MOUNTAIN SLOPE--UNTIL--
WHEEEEEEEEEEEE
--THE RAUCOUS SOUND OF A SCREECHING TRAIN WHISTLE KNIFES THRU THE PEACEFUL COUNTRY-SIDE--!

EEEEEEEEEE
WHO DARES DISTURB THE SLUMBER OF --HERCULES!

SO! AN IRON MECHANICAL MONSTER--HALTED BY A FALLEN TREE!
IT'LL TAKE DAYS TO LIFT THAT FALLEN SEQUOIA FROM THE TRACKS!
THAT MEANS WE'RE STUCK HERE--IN THE MIDDLE OF NOWHERE!
I'LL HAVE NO PEACE OR QUIET SO LONG AS THEY REMAIN! THEREFORE, IT IS UP TO HERCULES--!

STAND ASIDE, ALL! YOU SHALL SOON BE ON YOUR WAY AGAIN!
DIDJA HEAR THAT, WILLIE?
YEAH! WHY DOES EVERY NUT IN THE WORLD HAVE TO BUTT IN WHEN SOMETHING GOES WRONG?

BUT, A MINUTE LATER...
WILLIE! WILLIE! COME 'N PINCH ME! I GOTTA BE DREAMING!
IF YOU ARE, WE MUST BOTH BELONG TO THE SAME "DREAM-OF-THE-MONTH" CLUB!
ONE SIDE, MORTALS, WHILST HERCULES CLEARS THE TRACKS!
HE'S LIFTING THAT TREE AS EASY AS I LIFT MY PAYCHECK! WHA-WHAT'S HE GONNA DO?

EFFORTLESSLY, EASILY, WITH A CASUAL NONCHALANCE THAT MUST BE SEEN TO BE BELIEVED, THE MAN CALLED HERCULES LIFTS THE MONSTROUS FALLEN TREE IN HIS BARE HANDS, AND THEN, WITHOUT A MOMENT'S PAUSE, HURLS IT LIKE A SPEAR INTO THE SURROUNDING HILLS--!
D-DOES THAT ANSWER YOUR QUESTION, MARVIN?

MUST I DISPOSE OF THIS METAL OBJECT ALSO IN ORDER TO REMAIN UNDISTURBED??
N-NO! FOR THE LUVVA PETE, DON'T TOSS MY ENGINE OFF THE TRACKS!
WE'RE LEAVING RIGHT NOW! WE'LL BE OUT OF YOUR WAY IN MINUTES! HONEST! WE'RE GOING! WE'RE GOING!

GOING? WHERE ARE YOU GOING?
T-TO THE CITY! WE-WE'RE ALREADY BEHIND SCHEDULE!
ANH! THEN THERE ARE CITIES IN THIS STRANGE, MAD WORLD OF YOURS! GOOD! GOOD!
YOU SHALL TAKE ME WITH YOU!
SURE! SURE!

HERCULES HAS ALWAYS LOVED CITIES! IT IS THERE WHERE THE CROWDS ARE-- WHERE REVELING AND MERRY-MAKING ARE EVER TO BE FOUND!
AND WHO CAN ENJOY THE GOOD LIFE AS MUCH AS AN OLYMPIAN GOD?!!
TAKE ME THEN TO YOUR CITY! HERCULES COMMANDS!

MEANWHILE, UNAWARE OF THE PRESENCE ON EARTH OF ANOTHER IMMORTAL, THE SOMEWHAT MORE SERIOUS-MINDED SON OF ODIN IS OCCUPIED WITH MATTERS FAR REMOVED FROM REVELS OR MERRY-MAKING--
THWOK
THERE! NOW LET HIS CANNON BE FIRED!!
5

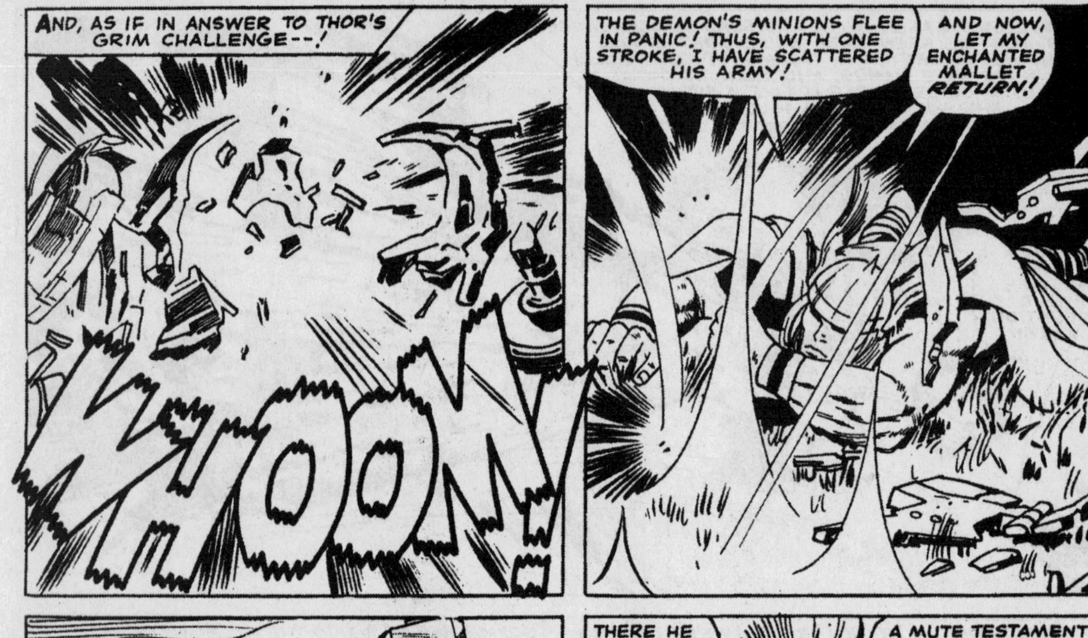
AND, AS IF IN ANSWER TO THOR'S GRIM CHALLENGE--!
WHOOM!
THE DEMON'S MINIONS FLEE IN PANIC! THUS, WITH ONE STROKE, I HAVE SCATTERED HIS ARMY!
AND NOW, LET MY ENCHANTED MALLET RETURN!

THWIPP!
SO BE IT!

THERE HE LIES--ALONE--COMPLETELY VANQUISHED--!
A MUTE TESTAMENT TO THE FOLLY OF POSSESSING GREAT POWER WITHOUT THE WISDOM TO USE IT JUSTLY!
HE IS MERELY STUNNED! THE NORN STONE PROTECTED HIM FROM ANY GREATER HARM--AS I KNEW IT WOULD!

BUT IT SHALL PROTECT HIM--IT SHALL SERVE HIM--NO MORE!

MY MISSION HERE IS ENDED! THE DANGER IS PAST!
BUT ALAS, THOR DOES NOT SUSPECT THE FAR GREATER DANGER WHICH HE SOON MUST FACE--!
6

FOR, AS THE MIGHTY THUNDER GOD MAJESTICALLY WATCHES THE LAST OF THE DEMON'S HORDES MELT AWAY IN THE TRACKLESS JUNGLE, HE CANNOT SUSPECT THAT HIS ORDEAL IS NOT YET ENDED -- NO, THE MOST SOUL-SEARING PART IS YET ABOUT TO BEGIN--!
AND NOW, BUT ONE LAST THING REMAINS TO BE DONE...

BEFORE RETURNING TO MY BELOVED JANE, I MUST BRING THE ENCHANTED STONE BACK SAFELY TO THE GOLDEN REALM...
IT SHALL BE THE WORK OF MERE MINUTES-- AND THEN, NOTHING SHALL PART ME FROM MY LOVED ONE AGAIN!
ON THEN-- TO BIFROST-- THE ETERNAL RAINBOW BRIDGE!!

THUS, SECONDS LATER--AS WE MERE MORTALS MEASURE TIME--!
SINCE REVEALING MY TRUE IDENTITY TO THE GIRL OF MY HEART, IT IS AS THOUGH A HEAVY WEIGHT HAS BEEN LIFTED FROM MY BOSOM!*
BUT, IN TRUTH, THE WRATH OF MY FATHER, NOBLE ODIN, SHALL BE BEYOND ALL MEASURE WHEN HE LEARNS WHAT I HAVE DONE!
*WE SAW IT LAST ISH, IN ONE OF MARVELDOM'S GREATEST DENOUEMENTS! --STAN.

THUS DOES THE THUNDER GOD GREET THE ALL-WISE-- UNAWARE THAT ODIN ALREADY KNOWS OF THE SECRET HIS SON HAS REVEALED--!
HAIL, MOST NOBLE FATHER!
ENTER! STAND BEFORE THE ROYAL PRESENCE!

I HAVE BROUGHT THE NORN STONE BACK TO ITS RIGHTFUL PLACE, SIRE--!
SO BE IT!
IF MY FATHER HATH NO DESIRE TO CONVERSE, THEN BY YOUR LEAVE, I RETURN TO EARTH!
I SAY THEE-- NAY!

THE FURY IN YOUR EYES-- THE THUNDER IN YOUR VOICE --FATHER-- YOU KNOW!
NOT FOR NOTHING AM I ODIN, THE ALL-WISE!! YES, BLOOD OF MY BLOOD--I KNOW!
BALDER!! COME YOU TO MY SIDE!!

YOU CALLED, SIRE?
THOR! MY FRIEND WHO ART MORE THAN BROTHER TO ME! I EMBRACE THEE!
SILENCE, COURAGEOUS ONE! THERE IS A TASK TO BE DONE--!

MY SON HATH BETRAYED HIS TRUST! YOUR BLADE, LOYAL BALDER! SMITE HIM!!

THOR MUST ENDURE THE RITUAL OF STEEL! AND, SHOULD HE SURVIVE--HE SHALL NEVERMORE SET FOOT UPON THE PLANET EARTH!
NO, FATHER! SHE WHOM I LOVE DWELLS THERE!
PUNISH ME AS YOU WILL-- BUT I CANNOT FORSAKE MY HEART!

THUNDER GOD, THOU HAST NO CHOICE! ODIN HATH SPOKEN!
NO! NOT ALL THE BLADES IN ASGARD--NOT ALL THE POWER IN THE UNIVERSE--SHALL HALT ME NOW!
MY STRENGTH--MY LIMBS--MY VERY LIFE ARE IN THY SERVICE, SIRE! BUT, EVEN A THUNDER GOD HAS THE RIGHT TO LOVE!

THEN, LIKE A *THUNDER-CLAP*, BEGINS THE *RITUAL OF STEEL*--!
HAVE *AT* HIM, WARRIORS! BY COMMAND OF LORDLY *ODIN*!
BACK!! BACK, I SAY!! *BACK* BEFORE THE POWER OF MY MALLET--*BACK*, BEFORE THE *RAGE* THAT DOTH FILL MY VERY *SOUL*--!
BY THE *GOLDEN SPIRES!!* HE DOTH BATTER US ASIDE, DESPITE OUR NUMBER! 
THOUGH EVERY BLADE IN ASGARD BE RAISED *AGAINST* ME--*THOR FIGHTS ON!* THOUGH THE HEAVENS THEM-SELVES TREMBLE AND QUAKE--*THOR FIGHTS ON!!*

AND, IN A DIFFERENT WORLD, AS THOR FIGHTS HIS GREATEST FIGHT, ANOTHER IMMORTAL--ONE WITH A TASTE FOR THE GOOD LIFE--FINDS THAT EARTH IS THE CLOSEST THING HE HAS EVER KNOWN TO OLYMPUS ITSELF--!
NOW, GET THIS, J.B.-- I SPOTTED JUST THE ONE WE'RE LOOKING FOR! I DON'T KNOW WHO HE IS! I SAW HIM COMING OUT OF GRAND CENTRAL STATION!
HE'S EVEN DRESSED FOR THE PART! HE'LL MAKE THE GREATEST HERCULES EVER FILMED!
DON'T WORRY! I WON'T LEAVE WITHOUT SIGNING HIM UP! YOU KNOW ME, J.B.!
WHO'S THE REFUGEE FROM MUSCLE BEACH, CHARLIE?
I DUNNO! BUT, IF YOU FIND OUT WHAT KINDA VITAMIN PILLS HE TAKES, ORDER ME A BUSHELFUL!
COME ON, GIRLS! STOP BEING SELFISH! LET ME GET NEXT TO HIM FOR A MINUTE!
NO NEED TO CROWD, DAMSELS! THIS PLACE DOTH PLEASE ME! I SHALL NOT SOON DEPART!
I TELL YA HE'S TOO GOOD TO BE TRUE! HE NOT ONLY LOOKS THE PART, HE EVEN SOUNDS LIKE HERCULES!
NO, J.B., I'M NOT PUTTIN' YA ON! HE'D MAKE KING KONG LOOK LIKE A POWDER PUFF!
THIS INSTRUMENT IS NOT UNLIKE MINE OWN LYRE! IN TRUTH, THIS IS A MOST SATISFACTORY WORLD!
I KNEW IT! HE'S A FOLK SINGER-- PLUGGING A NEW DISC!
BUT THEN, SUDDENLY, AN INTERRUPTION OCCURS FROM AN UNEXPECTED QUARTER--
AWRIGHT, THE PARTY'S OVER! GETCHA HANDS UP-- FAST! THIS IS A STICK UP!
THAT MEANS EVERY-BODY! WE DON'T WANNA GET ROUGH UNLESS WE HAVETA! REACH FOR THE CEILING!
THOUGH THE WORDS BE STRANGE, THE TONE IS UNMISTAKABLE! AND WORSE, THEY INTERRUPT MY MADRIGAL!
10

SCURVY KNAVES-- BEGONE!

I DUNNO WHO THAT CREEP IS, BUT NOBODY'S WRECKIN' THIS CAPER IF I CAN HELP IT!
BUKKA
BUK

WHAT MONUMENTAL INSOLENCE!! A MORTAL --A MERE MORTAL-- AND HE DOTH ATTACK HERCULES!!
THK!
THK!
THK!

OUT, THOU UNMITIGATED FLEA--AND BE THANKFUL THAT I BE IN GENTLE MOOD!
KUH-RASH!

OUTSIDE THE SUPPER CLUB, A TERRIFIED LOOKOUT IN THE GETAWAY CAR APPLIES FULL THROTTLE AS HE CATCHES A GLIMPSE OF THE TITAN WHO STRIDES TOWARDS HIM--
I DON'T KNOW WHAT'S GOIN' ON, BUT I AINT TAKIN' ANY CHANCES! THAT GUY'S TOO BIG TO PLAY PATTYCAKE WITH!
IT IS BEYOND BELIEF!! DO THESE M RTAL WEAKLINGS HOL THEIR LIVES SO CHEA THAT THEY WOULD ATTACK HERCULES?!!
CRACK!
SKREEEE

NONE MAY TRAIN WEAPONS AGAINST MY PERSON WITH IMPUNITY!
SKRUNCH

FOR, THRUOUT THE AGES IT HAS SURELY BEEN PROVEN--HERCULES IS INDEED MASTER OF ALL!

LET ALL WHO BEAR WITNESS REMEMBER--THE SON OF ZEUS MAY BE TRIFLED WITH NEVER!
SKRRRAK

AND, HIGH ABOVE THE INCREDIBLE SCENE, JANE FOSTER, PREPARING TO CHECK OUT OF HER HOSPITAL, HEARS THE COMMOTION BELOW--
THAT DEAFENING CRASH! AND NOW--THE POLICE SIRENS--WHAT CAN BE HAPPENING DOWN THERE?
IT'S HARD TO SEE CLEARLY FROM THIS HEIGHT, AND YET--!

THAT LARGE, POWERFUL FIGURE IN THE CENTER OF THE CROWD! SO MUSCULAR--SO BROAD-SHOULDERED! IT CAN ONLY BE--THOR! NO ONE ELSE COULD HAVE HURLED THAT LAMPPOST!
HE'S COME BACK TO ME--AS HE VOWED HE WOULD! MY LOVE HAS RETURNED!
12

THEN, AS JANE RACES BREATHLESSLY TO THE HOSPITAL ELEVATOR...
IT'S ALL RIGHT, OFFICER! I'LL TAKE THE RESPONSIBILITY! HE'S J.B. STARDUST'S NEW ACTING DISCOVERY--!
PROBABLY ANOTHER HOLLYWOOD PUBLICITY STUNT, HUH? I SHOULDA GUESSED!

I MUST GET TO HIM! I MUST REACH THOR BEFORE--OH!
I-I WAS WRONG! IT ISN'T HIM!
BUT THEN -WHO CAN HE BE?
OH! HE NOTICED ME RUSHING TOWARDS HIM! NOW HE'S COMING TO ME!

EVERYTHING ABOUT HIM--REMINDS ME OF THOR!! AND YET--HE-HE'S SO VERY DIFFERENT!!
I AM HERCULES!

MANY HAVE BEHELD ME! BUT ONLY IN THINE EYES DO I SEE--A FLAME WHICH MIGHT BE KINDLED!
HOLD IT, BIG BOY! J.B. WANTS ME TO FLY YOU TO THE COAST! THERE ARE PLENTY OF DOLLS OUT THERE!

HEED NOT THE MOUTHINGS OF INSECTS! HERCULES LISTENS TO NONE!
HIS STRENGTH IS LIKE THOR'S! BUT, HE'S MORE RECKLESS--MORE BRUTAL--!

THUS, LIKE A GIRL IN A TRANCE, JANE FOSTER ALLOWS HERSELF TO BE LED AWAY BY THE FORCEFUL, COMMANDING FIGURE OF THE IMMORTAL FROM OLYMPUS, WHILE, BACK IN ASGARD, WE FIND...
THE RAINBOW BRIDGE LIES JUST AHEAD!
NOW BARS MY WAY TO EARTH!
IT IS FUTILE! WE POSSESS NOT THE POWER TO STOP HIM!

SO, HEIMDALL! THY SENSITIVE EARS HAVE ALREADY WARNED THEE OF MY COMING!
BACK, GOD OF THUNDER! NONE MAY PASS SAVE BY ODIN'S COMMAND!

THY HAMMER SHALL AVAIL THEE NAUGHT! REMEMBER--MY URU SWORD DOTH POSSESS EQUAL POWER!

HE SPEAKS TRUE! BUT, I CAN TARRY NO LONGER! ODIN IS NOW CONTENT TO LET HIS WARRIORS PURSUE ME--!
YET, SHOULD HE HIMSELF ENTER THE FRAY, MY CAUSE WILL BE SURELY LOST!
THEREFORE, WHATEVER IS TO BE DONE --I MUST DO IT NOW!

HEIMDALL'S EARS! SENSITIVE ENOUGH TO WARN OF ANY DANGER--THEY SHALL NOW PROVE HIS UNDOING!

THEN, MOVING TOO SWIFTLY FOR THE EYE TO FOLLOW--TOO POWERFULLY FOR A MERE SWORD THRUST BY HEIMDALL TO INTERCEPT--THE MIGHTY THUNDER GOD STRIKES HIS ENCHANTED MALLET WITH FORCE ENOUGH TO CAUSE A SONIC BOOM--AS THE SUDDEN, EAR-SHATTERING SOUND CAUSES HEIMDALL TO CRUMBLE IN SHOCK--!

WHILE, BACK IN THE AWESOME THRONE ROOM...
I SURRENDER MY SWORD TO THEE, SIRE! LET THY HAND SLAY BALDER, IF IT BE THY WISH! I COULD NOT FIND IT IN MY HEART TO SMITE THE GOD OF THUNDER!
RISE, FAITHFUL ONE! THE FAULT IS NOT THINE, BUT RESTS WITH ME ALONE--!

THEN, THE ALL-SEEING EYES OF OMNIPOTENT ODIN TURN ONCE AGAIN TO THE FLEEING THUNDER GOD, AS THE VENGEFUL MONARCH PONDERS THE PUNISHMENT HE SHALL INFLICT UPON HIS REBELLIOUS SON--!

BACK TO EARTH-- AT LAST!
MY VERY SOUL HUNGERS FOR THE SIGHT OF MY BELOVED!

A MILLING CROWD-- ACROSS THE STREET FROM HER HOSPITAL!
CAN IT BE THAT JANE FOSTER IS IN DANGER?!!

PLUMMETING TO THE GROUND LIKE A STREAK, THE IMMORTAL HEARS--
FOR THE LUVVA PETE! ANOTHER ONE! THIS TOWN'S CRAWLIN' WITH HUMAN POWER-HOUSES!
ANOTHER ONE?? WHAT DO YOU MEAN? SPEAK, MORTAL --THOR COMMANDS!
ANSWER 'IM, CHARLIE! HE'S ONE GUY YOU DON'T WANNA KID AROUND WITH!

S-SEE FOR YOURSELF, MISTER! JUST LOOK THRU THAT SODA PARLOR WINDOW--!
DARE I BELIEVE MY EYES?!!

AHH! THIS LIQUID IS LIKE NECTAR OF THE GODS!
JANE! I HAVE RETURNED!
REALLY? I FORGOT YOU HAD BEEN AWAY!
-ULP!- IT-IT'S THOR!

I THOUGHT YOU LOVED ME--BUT AGAIN YOU LEFT, WITHOUT A WORD OF EXPLANATION! WELL, I'M THRU BEING LEFT BEHIND--WONDERING--NEVER KNOWING WHEN OR IF YOU'LL RETURN!
STOP! YOU KNOW NOT WHAT YOU SAY!
YOU MUST ALLOW ME TO EXPLAIN--!

DO YOU THINK THAT I WANTED TO BE PARTED FROM YOU??
IF YOU COULD BUT KNOW THE ODDS I FACED TO RETURN TO YOU--!
AND WHAT OF ME? WHAT OF THE LONG, LONELY HOURS-- THE EMPTY, ENDLESS DAYS--??

GREETINGS, GOD OF THUNDER! I KNEW WE WOULD ONE DAY MEET AGAIN!*
STAND ASIDE, HERCULES! 'TIS NOT WITH YOU I WISH TO SPEAK!
*THEY FIRST MET IN THE THOR ANNUAL #1, RIGHT? --STAN.

HOW CAME YOU TO BE HERE WITH HIM??
I MUST HEAR YOUR ANSWER!
HOLD, THUNDER GOD! STAND YOU AWAY! HERCULES SPEAKS!

NONE MAY IGNORE THE FAVORED SON OF ZEUS!!
AND NONE MAY RAISE VOICE TO A FEMALE WHOM HERCULES LOOKS UPON WITH FAVOR!

VERILY, IT IS BEYOND BELIEF!
TO THINK THAT ANOTHER WOULD SMITE THOR IN DEFENSE OF JANE FOSTER!!
16

SLOWLY, THE MIGHTY THUNDER GOD RISES TO HIS FEET, HIS EYES BLAZING WITH CATACLYSMIC FURY--HIS VERY SOUL CLAMORING FOR VENGEANCE!
BRAZEN ONE-- DEFEND THYSELF!

NEXT ISSUE:
THE BATTLE OF THE TITANS!

TALES OF ASGARD, HOME OF THE MIGHTY NORSE GODS!

the QUEEN COMMANDS

NONE BUT MARVEL'S STAN LEE COULD TELL SUCH A TALE! | NONE BUT MARVEL'S JACK KIRBY COULD DRAW SUCH A TALE! | NONE BUT MARVEL'S VINCE COLLETTA COULD INK SUCH A TALE! | NONE BUT MARVEL'S ARTIE SIMEK COULD BE SUCH A PUSSYCAT!

STAY YOUR HANDS, WARRIORS OF ASGARD! LET *THOR* BE YOUR SWORD--AS WELL AS YOUR *SHIELD!*

WE SEEK NO NEEDLESS BATTLE--THOUGH WE SURRENDER TO *NONE!*

THE WORDS OF THOR ARE HEAVY LADEN WITH WISDOM!
BUT, TO INSURE THAT YOU REMAIN PEACEFUL, WE SHALL DEMONSTRATE THE POWER OF OUR STING UPON YON QUIVERING MASS OF BLUBBER--!
I KNOW NOT OF WHOM HE SPEAKS!! BUT, SURELY IT CANNOT BE VOLSTAGG, WHO IS COURAGE INCARNATE!

HOLD, WINGED ONE! USE THY STING BUT ONCE, AND NO POWER SHALL SAVE THEE FROM THE VENGEANCE OF THOR!
SO SAY WE ALL!

BUT, BELOW DECKS, AT THAT VERY MOMENT, WE FIND...
IF THOR IS TOO COWARDLY TO BATTLE THE TROLLS, LET IT BE KNOWN THAT LOKI IS CUT FROM A DIFFERENT CLOTH!
MORE POTIONS-- MORE!! THE DEED IS ALMOST DONE!

THUS, WITHOUT WARNING, A STRANGE, PUNGENT VAPOR FILLS THE AIR, AND---
A MYSTIC POISON FELLS OUR RANKS! FLEE! FLEE!

THOUGH PAINFUL TO THE FLYING TROLLS, LOKI'S ENCHANTED VAPOR HAS NO EFFECT UPON THE WARRIORS OF ASGARD, AS AN ENRAGED THUNDER GOD SOON REALIZES--!
THERE! THERE IS THE SOURCE OF THE FATEFUL SUBSTANCE!!
WHAT TRAITOROUS FOOL HAS COMMITTED SO CATACLYSMIC A BLUNDER?? STEP FORTH! LET THE WITLESS CULPRIT BE THUS REVEALED!!

YOUR ANGER REVEALS YOUR ENVY, BROTHER! IT RANKLES YOU THAT IT WAS I WHO HAS SAVED OUR SHIP!
LOKI!! IN TRUTH, I SHOULD HAVE KNOWN!

YOU HAVE SAVED NOTHING, EVIL ONE! WHERE THOR HOPED FOR PEACE, YOU HAVE BUT ANGERED THE TROLLS!! OUR DANGER HAS BEEN MULTIPLIED!
CAN IT BE THE GOD OF THUNDER IS AFRAID??
SAY NO MORE-- LEST I FORGET YOU BE MY OWN HALF-BROTHER!

'TIS NOTHING THAT LOKI WISHES TO REMEMBER! ONE DAY I SHALL PROVE THAT IT IS I WHO SHOULD BE--
WAIT! WHAT IS THAT OMINOUS NOISE??
THE SWARM RETURNS!!
SURELY, YOU DID NOT BELIEVE YOUR MYSTIC VAPOR COULD KEEP THEM AT BAY FOR LONG!
NOW, STAND YOU ASIDE, WHILST THOR TAKES COMMAND!

But then, in the space of a single heartbeat--!
GRAPPLE RINGS!! THEY'VE CAUGHT ME-- BEFORE I CAN CAST A SPELL!
THE TROLLS KNOW WHO CREATED THE VAPOR!

WARRIORS ASSEMBLE!!
SAVE ME, THOR--!
WHOSOEVER ATTACKS ONE ARGONAUT, ATTACKS ALL!!

Meanwhile, a winged courier streaks toward the fateful isle of Thryheim, on which stands the sinister Hive of Stone--!
OUT OF MY WAY! I MUST ENTER THE HIVE! THE QUEEN COMMANDS!
5

LOKI IS OURS, MY QUEEN --AS YOU COMMANDED!
OF COURSE! ARE MY THOUGHTS NOT EVERYWHERE? EVEN NOW, I SENSE THE THUNDER GOD APPROACHING!
LET THE PREPARATIONS BE MADE--WE MUST HAVE A WELCOME FOR THE SONS OF ODIN!
By the golden gates of Asgard, you must join us next issue! So be it!

THE MIGHTY
THOR
MARVEL
COMICS
GROUP
126
MAR
APPROVED
BY THE
COMICS
CODE
AUTHORITY
12¢
IND.
"WHOM THE
GODS WOULD
DESTROY!"

THE MIGHTY THOR!
"WHOM THE GODS WOULD DESTROY!"
NOT EVEN HERCULES, SON OF ZEUS, MAY STRIKE THOR WITH IMPUNITY!
ANOTHER MIGHTY MARVEL INSTANT RESUMÉ:
HERCULES HAS COME TO EARTH! HE'S GOT THE BIG EYE FOR THOR'S CHICK!
GOLDILOCKS IS BUGGED, BUT GOOD!
SO, THEY'RE FIGHTING IT OUT!
THERE! THAT'S AS PAINLESS AS WE CAN MAKE IT!
CHAPTER II
FEATURING: THE LONG-AWAITED CLASH OF TITANS BETWEEN MIGHTY THOR and HERCULES!
YOUR OVERBEARING CONCEIT IS A STANDING JOKE IN OLYMPUS, THUNDER GOD! BUT NOW I'LL RID YOU OF IT-- FOREVER!
THEY SAID IT COULDN'T BE DONE! AND HERE ARE THE GUYS WHO ALMOST COULDN'T DO IT--
STAN LEE THE LITERARY LION!
JACK KIRBY THE PENCILLING PUSSYCAT!
V. COLLETTA THE DELINEATING DRAGON!
ARTIE SIMEK THE LETTERING LOOKS IT!

MY HAMMER AGAINST YOUR MACE! WE SHALL SEE WHICH IS THE STRONGER!
I'VE NEVER YET TASTED DEFEAT-- NOR SHALL I NOW!
NO! THEY MUSTN'T FIGHT OVER ME! IF--IF ONE OF THEM SHOULD BE HURT--OR WORSE--!
NEVER MIND THAT! DOES MY STORE INSURANCE COVER DAMAGE BY IMMORTALS?

I DO NOT SEEK TO HARM YOU! MERELY TO SHOW THAT POWER MISUSED IS POWER ABUSED!
WHAT MANNER OF WARRIOR ARE YOU? YOUR LIPS SPOUT FABLES, WHILST YOUR SINEWS ARE THE EQUAL OF HERCULES!

NAY, RASH ONE! THE POWER OF THOR IS EQUAL TO NONE! MY STRENGTH IS SUPREME!
AGAIN YOUR COLOSSAL EGOTISM FILLS MY SOUL WITH RAGE!

THE MORTAL FEMALE FOR WHOSE FAVOR WE BATTLE DESERVES BETTER THAN SUCH A VAIN, HUMORLESS DULLARD AS THEE!
DIM-WITTED CLOD! IF I BE HUMORLESS, IT IS NOT WITHOUT GOOD REASON!

FOR MONTHS, THE POWERS OF ASGARD AND EARTH HAVE CONSPIRED TO KEEP ME FROM MY BELOVED!
BUT, NO LONGER DO I ENDURE MY FATE IN STONY SILENCE! NOW, THE SON OF ODIN STRIKES BACK!
I HAVE MISJUDGED HIM! NO DULLARD IS HE! INSTEAD, HE IS TRULY TORTURED BY A SOUL IN TORMENT!

MEANWHILE, ON THE FABLED RAINBOW BRIDGE WHICH SPANS THE INFINITE VOID BETWEEN EARTH AND ASGARD, A SOLITARY FIGURE SLOWLY RISES...
TRULY MUST THE MADNESS BE UPON THE GOD OF THUNDER!
HE HATH USED HIS AWESOME POWER TO OVERCOME HEIMDALL, GUARDIAN OF THE BRIDGE! SURELY, HE MUST KNOW THE DREAD PRICE WHICH A VENGEFUL ODIN WILL FORCE HIM TO PAY!

AND, THRUOUT THE GOLDEN REALM, AS THE WARRIORS OF ASGARD RECOVER FROM THE INDESCRIBABLE ONSLAUGHT OF MIGHTY THOR, ALL SEEM TO SHARE THE SAME SOLEMN THOUGHT...
WHAT PUNISHMENT WILL THOR RECEIVE AT THE HANDS OF REGAL ODIN?
IT CHILLS ME TO THE MARROW WHEN I THINK UPON IT!

IT CHILLS THE HEART OF THE THUNDER GOD'S CLOSEST FRIEND, AS WELL--AS BALDER THE BRAVE ATTEMPTS TO SOFTEN THE CATACLYSMIC WRATH OF HIS LIEGE...
HARK YOU, SIRE! THY SON WAS MOTIVATED BY LOVE OF A FEMALE --IS HE NOT MORE DESERVING OF PITY THAN RETRIBUTION?
LET THY VOICE BE STILL, LOYAL BALDER! I BE NOT MOVED!
I RESPECT THY DEVOTION--BUT MY LAW IS THE LAW SUPREME--AND NONE MAY BREAK IT!
MINE EARS SHALL HEAR NO MORE ENTREATIES! NOR SHALL THE VOICE OF ODIN MOUTH WORDS OF FORGIVENESS!

THOR HAS DARED TO PIT HIS WILL AGAINST MINE! FOR THAT, HE MUST PAY!
AND, BY THE TOWERING SPIRES OF ASGARD, HOW HE SHALL PAY!

THEN, TURNING DARKLY TO THE COSMIC CRYSTAL FROM WHICH NOTHING ON EARTH CAN BE HIDDEN, THE LORD OF ASGARD MUTTERS SOFTLY...
ALL THAT NOW REMAINS IS THE CHOICE OF PUNISHMENT! A CHOICE I SHALL NOT LONG DELAY!

BUT, IN THE MORTAL WORLD BELOW, THOR CONTINUES HIS THUNDEROUS ONSLAUGHT--UNAWARE OF THE DIRE FATE WHICH AWAITS HIM--!
HIS ENCHANTED HAMMER MAKES A LIVING MOCKERY OF MINE OWN MACE--EVEN AS THE POWER OF HIS LIMBS IS EASILY THE EQUAL OF MINE OWN!
BACK, THOU BLUSTERING BRAGGART! WELL MAY THOU THANK WHATEVER GODS THOU PRAYEST TO THAT I HURL MY HAMMER NOT TO DESTROY, BUT TO HUMBLE THEE!
LET NO MORTAL FEEL THE PANGS OF FEAR! ONLY HERCULES IS TARGET FOR MY URU MALLET! ALL OTHERS SHALL BE UNSCATHED!
HIS HAMMER RETURNED TO HIM--PASSING OVER THE HEADS OF THE MORTAL ASSEMBLAGE!
BE THOU WARNED, SCION OF ASGARD! NOW THAT THE FULL MEASURE OF THY STRENGTH IS REVEALED, I HUNGER FOR MORE BATTLE!
FOR NOTHING PLEASES THE HEART OF HERCULES SO MUCH AS A FOE WHO CAN OFFER A CHALLENGE TO MY MATCHLESS POWER!
HE IS AS THOR HAD BEEN, IN THE HALCYON DAYS OF YORE! HE THRIVES ON COMBAT AS THE BLOSSOMS THRIVE ON RAIN!
BUT I AM TOO HEAVILY-LADEN WITH CARE TO TREAT THIS ENCOUNTER AS A LARK! IT MUST BE ENDED--AND SOON!
SSKKRUNTCH!
HAH! HOW PUNY ARE THE PRODUCTS OF MERE MORTALS!! HOW THEY SHATTER AND CRUMBLE BEFORE THE MIGHT OF HERCULES!
STRENGTH ALONE IS A HOLLOW VIRTUE, SON OF ZEUS!
WITHOUT CONSCIENCE, WITHOUT RESPECT FOR THOSE WHO MAY BE WEAKER THAN THEE--THY POWER RESTS ONLY ON PILLARS OF SAND!

SUDDENLY, THE UNPREDICTABLE GREEK IMMORTAL HURLS HIMSELF FROM THE WRECKED VEHICLES, LEAPING AT HIS CAPED FOE WITH THE FORCE OF A JUGGERNAUT--!
FIE UPON CONSCIENCE!! I LEAVE OTHERS TO DWELL UPON THE RIGHT AND WRONG OF MATTERS!
AS FOR ME, THE ECSTASY OF BATTLE IS REWARD ENOW!

I HAVE WARNED THEE FOR THE FINAL TIME! TILL NOW, I HAVE STAYED MINE ARM FROM UNLEASHING A FATAL BLOW --BUT YOU LEAVE ME NO CHOICE--!
DO THEN THY WORST, THUNDER GOD! NO GROUNDLESS THREAT SHALL PUT HERCULES TO ROUTE!

BY THE MAJESTY OF MIGHTY OLYMPUS!! NEVER BEFORE HAS ANY BEING BROKEN THE GRIP OF HERCULES TO ESCAPE MY MOST POTENT BLOW!

EVEN ON THY BACK, THOU ART A FOE TO BE FEARED! BUT, MY MACE SHALL GIVE THEE PAUSE!
THOR IS NOT IMPRESSED! THY WORDS DO LITTLE MORE THAN BOLSTER THINE OWN FALTERING CONFIDENCE!

ONCE MORE, THE MATCHLESS POWER OF THE THUNDER GOD ENABLES HIM TO ROLL CLEAR OF HERCULES' CYCLONIC BLOW, AS THE IMMORTAL'S MACE SHATTERS THE VERY GROUND BENEATH THEM, CAUSING THE TWO TITANIC COMBATANTS TO PLUNGE ATOP A SPEEDING TRAIN IN THE SUBWAY TUNNEL BELOW...!
WHOOOM!

OBLIVIOUS TO ALL AROUND THEM, THE TWO RAMPAGING GOLIATHS FIGHT ON, AS THE SPEEDING STEEL CAR BENEATH THEIR FEET ROARS TOWARDS ITS NEXT STOP--AN ELEVATED OPEN-AIR STATION--!
ONCE AGAIN I BESEECH THEE, HERCULES--HEED MY WORDS! LET THIS SENSELESS BATTLE CEASE!
THY PLEA--COMING FROM ANY OTHER LIPS--WOULD BESPEAK RANK COWARDICE!
YET, I KNOW 'TIS NOT FEAR--BUT CONCERN THAT CAUSED THY UTTERANCE!

BUT THE VERY PRIDE OF HERCULES IS AT STAKE! THE VICTORY MUST BE MINE ERE MY ARM WILL BE STILLED!
SO BE IT! UPON THINE OWN HEAD THEN SHALL BE THAT WHICH BEFALLS!
THAT NOISE! THAT POUNDING! WHAT'S HAPPENING UP THERE!
WE'VE REACHED THE STATION! EVERYONE OUT--QUICKLY!

WE CAN END THIS AT ONCE, GOD OF THUNDER! MERELY MOUTH THE WORDS--I YIELD TO THEE!
MAY I NE'ER GAZE UPON VALHALLA ERE SUCH WORDS ESCAPE THE LIPS OF THOR!
THE SUBWAYS WERE BAD ENOUGH TILL NOW--BUT THIS IS RIDICULOUS!

ONE FINAL BLOW--WITH ALL MY STRENGTH--WOULD SURELY END THIS USELESS AFFAIR!
AND YET, I CANNOT BRING MYSELF TO DEAL SO HARSHLY WITH THE SON OF ZEUS!

I AM TRULY CERTAIN THAT HERCULES IS HEADSTRONG RATHER THAN EVIL--LIKE A SMALL CHILD WHO HAS BEEN UNDISCIPLINED SINCE BIRTH!
SURELY THE LUST FOR BATTLE HAS FADED FROM THEE BY NOW, OLYMPIAN!
NAY, THUNDER GOD! MORE THAN EVER DO I LONG TO RAISE MY MACE IN TRIUMPH!

NOW, HERE--ON THIS SITE WHERE AGED BUILDINGS ARE BEING DEMOLISHED, WE CAN REACH OUR ULTIMATE MOMENT OF TRUTH--WITH NONE TO INTERFERE!
CAUTION
YOUR HUNGER FOR BATTLE IS A DISEASE --AND THE HAMMER OF THOR SHALL SUPPLY THY CURE!

NOT WHILST HERCULES CAN HURL THE FIRST BLOW! LET THIS TEACH THEE CAUTION, ASGARDIAN!
THOK
VERILY, THOU ART BEYOND ALL REASON! THUS, IF ONLY FORCE SHALL PREVAIL--!
FORCE THEN SHALL IT BE THAT BRINGS THEE TO THY KNEES!

NEVER BEFORE HAVE ANY FAILED TO FALL PROSTRATE WHEN STRUCK BY HERCULES!!
BUT, THY STRENGTH MERELY WHETS MY APPETITE FOR FURTHER SPORT!
THOU SHALT NO LONGER CALL IT SPORT AFTER THOR HATH DONE WITH THEE!
RRAKK!

THWPP!
HAH! USING THE STEEL TREAD OF A VEHICLE AS A WHIP AGAINST HERCULES!! A BRILLIANT STRATAGEM, THUNDER GOD--!
A PITY IT IS DOOMED TO FAILURE!

AHH, THE REJOICING--THE BACCHANALIAN REVELING--WHICH SHALL FILL ALL OF OLYMPUS--WHEN IT IS LEARNED THAT HERCULES HATH FELLED THE MIGHTY THOR!
AND, HOW FITTING IT SHALL BE TO ACHIEVE MY GREATEST VICTORY BY MEANS OF AN ANCIENT OLYMPIAN SPORT--

MAYHAP EVEN THOU HAST HEARD OF THE GRECIAN PROWESS AT THROWING THE DISCUS!!

SO FAST DO THE HEAVY FLYING OBJECTS ZOOM THRU THE AIR, THAT EVEN THE SPEED OF THOR IS NOT SUFFICIENT TO SAVE HIM FROM THE BATTERING IMPACT....!
RROOOM!

AND NOW, WHILST THOU ART STILL IN STATE OF SHOCK--
THE FINAL BLOW SHALL BE STRUCK--AS ONLY THE FABLED FIST OF HERCULES CAN STRIKE IT!

BUT, A SPLIT-SECOND LATER--
A STRONGER ARM! A STOUTER HEART! A NOBLER SOUL! AND NONE DOTH HERCULES POSSESS, THOU BLABBERING, BLUSTERING, BOASTFUL BUFFOON!
BY THE CLOVEN HOOVES OF PAN!! WHAT DOTH IT TAKE TO DEFEAT THE SON OF ODIN??!

WONDER BEYOND WONDERS!! THOU DOST HAVE FIRE IN THY VEINS--AS WELL AS THUNDER IN THY FISTS! YEA, 'TIS NOT SOME MEALY-MOUTHED CABBAGE I DO BATTLE WITH! THOU ART AS CAPABLE OF ANGER AS HERCULES HIMSELF!
ANGER??! BY THE BRISTLING BEARD OF ODIN, THOU KNOWEST NOT THE MEANING OF THE WORD! NOT ALL THE FURY IN THE HEAVENS--NOT ALL THE SAVAGERY ON EARTH--CAN EQUAL THE SENSES-SHATTERING CYCLONE OF RAGE WHICH IS THOR, WHEN SEIZED BY A POUNDING PAROXYSM OF WRATH!

FINALLY, AFTER LONG MOMENTS OF PAINFUL CONTEMPLATION, THE DEEP VOICE OF ODIN SLOWLY FILLS THE CHAMBER...

GIVE EAR TO THE JUDGMENT OF THY LIEGE! I SHALL CAUSE THE POWER OF THOR TO EBB FROM HIS LIMBS--UNTIL IT BE BUT HALF THAT WHICH HE RIGHTFULLY POSSESSES!

BUT, MOST ALL-WISE--IF THOU CAUSE HIM TO LOSE HALF HIS POWER NOW--WHILST HE NEEDS IT MOST, IN BATTLE WITH HERCULES --IT IS POSSIBLE THAT DEATH ITSELF MAY BE HIS FATE!

SILENCE! MY SON IS A GOD! NO LESSER PUNISHMENT WOULD BE SEEMLY! I HAVE SPOKEN!

*MIDGARD: THE ASGARDIAN NAME FOR EARTH! --LEGENDARY STAN!

AND, AT THAT VERY INSTANT, AN UNIMAGINABLE DISTANCE AWAY--!
WHAT IS THIS?
THOU, WHO HAST ENDURED MY MIGHTIEST BLOWS-- INJURED BY A MERE BOLT OF LIGHT??!
UHHHHH--!
OR, CAN IT BE THAT MY ATTACK HATH FINALLY WEAKENED THEE--AS IT WAS INTENDED TO DO?!!
BOM!
WHAT HAS BEFALLEN ME? FOR THE FIRST TIME, I AM TRULY STAGGERED BY A SINGLE BLOW!
HAH! THOUGH THE THUNDER GOD'S STRENGTH IS WANING AT LAST, THE POWER OF HERCULES IS AS TITANIC AS BEFORE! THEREFORE, I SHALL NOW PROVE 'TIS HERCULES WHO IS MIGHTIEST OF ALL-- IN A MANNER THAT BEFITS SO MONUMENTAL AN OCCASION--!
SO LONG AS THE MEMORY OF MANKIND ENDURES, THIS SHALL BE ACCLAIMED AS THE GREATEST SINGLE FEAT IN RECORDED HISTORY!
THERE CAN BE NO DENYING!! THIS MOMENT SUPREME BELONGS TO HERCULES-- NOW--AND FOREVER!
WHAT BALLADS SHALL BE SUNG! WHAT LEGENDS SHALL BE TOLD! WHAT MEMORIES SHALL THIS GLORIOUS MOMENT EVOKE!!
KRRRAKKA-BOOM!

THEN, WITH THE EASE OF A MAN CASUALLY FLIPPING A CHEWING-GUM WRAPPER AWAY, THE TITAN FROM OLYMPUS HURLS THE GUTTED BRICK HOUSEFRONT AT THE NOW-WEAKENED THUNDER GOD--!
WHROOOM!
MY STRENGTH HAS FINALLY FAILED ME! BUT--MY ENCHANTED HAMMER SHALL SERVE TO KEEP THE WALL FROM ENGULFING ME!!
ONCE BEFORE THE WRATH OF ODIN CAUSED HALF MY POWER TO BE SHORN FROM MY LIMBS!* AM I NOW BEING PUNISHED SO AGAIN??
*AS SEEN, LO, THESE MANY MONTHS AGO-- BUT ONLY ODIN REMEMBERS WHEN!-- -- EMBARRASSED STAN.
EVEN WITH THE AID OF MY URU MALLET, I CAN NO LONGER BEAR THE INDESCRIBABLE PRESSURE--!
I MUST RELEASE IT SUDDENLY-- AND PRAY I CAN ROLL ASIDE IN TIME!
THOOOM!
BY THE GOLDEN GIRDLE OF VOLSTAGG-- I AM SAVED!
SAVED? NOT SO, DEFEATED ONE! NOT WHILST THY LIMBS HAVE TURNED TO JELLY--NOT WHILST I STILL AWAIT THY WORDS OF ABJECT SURRENDER!
I AM HELPLESS BEFORE HIM--AND HE KNOWS THIS FULL WELL! BUT I SHALL NEVER YIELD!
MAYHAP WHEN STRENGTH HAS DEPARTED, NATURAL CUNNING YET MAY SERVE!
SINCE THY STRENGTH HATH DESERTED THEE, HERCULES' ZEST FOR BATTLE IS GONE! THEREFORE, LET US PUT AN END TO THIS FARCE! PREPARE FOR THINE UNDOING, PITIFUL ONE!

BUT, ALTHOUGH KNOWING HE IS NO LONGER A MATCH FOR HERCULES, THE IMMORTAL AVENGER IS STILL GOD OF THUNDER--STILL A FIGHTER--TO THE END--!
THOR IS NOT DEFEATED YET!
BRAK
IT IS AS I FEARED! HE SEEMED NOT TO FEEL THE BLOW!

IF THAT IS ALL THE FORCE THOU CANST MUSTER--THE END SHALL BE SOONER THAN I THOUGHT!
UNHHHH--!

VALOR IN VICTORY COMES EASILY! BUT, HAS EVER MAN OR IMMORTAL BEEN SO VALOROUS IN DEFEAT AS THE SON OF ODIN AT THIS MOMENT--?
IF THIS IS TO BE MY FINAL HOUR, THEN LET IT BE CROWNED WITH GLORY! LET ME MAKE ONE LAST SUPREME EFFORT--!
SEE HOW THOU DOEST STRAIN TO LIFT YON VEHICLE! WHEN FIRST WE BATTLED, IT WOULD HAVE BEEN BUT A TRIFLING TASK FOR THEE!

NOW TO HURL IT AT--UNHHHHH TOO HEAVY--!
NO! NO I MUST NOT BEND BENEATH THE WEIGHT--NOT NOW--!

BUT, TRY AS HE MAY, THE GALLANT THUNDER GOD CANNOT PREVAIL AGAINST THE TONS OF STEEL WHICH HE HAD VAINLY TRIED TO HURL AT HIS SNEERING FOE--!
PERHAPS--'TIS BEST TO END THIS WAY! WITHOUT MY POWER--I AM USELESS!
NOW THAT MY LIMBS HAVE FAILED ME--NOTHING REMAINS--SAVE DEATH!

HOLD, GOD OF THUNDER! THOU SHALT NOT SO EASILY DEPRIVE ME OF MY VICTORY!
CHAK!

ON THY FEET, ASGARDIAN! MOUTH THE WORDS I AM WAITING TO HEAR! TELL HERCULES THAT THOR ABJECTLY SURRENDERS! SPEAK, VANQUISHED ONE!
NEVER! NOT WHILE BREATH REMAINS WITHIN ME! NOT WHILE LIFE ENDURES!

STILL THOU FIGHTEST ON?!! STILL THOU STRIKETH AT THY MASTER?!! THOU ART TRULY MAD!

AND THIS THEN SHALL BE THY PAEAN OF DEFEAT!

HE WON! HERCULES BEAT THOR!
WHAT A FIGHT!
SO! THE WORLD HAD BEEN WATCHING! 'TWAS TO HAVE BEEN EXPECTED! AND NOW, THE JACKALS GATHER 'ROUND THE LION!
WOTTA STORY! WHAT PICTURES! IT'LL BE THE GREATEST SENSATION SINCE D-DAY!
FROM NOW ON, THOR'LL BE A HAS-BEEN! THE CHAMP IS DEAD--LONG LIVE THE CHAMP!

OBLIVIOUS TO THE FALLEN THUNDER GOD, THE EXUBERANT CROWD MILLS AROUND THE SMILING HERCULES--CHEERING THE VICTOR, AS CROWDS HAVE DONE SINCE TIME IMMEMORIAL--!
HERCULES--YOU'RE THE GREATEST!
I GOTTA SHAKE HIS HAND--I JUST GOTTA!
YAY FOR HERCULES!
BUT THEN, ONE BREATHLESS FIGURE SHOULDERS HIS WAY THRU THE JOSTLING THRONG--
HERCULES--REMEMBER ME? I'M THE ONE WHO OFFERED YOU A MOVIE CONTRACT BEFORE!* THE OFFER STILL GOES, HANDSOME! WE'LL MAKE YOU FAMOUS!
YOU WILL MAKE HERCULES FAMOUS??!
*THEY MET IN THOR #125, TO BE EXACT!--STICKLER STAN!

THINK OF IT, BIG FELLA! YOUR OWN SWIMMING POOL! BEAUTIFUL STARLETS! FAN CLUBS! TV RESIDUALS!
I ACCEPT! THE WORLD MUST NOT BE DEPRIVED OF MY GREAT TALENT!

MAN! THAT CAT'S THE LIVIN' END! HE COMES ON LIKE GANGBUSTERS!
HE'S NO HANDSOMER THAN THOR--BUT THERE'S SOMETHING ABOUT HIM--HE'S SO DEVIL-MAY-CARE!

HERCULES--GONE! THE CROWD--DRIFTING AWAY... THEN IT'S TRUE--IT REALLY HAPPENED--!
I HAVE BEEN DEFEATED--AT LONG LAST!
AND NONE THERE ARE--WHO STAY BEHIND--WITH A LOSER--!

HEY, GANG--LOOK! THE THUNDER GOD'S BACK WITH US AGAIN! HOW ABOUT THAT?
HUH! IF YA ASK ME, HE SHOULDA STAYED IN BED!
FROM WHERE I SIT, HIS THUNDER SOUNDS MORE LIKE A SHAKY SQUEAK!

SO! IT HAS COME TO THIS! MIGHTY THOR IS NAUGHT BUT AN OBJECT OF RIDICULE FOR THE MASSES!
THOR! OH, THANK HEAVENS YOU'RE ALL RIGHT! AT LAST I'VE FOUND YOU!

YOU! WHY DO YOU REMAIN BEHIND? HAS VICTORIOUS HERCULES NO TIME FOR THEE NOW??
DON'T SAY THAT, MY DARLING! YOU KNOW IT'S YOU I LOVE! IT'S ALWAYS BEEN YOU! IT'S ONLY BEEN YOU!
I ACTED LIKE A FOOL! I ONLY WANTED TO MAKE YOU JEALOUS-- NOTHING MORE!

I'LL HEAR NO MORE! WHATEVER YOUR MOTIVES, YOU HAVE SET IN MOTION FORCES WHICH CANNOT NOW BE STOPPED!
DESTINY HATH DEALT US A MOST TRAGIC BLOW, MY BELOVED!
WH-WHAT DO YOU MEAN BY THAT?

I AM NO LONGER THE ONE I WAS! NO LONGER AM I WORTHY TO WEAR THE MANTLE OF THUNDER GOD! NO LONGER AM I WORTHY OF THEE, JANE FOSTER!
NOW MUST I LEAVE THEE! NEVER SHALL WE MEET AGAIN--UNTIL I CAN RE-GAIN MINE HONOR!
NO! YOU CAN'T--! I DON'T CARE THAT YOU WERE BEATEN--!
BUT THOR CARES! THOR MUST CARRY THE SCAR-- FOREVER!

SUDDENLY, A BOOMING VOICE THUNDERS IN JANE FOSTER'S BRAIN! THE VOICE OF ODIN, LORD OF ASGARD--A VOICE QUIVERING WITH DESPERATE PRIDE--!
MY SON WAS NOT BEATEN! HIS VICTORY WAS STOLEN FROM HIM--STOLEN BY A SHAMED AND REMORSEFUL FATHER!

HE FOUGHT LIKE THE TRUE SON OF ODIN--HE BORE HIS DEFEAT LIKE A GOD! BUT NOW--HE HATH NEED OF THEE! HE HATH DONE PENANCE ENOUGH! GO TO HIM, WOMAN!
I WILL! OH, I WILL!

SPECIAL BULLPEN NOTE:
DO NOT EVEN TRY TO GUESS WHAT OUR NEXT ISSUE WILL BE--!
SUFFICE IT TO SAY THAT IT SHALL EXCEED THY FONDEST HOPES, THY MOST EXTRAVAGANT EXPECTATIONS! WE HAVE SPOKEN!

TALES OF ASGARD, HOME OF THE MIGHTY NORSE GODS!
THE "SUMMONS!"
KNOW YOU, QUEEN ULA, MY MEN AND I ARE ON A ROYAL QUEST UNDER ORDERS OF LORDLY ODIN HIMSELF! YET, YOU HAVE DARED TO CAPTURE MY STEP-BROTHER, LOKI.!!
ONLY TO BRING YOU TO MY SIDE, MIGHTY THOR!
AM I NOT QUEEN OF THE FLYING TROLLS? THERE IS NOTHING ULA DOES NOT DARE!
SCRIPT: STAN LEE
ART: JACK KIRBY
INKING: V. COLLETTA
LETTERING: ARTIE SIMEK
SO BE IT!!
THOR--! ENOUGH TALK! LET ME BE FREED!

REMEMBER, GOD CF THUNDER, THIS IS THRYHEIM--THIS IS MY DOMAIN! 'TIS I WHO AM THE POWER HERE!

NAY, MY QUEEN! WHERE E'ER A TRUE WARRIOR OF ASGARD TRODS, 'TIS THERE THAT POWER REPOSES! NOW LET LOKI BE UNSHACKLED!

'TIS NO EMPTY THREAT I UTTER! MY WARRIORS ARE AS LIMITLESS AS THE SANDS ON THE SHORE!
YOU CANNOT REFUSE HER, THOR! YOU MUST SACRIFICE YOURSELF, FOR THE GOOD OF THE REST!
SILENCE, BASE LOKI! EVEN AT SUCH A MOMENT, YOU THINK ONLY OF YOURSELF! YOU SHAME THE NAME OF VALOR!

SUDDENLY, SILENTLY--UTTERLY WITHOUT WARNING--A SENSES-SHATTERING BURST OF ANTI-ENERGY FILLS THE AIR--A FLASH WHICH INSTANTLY FELLS THE LEGION OF FLYING TROLLS...
WHHT!

ONLY WE TWO STILL REMAIN CONSCIOUS! WHAT HAS BEFALLEN MUST TRULY BE A SIGN FROM OMNIPOTENT ODIN HIMSELF!
FASTER! FASTER! ONCE AWAY FROM THIS ACCURSED STONE BEEHIVE MY POWER WILL AGAIN RETURN TO ME!

IS THAT ALL THAT CONCERNS YOU, LOKI? DOES NAUGHT BUT THE THOUGHT OF POWER OCCUPY THY MIND?
ALL ELSE IS EMPTY-- MEANINGLESS! POWER IS ALL!

MEANWHILE, BACK AT THE VALIANT ODINSHIP, WE FIND...
FASTER, THOU LAGGARDS! ROW EVER FASTER! WE MUST RESCUE THOR!
AND WHY DOES YOUR BACK NOT BEND OVER YONDER OAR AS WELL, BLUSTERING VOLSTAGG?
I?? I MUST SAVE MY STRENGTH, KRODA! FOR I SHALL LEAD THE ATTACK UPON THE STONE HIVE!
THINK, THOU WITLESS OAF, HOW ONE BLISTER UPON THIS MIGHTY FINGER COULD LOSE AN ENTIRE BATTLE FOR ASGARD!
DO NOT FEAR, GALLANT VOLSTAGG--WE HAVE BLISTER OINTMENT AMONGST OUR STORES!
THEREFORE, AS ACTING CAPTAIN, IN THE ABSENCE OF THOR, I ORDER THEE TO ROW WITH THE OTHERS!
WILLINGLY DO I OBEY, LOYAL BALDER!
BUT, 'TIS TRULY A PITY THAT SUCH SEATS ARE BUILT FOR FAR LESSER MEN THAN MOUNTAINOUS VOLSTAGG!
HAVE A CARE, ENORMOUS ONE, LEST THOU JOSTLE HALF OUR CREW INTO THE SEA!
BUMBLING BUFFOON! THERE IS NO ROOM HERE FOR THEE!
LET THE ROWING DESIST! WE HAVE RETURNED!
MIGHTY THOR! THOU HAST RESCUED THY BROTHER! ODIN BE PRAISED!
RESCUED INDEED! 'TWAS THE MEREST ACCIDENT! ANY MIGHT HAVE DONE THE SAME!
MAYHAP--BUT THE HAND IS THOR'S THAT HOLDS THEE!

VOLSTAGG WAS BUT MOMENTS BEHIND THEE, THOR! HAD YOU NOT RESCUED LOKI, THE FLYING TROLLS WOULD HAVE ANSWERED TO ME! I WOULD HAVE CRUSHED THEM LIKE FLEAS!
ODDS BLOOD, BELLOWING ONE--IN TRUTH, THOU MIGHT HAVE TALKED THEM TO DEATH!
NONE BUT ODIN, THE ALL-WISE, COULD HAVE SAVED US!
FOR ONCE MY BROTHER SPEAKS THE TRUTH! ODIN DID IT FOR ME! THE LIFE OF LOKI IS TOO PRECIOUS TO BE PLACED IN JEOPARDY!

THE MIGHTY THOR
APPROVED BY THE COMICS CODE AUTHORITY
127 APR
MARVEL COMICS GROUP
12¢
IND.
"The HAMMER and The HOLOCAUST!"

THE MIGHTY THOR!
"THE HAMMER AND THE HOLOCAUST!"
THOR... WAIT! EVEN THOUGH HERCULES HAS DEFEATED YOU IN BATTLE... NOTHING HAS CHANGED BETWEEN US!
I.. I LOVE YOU AS MUCH AS EVER, MY DARLING...!
BEGONE, JANE FOSTER...!
YOU NO LONGER SPEAK TO MIGHTY THOR! INSTEAD, YOU SEE BEFORE YOU A HOLLOW MOCKERY OF HIM WHO HAD BEEN GOD OF THUNDER!
AS PUNISHMENT FOR MY RASH DEFIANCE OF HIS WILL, MY FATHER HATH STRIPPED ME OF HALF MY POWER! I KNOW NOT WHAT FURTHER INDIGNITY MAY AWAIT ME!
BUT, THE GUILT WAS MINE ALONE! SO MUST THE PENANCE BE MINE! NONE SHALL SHARE IT WITH ME!
POSSIBLY THE MOST MAGNIFICENT CHRONICLE OF THOR EVER PRESENTED, BY...
STAN LEE, WRITER
JACK KIRBY, ARTIST
VINCE COLLETTA, DELINEATOR
SAM ROSEN, LETTERER

NO! YOU CANNOT EXPECT ME TO FORSAKE YOU NOW... NOT WHEN YOU NEED ME THE MOST!
WHEN I SAW YOU DEFEATED BY HERCULES, I REALIZED HOW MUCH I TRULY LOVED YOU...!

SAY NO MORE! THOUGH THY WORDS ARE THE WORDS OF LOVE... THEY DO CARRY THE SEEDS OF PITY... PITY FOR THE FALLEN THOR!
HAVE I NOT BEEN HUMBLED ENOUGH? MUST I BECOME AN OBJECT OF SYMPATHY, AS WELL?

NO! BY THE POWER WHICH STILL IS MINE, I SHALL FLEE FROM THE SIGHT OF MORTAL EYES! I SHALL ENDURE WHATEVER FATE AWAITS ME... ALONE!
EVEN IN DEFEAT, THERE MUST BE A FINAL DIGNITY!

BUT, WHAT OF ME?? WHAT IF YOU SHOULD NEVER RETURN? HOW COULD I BEAR TO SPEND THE REST OF MY LIFE WITHOUT YOU?
'TIS BETTER THUS! REMEMBER ME AS I WAS, MY BELOVED... REMEMBER THE BRIEF HAPPINESS WE HAVE KNOWN...

THOR! MY DARLING... COME BACK...!
FOR ONE BRIEF, FLEETING INSTANT OF ETERNITY, A GOD HATH DARED TO LOVE A MORTAL! TILL THE UNIVERSE CRUMBLES, MY HEART IS EVER THINE!
LET THAT BE OUR EPITAPH... AND OUR GLORY!
2.

MEANWHILE, AS THE VICTORIOUS HERCULES IS EN ROUTE TO HOLLYWOOD TO STAR IN A MOTION PICTURE PICTURE SERIES BASED UPON HIS EXPLOITS, WE TURN TO STARDUST STUDIOS, WHERE FEVERISH PREPARATIONS ARE NOW IN PROGRESS...

IMAGINE THE NEW PRODUCER DESIGNING HIMSELF AN OFFICE LIKE THIS! HE MUST THINK HE'S SOME KINDA TIN GOD OR SOMETHIN'!

BOY, THIS TAKES THE CAKE! THEY'RE REDESIGNING THE WHOLE BLAMED STUDIO JUST ON ACCOUNTA THE NEW HERCULES MOVIE!

YEAH! THEY EVEN HIRED A SPECIAL PRODUCER FOR THE PICTURE... SOME NUT NAMED PLUTO!

DIDJA GET A LOOK AT 'IM YET? FIRST TIME I SAW HIM, I THOUGHT HE WAS WEARIN' A FRIGHT MASK!
SPEAKIN' OF FRIGHT MASKS.. THAT CRAZY GIZMO YOU'RE JOCKEYIN' INTO HIS OFFICE MUSTA BEEN LEFT OVER FROM LAST YEAR'S HALLOWEEN PARTY!
I WONDER WHERE THEY DUG PLUTO UP FROM? I NEVER HEARD OF 'IM WORKIN' AROUND THE STUDIOS BEFORE!
THE WAY I HEARD IT, HE CONVINCED MR. STARDUST THAT HE WAS AN EXPERT ON THE LEGENDS OF HERCULES! HE MUST'VE GIVEN 'EM A REAL SNOW JOB!
YOU CAN SAY THAT AGAIN!

SILENCE! YOU HAVE BEEN ENGAGED TO WORK... NOT TO SPEAK DISPARAGINGLY OF YOUR BETTERS! HOW COULD YOU EVEN HOPE TO FATHOM THE TRUTH ABOUT ONE SUCH AS I??
S-SORRY, MR. PLUTO! NO OFFENSE MEANT! WE'LL GET RIGHT TO WORK!
NO WONDER STARDUST HIRED 'IM! WHO'D HAVE THE NERVE TO SAY "NO" TO A CREEP LIKE THAT?

EXACTLY SIXTY MINUTES LATER, PLUTO SPEAKS AGAIN..!
GET OUT, ALL OF YOU! YOU ARE DISMISSED! I WISH TO BE ALONE NOW!
BUT STAND BY FOR FURTHER ORDERS! YOU ARE NOT TO LEAVE THE STUDIO GROUNDS! NOW GO!
YES SIR! RIGHT AWAY! Y-YOU WON'T HAVETA TELL US TWICE!

THEN, ONCE ALONE IN HIS HAUNTINGLY STRANGE, SECURELY LOCKED OFFICE, PLUTO MAKES A MYSTIC PASS WITH HIS HAND, AS THE MOLECULES IN THE AIR SEEM SUDDENLY TO REARRANGE THEMSELVES INTO A FANTASTIC, FLAMING IMAGE...
SPEAK, SLAVE! HOW GOES MY UNDERWORLD DOMAIN IN MY ABSENCE? DO THE FIRES STILL BURN?
ALL IS WELL, MASTER... AS IT HAS EVER BEEN... AS IT SHALL EVER BE!
NAY, SLAVE... FOR THE FIRST TIME IN AGES... THERE SHALL BE A CHANGE! NOW HEED THE WORDS OF PLUTO..!

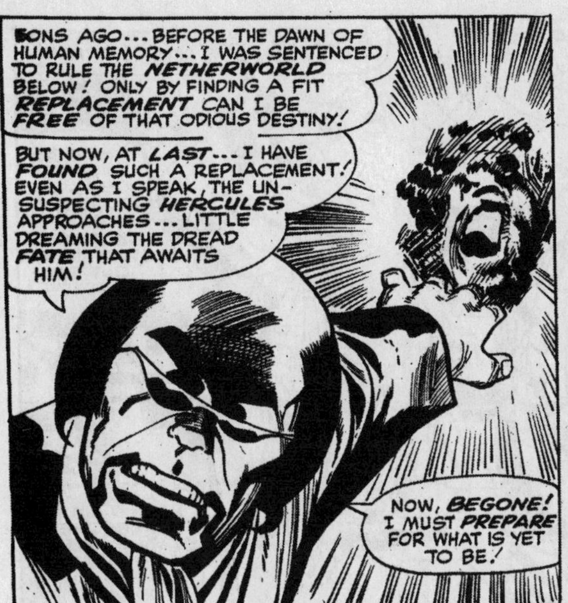
EONS AGO... BEFORE THE DAWN OF HUMAN MEMORY... I WAS SENTENCED TO RULE THE NETHERWORLD BELOW! ONLY BY FINDING A FIT REPLACEMENT CAN I BE FREE OF THAT ODIOUS DESTINY!
BUT NOW, AT LAST... I HAVE FOUND SUCH A REPLACEMENT! EVEN AS I SPEAK, THE UN-SUSPECTING HERCULES APPROACHES... LITTLE DREAMING THE DREAD FATE THAT AWAITS HIM!
NOW, BEGONE! I MUST PREPARE FOR WHAT IS YET TO BE!

THUS DO FORCES BEYOND HUMAN KEN WEAVE A MIGHTY WEB OF WONDER! BUT NOW, WE MUST TURN ONCE MORE TO THE NOBLEST IMMORTAL OF ALL...
NO LONGER DO I HAVE STOMACH FOR THE STIFLING CITY!
I MUST FLY TO A PLACE FIT FOR A GOD TO THINK!

FOR, THOUGH MY POWER HATH BEEN HALVED... IT IS STILL A FORCE THAT CAN ALTER WORLDS!
BUT, AS SURELY AS NIGHT DOTH FOLLOW DAY, I HAVE REACHED A TURNING POINT... A MOMENT OF GRAND DECISION!

I MUST YET DECIDE WHAT USE TO MAKE OF MY REMAINING POWER..
OR, SHALL I CAST OFF THE MANTLE OF THUNDER GOD? HAS IT BEEN PROVEN THAT MIGHTY THOR HATH BEEN FOUND.. UNWORTHY?

AND SO, SILENTLY SEATED UPON A LONELY PROMON-TORY, THE SON OF ODIN SEARCHES HIS SOUL... WRACKED BY DOUBTS, PLAGUED BY UNCERTAINTY, TORTURED BY CONSCIENCE..!
TRULY, THERE CAN BE NO MORE ANGUISHED SPIRIT, THAN THAT OF A GOD IN TORMENT..!

BUT, THE INDESCRIBABLE AGONY OF THOR IS MATCHED BY THAT OF LORDLY ODIN, WHO CAN BEAR TO OBSERVE THE SIGHT NO LONGER FROM HIS VANTAGE POINT IN FABLED ASGARD---
ENOUGH! I CAN ENDURE THE TORTURED VISAGE OF MY ERRANT SON NO MORE!
5.

WHAT TOWERING MADNESS POSSESSED ME??! TO THINK THAT ODIN WOULD THUS BETRAY THE FLESH OF HIS FLESH!
NAY, SIRE! PUNISHMENT IN THE NAME OF JUSTICE IS NEVER BETRAYAL!
FURTHER-MORE, 'TWAS NOT THEE... BUT SEIDRING WHO METED OUT THY SENTENCE!
I DID IT WITH THE AWESOME ODIN POWER WHICH THOU DIDST BESTOW UPON ME!

EVEN MIGHTY ODIN HAD NOT THE HEART TO DEAL SO HARSHLY WITH HIS SON... SO HE GAVE ME THE POWER!

AND, IN HIS MONUMENTAL SORROW, HE HATH FORGOTTEN THAT I STILL POSSESS HIS ODIN POWER... THE GREATEST POWER OF ALL!
SEIDRING! TO MY SIDE! I HAVE A MISSION FOR THEE!

NAY, ETERNAL ONE! I OBEY THEE NO LONGER! 'TIS I WHO NOW POSSESS THE POWER!
YOU DARE...??!!

VERILY, MY LORD... I DARE!
KNOW YOU THEN THAT ODIN CALLS THEE TRAITOR!
THY NAME SHALL LIVE IN INFAMY, SO LONG AS MEMORY ENDURES!
6.

THOUGH THE POWER NOW IS THINE... THE HERITAGE BE ODIN'S! STRIKE AS THOU WILT... I FIGHT WHILST THERE BE BREATH WITHIN ME!
EMPTY WORDS, MY LORDS! NONE CAN WITHSTAND THE ODIN POWER... NAY, NOT EVEN HE FOR WHOM IT WAS NAMED!

IT CANNOT END THUS! THOU ART NOT FIT TO RULE! POWER, WITHOUT CONSCIENCE, MUST BE ITS OWN UNDOING!

NOBLE WORDS, MY LORD! A PITY THEY COULD NOT STEM THE FURY OF THE ODIN POWER!
THY REIGN IS ENDED! THE ERA OF SEIDRING, THE ALL-POWERFUL, HAS NOW BEGUN!

SEIDRING! WHAT FATE HATH BEFALLEN OMNI-POTENT ODIN?
BACK, BALDER! LOWER THY HEAD! PAY HOMAGE TO THE NEW OVERLORD OF ASGARD!

ODIN IS DETHRONED! I AM THE POWER NOW! SWEAR ALLEGIANCE TO SEIDRING, OR FACE THE FURY OF THE ODIN POWER!
ALLEGIANCE TO SUCH AS THEE?? I WOULD SUFFER DAMNATION FIRST!
7.

AND, EVEN AS BRAVE BALDER HURLS HIS CHALLENGING CRY OF DEFIANCE, A BROODING FIGURE SLOWLY STRIDES THE GLEAMING RAINBOW BRIDGE TO ASGARD...
I MUST RETURN TO FACE MY FATHER! NO MATTER WHAT THE COST, LET ME ACQUIT MYSELF WITH HONOR!

ON AND ON, ACROSS THE SEEMINGLY-ENDLESS SPAN, WALKS THE GOD OF THUNDER, UNTIL AT LAST HE REACHES THE TOWERING GATES OF ETERNAL ASGARD, ONLY TO FIND...
HEIMDALL! GUARDIAN OF THE BRIDGE! IMPRISONED IN A BLOCK OF ETHEREAL FORCE!
TURN BACK, NOBLE THOR! EVEN THY MIGHT CANNOT SAVE ASGARD FROM WHAT AWAITS THEE BEYOND THE GATES!

BUT, THE SON OF ODIN DOES NOT TURN BACK! HIS HEART HEAVILY POUNDING WITHIN HIM, THE GOD OF THUNDER STORMS INTO THE STRANGELY SILENT CELESTIAL CITY...
ONLY MY FATHER'S ODIN POWER CAN CONTROL THE PROPERTIES OF ETHEREAL FORCE!
BUT, SURELY THE ALL-WISE WOULD NEVER TREAT FAITHFUL HEIMDALL IN SUCH MANNER!

WARRIORS OF ASGARD! IMPRISONED BY ETHEREAL ENERGY BANDS! WHAT MADNESS IS THIS??
TURN BACK, GOD OF THUNDER... LEST THOU TOO SUFFER OUR FATE!
WHAT HATH TRANSPIRED FOR ODIN TO RELEASE SUCH FURY??
'TIS NOT THY FATHER'S DOING, MIGHTY ONE! HE SUFFERS A FATE NO BETTER THAN OURS!
8

WITH THOSE FATEFUL WORDS RINGING IN HIS EARS, THE THUNDER GOD THROWS CAUTION TO THE WINDS, RACING TO THE HEART OF THE CITY, UNTIL HE SEES...
BALDER! THOU TOO ART FROZEN INTO IMMOBILITY, AS ARE THY COMRADES AT ARMS! BY WHOSE HAND, LOYAL ONE? WHO HATH DONE THIS DIRE DEED ??
IF ANY HARM HATH BEFALLEN NOBLE ODIN..!

MORE THAN HARM HAS COME TO THY FATHER, THUNDER GOD! HE HATH LOST A UNIVERSE!
A RING OF CELESTIAL FLAME.... DRAWING CLOSER TO ME!
AND THAT VOICE! A VOICE I HAVE HEARD BEFORE! A VOICE MY FATHER ONCE DID TRUST...

...THE VOICE OF SEIDRING, THE MERCILESS!
AY, SON OF ODIN... 'TIS I WHO NOW RULE ASGARD ... AND HENCE, THE WORLD! YOU HAVE SEEN THE FATE OF THOSE WHO DEFIED ME... BUT, YOU NEED NOT SHARE THAT FATE..!

SWEAR ALLEGIANCE TO ME, AND THOU SHALT BE MY OWN RIGHT ARM!
ODIN DOES NOT DESERVE THY LOYALTY! DID HE NOT HUMBLE THEE BEFORE HERCULES? HATH HE NOT STRIPPED THEE OF HALF THY POWER?
TRUE, SEIDRING! MY FATHER HATH DONE ALL THAT... AND MORE! AND THIS IS MY REPLY..

MAY THY FLAMES CONSUME ME THROUGHOUT ETERNITY, ERE I TURN MY BACK UPON HIM WHO HATH SIRED ME... UPON ODIN, THE TRUE RIGHTFUL MASTER OF ALL!
FOOL! THOU HAST SEALED THY DOOM! THE FLAMES WHICH SURROUND THEE ARE BUT AN ILLUSION, CREATED TO TEST THY METTLE...
BUT NOW... THE ODIN POWER WHICH THOU SHALT FACE WILL BE NO MERE ILLUSION..!
9.

AND, IN HOLLYWOOD, A FANTASTICALLY GARBED, BREATH-TAKINGLY BEAUTIFUL FEMALE ENTERS THE OFFICE OF THE ONE CALLED PLUTO...
COME IN! I HAVE BEEN WAITING FOR YOU!
OF COURSE! DO NOT MEN WAIT FOR ME ALWAYS?

AND WHAT OF MY COSTUME? DOES IT SUIT THE ROLE YOU WISH ME TO PLAY?
INDEED! IT TRULY BEFITS THE ONE WHO IS QUEEN OF THE AMAZONS!
ARE YOU CERTAIN YOU HAVE REHEARSED YOUR PART TO PERFECTION?

DO NOT FEAR! I SHALL NOT FAIL!
HERCULES CANNOT HELP BUT LOSE HIS HEART TO ME!
AND, HE SHALL REGRET IT...FOREVER-MORE!

TRUE... TRUE! BUT, YOU ARE MERELY ONE SEGMENT OF MY MASTER PLAN!
THIS INNOCENT-LOOKING CONTRACT IS STILL ANOTHER... AN EQUALLY DIABOLICAL GAMBIT!

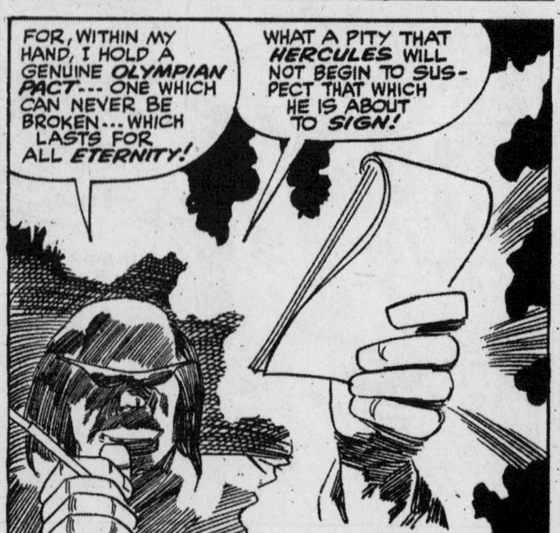
FOR, WITHIN MY HAND, I HOLD A GENUINE OLYMPIAN PACT--- ONE WHICH CAN NEVER BE BROKEN...WHICH LASTS FOR ALL ETERNITY!
WHAT A PITY THAT HERCULES WILL NOT BEGIN TO SUSPECT THAT WHICH HE IS ABOUT TO SIGN!

BUT, EVEN AS THE MIGHTY-MUSCLED SON OF ZEUS INNOCENTLY APPROACHES THE MYSTERIOUS STUDIO, WE CANNOT AFFORD TO MISS THE SPECTACULAR TABLEAU WHICH AWAITS US IN ASGARD...
HOW CAN YOU EXPECT TO ATTACK ONE WHO POSSESS THE ODIN POWER?
SEE HOW EASILY I DISTORT THE FABRIC OF SPACE ITSELF TO DEFLECT THY BLOW!
NO MATTER, EVIL ONE...
.. DO AS THOU WILT... THOR FIGHTS ON!
10

THE SON OF ODIN HATH KNOWN THE BITTER TASTE OF DEFEAT IN THE PAST... BUT HE HATH NEVER THE IGNOMINY OF SURRENDER!
THEN THAT SHALL BE MY GREATEST TRIUMPH! NEVER SHALL I REST UNTIL I HAVE WRENCHED THE WORD "ENOUGH" FROM THY TREMBLING LIPS!

THEN, WITH A CASUAL GESTURE, THE EVIL SEIDRING DIRECTS A POTENT RAY INTO THE COSMOS... CATCHING A TRIO OF PLANETOIDS LIKE FISH IN A NET...!

...AS, WITH STILL ANOTHER DISDAINFUL MOTION, HE DIRECTS THEM... WITH UNABATED SPEED... AT THE HAPLESS GOD OF THUNDER...!
AFTER BUT A FEW MOMENTS' SAMPLING OF MY LIMITLESS POWER, ARROGANT ONE, THE WORDS OF SURRENDER WILL SEEK THY LIPS WITH MOST AGONIZING SWIFTNESS!

BUT, THE IMMORTAL AVENGER DARTS, LEAPS, SWERVES, RACES... FRANTICALLY ELUDING THE DEADLY SPACE MISSILES... FIGHTING TILL THE END... AND PLANNING ALL THE WHILE...!
IF I DROP TO THE GROUND NOW, MAYHAP FORTUNE WILL FAVOR ME...!

UNEXPECTEDLY HURLING HIMSELF ONTO THE COLD MARBLE FLOOR, THE PRINCE OF ASGARD BARELY ESCAPES THE CATACLYSMIC IMPACT OF THE THREE METEORITES AS THEY DEAFENINGLY HURTLE INTO EACH OTHER!
11.

I THANK THEE, GOD OF THUNDER, FOR PROVIDING ME SUCH SPORT!

AND NOW, LET THE GAME CONTINUE...
IS THERE NO END TO THIS MADNESS?? A STRANGE GLOBULAR SUBSTANCE BURSTS FORTH FROM THE GROUND BENEATH ME...!

THEN, BEFORE THE VALIANT ASGARDIAN CAN MAKE ANOTHER MOVE, A MYSTIC, IRRESISTIBLE FORCE PULLS HIM INTO THE CENTER OF THE FANTASTIC GLOBULE!

I'M BEING WHIRLED ABOUT... IN A VORTEX OF LIQUIFIED WOLFBANE!
USING THE POWER HE HATH STOLEN FROM MY FATHER, SEIDRING TOYS WITH ME AT WILL!

THOU CANST NOT BREAK FREE OF YON GLOBULE.. AND LO, THE WOLFBANE SHALL DRAIN THE LAST REMAINING BREATH FROM THY BODY!
THEREFORE, THOU HAST NO CHOICE BUT TO SURRENDER!

NEVER, THOU BASEST OF VILLAINS!!
THOUGH THIS BREATH BE MINE LAST... I SAY THEE... NEVER!
12.

BUT, NO SOONER HAS THOR HURLED HIS DEFIANT WORDS BACK AT SEIDRING, THAN THE DEADLY BUBBLE BURSTS... UNABLE TO CONTAIN THE DYNAMIC FORCE OF THE THUNDER GOD, WHO HAS NEVER CEASED STRUGGLING WITHIN!
I'M FREE!! THE FURY OF THE GLOBULE HATH SPENT ITSELF!

WHAT MANNER OF BEING ART THOU? KNOWING FULL WELL THAT NAUGHT CAN EQUAL THE SUPREME ODIN POWER, STILL THOU FIGHTEST ON!
AND YET, THERE CAN BE BUT ONE RESULT...
NOW, THUNDER GOD... PREPARE FOR THY DOOM!

A THOUSAND TIMES NAY, SCION OF DARKNESS! I PREPARE FOR BATTLE... AS I HAVE EVER DONE!
THE POWER IS THINE... BUT THE CAUSE IS MINE! MY HAMMER STRIKES FOR JUSTICE!

SO SAYING, THE RAGING, RAMPAGING GOD OF THUNDER SWINGS HIS URU MALLET AS ONLY THE MIGHTY THOR CAN... SHATTERING ALL ABOUT HIM, AND HURLING THE FRAGMENTS AT HIS AWE-STRICKEN FOE...!

BUT, STILL THE ODIN POWER IS SEIDRING'S... AND, WITH THE MEREST FLICK OF A FINGER, THE EVIL USURPER CREATES AN IMPENETRABLE CRYSTAL SHIELD ABOUT HIM, WHEREIN HE STANDS, SECURE FROM ANY AND ALL HARM!
DO THY WORST, ACCURSED ONE! THE ULTIMATE ANSWER SHALL YET BE MINE!

NO MATTER WHAT THE POWER... NO MATTER WHAT THE THREAT... THIS DO I SAY UNTO THEE... THOU SHALT NEVER RULE HALLOWED ASGARD!
WHAT!! THOU DARE, SPEAK THUS TO ME??!

VERILY... I DARE!
STILL AM I GOD OF THUNDER AND LIGHTNING! STILL DO I WIELD MINE HAMMER!
WHOO OM!

MOVING WITH DAZZLING SPEED, MIGHTY THOR CAUSES A SUDDEN BURST OF LIGHTNING... SO ELECTRIFYING ... SO INTENSE... THAT THE SINISTER SEIDRING IS TEMPORARILY BLINDED BY ITS BRILLIANCE...
THE PAINFUL BRIGHTNESS... I CANNOT SEE!

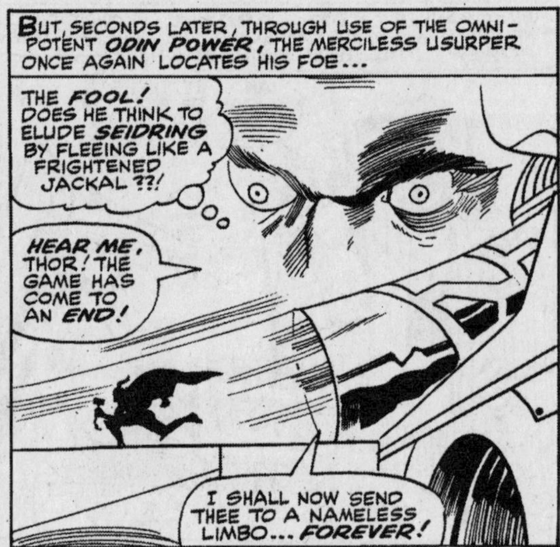
BUT, SECONDS LATER, THROUGH USE OF THE OMNIPOTENT ODIN POWER, THE MERCILESS USURPER ONCE AGAIN LOCATES HIS FOE...
THE FOOL! DOES HE THINK TO ELUDE SEIDRING BY FLEEING LIKE A FRIGHTENED JACKAL ??!
HEAR ME, THOR! THE GAME HAS COME TO AN END!
I SHALL NOW SEND THEE TO A NAMELESS LIMBO... FOREVER!

BUT, THE MIGHTIEST OF AVENGERS WAS NOT RUNNING IN AIMLESS PANIC...
THE ODIN SWORD AT LAST! IF I CAN BUT TOUCH ITS ENCHANTED HILT..!
FOR HERE, IN THE GREATEST CHAMBER OF THE PALACE ROYAL, REPOSES THE MOST AWESOME WEAPON IN ALL THE UNIVERSE...
14

REALIZING WHAT THOR'S *OBJECTIVE* IS, SEIDRING FEELS THE ICY PANGS OF FEAR FOR THE FIRST TIME, AS HE STRIKES WILDLY... DESPERATELY...

I DARE NOT UNLEASH A MAJOR BLOW, FOR FEAR OF TOUCHING YON *ODIN SWORD!*

AS ALL OF ASGARD KNOWS FULL WELL, WHEN FALLS THE *ODIN SWORD,* THE COSMOS ITSELF SHALL *VANISH!*

THUS I STRIKE THE THUNDER GOD WITH NOTHING STRONGER THAN A CAREFULLY AIMED BOLT OF *ENERGY!*

BUT, THOUGH WEAKENED TO THE POINT OF FINAL COLLAPSE, *STILL* THE SON OF ODIN WILL NOT YIELD...

I CANNOT STOP *NOW!* CANNOT WALLOW IN DEFEAT SO NEAR TO *VICTORY!*

I *MUST* REACH THE SWORD... THOUGH IT COST ME MY VERY *LIFE!*

AND THEN, AS THE CONFUSED, FEARFUL SEIDRING WATCHES IN MOUNTING PANIC, NOT DARING TO LAUNCH A NEW ATTACK UPON ONE SO CLOSE TO THE *ODIN SWORD,* THOR MAKES HIS MOVE...!

BY THE TOWERING SPIRES OF ASGARD...

MAY ODIN GRANT THAT I DO NOT FAIL!

AND THEN... AT LAST... THE PRIZE IS *WON!*

SEIDRING... HEED MY WORDS!

RETURN THE *ODIN POWER,* OR I *DROP* THE GREAT SWORD!

THOU KNOWEST FULL WELL WHAT SUCH A MOVE WOULD *MEAN!* AND KNOW YOU THIS... I HAVE THE WILL TO *DO* IT!

DECIDE, EVIL ONE! RETURN THE POWER TO MY NOBLE FATHER... OR ALL SHALL *PERISH!*

I DO NOT UTTER IDLE WORDS! WHAT ASGARDIAN WOULD NOT PREFER *DEATH* TO BEING RULED BY SUCH AS *THEE??!*

YOU CHOOSE NOT TO SPEAK! THEN MUST THE SWORD BE DROPPED! LET THIS MOMENT BE UPON *THY* HEAD, TRAITOR... FOR ALL ETERNITY

NO! NO! DO NOT *DROP* IT! THE VICTORY IS *THINE!* I YIELD! SEIDRING *YIELDS!*

IF THE *ODIN POWER* CANNOT DEFEAT ONE LONE WARRIOR.. THEN TRULY IT DOTH NOT MERIT SO MANY LIVES!

'TWAS NOT MERELY ONE LONE WARRIOR.. THOU DIDST BATTLE WITH *THOR!*

THOU MUST STAND AWAY FROM YON SWORD! THE SLIGHTEST JAR... THE SMALLEST MOVE... COULD SPELL DISASTER!
LET THE POWER BE ODIN'S ONCE MORE! SEIDRING YIELDS! THE BATTLE IS ENDED!

AND THEN, A MAJESTIC FIGURE APPEARS BEFORE THEIR EYES..BATHED IN AN AURA OF SHIMMERING, CRACKLING FORCE...!
THE POWER IS MINE ONCE AGAIN! SO BE IT!
ODIN!!

GET THEE FROM MINE SIGHT, THOU BASE BETRAYER!
TIME ENOW TO DEAL WITH THEE LATER! FOR TRULY, THERE BE NO PLACE IN THE UNIVERSE FOR THEE TO HIDE FROM MINE VENGEANCE!
VERILY, IT DOTH GRIEVE MY HEART TO REMEMBER HOW ONCE I HELD HIM IN HIGHEST ESTEEM!

BUT, WHAT OF THOR? WHAT OF HIM WHO IS MY SON?

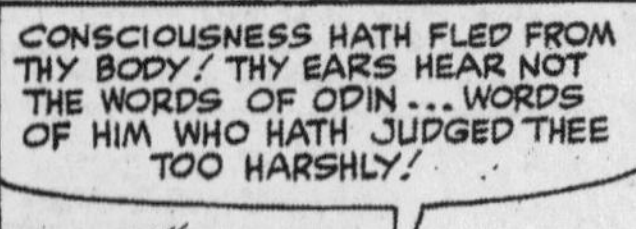
CONSCIOUSNESS HATH FLED FROM THY BODY! THY EARS HEAR NOT THE WORDS OF ODIN... WORDS OF HIM WHO HATH JUDGED THEE TOO HARSHLY!

THOUGH I AM SAID TO BE ALL-WISE IN ALL MATTER OF THINGS... MY WISDOM FLED WHEN I TURNED AGAINST THEE... MY SON!

FOR, ABOVE ALL ELSE, I HOLD THIS TRUE...
THOU ART THE NOBLEST ASGARDIAN OF ALL!
NEXT ISSUE:
THE SECRET OF PLUTO!
--SO BE IT!
16

TALES OF ASGARD, HOME OF THE MIGHTY NORSE GODS
"THE MEANING OF... RAGNAROK!"
MIGHTY THOR AND HIS HARDY BAND OF ARGONAUTS HAVE BEEN SUMMONED BACK TO ASGARD BY IMPERIAL ORDER OF THE ALL-WISE ODIN! AFTER A PERILOUS VOYAGE IN SEARCH OF THE FORCES OF EVIL WHICH THREATEN THE GOLDEN REALM, THEY LEARN AT LAST THAT THE DEADLY DANGER IS TO BE FOUND IN ASGARD ITSELF!
HEED YOU THE WORDS OF VOLLA, THE PROPHETESS! BEWARE! THE DAY OF RAGNAROK DRAWS EVER CLOSER!
SCRIPT: STAN LEE
PENCILLING: JACK KIRBY
DELINEATION: VINCE COLLETTA
LETTERING: ARTIE SIMEK
WE HAVE SPOKEN!!
1

RAGAROK! THE VERY WORD HAS THE POWER TO MAKE IMMORTALS TREMBLE! RAGNAROK! THE MOST DREADED DANGER OF ALL TIME! RAGNAROK! THAT WHICH HAS BEEN PREDICTED! THAT WHICH FORCE IN ALL THE UNIVERSE CAN PREVENT! SUCH IS--RAGNAROK!!!
AT LAST, OMNIPOTENT ODIN HATH CONFESSED THE TRUE REASON HE DISPATCHED US UPON OUR QUEST!
WE HAD BEEN TOO LONG WITHOUT BATTLE--TOO LONG WITHOUT PURPOSE! OUR TEMPERS WERE FRAYED--OUR SWORD EDGES BLUNTED!
'TIS TRUE, GOD OF THUNDER! A WARRIOR WITH NO MISSION IS LIKE UNTO A SHIP WITH NO RUDDER!
STAY YOUR TONGUES! THE PROPHETESS BEGINS TO SPEAK! 'TIS RAGNAROK WHICH MOST CONCERNS US NOW!

LET ALL BE SILENT! BY THE POWER OF PROPHECY WHICH I HAVE BEQUEATHED HER, LO, THOSE MANY AGES AGO--VOLLA SHALL GIVE VOICE!
I COMMAND THE VAPORS OF TIME TO RISE ABOUT ME!! LET THEIR MYSTICAL MISTS ENGULF US ALL! LET THE FUTURE STAND THUS REVEALED! LET NO ONE MOVE! LET NONE BREAK THE SOLEMN SPELL!
SWIRL, SHADOWY VAPORS!! NOW SHALL WE SEE WHAT IS TO BE!

SLOWLY--SLOWLY--THE MURKY MISTS BEGIN TO CLEAR--AS THE FIRST SIGNS OF RAGNAROK BECOME DIMLY VISIBLE! THE LIGHT FROM THE STARS BEGINS TO FADE, WHILE SOUL-SEARING FROST AND NEVER-ENDING STORM COVER THE GOLDEN LAND--!
ALL THAT YOU SHALL BEHOLD, IMMORTALS OF ASGARD, HAS BEEN PROPHESIED!! NOW OBSERVE YOUR FUTURE--AND TREMBLE!

GOADED BY NAMELESS FEAR--BY AN EVER-GROWING DREAD OF CERTAIN DOOM, FRIEND TURNS AGAINST FRIEND, BROTHER AGAINST BROTHER, IN A SENSELESS ORGY OF SAVAGE COMBAT--!

AS CHAOS AND CARNAGE ENVELOP THE REALM; AS A FURY AKIN TO MADNESS SWEEPS THE VERY SOUL OF ASGARD; THERE ARE THOSE WHO CRUMBLE BENEATH THE STRAIN--WHO JOIN THE RANKS OF THE FORCES OF EVIL--LEADING THEM IN ENDLESS ARRAY ACROSS THE SWEEPING SPAN OF *BIFROST,* THE RADIANT RAINBOW BRIDGE--!

THIS THEN IS THE ULTIMATE BETRAYAL--THE ULTIMATE ACT OF TREASON! BUT, SINCE THE WORLD BEGAN, THERE HAS NEVER BEEN A PROVOCATION SUCH AS THIS--THERE HAS NEVER BEEN A DAY SUCH AS THE DAY OF--*RAGNARAK!*

BUT, SEEING THE DREADED DENIZENS OF EVIL AS THEY STREAM TOWARDS ASGARD IN EVER-INCREASING NUMBER, THE HANDFUL WHOSE LOYALTY HAS NEVER WAVERED *DESTROYS* THE LAST LINK BETWEEN MAN AND IMMORTAL--DESTROYS THE HALLOWED *RAINBOW BRIDGE!*

FIRST TO MEET THE IRRESISTIBLE ATTACK IS FAITHFUL *HEIMDALL,* WHOSE LAST KNOWN ACT OF DEVOTION IS TO SOUND THE *ALARM*--BEFORE HE IS SWALLOWED UP FOREVER IN THE INSANE PHANTASMAGORIA OF BATTLE--!

WHILST THE MIGHTY GOD OF THUNDER, FIGHTING AS NEVER BEFORE, LEADS THE FLOWER OF ASGARD'S IMMORTAL WARRIORS IN AN ATTACK DESTINED TO SHATTER THE VERY FABRIC OF TIME AND SPACE!

IN THE NAME OF OMNIPOTENT ODIN--IN THE NAME OF ETERNAL ASGARD--BY THE POWER OF MY HAMMER--FOR THE GLORY OF OUR CAUSE--ONWARRRRD--TO VICTORY!

IT IS THEN THAT THE TWO SONS OF ODIN--THE GOD OF THUNDER AND THE PRINCE OF EVIL--MEET IN DEADLY COMBAT--FOR THE LAST TIME--AS THE WORLD ABOUT THEM IS CONSUMED BY BATTLE--!

FOR, THERE CAN BE NO VICTORY--THERE CAN BE NO SURVIVORS--THERE CAN BE NAUGHT BUT THE DISSOLUTION OF THE LAND WHERE IMMORTALS HAVE DWELLED!

--UNTIL, AT LAST, ALL ASGARD TREMBLES UNDER THE GREATEST UPHEAVAL EVER KNOWN--AS THE SEETHING AND SWELLING OF THE MIGHTY OCEANS SIGNAL THE COMING OF THE FINAL ENEMY--THE ULTIMATE DESTROYER--
5

AS LO, THERE SHALL APPEAR THE MIDGARD SERPENT--PROCLAIMING THE DAY OF RAGNAROK!! RAGNAROK--THE TIME THE GODS THEMSELVES SHALL PERISH! RAGNAROK--THE END OF THE WORLD!!
NEXT: THE SENSES-STAGGERING SPECTACLE THAT NONE BUT MIGHTY MARVEL WOULD DARE TO ATTEMPT--
"AFTERMATH!"

THE MIGHTY
THOR
APPROVED BY THE COMICS CODE AUTHORITY
128
MAY
MARVEL COMICS GROUP
12¢
IND.
GOD OF THUNDER and SON OF ZEUS
FACE
"THE POWER OF PLUTO!"

THE MIGHTY THOR!
"THE POWER OF PLUTO!"
AT LAST, MIGHTY THOR HAS REDEEMED HIMSELF IN THE EYES OF HIS ROYAL FATHER, ODIN, BY DEFEATING THE EVIL SEIDRING! BUT, EVEN A GOD CAN BE INJURED BY BOLTS OF FUNDAMENTAL ENERGY SUCH AS THOSE WHICH THE DESPERATE TRAITOR HAS HURLED AT THE IMMORTAL AVENGER--!
LET SILENCE REIGN! THE GOD OF THUNDER DOTH TAKE HIS REST!! BY ORDER OF IMPERIAL ODIN!
HE SLEEPS! 'TIS GOOD! SOON, THE STRENGTH WHICH IS HIS BIRTHRIGHT SHALL RETURN TO YON NOBLE BODY!
CONCEIVED IN GRANDEUR AND PRODUCED IN GLORY, BY:
STAN LEE, WRITER
JACK KIRBY, PENCILLER
VINCE COLLETTA, INKER
ARTIE SIMEK, LETTERER
VERILY, WE HAVE SPOKEN!
1

LATER, THE MOST REGAL PRESENCE IN ALL THE CELESTIAL REALM ENTERS THE HEAVILY-GUARDED CHAMBER...
HOW FARES THE SON OF MY HEART, PHYSICIAN?
HE HATH TOTTERED AT THE BRINK OF THE ETERNAL SLEEP, MY LORD ODIN...
...BUT, THE GLOWING STRENGTH OF HIS LIMBS, COUPLED WITH THE MATCHLESS COURAGE OF HIS SPIRIT, SHALL SURELY RESTORE THY PRINCELY OFF-SPRING TO THY BOSOM, SIRE!

IN A FIT OF ROYAL RAGE, WHICH I SHALL REGRET TILL THE END OF TIME, I DID *DEPRIVE* HIM OF HALF HIS GODLY POWER!
O, MOST RASH AND SHAMEFUL DEED! UPON THE OPENING OF HIS EYES, THAT POWER SHALL BE *RESTORED*--AS SURELY AS THE HEAVENS ENDURE!

BUT NOW, I MUST GET ME HENCE TO THE UNSPEAKABLE *VILLAIN* WHO HATH COMMITTED SO FOUL AN ACT OF TREASON UPON THE GOLDEN REALM!
ONWARD--TO THE *JUDGMENT SEAT!*

THE TIME IS COME!
THE MOMENT OF *RETRIBUTION* IS AT HAND!

BRING THEN FORTH THE TRAITOR--*SEIDRING!*
NO! NO! MERCY! *MERCY!* I DARE NOT FACE THE WRATH OF *ODIN!*

MERCY, OMNIPOTENT LORD! MERCY UPON ONE WHO WAS MADDENED BY LUST FOR POWER!
THINE ABJECT WHIMPERING PROFANES MY VERY EARS!

THOU, WHOSE HEART BE COLDER THAN THE WINDS OF SPACE--WHOSE AMBITION BE DEADLIER THAN A SERPENT'S STING--THOU DARE SPEAKEST TO ME OF MERCY??!
FOR POWER DIDST THOU LUST--AND POWER SHALT THOU RECEIVE! THIS THEN BE THY SENTENCE--

THOU SHALT HAVE A KINGDOM OF THINE OWN--A KINGDOM TO RULE FOR ALL THE DAYS THOU SHALT LIVE...
I GRANT THEE THE POWER--FOREVER!

I HAVE BEEN TRANSPORTED--TO ANOTHER PART OF THE UNIVERSE --BEYOND THE GOLDEN VALE OF ASGARD!
THERE--OVER THE HORIZON--LIVING FORMS--COMING CLOSER--CLOSER--

BEHOLD! THE PROPHECIES HAVE COME TRUE!
AT LAST! A KING HAS BEEN SENT TO US!
ROCK TROLLS! THE UGLIEST--MOST BESTIAL CREATURES OF ALL! EVEN DEATH IS PREFERABLE TO THE COMPANY OF SUCH AS THESE!
WE SHALL NEVER LET HIM GO!
THIS THEN IS MY FATE--TO RULE THESE MONSTROUS BEINGS--ON THIS BARREN, FORSAKEN WORLD--FOREVER!
3

BUT NOW, LET US TURN OUR ATTENTION BACK TO THE VERDANT PLANET EARTH, WHERE WE FIND THE POWERFUL HERCULES TOURING A SPECIALLY-BUILT MOVIE SET BEHIND THE GATES OF STARDUST STUDIOS...
I MARVEL AT SUCH HANDIWORK! TO THINK THAT MERE MORTALS COULD CREATE A SCENE WHICH SO TRULY RESEMBLES MY NATIVE OLYMPUS!
KEEP IT UP, HERKY BABY! YOU'RE BEGINNING TO SOUND JUST LIKE YOU REALLY ARE THE SON OF ZEUS!
OKAY, YOU GUYS-- LET'S KNOCK OFF! IT'S TIME FOR OUR COFFEE BREAK!
4

TO THINK THAT I--THE HERO OF HEROES--SHALL SPEND MY TIME IN PLAY-ACTING FOR THE AMUSEMENT OF MORTALS! WHAT A MONUMENTAL JEST! HOW THE HEAVENS THEMSELVES SHALL ROCK WITH LAUGHTER!
OKAY, HERK--DON'T LET'S OVER-DO THE OLYMPUS BIT, HUH? WE'VE GOT COMPANY NOW!
HERE COMES YOUR LEADING LADY! MAN, TAKE A SQUINT AT THAT GET-UP!

MY CONGRATULATIONS, FAIR ONE! VERILY, THOU DOEST LOOK LIKE A TRUE QUEEN OF THE AMAZONS!
THAT'S THE NAME OF THE GAME, BIG BOY!

YOU'RE NOT EXACTLY HARD TO TAKE EITHER, TALL, DARK, AND DELICIOUS!
I DON'T KNOW WHERE THEY FOUND YOU, BUT IT MUST HAVE BEEN A GREAT SPOT FOR PROSPECTING!

OKAY, HERC--THERE'LL BE PLENTY OF TIME FOR SWEET-TALK LATER! RIGHT NOW, I'VE GOT TO TAKE YOU TO MEET THE PRODUCER!
NONE TAKE HERCULES! THE SON OF ZEUS WALKS WHERE HE CHOOSES!
SURE, PAL--SURE! IF YOU WANNA LIVE THE ROLE, THAT'S YOUR BIZ!

BUT YOU BETTER PLAY IT COOL WITH THE TOP BRASS! RUB 'EM THE WRONG WAY, AND THEY'LL TURN YOU IN FOR STEVE REEVES!
I BEGIN TO WEARY OF THY PRATTLE! WHAT IS THIS THAT DOTH APPROACH ME?
I DUNNO! NEVER SAW IT BEFORE!
5

THIS IS YOUR SCREEN TEST, HERCULES! DEFEND YOURSELF!
I-I'D BETTER GO AND RE-READ THE CONTRACT!

YOUR OPPONENT IS MERELY A MECHANICAL DEVICE, CREATED BY OUR STUDIO TECHNICIANS, TO SEE HOW YOU PHOTOGRAPH IN A FIGHT SCENE!
THOU SHALT GET MORE THAN THOU BARGAINED FOR!
I'LL REND IT ASUNDER WITH BUT A SINGLE BLOW--!

NO! WE HAVE SEEN ENOUGH! THE TEST IS OVER!
A SUDDEN WALL OF LIVING FLAME! TRULY, THY TECHNICIANS ARE MASTERS OF THEIR ART!

INDEED! YOUR ROBOT FOE WAS FAR TOO EXPENSIVE FOR US TO ALLOW YOU TO DAMAGE IT!
YOU ARE ALL I HAVE HEARD YOU ARE! THE ROLE IS YOURS!

I SHALL MAKE YOU THE GREATEST STAR OF ALL TIME! YOUR NAME WILL BECOME A HOUSEHOLD WORD!
KNOW YOU NOT THAT THE NAME HERCULES HATH BEEN HAILED FOR AGES THRUOUT THE KNOWN UNIVERSE?!!

BUT, AS AN UNSUSPECTING HERCULES PREPARES TO DINE, LITTLE DREAMING OF THE FATEFUL TRAP HE IS STUMBLING INTO, WE TURN OUR ATTENTION TO HALLOWED ASGARD, WHERE A ROYAL ICE-SKIMMER GLIDES AROSS THE FROZEN SEA OF MARMORA...

MY LORD BALDER! THOU MUST PROTECT OUR NOBLE PASSENGER TILL THE DANGER BE PAST!
FEAR THEE NOT, PILOT! I STAND FOR THOR!
KRASH
RRRRRRR
BACK, THOU BLACK-HEARTED DEMON FROM THE ICY DEPTHS! NO HARM SHALL COME TO THE GOD OF THUNDER WHILST BALDER STILL LIVES!
RRAK!
LOYAL FRIEND-- SAVE THYSELF!
THOUGH MY STRENGTH DOTH NOT MATCH THE FULL EXTENT OF THINE, MIGHTY ONE-- STILL IS BALDER A WARRIOR BORN!
YOU DID IT! YOU HURLED HIM FROM THE SHIP WITH ONE FELL SWOOP!
NOW, PILOT-- BEGONE! WE HAVE HERE TARRIED LONG ENOW!
THOU ART STILL TOO WEAK FOR SPORT SUCH AS THIS, VALIANT THOR!
TRUE, FAITHFUL FRIEND! BUT, MY STRENGTH RETURNS WITH EACH PASSING MOMENT--!
SOON, BALDER-- SOON SHALL I BE GOD OF THUNDER IN FACT AS WELL AS NAME! AND THEN --LET HERCULES BEWARE!

AND, EVEN AS A VENGEFUL THOR MENTIONS THE OLYMPIAN STRONGMAN...
I TRUST YOU ARE AMUSED BY THE ENTERTAINMENT I HAVE PROVIDED FOR YOU, HERCULES!
THIS IS A MINOR TABLEAU FROM ONE OF THE AMAZONIAN BATTLE SCENES WHICH OUR EPIC SHALL FEATURE!
AHHH! SUCH ZEST! SUCH SPIRIT! SUCH VIGOR! YONDER BEAUTY DOES THE IMMORTAL WARRIOR QUEEN PROUD INDEED!
NOW PARRY! NOW THRUST! HAH-- HAVE AT YOU!
KLANNNG

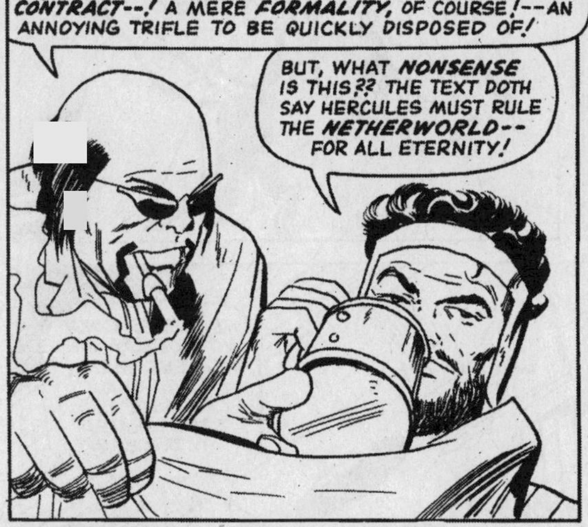
OH, BEFORE WE FORGET--IF YOU WILL JUST SIGN THIS CONTRACT--! A MERE FORMALITY, OF COURSE!--AN ANNOYING TRIFLE TO BE QUICKLY DISPOSED OF!
BUT, WHAT NONSENSE IS THIS?? THE TEXT DOTH SAY HERCULES MUST RULE THE NETHERWORLD-- FOR ALL ETERNITY!

OH, DID I NOT TELL YOU? IT IS MERELY THE THEME OF OUR PICTURE! SURELY THE POWERFUL HERCULES IS NOT AFRAID TO SIGN?
ACCORDING TO THE PLOT OF THE MOVIE, YOU CONQUER THE ENTIRE NETHERWORLD---BY DEFEATING PLUTO IN BATTLE! AND I REMAIN AT YOUR SIDE ALL THE TIME!
HMMM! THAT THOUGHT DOTH PLEASE ME GREATLY!

ENOUGH TALK, THEN! HEREWITH, THE THUMB-PRINT OF HERCULES! THE PACT IS SEALED!

I'VE WON! AFTER ALL THESE AGES--YOU SIGNED IT WILLINGLY!
AN OLYMPIAN CONTRACT-- WHICH CAN NEVER BE CANCELLED! I'M FREE--AT LAST, I'M FREE!
THY VOICE-- THY DEMEANOR-- THEY HAVE CHANGED!

HERE! LET ME REMOVE THESE WORTHLESS GLASSES! NOW LOOK, HERCULES-- LOOK INTO MY EYES! LOOK DEEP--DEEP--AND TELL WHAT YOU BEHOLD!
YOU! IT CAN BE NO OTHER! 'TIS PLUTO-- LORD OF THE NETHER-WORLD!
AND, WHAT OF ME, MAN OF OLYMPUS?
HYPPOLITA-- QUEEN OF THE AMAZONS! THEN, THIS BE NOT PLAY-ACTING!
NO, HERCULES--I AM HYPPOLITA-- I AM THE ONE YOU SPURNED THOSE LONG YEARS AGO--THE ONE WHO SWORE SHE'D HAVE HER REVENGE UPON THEE!
YOU ARE UNDONE, HERCULES--DOOMED TO RULE THE ACCURSED NETHERWORLD-- FOREVER!
NAY! NOT I! NOT THE SON OF ZEUS!
YOU HAVE NO CHOICE, HERCULES! YOU HAVE SIGNED THE OLYMPIAN CONTRACT!
AND NOW, LET THE FLOOR BENEATH US PART--FOR HERCULES MUST DESCEND THE STAIRWAY--TO HIS ETERNAL FATE!
HERCULES DOTH NOT YIELD! THE HEAVENS THEM-SELVES SHALL CRUMBLE ERE I BE DEFEATED BY TRICKERY!
FARE THEE WELL, DECEIVED ONE! NEVERMORE SHALT THOU REJECT THE LOVE OF A QUEEN!
10

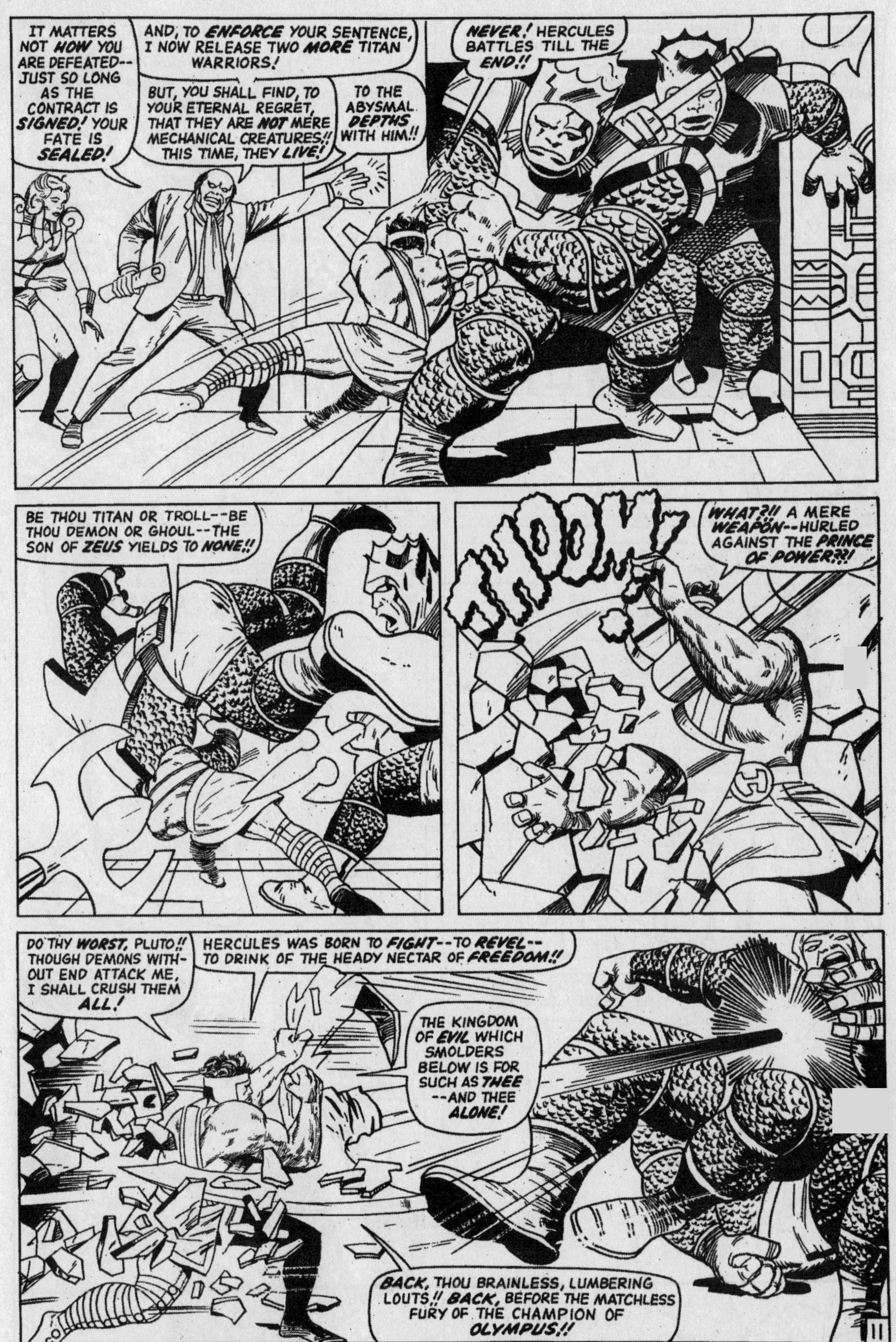
IT MATTERS NOT HOW YOU ARE DEFEATED-- JUST SO LONG AS THE CONTRACT IS SIGNED! YOUR FATE IS SEALED!
AND, TO ENFORCE YOUR SENTENCE, I NOW RELEASE TWO MORE TITAN WARRIORS!
BUT, YOU SHALL FIND, TO YOUR ETERNAL REGRET, THAT THEY ARE NOT MERE MECHANICAL CREATURES!! THIS TIME, THEY LIVE!
TO THE ABYSMAL DEPTHS WITH HIM!!
NEVER! HERCULES BATTLES TILL THE END!!
BE THOU TITAN OR TROLL--BE THOU DEMON OR GHOUL--THE SON OF ZEUS YIELDS TO NONE!!
THOOM!
WHAT?!! A MERE WEAPON--HURLED AGAINST THE PRINCE OF POWER?!!
DO THY WORST, PLUTO!! THOUGH DEMONS WITHOUT END ATTACK ME, I SHALL CRUSH THEM ALL!
HERCULES WAS BORN TO FIGHT--TO REVEL--TO DRINK OF THE HEADY NECTAR OF FREEDOM!!
THE KINGDOM OF EVIL WHICH SMOLDERS BELOW IS FOR SUCH AS THEE --AND THEE ALONE!
BACK, THOU BRAINLESS, LUMBERING LOUTS!! BACK, BEFORE THE MATCHLESS FURY OF THE CHAMPION OF OLYMPUS!!
11

MEANWHILE, IN GLITTERING ASGARD, MIGHTY THOR JOUSTS LIKE A MASTER, AS HIS STRENGTH RETURNS WITH EVER-INCREASING SPEED--
HAVE AT THEE, VALIANT VOLSTAGG!! LOOK TO THY DEFENSES!
SURELY THOU SPEAKEST IN JEST, THUNDER GOD!
VOLSTAGG IS A ROCK --A MOUNTAIN --WHICH NONE CAN TOPPLE!

THEN TRULY, A MIRACLE IS NOW UPON US--!
THOR HATH MOVED A MOUNTAIN!
O INFAMOUS MOMENT! WHO WILL E'ER BELIEVE SO IMPOSSIBLE AN EVENT??! WHO WILL--GLUGGG!

MOMENTS LATER, THE MOST REGAL IMMORTAL OF ALL ENTERS THE GREAT JOUSTING AREA....!
MY HEART REJOICES--FOR THE GOD OF THUNDER HATH RECOVERED FULLY HIS MATCHLESS POWER!
MOST HONORED FATHER--
--THY SON CRAVES A BOON!
THOU HAST BUT TO ASK--!

NOBLE SIRE, GRANT ME LEAVE TO RETURN TO EARTH!! FOR, NEVER SHALL MINE HONOR BE RETORED--NEVER SHALL MINE HEART KNOW TRANQUILITY--UNTIL I HAVE REDEEMED MYSELF--IN BATTLE WITH THE SON OF ZEUS!!

FULL WELL DO I KNOW THE ANGER THAT RAGES IN THY SOUL! I DO GRANT THEE LEAVE! SO BE IT!
AND KNOW THOU ALWAYS--WHERE E'ER THE THUNDER-GOD GOEST, THE BLESSING OF ODIN SHALL FOLLOW!

IF YOUR MORTAL EYES WERE TO SCAN THE HEAVENS AT THIS MOMENT, YOU WOULD THINK YOU WERE VIEWING A FIERY COMET, BLAZING A TRAIL TOWARDS EARTH--
--BUT, THE TRUE ASGARDIAN WOULD KNOW IT IS THOR, TRAVELLING AS ONLY AN IMMORTAL CAN!
12

GUIDED BY HIS ENCHANTED URU MALLET, THE MIGHTY AVENGER IS UNERRINGLY BROUGHT TO THE VERY SPOT WHERE WE LAST LEFT HERCULES--!
A SHAMBLES, HERE IN THE CINEMA CAPITAL OF THE WORLD!
HAS THE OLYMPIAN TITAN SO SOON BECOME A RAMPAGING DESTROYER?? OR, IS OTHER SAVAGERY AFOOT?

A CREATURE FROM THE DOMAIN WHICH BLAZES BELOW--DEFEATED IN BATTLE!
THERE IS MORE TO THIS THAN FIRST MEETS THE EYE! THERE IS DEMONIAC DANGER ALL ABOUT ME!

THEN, AT LAST--DRAWN BY THE DEAFENING SOUND OF COMBAT, THE GOD OF THUNDER STRIDES UNHESITATINGLY FORWARD, UNTIL HE SEES--
BESTIAL DENIZENS OF THE NETHERWORLD--ATTACKING THE LONE HERCULES!!
WHATE'ER THE PROVOCATION, MY BLOOD VERILY BOILS IN LOATHING AT SO UNEQUAL A TABLEAU!
BASEST OF VILLAINS!! THOUGH THY NUMBERS BE LIMITLESS, MY MACE SHALL CRUSH EACH OF THEE IN TURN!

NO LONGER NEED HERCULES BATTLE ALONE!!
THOSE WHO ATTACK IN COWARDLY NUMBER SHALL ALSO FACE THE FURY OF THE THUNDERING HAMMER OF THOR!
THE THUNDER GOD!! STAY BACK, ASGARDIAN!! THOU HAST NOT THE MIGHT TO DEAL WITH SUCH AS THESE!!

NEVERMORE SHALT THOU UTTER SUCH STINGING WORDS, OLYMPIAN!
BEHOLD, RASH BRAGGART-- BEHOLD THE TRUE POWER OF THE SON OF ODIN!!

THY STRENGTH-- THY VALOR--THEY ARE WORTHY OF HERCULES, HIMSELF!!
WHY DIDST THOU NOT BATTLE IN SUCH MANNER WHEN LAST WE FOUGHT??
TIME ENOW FOR TALK AFTER OUR TASK HERE BE DONE!

LET US END THIS CHARADE WITH GREATEST SPEED--FOR THERE IS A GREATER SCORE TO BE SETTLED BETWEEN OURSELVES!
BY MY BEARD, I UNDERSTAND THEE NOT, THUNDER GOD!!
BUT, IT SHALL BE EVEN AS THOU SAYEST!
14

AND, AS THE CYCLONIC BATTLE CONTINUES TO RAGE, UNABATED--
OUR WARRIORS FALL BACK!!
LET THE STINGING SWORD OF HYPPOLITA BE ADDED TO THEIR NUMBER!
NO! STAND ASIDE! THE NEWLY-ARRIVED GOD OF THUNDER IS A FORCE I HAD NOT CONJURED WITH!
THROK
THE FINAL VICTORY MUST BE MINE!! HERCULES HAS INDEED AFFIXED HIS MARK TO AN OLYMPIAN CONTRACT!
THEREFORE, WE SHALL TAKE OUR CASE TO THE ONE BEING WHO CAN FORCE THE PRINCE OF POWER TO OBEY!
BE THEN PREPARED, AMAZON QUEEN--!
WE NOW EMBARK UPON THE GREATEST JOURNEY OF ALL--WE GO TO FABLED OLYMPUS--TO CONFRONT THE AWESOME ZEUS, HIMSELF!
LET THE IMMORTAL PRINCES FIGHT ON--THEIR CAUSE IS DOOMED TO FAIL!
WITH ALL THE DARK POWER OF THE NETHERWORLD AT MY DISPOSAL, THE VICTOR CAN BE NONE BUT--PLUTO!
AND NOW, LET US BEGONE--!!
DIDST THOU OBSERVE, ASGARDIAN?? THE EVIL ONE AND HIS HANDMAIDEN HAVE VANISHED!
THE TRIUMPH IS MINE!
NOT UNTIL THOU HAST DEALT WITH ME, BLUSTERING ONE!
BUT FIRST--CATCH THOU THIS PILLAR AS IT FALLS!!
FTOOM

NEXT ISSUE: "THE VERDICT OF ZEUS!"

TALES OF ASGARD, HOME OF THE MIGHTY NORSE GODS
"AFTERMATH!"
SCRIPT: STAN LEE
PENCILLING: JACK KIRBY
DELINEATION: VINCE COLLETTA
LETTERING: S. ROSE
ACCORDING TO VOLLA, THE PROPHETESS, THE DAY OF RAGNAROK IS ALMOST AT HAND! RAGNAROK... THE END OF THE WORLD!! EVEN AS VOLLA SPEAKS, THE ASSEMBLED GODS WITNESS, IN THEIR IMAGINATION, THE LAST AGONIZING MOMENTS OF ASGARD, AS SHE PREDICTS THE GOLDEN REALM BEING WRACKED BY FIRE, FLOOD, AND THE FLAMES OF BATTLE..!

THEN AS THE UNIVERSE-SHAKING BATTLE CONTINUES TO RAGE, AS FORCES BEYOND THE SCOPE OF HUMAN COMPREHENSION ARE UNLEASHED AT WILL, ASGARD ITSELF IS FINALLY TORN ASUNDER BY A MONUMENTAL EXPLOSION, WHICH SHAKES THE VERY FOUNDATIONS OF INFINITY ITSELF!!

FINALLY, NOTHING REMAINS... BUT *SILENCE!!* SILENCE...AND GRIM, UTTER, ENDLESS DESOLATION... THE AWESOME REMNANTS OF AN AGE, A GLORY, THAT IS FOREVER GONE..!

LO, THE CENTURIES TURN TO AGES, AND THE AGES TO EONS, AS THE SEAS SLOWLY RETURN AND VAST CONTINENTS TAKE FORM, RISING FROM THE RESTLESS WATERS...

IN TIME, VEGETATION BURSTS FORTH OVER THE LAND, AS AN ABUNDANCE OF GREENERY... OF LUSH, VERDANT FLORA ONCE AGAIN FILLS THE AIR WITH THE SCENT OF REAWAKENED *LIFE!*

AND, IN TIME, THIS NEW RACE SPAWNS A NEW CIVILIZATION... A NEW GOLDEN AGE... A NEW *REBIRTH*, AS GLORIOUS AS ANY THE WORLD HAS EVER KNOWN!

FOR, *THIS* IS THE DESTINY OF GOD AND MAN ALIKE... *THIS* IS THE LESSON SUPREME... ALL THAT LIVE MUST DIE... *BUT*, ALL THAT DIE SHALL *LIVE!*

AS SURELY AS RAGNAROK ITSELF, LET ALL WHO READ THESE WORDS KNOW FULL WELL THAT NEW WONDERS SHALL UNFOLD NEXT ISSUE---!
WE HAVE SPOKEN!!

5.

THE MIGHTY THOR
MARVEL COMICS GROUP
129 JUNE
APPROVED BY THE COMICS CODE AUTHORITY
12¢
IND
"THE VERDICT OF ZEUS!"

THE MIGHTY THOR!
"THE VERDICT OF ZEUS!"
NO MATTER HOW SOPHISTICATED NEW YORKERS MAY BE, WHEN THE NOBLE FIGURE OF THE GOD OF THUNDER HURTLES DOWN FROM THE SKIES ABOVE, YOU CAN BE SOMEWHAT CERTAIN HE'LL RECEIVE MORE THAN A PASSING GLANCE--!
IT'S MIGHTY THOR! IF ONLY I HAD MY CAMERA!!
HARKEN, YE!
STAN LEE, WRITER
JACK KIRBY, PENCILLER
VINCE COLLETTA, INKER
ARTIE SIMEK LETTERER
YEA, VERILY!
1

ONCE OVER THEIR INITIAL FEELING OF AWE AND ASTONISHMENT, THE PASSERSBY SOON MUSTER UP ENOUGH NERVE TO CROWD AROUND THE COSTUMED IMMORTAL, PLYING HIM WITH ENDLESS QUERIES--
THERE'S BEEN A LOT OF TALK ABOUT YOU RUNNIN' INTO HERCULES ON THE COAST, THOR! THEY SAY YOU BEAT 'IM TO A FARE-THEE-WELL THIS TIME!
IS IT TRUE??
NONE CAN BEST THE PRINCE OF POWER THUS EASILY!
YET, YOU MAY SAY I ACQUITTED MYSELF WITH HONOR!
WHAT HAPPENED TO HERCULES? WHERE IS HE NOW?
WHY'D YOU LET HIM GET AWAY?

I FEAR IT CANNOT BE SAID THAT HERCULES HAS TRULY "GOTTEN AWAY"!
BUT, IT IS BEST THAT THESE MORTALS DO NOT LEARN THAT PLUTO HAS TRICKED THE PROUD OLYMPIAN INTO REPLACING HIM AS CUSTODIAN OF THE DREAD NETHERWORLD --FOREVER!*
BUT, IF HE DIDN'T ESCAPE, THEN WHERE IS HE?
WHY'D YOU RETURN TO NEW YORK? IS THERE TROUBLE BREWING?
WADDAYA KNOW?!! IT'S THE THUNDER GOD, HIMSELF!
*ANOTHER SNEAKY, SUGAR-COATED SUBLIMINAL SUMMARY! --SLY STAN.
WHAT ABOUT THE AVENGERS? WHEN ARE YOU GONNA REJOIN THEM? EVERY-ONE'S BEEN ASKING--!
HEY! LET'S SEE YA DO SOME TRICKS WITH THAT JAZZY HAMMER OF YOURS, HUH? C'MON, SHOW US WHATCHA CAN DO!
BACK, ALL OF YOU! STAND YE BACK! THE ENDLESS PRATTLE OF THY VOICES PROVES WEARISOME TO MINE EARS!
WHO DOES HE THINK HE IS? WE'VE GOT A RIGHT TO SAY WHAT WE WANT!

WAIT, THOR! I WANT YOUR AUTOGRAPH FOR MY KIDS!
QUICK! TEAR OFF A PIECE OF HIS CAPE--FOR A MEMENTO!
ONE LOCK OF HIS HAIR! THAT'S ALL I WANT-- JUST ONE!
YOU CAN USE SOME HELP, FELLA! C'MON, HOP INTO MY HACK!
THE GOD OF THUNDER-- IN A PUBLIC CONVEYANCE??
BUT THEN-- WHY NOT?

WHERE TO, PAL? YOU NAME IT--I'LL GETCHA THERE!
MY DESTINATION IS THE TOWN TOWERS, ON EAST 75TH STREET!
SURE! I KNOW THE PLACE!
SIT BACK 'N RELAX, CURLY! I'LL HAVE YA THERE IN NO TIME!

YOU GOTTA EXCUSE THEM RUBBER-NECKS, MISTER! THEY DON'T REALIZE THAT YOU IMMORTALS CAN GET SICK OF CROWDS JUST LIKE ANY ORDINARY JOE!
THE WAY I SEE IT, YOU AINT MUCH DIFFERENT THAN A GUY LIKE ME--!

YOU CARRY A NUTTY HAMMER AND WEAR THEM WINGS ON YER HAT, WHILE I DRIVE ME A HACK AND WEAR A BUTTON IN MY CAP!
BUT, I'LL BETCHA YOU WORRY ABOUT DAMES, 'N POLITICS, 'N THE WORLD SERIES JUST LIKE ME 'N EVERYBODY ELSE!
YOU ARE QUITE A PHILOSOPHER, MY FRIEND!

SURE! WHAT CABBIE AINT? BUT, I BEEN AROUND, TOO! I CAUGHT ME A BULLET AT ANZIO, IN THE BIG WAR!
THEN YOU TOO HAVE DONE YOUR SHARE FOR FREEDOM!
YEAH, JUST LIKE YOU! I READ PLENTY ABOUT YOU, PAL!
IN SPITE OF THEM CRAZY GOLDEN CURLS, YOU'RE AN A-1 JOE IN MY BOOK!

I HAVE RECEIVED PLAUDITS AND ACCOLADES FROM THE HIGHEST AND MIGHTIEST OF MEN AND IMMORTALS--YET, THE WORDS YOU HAVE SPOKEN SHALL GLADDEN MY HEART FOR AS LONG AS MEMORY ENDURES!
IF THAT MEANS WHAT I THINK IT DOES, I'M MUCH OBLIGED, MISTER!
NOW, HERE WE ARE--THE TOWN TOWERS, JUST LIKE YA SAID!
TAXI
IT'S DULL--BUT IT'S A LIVING!
HO HUM--ANOTHER CAB DOOR TO OPEN--ANOTHER PALTRY TIP!

GOOD HEAVENS!! IT--IT'S THE GOD OF THUNDER!!
WHAT DOES ONE DO IN HIS PRESENCE? BOW? TIP ONE'S HAT?
HOW SHALL I CORRECTLY ADDRESS HIM?
ACCEPT MY THANKS FOR YOUR ASSISTANCE!
SURE, CURLY! I'LL SEE YA AROUND, HEAR?
TAXI
BE SURE TO KEEP YER NOSE CLEAN, PAL!

YOU--YOU SPOKE TO HIM AS THOUGH HE'S JUST AN ORDINARY FARE!
WHY NOT? HE'S A REAL SWINGER, THAT GUY! HIM 'N ME'S BUDDIES! HE TAKES MY HACK WHENEVER HIS HAMMER'S ON THE BLINK!
BUT AN ORDINARY FARE HE AINT! HE CLEAN FORGOT ABOUT PAYIN' ME!

MOMENTS LATER--
A COSTUME PARTY--ON THIS FLOOR--AND I WASN'T INVITED!!
I HOPE I SHALL FIND JANE FOSTER AT HOME! IT IS IMPORTANT THAT I SPEAK WITH HER!
BUT, RIGHT NOW, IT'S MORE IMPORTANT FOR US TO TURN OUR ATTENTION TO FAR-OFF OLYMPUS! READY? THEN, LET'S GO--!

OLYMPUS-- WHERE REIGNS THE SPIRITED ZEUS, FATHER OF HERCULES, SUPREME SOVEREIGN OF ALL HE SURVEYS--!
AHHH, MY LORD ZEUS, HOW MERRY IS THY CELEBRATION! WHERE, BUT IN ETERNAL OLYMPUS, CAN SUCH REVELS CONTINUE WITHOUT END?!!
IN TRUTH, MY MERRY DIONYSIUS, WHEN THERE ARE NO BATTLES LEFT TO FIGHT--NO ENEMIES TO OVERCOME--THEN 'TIS TIME TO PARTAKE OF FROLIC AND OF GAMBOLS IN THIS HALCYON CLIME!
BUT SOFT! I FEEL THE PRESENCE OF EVIL APPROACHING! THE SUBTLE SCENT OF MENACE PERVADES THE VERY AIR WE BREATHE!
WE WISH YOU COULD HEAR THE JOYOUS MUSIC WHICH FILLS THE HALLOWED AIR OF OLYMPUS--BUT, ALAS, MORTAL--SUCH GODLIKE MELODIES ARE NOT FOR SUCH AS THEE! AND SO--ON WITH OUR TITANIC TALE--
4

SUDDENLY, THE REVELS CEASE, IN THE SPACE OF A SINGLE HEARTBEAT--AS THE GRIM, FOREBODING FIGURE OF PLUTO, PRINCE OF DARKNESS, MYSTICALLY TAKES SHAPE--IN FULL REGALIA AS EX-MONARCH OF THE NETHERWORLD--!

BUT, EVEN AS THE THUNDERSTRUCK ZEUS RECOILS IN STUNNED SURPRISE, THE LONELY FIGURE OF THE PRINCE OF POWER SCALES THE MASSIVE PEAK OF MOUNT OLYMPUS-- COMPLETING A CLIMB WHICH VERILY DEFIES MERE HUMAN COMPREHENSION--!
I MUST REACH THE THRONE OF ZEUS! ONLY HE CAN FREE ME FROM THE DIRE TERMS OF THE OLYMPIAN CONTRACT TO WHICH I SO BLINDLY AFFIXED MY MARK!
I, WHO AM HERCULES-- WHO AM POWER INCARNATE --WHO HAVE BESTED EVERY FOE--MET EVERY DANGER-- SURMOUNTED EVERY OBSTACLE --I CANNOT BEAR THE THOUGHT OF AN ETERNITY, SPENT IN THE SHADOWY DESOLATION OF THE NETHERWORLD!
AHH--THE SUMMIT AT LAST! NOW TO-- STAY! WHAT IS THIS?!!
A YELLOW-CRESTED TITAN!! FIERCEST AND MOST POWERFUL OF ALL THE SAVAGE BREED!
STAND THOU ASIDE, MONSTROUS MARAUDER! HERCULES SO COMMANDS!
BUT, THE DIM-WITTED, RAMPAGING CREATURE IS TOO CONSUMED WITH SAVAGERY, WITH UNREASONING HATRED, TO DO AUGHT BUT STRIKE OUT--
WHOOM!
6

I AM ON A MISSION MOST URGENT! GLADLY WOULD I HAVE LET THEE GO THY WAY, SINCE THOU ART OF NO IMPORT TO ME!
BUT NOW, THOU HAST AROUSED THE FLAMING ANGER OF HERCULES!!!
LET THE NETHERWORLD WAIT! LET THE PLANETS BE STILLED! NOTHING SHALL SAVE THEE NOW!
KRAKK!
TOOM
SKAKK!
BAM!
SLOWLY, THE OLYMPIAN IMMORTAL TURNS FROM HIS FALLEN FOE, AND, WITHOUT A BACKWARD GLANCE, CONTINUES ON HIS WAY! SO REPLETE WITH VICTORY IS HIS PAST, THAT ONE ADDITIONAL TRIUMPH IS OF VIRTUALLY NO CONSEQUENCE--TO HERCULES!
NOW, TO SEEK AUDIENCE WITH HONORED ZEUS!
7

A SHORT TIME LATER, HIS DESTINATION REACHED, HERCULES ENTERS THE GLEAMING CASTLE--
'TIS MOST PASSING STRANGE! THOUGH I AM SEEN BY ALL, NONE THERE ARE WHO APPROACH ME!
THEN, SUDDENLY--
ZUMM!
ADVANCE NO FURTHER, TRAGIC OFFSPRING! THERE CAN BE NO SANCTUARY FOR THEE IN OLYMPUS!
THE VOICE OF MY FATHER! THEN--HE ALREADY KNOWS!
IS MY PLEA TO BE THUS DENIED--ERE I AM ALLOWED TO PRESENT IT?
MY SON--I KNOW THOU HAST BEEN GROSSLY DECEIVED! YET, THOU DIDST SIGN THE COMPACT--AND, MORE PRECIOUS TO THY FATHER THAN LIFE ITSELF IS--HONOR!
THOU MUST BE TRUE TO THY DEED! THOUGH THOU BE FAVORED ABOVE ALL IN MINE EYES, I DO BANISH THEE TO THE NETHERWORLD!
HEAR ME, MY FATHER! A CHANCE IS ALL I CRAVE! THE CHANCE TO FIGHT FOR MY FREEDOM!
I BEG NO FAVOR--I ASK NO PITY! BUT, I AM HERCULES!! I KNOW NOT HOW TO YIELD!
ALAS, MY SON! THY PRIDE HATH BEEN THY DOWNFALL! NOW MUST THOU LEARN THE LESSON OF--HUMILITY!
MY ONLY CHANCE! I MUST FIND A CHAMPION WHO WILL DO BATTLE IN MY BEHALF!
BUT WHERE IN THE UNIVERSE IS THERE ONE SO SELFLESS??!
FIND YE ONE WHO WILL FIGHT IN THY STEAD! ONE WHO WILL RISK THE NETHERWORLD, HIMSELF TO SAVE THEE!
8

AND, EVEN AS HERCULES PONDERS HIS FATE, ON THE PLANET EARTH A DOOR SLOWLY OPENS, AND THE GOD OF THUNDER BEHOLDS--
A FEMALE! ONE WHOM I HAVE NEVER SEEN BEFORE--AND YET--SHE IS STRANGELY FAMILIAR!
YOU WISH TO SEE JANE FOSTER?
THOR! IT'S YOU--AT LAST!
JANE! I HAVE RETURNED!

I KNEW YOU'D COME BACK! I KNEW NOTHING COULD CRUSH YOUR FIGHTING SPIRIT--YOUR PROUD HEART--NOT EVEN HERCULES!
MY DARLING! MY OWN TRUE LOVE! IF ONLY I COULD KNOW THAT YOU'LL NEVER LEAVE ME AGAIN!
EVEN A THUNDER GOD MAY NOT PREDICT THE FUTURE, MY BELOVED!

OH, FORGIVE ME! I ALMOST FORGOT--!
THOR, THIS IS TANA NILE, MY NEW ROOMMATE! TANA HAS JUST MOVED TO THE CITY, LOOKING FOR A JOB!
IT WAS MOST KIND OF JANE TO LET ME SHARE THIS APARTMENT WITH HER!

YOU SPEAK ENGLISH PERFECTLY! AND YET, YOU DO NOT SOUND LIKE A NATIVE OF THIS LAND!
YOU ARE RIGHT, GOD OF THUNDER! I COME FROM--A DISTANT PLACE!
BUT, THERE IS NO NEED TO DISCUSS THAT NOW!

THEN, WITHOUT CONSCIOUS THOUGHT, THE SON OF ODIN BENDS HIS KNEE, KNEELING, AS THOUGH IN THE PRESENCE OF A REGAL BEING--!
THERE IS SOMETHING ABOUT HER--SOMETHING WHICH JANE CANNOT RECOGNIZE--SOMETHING STRANGELY MAJESTIC!
MAY THE STARS OF ASGARD SHINE UPON THEE, TANA NILE!
THANK YOU, THOR!

THOR! YOU TOO?
SHE IS NAUGHT BUT A MORTAL FEMALE, AND YET--I FELT COMPELLED TO MAKE OBEISANCE!
'TIS CERTAIN AN ENIGMA IS UPON US!

TANA SEEMS TO AFFECT EVERYONE THE SAME WAY! I-I DON'T UNDERSTAND IT!
HOW DID YOU MEET? FROM WHENCE DOES SHE COME?
ACTUALLY, I KNOW ALMOST NOTHING ABOUT HER! I PUT AN AD IN THE PAPER FOR A ROOMMATE TO SHARE EXPENSES, AND TANA WAS THE FIRST TO ANSWER!
BUT, ENOUGH OF HER, MY DARLING! LET'S TALK ABOUT US!
IN TRUTH, MY LOVED ONE, THERE IS MUCH FOR US TO DISCUSS!
SINCE A GOD MAY NOT WED A MORTAL, THE TIME HAS COME FOR ME TO SHED THE MANTLE OF IMMORTALITY!
THOR!! YOU MEAN--YOU'D BECOME DR. DON BLAKE--FOR THE REST OF YOUR LIFE?!!
ALTHOUGH IT IS WHAT I HAVE PRAYED FOR, YOU CANNOT MAKE SUCH A GRAVE DECISION SO QUICKLY! YOU-YOU'D BE GIVING UP SO MUCH--!
BUT, CONSIDER THE GAIN! IS ALL THE GLORY OF ASGARD WORTH ONE EMBRACE FROM THE WOMAN I LOVE?
ONCE AGAIN I SHALL LEAVE YOU, MY DEAREST! BUT, IT SHALL BE FOR THE FINAL TIME!
I MUST RETURN TO THE COURT OF ODIN, THERE TO TELL MY FATHER OF MY DECISION--THERE, TO RENOUNCE MY GODLY HERITAGE--FOREVER!
THOR! YOU --YOU REALLY MEAN IT?!!
AS SURELY AS THE SUN DOTH RISE EACH MORNING--AS SURELY AS THE RAINS DO FALL --THIS DO I MEAN, JANE FOSTER! I SHALL TAKE THEE FOR MY BRIDE--OR PERISH IN THE STRIVING!
MY DARLING--I-I'VE WAITED SO LONG TO HEAR YOU SAY THAT--YET NOW, I'M SUDDENLY AFRAID!
LET FEAR BE BANISHED FROM THY HEART! NOTHING SHALL EVER AGAIN KEEP US APART!
BUT, EVEN AS THE THUNDER GOD SPEAKS, A PAIR OF COLD, UNBLINKING EYES NEVER LEAVE HIS FACE--
THOR MUST NOT RETURN TO EARTH AGAIN! FOR, IF HE SHOULD, IT WOULD SPOIL ALL MY CAREFULLY LAID PLANS!
AND, I HAVE COME TOO FAR TO BE STOPPED NOW!

MOMENTS LATER, AFTER A BRIEF BUT TENDER FAREWELL...
NOW TO RETURN TO THE GOLDEN REALM...
...PERHAPS FOR THE FINAL TIME!

SHOOSH!

CREATING A SPACE/TIME-DISTORTING VORTEX, THE IMMORTAL AVENGER REACHES THE FABLED RAINBOW BRIDGE TO ASGARD JUST IN TIME TO SEE--
BRAVE BALDER--ABOUT TO SET FORTH UPON SOME MISSION! I MUST GREET THE MOST FAITHFUL OF ALL WHO SERVE THE THRONE!
MIGHTY THOR!! YOU HAVE SAVED ME FROM MY INTENDED JOURNEY!

GIVE WORDS TO THY THOUGHT, LOYAL ONE! OF WHAT NATURE WAS THY MISSION?
I AM UNDER DIRECT ORDERS OF NOBLE ODIN HIMSELF! HE COMMANDED ME TO LOCATE YOU!
FOR WHAT PURPOSE, VALIANT FRIEND?

HE MUST TELL YOU THAT HIMSELF!
SUFFICE IT TO SAY THAT HE IS SORELY DISTURBED! I AM ORDERED TO BRING YOU TO HIM AT ONCE!
11

BUT WHY, BRAVE BALDER? WHAT CAN BE AMISS?
HAVE YOU FORGOTTEN THUS SOON? 'TIS THE LONG-AWAITED DAY OF THE THREE WORLDS!
THE DAY OF MOMENTOUS DECISION FOR THE GOD OF THUNDER--AS PREDICTED IN THE BOOK OF ENCHANTERS!
ALAS--THAT IT SHOULD FALL AT SUCH A TIME!

GOOD MY LORD--THOU HAST SUMMONED ME!
COME FORTH, SON OF MY HEART! 'TIS TIME FOR ME TO SEND THEE THRU THE DOORWAY TO ALL THE WORLDS!
THOUGH I BE SORELY TROUBLED AT THE FATE THAT MAY BEFALL THEE --IT MUST BE DONE!

'TIS THY DUTY TO WAIT IN LIMBO, MY SON!
FOR, ON THIS FATEFUL DAY, THE WHISPERING WIND SHALL CALL THEE--
--AND, THOU MUST FULFILL THY DESTINY BY FOLLOWING WHERE'ER IT MAY LEAD! SO HATH IT BEEN WRITTEN!

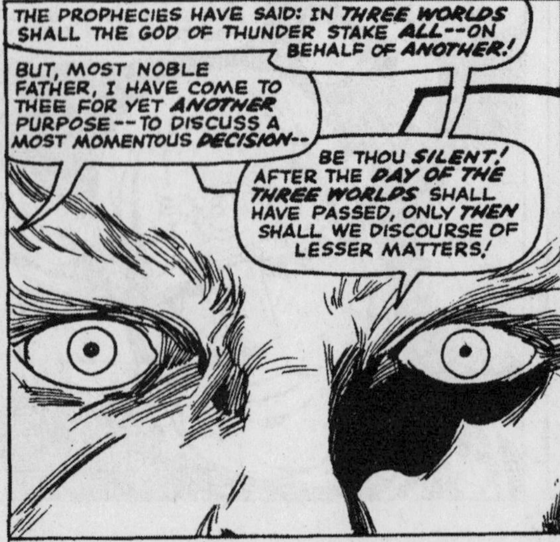
THE PROPHECIES HAVE SAID: IN THREE WORLDS SHALL THE GOD OF THUNDER STAKE ALL--ON BEHALF OF ANOTHER!
BUT, MOST NOBLE FATHER, I HAVE COME TO THEE FOR YET ANOTHER PURPOSE--TO DISCUSS A MOST MOMENTOUS DECISION--
BE THOU SILENT! AFTER THE DAY OF THE THREE WORLDS SHALL HAVE PASSED, ONLY THEN SHALL WE DISCOURSE OF LESSER MATTERS!

NOW, MIGHTIEST OF THE MIGHTY--NOBLEST OF THE NOBLE--PREPARE THYSELF!!
I SEND THEE TO LIMBO! THERE, WHAT IS TO BE--SHALL BE!
I MUST BE TRUE TO MY DESTINY! FIRST, MY DUTY SHALL BE DONE! AND THEN--MY MOMENT OF GREATEST DECISION!

THEN, FASTER THAN THE FLICKER OF AN ASGARDIAN EYE, THE MOST HEROIC IMMORTAL OF ALL FINDS HIMSELF IN THE DOMAIN OF DESOLATION--THE EVER-CHANGING, EVER-ETERNAL SHADOWY REALM OF NOWHERE--THE LEGENDARY LAND OF LIMBO--
HERE MUST I REMAIN, TILL THE WINDS OF THE WORLD SUMMON ME--TO DO BATTLE FOR ANOTHER!
I KNOW NOT OF THE PERILS THAT AWAIT ME, BUT THIS DO I VOW--THE GOD OF THUNDER SHALL FACE THEM--AS BEFITS THE SON OF IMPERIAL ODIN!
THUS DO WE LEAVE MIGHTY THOR, ENGULFED BY EMPTINESS--AS ONCE AGAIN WE TURN OUR ATTENTION TO THE PRINCE OF POWER, IN FABLED OLYMPUS--

ARES! I CRAVE A BOON! BECAUSE I SIGNED AN OLYMPIAN CONTRACT, MY ARM MAY NO MORE BE LIFTED IN BATTLE!
I MUST FIND ONE WILLING TO RISK ALL IN ORDER TO FIGHT--TO DARE--FOR THE CAUSE OF HERCULES!
THEN THOU MUST SEEK HIM ELSE-WHERE, SON OF ZEUS!

LONG HAVE I DESPISED THY BLUSTERING MANNER--THY VAIN CONCEIT--THY OVER-POWERING STRENGTH--STRENGTH WHICH, BY RIGHTS, SHOULD HAVE BEEN MINE!
NOW, STAND THOU ASIDE! I MUST EVER PRACTICE HURLING MY FATEFUL JAVELINS!
THEN--THOU DOTH REFUSE ME?!!
AY! LOOK NOT TO ARES FOR SUCCOR!

GOD OF WAR THOU ART CALLED! WHERE THEN IS THY WARLIKE SPIRIT? WHERE THEN THY LUST FOR COMBAT??
UNHAND ME, DOOMED ONE! EVEN ARES IS NOT WITLESS ENOUGH TO DO BATTLE WITH MIGHTY PLUTO--AND HIS DEADLY LEGIONS!

NEVER SHALL I FORGET HOW THOU HAST TURNED THY BACK UPON THY FELLOW OLYMPIAN...BASE, BLACK-HEARTED COWARD!
REMEMBER THEN, HERCULES--AS THOU SPENDEST ETERNITY IN THE NETHERWORLD!

WITHOUT ANOTHER WORD--WITH GRIM, BURNING DESPERATION GNAWING AT HIS HEART, THE PRINCE OF POWER SWIFTLY TURNS AWAY!
ONLY SECONDS OF FREEDOM ARE LEFT TO ME!
I MUST FIND A CHAMPION TO STRIKE FOR HERCULES--OR ALL IS LOST--FOREVER!

IN THE DISTANCE--'TIS HERMES--MOUNTED UPON HIS FLYING CHARIOT!
HERMES--WHO KNOWS NOT THE MEANING OF FEAR! HERMES, WHOSE SPEED IS ALMOST THE EQUAL OF MY OWN STRENGTH!
HE PREPARES TO EMBARK UPON A NEW QUEST!! I MUST REACH HIM 'ERE HE DEPARTS!
HERMES!! STAY THY FLIGHT!! 'TIS HERCULES WHO CALLS!!
UP, MY PEERLESS STEEDS! GET THEE TO FLIGHT!

FOOSH!
FASTER! EVER FASTER, MY VALIANT STALLIONS! WE HAVE A UNIVERSE TO CROSS 'ERE THE CURTAINS OF DARKNESS GATHER!
HERMES!! THOU MUST NOT GO! MY LIFE IS AT STAKE!!
HE HEARS ME NOT! THE THUNDER OF HIS CHARIOT DOTH DROWN MY FUTILE PLEA!!

BUT HARK--THE SANDS OF TIME HAVE RUN OUT! IN TRUTH, THE SON OF ZEUS IS SURELY UNDONE!
NONE THERE ARE WHO CAN SAVE HERCULES NOW!

HOW DARK GROW THE SKIES ABOVE ME! HOW HEAVY LADEN WITH DREAD IS THE AIR I BREATHE!
MY TIME IS COME! THE NETHERWORLD CALLS OUT TO ME!
AND, FOR THE FIRST TIME--SINCE THE DAWN OF CONSCIOUS-NESS--HERCULES KNOWS AT LAST--THE MEANING OF --FEAR!

AND THEN, A VOICE RINGS OUT! A VOICE TOTALLY LACKING IN PITY, IN WARMTH, IN ANY SEMBLANCE OF HUMAN EMOTION OR FEELING-- THE VOICE OF PLUTO, THE INEXORABLE!
PREPARE THYSELF, HERCULES! THOU HAST SIGNED THE OLYMPIAN CONTRACT-- NOW MUST THOU PAY THE PRICE!
EVEN AS I SPEAK, MY LEGIONS APPROACH FROM THE LAND BELOW --TO TAKE THEE TO THY FATE!

AFTER ALL THESE AGES, I AM FREED AT LAST--WHILE THOU SHALL SERVE IN MY PLACE-- TILL TIME ITSELF DOTH VANISH!
ARISE, DENIZENS OF THE ABYSMAL DEPTHS--ARISE, AND CLAIM THY NEW KING!

A HUNDRED SPEARS?!! LEVELLED AGAINST HERCULES?!! LEVELLED AGAINST ONE WHO HATH THE POWER TO TURN ASIDE A THOUSAND TIMES A HUNDRED?!!
BUT, THY STRENGTH IS USELESS NOW! SINCE SIGNING THE PARCHMENT, THOU ART FORBIDDEN TO STRIKE A SINGLE BLOW!

ONLY ANOTHER MAY DO BATTLE IN THY BEHALF! BUT, NONE WOULD BE SO FOOLHARDY! PREPARE THYSELF THEN--TO YIELD--!
NAY! SOMEWHERE--SOMEWHERE IN THE VAST, LIMITLESS UNIVERSE THERE MUST MUST BE ONE-- ONE WHO WILL HEED MY CALL--!!!

AND, IN THE LAND OF LIMBO--ONE THERE IS WHO HEARS THE DESPERATE CRY WHICH IS CARRIED BY THE ENCHANTED WINDS--!
IT CANNOT BE--IT MUST NOT BE--THAT THE PRINCE OF POWER--THAT HERCULES-- WHO HATH NEVER BEEN DEFEATED IN BATTLE--SHALL BE TAKEN WITHOUT AN ARM UPRAISED--WITHOUT A BLOW BEING STRUCK--!
HERCULES!! THEN IT MUST BE HE FOR WHOM I AM FATED TO DO BATTLE!

SURELY THERE IS NONE MORE WORTHY--NONE MORE DESERVING--THAN THE SON OF ZEUS!
IF THE POWER OF THE THUNDER GOD CAN AID THE OLYMPIAN-- THEN SO BE IT!
15

WITH A DEAFENING ROAR THE WINDS SUDDENLY CEASE THEIR SWIRLING, AND--WHEN THE MISTS HAVE CLEARED, THE IMMORTAL AVENGER FINDS HIMSELF IN--
OLYMPUS!! THE REALM OF REGAL ZEUS!
IT IS HERE THEN THAT MY DESTINY AWAITS ME!

AHEAD OF ME--THE HUBBUB OF VOICES--AND ONE MORE POWERFUL, MORE DESPERATE THAN ANY OTHER--THE VOICE OF HERCULES!
HERCULES--HE WHO HAD BEEN MY FOE--HE, FOR WHOM I AM NOW PREPARED TO RISK ALL ON THE FIELD OF BATTLE--AGAINST UNKNOWN ODDS!

SEIZE HIM! FEAR NOT HIS STRENGTH--HE IS FORBIDDEN TO EMPLOY IT SO LONG AS I HOLD THIS CONTRACT!
LET ME THEN BE TAKEN! OF WHAT USE IS IT TO REMAIN IN A WORLD WHERE NONE WILL STAND UP FOR ANOTHER WHO HATH BEEN UNJUSTLY USED?
ALL HAIL THE NEW LORD OF THE NETHERWORLD! PLUTO IS THUS FREED--WHILST HERCULES SHALL SERVE IN HIS STEAD--FOREVER!
THE TIME OF VALOR IS PAST! THE AGE OF THE WARRIOR IS DEAD! LET HERCULES THEN PERISH WITH THEM!

HAH! IT IS THINE OWN ACCURSED POWER WHICH HAS PROVEN TO BE THINE UNDOING! ONLY ENEMIES HAST THOU MADE IN BATTLE--NEVER FRIENDS!
16

I SAY THEE NAY, EMPEROR OF EVIL! ONE THERE IS WHO SHALL FIGHT FOR THE PRINCE OF POWER!
LET THY WARRIORS GATHER! LET THY OWN AWESOME FORCES BE ASSEMBLED! AGAINST THEM ALL, I SHALL PREVAIL!
IMPOSSIBLE!! NONE THERE ARE WHO WOULD DARE--!!

NONE--SAVE A WARRIOR BORN!
THE GOD OF THUNDER DARES!!
NEXT ISSUE:
INTO THE NETHERWORLD!

TALES OF ASGARD, HOME OF THE MIGHTY NORSE GODS
"THE HORDES OF HAROKIN!"
Know Ye This:
IT HATH BEEN PREDICTED THAT TRAITOROUS LOKI, BY UNITING THE FORCES OF EVIL, WOULD ONE DAY BE RESPONSIBLE FOR RAGNAROK, THE END OF THE WORLD!
THEREFORE, IMPERIAL ODIN DOTH ISSUE A GRIM COMMAND...
NO! NO! I AM INNOCENT! IT IS LIES-- ALL LIES!! SPARE ME--!
TO THE WELL OF ETERNAL SLEEP WITH HIM! I HAVE SPOKEN!
FABULOUSLY WRITTEN BY... STAN LEE
FANTASTICALLY DRAWN BY... JACK KIRBY
FASTIDIOUSLY INKED BY....... V. COLLETTA
FINALLY LETTERED BY......... ARTIE SIMEK
1

THUS, IT COMES TO PASS THAT THE HALF-BROTHER OF THOR IS SENTENCED TO PAY FOR FOUL DEEDS EARLIER COMMITTED--AND DARK DEEDS YET UNDONE--!
SO BE IT!
NO SOONER DOES THE PRINCE OF EVIL HURTLE INTO THE DREADED WELL, THAN A BARRAGE OF VAPORS INSTANTLY ENGULFS HIM, PLACING HIM IN A PAINLESS STATE OF UNENDING SUSPENDED ANIMATION....!
HONORED SIRE! THOUGH LOKI IS SURELY DESERVING OF HIS FATE, STILL IS HE MY BROTHER--STILL IS HE THY SON--!
HOLD THY TONGUE, THUNDER GOD!
THINK YOU THAT ODIN BE NOT AS SORELY GRIEVED AS THEE? THINK YOU MY HEART DOTH NOT BEAT HEAVY WITHIN MY BREAST?
YET, THE LORD OF ASGARD MUST BE FIRST A MONARCH --AND THEN A FATHER! I SHALL HEAR NO MORE!
FOR LONG, POIGNANT MOMENTS --AS OMNIPOTENT ODIN COVERS HIS REGAL FACE WITH A BATTLE-WEARY HAND--A HEAVY, SOMBER SILENCE FILLS THE GREAT CHAMBER--THE SILENCE OF A FATHER--WEEPING WITHOUT TEARS!
2

BUT THEN, AT LAST, THE SPELL IS SHATTERED BY THE STENTORIAN VOICE OF THE SOVEREIGN OF ASGARD--!
REMAIN WHERE THOU ART, GOD OF THUNDER!
AND NOW, LET HOGUN, VOLSTAGG, AND FANDRAL APPROACH THE ROYAL PRESENCE!
--AHH!-- NOW SHALL MY HEART SING-- FOR A MISSION IS IN THE OFFING!

THE LIFE OF HOGUN, THE GRIM IS THINE, NOBLE ODIN--FOR THOU ART TRULY ASGARD!
SO TOO SPEAKS VOLSTAGG, SIRE! I, THE EAGLE OF WARRIORS, FLY TO THY SERVICE!
THOUGH A THOUSAND KNAVES OPPOSE ME, THE BLADE OF FANDRAL, THE DASHING, SHALL SING FOR MY LORD!
THEN COME YE FORTH-- ALL-- AND HEED MY WORDS--!

TO THE LAND OF MUSPELHEIM SHALT THOU JOURNEY--THERE TO FETCH FOR THY LIEGE THE ENCHANTED WARLOCK'S EYE FROM THE TEMPLE OF MYSTICS!
ONLY BY KEEPING SUCH WEAPONS FROM THE FORCES OF EVIL CAN THE DAY OF RAG-NAROK BE POST-PONED!
THEN GET THEE HENCE, MY WARRIORS! MAY THE EYES OF ASGARD BE EVER UPON THEE!

BUT, EVEN AS ODIN SPEAKS, CALAMITY HAS ALREADY STRUCK! AT A FAR OUTPOST, NEAR THE LAND OF MUSPELHEIM, A FATEFUL ALARM RINGS OUT--!
TO ARMS!! TO ARMS!! THE HORDES OF HAROKIN ATTACK!
BEHOLD! IN THE DISTANCE-- MUSPELHEIM IS ALREADY AFLAME! HAROKIN HATH BROKEN THRU!
HE HATH SEIZED THE WARLOCK'S EYE!
THEN-- TRULY WE ARE UNDONE!

THE EYE IS MINE! NOW LET US STRIKE! NO POWER IN THE UNIVERSE CAN STEM THE TIDE!! TODAY, IT IS MUSPELHEIM!! TOMORROW-- ASGARD ITSELF!!
'ERE I AM DONE, THE ENTIRE COSMOS SHALL PAY HOMAGE TO HAROKIN--WHILE ALL THAT LIVE SHALL BE TRAMPLED UNDER FOOT BY MY INVINCIBLE HORDES!

NEXT ISSUE:

"THE FATEFUL CHANGE!"

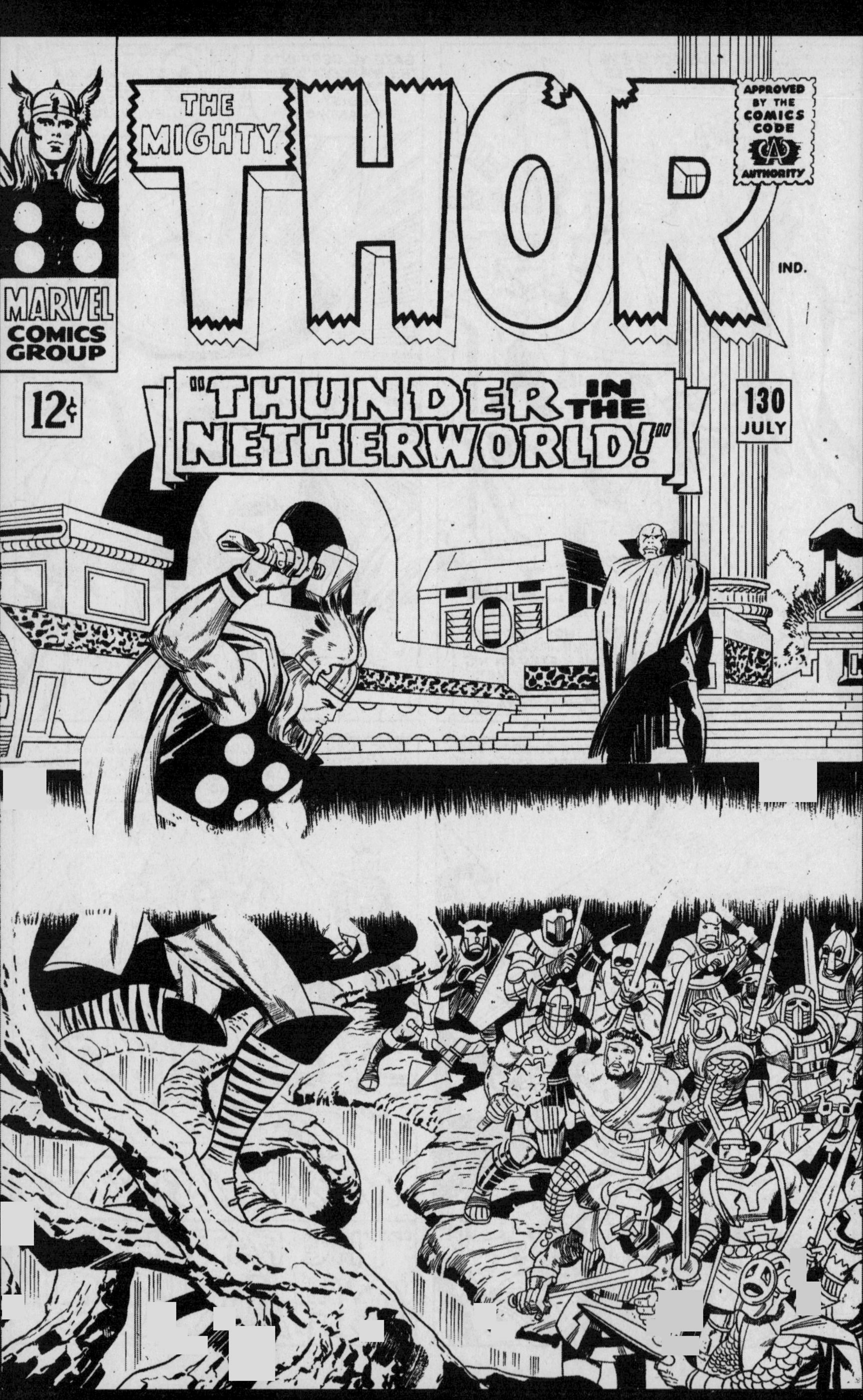

THE MIGHTY
THOR
APPROVED BY THE COMICS CODE AUTHORITY
IND.
MARVEL COMICS GROUP
12¢
"THUNDER IN THE NETHERWORLD!"
130
JULY

THE MIGHTY THOR!
"THUNDER IN THE NETHERWORLD!"
PLUTO! LET THY WARRIORS GATHER! LET THINE OWN AWESOME POWERS BE ASSEMBLED! THOR, SON OF ODIN, ACCEPTS THY CHALLENGE!
THE GOD OF THUNDER SHALL BATTLE TO SAVE HERCULES!
CONSIDER WELL, MIGHTY ONE! IF THOU SHOULDST FIND DEFEAT AT THE HANDS OF MY SUBJECTS, THEN THOR MUST TAKE THE PLACE OF HERCULES AS RULER OF THE DREADED NETHERWORLD-- FOR ALL ETERNITY!
LET US PROCLAIM A PROUD PAEAN OF PRAISE FOR MARVEL'S MOST PROLIFIC PURVEYORS OF PEERLESS PAGEANTRY--
STAN THE MAN LEE, WRITER
JACK KING KIRBY, ARTIST
VINCE THE PRINCE COLLETTA, DELINEATOR
ARTIE PUSSYCAT SIMEK, LETTERER
1

IT IS SAID THAT THOU ART ENEMY OF HERCULES! WHAT CAUSES THEE, THEN, TO RISK THY LIFE AND LIBERTY FOR THE ARROGANT OLYMPIAN?
THOUGH THE SON OF ZEUS HATH DONE BATTLE WITH ME IN THE PAST, HE HATH ACQUITTED HIMSELF AS AN IMMORTAL SHOULD!
THE POWER OF HIS ARM DOTH MATCH THE VALOR IN HIS HEART! THOU DIDST NOT DEFEAT HIM IN FAIR COMBAT!
IT IS NOT FIT THAT ONE SO VALIANT BE DOOMED--WITH NONE TO BE HIS CHAMPION!
I KNOW NOT WHAT MADNESS IS UPON THEE--BUT THE DIE IS CAST!

MYSTIC FINGERS OF FLAME--RISING ALL ABOUT ME! THUS DOES EVIL PLUTO SEAL HIS COMPACT!
THE PRINCE OF POWER IS ALREADY TRAPPED WITHIN THE SMOULDERING NETHERWORLD!
AND NOW I SHALL SEND THEE TO JOIN HIM!

THOUGH HE IS FORBIDDEN TO DO BATTLE FOR HIS FREEDOM, THOR MUST FIGHT EVERY INCH OF THE WAY--
NEVER HAS A CAUSE BEEN MORE HOPELESS! NEVER HAS MAN OR IMMORTAL FACED SUCH AWESOME ODDS!

AND NOW-- AWAY WITH THEE!
THE ENTRANCE TO MY REALM LIES THERE--AT THY FEET! ONE STEP FURTHER, AND THOU SHALT ENTER THE PORTALS OF BLAZING ENERGY--TO RETURN NEVERMORE!
ENTER, I SHALL! AND RETURN I SHALL!! THUS SPEAKS THE THUNDER GOD!

SLOWLY, SAVAGELY, THE UNSEEN ELEMENTS OF INFINITY ALTER THEIR ENDLESS PATTERN--AND THEN, WITHOUT WARNING --THE MISTS CLEAR-- AND THOR BEHOLDS--

THE ETERNAL NETHERWORLD-- THE MOST DREADED REALM OF ALL!

'TIS HERE I SHALL GAIN FOR HERCULES HIS FREEDOM--OR LOSE MINE OWN --TILL THE END OF TIME!

AND THEN, UTTERLY WITHOUT WARNING--
THE CRAVEN CERBERUS-- WHOSE NAME IS SPOKEN IN WHISPERS THRUOUT THE UNIVERSE!
STAND FAST, INTERLOPER! I BE CERBERUS, GUARDIAN OF THE DEPTHS.!!
NO FURTHER SHALT THOU GO--UNLESS IT BE ON THY KNEES, IN ABJECT SUBMISSION AND SURRENDER!
ALL WHO DWELL BELOW MUST CRINGE IN FEAR BEFORE MY MIGHT!
THE GOD OF THUNDER DEFERS TO NONE!
THEN THE GOD OF THUNDER DIES!
THOOM
NOT SO, THOU MURDEROUS ABHORRENCE.! 'TIS AN ASGARDIAN WHO FACES THEE!
CLANNG
THEN LET IT BE AN ASGARDIAN WHO FALLS BENEATH MY HELMET'S RAY OF DESTRUCTION!
ZZZISSSS
THE SPEED OF THOR DOTH MAKE A MOCKERY OF THEE AND THY WEAPON.!
AND NOW--PREPARE TO FEEL THE THUNDER OF MINE OWN HAMMER!
4

THINE EMPTY THREATS ARE LIKE UNTO THINE OWN SIZE, CERBERUS--
--TRULY AWESOME TO BEHOLD--YET, AS ODIN IS MY JUDGE, THEY BE WITHOUT SHADOW OR SUBSTANCE!

READY THYSELF THEN--
--WITH FOE SUCH AS THEE, THE HAND OF THOR SHALL NOT BE STAYED IN THE NAME OF MERCY--!

BRAKOOM!

AT THAT VERY INSTANT, AN INCALCULABLE DISTANCE AWAY, IN A NEW YORK APARTMENT, WE FIND--
SINCE REVEALING HIS TRUE IDENTITY TO ME, MY BELOVED HAS GONE TO ASGARD, TO RENOUNCE HIS IMMORTAL HERITAGE--SO THAT WE CAN BE MARRIED HERE ON EARTH!
WELL! I SEE THAT MY ROMANTIC ROOMMATE IS STILL OBSESSED WITH THOUGHTS OF THE GOD OF THUNDER!
BUT, HE SHOULD HAVE RETURNED TO ME LONG BEFORE THIS! AND YET--NOT A WORD SO FAR--!

OH, TANA--TANA! I NEVER THINK OF HIM AS THE THUNDER GOD! TO ME, HE'S MERELY THE ONLY MAN I COULD EVER SO DESPERATELY LOVE--!
LOVE!!
AN EMOTION FIT FOR ONLY FOOLS--AND WEAKLINGS!
GREEK MYTHS

LET YOUR KNEES GROW WEAK! LET THE STRENGTH EBB FROM YOUR BODY! FROM THIS MOMENT HENCE YOU ARE NO LONGER MISTRESS OF YOUR OWN WILL!

I MUST REMOVE YOU FROM THIS PLACE BEFORE THE MIGHTY THOR CAN REAPPEAR! FOR HE--OF ALL WHO LIVE--MUST NEVER LEARN MY SECRET!

CEASE THY STRUGGLES, HERCULES!
ONCE THIS CROWN DOTH SIT UPON THY HEAD, THIS WORLD BECOMES THY DOMAIN--AND PRISON AS WELL--UNTIL TIME ITSELF SHALL EXIST NO MORE!
PLACE IT UPON HIM! THE LAW OF OLYMPUS FORBIDS THAT HE RESIST!

NAY! NAY! I AM A WARRIOR BORN! IF I MUST KNOW DEFEAT, LET IT BE IN BATTLE! LET IT BE AT THE HANDS OF A MORE POWERFUL FOE!
BUT NOT THIS! BY THE TOWERING SPIRES OF ETERNAL OLYMPUS--NOT THIS!
THE PRINCE OF POWER CANNOT RULE THE DREGS OF THE UNIVERSE!! HATH REASON FLED?? HATH JUSTICE PERISHED??

BUT THEN, A BOOMING COMMAND THUNDERS THRU THE GREAT CHAMBER--
STAND AWAY, SCIONS OF EVIL! THE SON OF ZEUS IS NOT YET THINE!
NOT SO LONG AS THE HAMMER OF THOR CAN STRIKE IN HIS BEHALF!

THE GOD OF THUNDER!! THEN, ONE THERE IS WILLING TO RISK ALL FOR HERCULES!
ONCE, I CALLED THEE ENEMY! NOW, UPON TRUER FRIEND MINE EYES HAVE NEVER FEASTED!

BUT, BEFORE THE POWERFUL OLYMPIAN CAN ADVANCE ANOTHER STEP, HE IS STOPPED IN HIS TRACKS BY THE ENCHANTMENT OF THE PACT HE HAS SIGNED!
DESIST, HERCULES! IT IS FORBIDDEN THAT THOU LIFT THY HAND IN BATTLE! ONLY ANOTHER MAY DO SO FOR THEE!

MIGHTY THOR--THOUGH I HAVE POWER ENOW TO SHAKE THE UNIVERSE--'TIS THEE WHO MUST STRIKE IN MY BEHALF!
I PRAY THAT THINE ARM BE STRONG, AND THINE EYE BE TRUE! KNOW YOU THAT HERCULES COULD WISH NO NOBLER CHAMPION!

MY HEART GRIEVES TO SEE PROUD HERCULES THUS STRIPPED OF HIS AWESOME POWER!
NONE CAN KNOW AS WELL AS I WHAT THE LOSS OF STRENGTH CAN MEAN TO A WARRIOR BORN!
SO! ALL THE HORDES OF PLUTO OPPOSE ME IN A BODY! THIS THEN IS THE TEST SUPREME!

BY THE BRISTLING BEARD OF ODIN-- I SHALL NOT FAIL!
HAVE AT THEE, THEN! TO ARMS, ONE AND ALL! THE GOD OF THUNDER STRIKES--!

KRRAK!

WE'D LIKE TO LETTER A LOT OF NEW **SOUND EFFECTS** IN THIS FRANKLY FABULOUS PANEL--HONEST! BUT, JUST BETWEEN US, WE CAN'T THINK OF A SINGLE ONE THAT COULD DO JUSTICE TO THE IMPACT, THE FURY, THE SHEER CATACLYSMIC **POWER** OF THOR'S ATTACK--!

BACK, YE HOSTS OF PILLAGE AND PLUNDER!! **BACK**, YE HARBINGERS OF DOOM AND DESPAIR! BACK, **BACK**, BEFORE THE SHATTERING WRATH OF **THOR**!

BUT, BEFORE THE FATAL BLAST CAN STRIKE ITS IMMORTAL TARGET, THE MIGHTY THOR MOVES AS ONLY A THUNDER GOD CAN-- SEIZING AN ARMFUL OF HAPLESS FOES AND USING THEM AS ARMORED SHIELDS AGAINST THE DEADLY CANNON--!
THE SON OF ODIN IS NO WHIMPERING TARGET, TO BE STRUCK AT WILL BY SUCH AS THEE!
AND NOW, I MUST STRIKE BACK FORTHWITH, ERE ANOTHER VOLLEY CAN BE FIRED!
THE SHELL HATH STRUCK OUR OWN WARRIORS! THE COSMIC SLEEP SHALL ENFOLD THEM FOR A CENTURY!

ASGARD FOREVER!!

BEEANG!

STRIKING THE AWESOME CANNON DEAD CENTER, THE HAMMER OF THOR RENDS IT IN TWAIN, AS THE MADLY-SPINNING IRON WHEELS INEXORABLY HURTLE THRU THE WALLS THEMSELVES--
ANOTHER CHALLENGE HATH BEEN MET! BUT, THE DEADLY PITFALLS OF THE NETHERWORLD ARE VERILY WITHOUT LIMIT!
EVEN NOW, THE MINIONS OF PLUTO CONTRIVE TO CRUSH ME WITH SOME NEW DEVICE!

AND, THE PROPHETIC MUSINGS OF THOR BEAR FRUIT A SPLIT-SECOND LATER--
THE WEAPONS OF THE NETHERWORLD ARE WELL-NIGH INEXHAUSTIBLE, THUNDER GOD--
--AS YOU SHALL FORTHWITH SEE!
THE LEVER HE PUSHES! WHAT DREAD DANGER DOTH THAT PORTEND?

THE FLOOR BENEATH MY FEET HATH DROPPED AWAY! A GLASS-LIKE CAGE NOW SURROUNDS ME!
I AM BEING SWIFTLY, SILENTLY LOWERED-- BUT--TO WHENCE--?
PREPARE TO BE RENDERED HELPLESS, DOOMED ONE--FOR THOU ART FINALLY TRAPPED--WITHIN A SHATTERPROOF TURBULENCE CHAMBER!
PLUTO'S TURBULENCE TRAP!! ARTIFICIAL WIND PRESSURE DESIGNED TO SLAY ANYTHING THAT LIVES!

AND SO FAREWELL, IMMORTAL OF ASGARD --FAREWELL--FOR THE FINAL TIME!
WHOOOSH

WHILE, BACK IN NEW YORK--AT THAT SELFSAME SECOND--
ALL OF A SUDDEN--I FEEL A COLD CHILL--AS THOUGH AN ICY WIND IS CLUTCHING MY HEART!
PUT EVERY OTHER THOUGHT OUT OF YOUR MIND! YOU MUST OBEY ONLY ME!
NOW--DEPART!
I MUST OBEY--ONLY YOU--!

GO! AS FAR FROM HERE AS POSSIBLE! DO NOT LOOK BACK! DO NOT RETURN! THOR MUST NEVER FIND YOU AGAIN!
THOR MUST--NEVER--FIND ME--AGAIN--!
GO! GO! GO!
I DO NOT--UNDERSTAND--AND YET--I KNOW--I CAN NEVER--DISOBEY YOU--!

IF HE LIVES, I KNOW THAT THE THUNDER GOD WILL RETURN FOR THE ONE HE LOVES!
BUT, WHEN HE FINDS HER GONE, HE WILL LEAVE! HE WILL SEARCH THE FARTHEST REACHES OF SPACE FOR HER! AND THUS MUST IT BE!
THE FATE OF JANE FOSTER DOES NOT MATTER! SHE IS MERELY A PAWN--IN A FAR GREATER GAME OF CELESTIAL CHESS!
11

LOOK AT THEM, SCAMPERING IN THE STREET BELOW! POOR UNSUSPECTING MORTALS! SO PITIFULLY WEAK--SO TOTALLY HELPLESS!
OF ALL THOSE TEEMING MILLIONS, NOT ONE IS AWARE OF THE DARK DESTINY WHICH SO SURELY AWAITS THEM!

BUT NOW, I HAVE MADE CERTAIN THAT THE SON OF ODIN SHALL NOT INTERFERE WITH MY SECRET PLAN...
THUS, I AM FREE TO ACT--TO CAST ASIDE THE FOOLISH CLOAK OF MORTALITY!
THEN WHEN MY PLAN BEARS FRUIT AT LAST--LET MANKIND BEWARE!

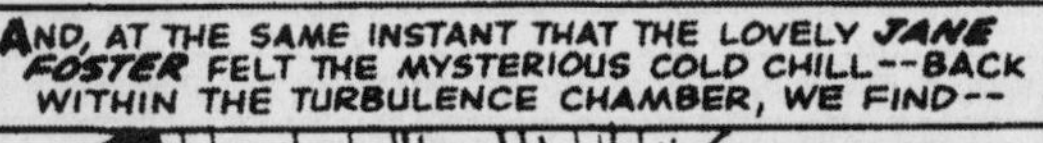
AND, AT THE SAME INSTANT THAT THE LOVELY JANE FOSTER FELT THE MYSTERIOUS COLD CHILL--BACK WITHIN THE TURBULENCE CHAMBER, WE FIND--

A STRANGE, ICY SENSATION SEEMS TO CLUTCH AT MY HEART--AS THOUGH ONE WHOM I LOVE IS IN DIRE DANGER!

THUS IT IS THAT THOR DOES NOT RISE TO HIS FEET WHEN THE TURBULENCE ENDS--FOR HIS BRAIN STILL IS SEETHING--
CAN IT BE JANE? CAN SOME NEW, DEADLY PERIL BE MENACING HER ON THE SURFACE OF EARTH?
OR, IS IT MY FATHER? DOTH THE ETERNAL RAINBOW BRIDGE TREMBLE ONCE AGAIN BENEATH AN INVADER'S BOOT?!!

NAY! I MUST BANISH SUCH THOUGHTS FROM MY BRAIN! THERE IS BATTLE STILL TO BE WON, HERE IN THE KINGDOM OF PLUTO--!
THE THUNDER GOD LIES MOTIONLESS!
HE HATH BEEN OVER-COME!
SEIZE HIM! THE VICTORY IS OURS!

BUT, BEFORE ANOTHER MOVE CAN BE MADE--
CLANNG!
HE LIVES! THOR STILL LIVES!
HIS HAMMER HATH FREED HIM WITH BUT ONE BLOW!
12

BEHOLD HIS FIGHTING STANCE-- HIS BLAZING EYES-- THE WAY HIS LIMBS DO STRAIN, AS THOUGH ANXIOUS TO HURL THEMSELVES INTO BATTLE!

LOOK TO THY DEFENSES, EVIL ONES--!

NEVER HATH THE NETHERWORLD KNOWN HIS LIKE!

IN THE NAME OF IMPERIAL ASGARD-- BY THE GRACE OF OMNIPOTENT ODIN--

NOW STRIKES THOR!!

WHROOOOOM!

BUT, NO SOONER HAS THE CRUSHER BEEN DISPATCHED, THAN...
ARCHERS! FIRE AT WILL!
THWITT
THWITT
ARROWS!! STILL THEY DARE TO TEST MY METTLE!!
THE MARKSMEN STAND ATOP YON STONE DEMON IDOL--WHILE THOR SEEMS DEFENSELESS BELOW!
BUT, IF THE IDOL ITSELF SHALL CRUMBLE--THEN THE ARCHERS TOO MUST TOPPLE INTO BLEAK DEFEAT!
SO BE IT!!
KARAA

YET, STILL THE RUTHLESS, SEEMINGLY UNENDING ATTACK CONTINUES--
NOW I AM CONFRONTED BY AN ARMY OF FLAME-THROWERS!! BUT, MY SWIRLING HAMMER SHALL DISPEL THEIR FIERY BLASTS!
WHOOOSH
DO THY WORST, CREATURES OF THE DARK!! THY REALM ITSELF SHALL CRUMBLE ERE THE GOD OF THUNDER TASTES DEFEAT!

SUDDENLY, A NEW VOICE RINGS OUT--
ENOUGH! LET THE COMBAT CEASE!!
PLUTO!

WITHIN A MATTER OF MINUTES, YOU HAVE TORN DOWN WHAT IT HAS TAKEN ME AGES TO CREATE!
I CAN WITNESS NO FURTHER DESTRUCTION TO THE REALM I HAVE RULED SINCE THE DAWN OF TIME!

MY SUBJECTS WOULD FIGHT TO THE END IF I WISH IT--BUT YOUR POWER IS TOO GREAT! IT WOULD AVAIL ME NOTHING!
THY PLACE IS HERE, PLUTO! THOU WOULDST NOT HAVE FOUND CONTENTMENT IN THE WORLD ABOVE!
YOU ARE RIGHT, THUNDER GOD! I KNOW THAT NOW!

I SHALL FREE THEE OF THY FATE, OLYMPIAN!
THEN--MIGHTY THOR HAS TRIUMPHED?!!
AY! THE ORDEAL IS ENDED!

NEXT ISSUE:

THE STRANGE SECRET OF TANA NILE!

WE HAVE SPOKEN!

TALES OF ASGARD, HOME OF THE MIGHTY NORSE GODS
"THE FATEFUL CHANGE!"
MY GLORIOUS RECORD PROVES THAT VOLSTAGG KNOWS NOT THE MEANING OF FEAR! BUT, WHY DO WE RACE SO QUICKLY INTO A LAND WHERE DEATH LURKS EVERYWHERE?
YON CITY OF MUSPELHEIM HAS FALLEN TO THE HORDES OF HAROKIN! WE MUST LIBERATE THE LAND WHILE WE CAN!
TRUE, HOGUN! YET, I PERCEIVE NO SIGNS OF BATTLE! HOW DID HAROKIN ACHIEVE HIS CONQUEST?
THERE CAN BE BUT ONE ANSWER, FANDRAL...
...HAROKIN HAS SEIZED THE ENCHANTED WARLOCK'S EYE! POSSESSING IT, NONE CAN STAND AGAINST HIM!
SCRIPT: STAN LEE
ART: JACK KIRBY
INKING: VINCE COLLETTA
LETTERING: SAM ROSEN
COSTUMES: ASGARD HABERDASHERY
1

SEE HOW HAROKIN'S BARBARIANS DISPORT THEMSELVES IN FIERCE AND SAVAGE MANNER!
YET, NO TRACE OF THE DEFENDERS OF MUSPELHEIM DO I SEE! IN TRUTH, THE VICTORS HAVE CONSIGNED THE VANQUISHED TO THE DUNGEONS!
HAIL, HAROKIN, CONQUEROR OF ALL! HAIL WARLOCK'S EYE, WHEREIN LIES HIS MATCHLESS POWER!
ENOUGH SPEECH-MAKING! 'TIS A TIME FOR WILD CAROUSING!

HOGUN! BEHIND THEE! WE HAVE BEEN DISCOVERED! THE LEGIONS OF HAROKIN ATTACK!
DEATH TO THE INTRUDER! NOT AN ASGARDIAN SHALL REMAIN ALIVE!
'TIS THOU WHO SHALL TASTE DEFEAT.. THOUGH THY NUMBERS BE ENDLESS!

KNOW YOU 'TIS HOGUN, THE GRIM YOU FACE! HOGUN, DOTH LIVE FOR BATTLE!
LET HIM WHO HATH TIRED OF LIFE ADVANCE-- ADVANCE TO FEEL THE POWER OF HOGUN'S BATTLE MACE!

NAY, GRIM ONE! THOU MAY NOT HAVE ALL THE COMBAT TO THYSELF! FANDRAL WOULD SHARE THE EXALTATION WITH THEE!
THOUGH MY EVERY LIMB ACHES TO JOIN THEE, I MUST MAKE THE SUPREME SACRIFICE AND TURN MY ATTENTION ELSEWHERE!
FOR ANOTHER HATH NEED OF VOLSTAGG'S AWE-SOME MIGHT!

SHOULDST THOU NEED HELP, DASHING FANDRAL --- SAY BUT TO THYSELF: "WHAT WOULD MIGHTY VOLSTAGG DO IF HE WERE SORELY PRESSED?"
NOW MUST I HASTEN TO THE SIDE OF THE GOD OF THUNDER!
WE SHALL FOLLOW THEE SOON, GARGANTUAN ONE! NONE IN THIS MOTLEY GROUP ARE WORTHY METTLE FOR OUR SKILL!

BUT, WHILE THE LUMBERING VOLSTAGG SEARCHES IN VAIN, THOR HAS ALREADY FOUND THE ONE HE SOUGHT...
GOD OF THUNDER OR NO... THOU CANNOT MATCH THE BATTLE PROWESS OF HAROKIN!
FIE! A DOZEN LIKE THEE CAN I DEFEAT WITHOUT THE SLIGHTEST EXERTION!
CRRAKK!
YOU LIE, THUNDER GOD!
NONE SPEAK THUS RUDELY TO THE SON OF ODIN!!
WOK!
I HAVE FELLED HIM...YET, THE BATTLE IS NOT YET ENDED!
I MUST RECOVER THE WARLOCK'S EYE... THOUGH ONLY HAROKIN MAY COMMAND ITS APPEARANCE...
STRANGE...I HAD NOT EARLIER NOTICED HIS APPEARANCE! IN TRUTH, HE DOTH RESEMBLE ME!
4.

I BEGIN TO PERCEIVE THE GLIMMER OF A PLAN! IF NONE BUT HAROKIN CAN ORDER FORTH THE WARLOCK'S EYE...
...THEN, WHY SHOULD NOT THE GOD OF THUNDER ACTUALLY BE HAROKIN?

THUS, MOMENTS LATER...
WE MUST TELL HAROKIN OF THE DANGER THAT THREATENS OUR LEGIONS!
THERE IS NOT A MINUTE TO LOSE!
IF TWO ASGARDIANS BE AMONG US ...HOW MANY OTHERS MAY ALSO BE LYING IN WAIT?

MASTER OF BARBARIANS, WE SALUTE THEE!
WE ARE UNDER ATTACK, HAROKIN...THERE BE WARRIORS OF ASGARD AMONGST US! WHAT IS THY COMMAND?

THERE CAN BE BUT ONE RESPONSE...
WE MUST EMPLOY THE WARLOCK'S EYE! WITH SUCH A WEAPON, EVEN ASGARD SHALL CRUMBLE BENEATH OUR HEELS!
NEXT ISSUE: "THE WARLOCK'S EYE!"
5.

THE MIGHTY

THOR

131
AUG
IND.

APPROVED BY THE COMICS CODE AUTHORITY

12¢

"THEY STRIKE FROM SPACE!"

THE MIGHTY THOR!
"THEY STRIKE FROM SPACE!"
REJOICE, YE MARVELITES! MIGHTY THOR HAS WON FREEDOM FOR HERCULES BY DEFEATING THE FORCES OF PLUTO IN DEADLY COMBAT! AND NOW, FLUSHED WITH TRIUMPH, THE TWO IMMORTALS APPEAR IN THE FABLED REALM OF ZEUS...
WE'VE DONE IT, THUNDER GOD! WE'VE PIERCED THE DIMENSIONAL BARRIER! I'VE RETURNED TO OLYMPUS --AT LAST!
SCRIPT........SMILIN' STAN LEE
ART..........JOLLY JACK KIRBY
INKS.........VIVACIOUS V. COLLETTA
LETTERING...AFFABLE ARTIE SIMEK
CELESTIAL GUIDED TOURS.... HONEST IRVING FORBUSH
1

SO! YOU THOUGHT YOURSELVES RID OF THE PRINCE OF POWER!
BUT, THE SON OF ODIN HATH WAGED THE FIGHT WHICH WAS FORBIDDEN TO ME--AND NOW--HERE STANDS HERCULES!
OVERBEARING BRAGGART! BETTER THOU HAD REMAINED IN THE NETHERWORLD!
'TIS ARES, COLD-HEARTED GRECIAN GOD OF WAR WHO SPEAKS!

NAH! I STILL HAVE A SCORE TO SETTLE WITH THE COWARD WHO WOULD NOT WIELD HIS SWORD IN HERCULES' BEHALF!
SO LONG AS ZEUS FAVORS THEE ABOVE ARES, THOU SHALT EVER BE MINE ENEMY!
AND THOSE WHO AID THEE, AS WELL!

'TIS TIME FOR THOR TO TAKE HIS LEAVE!
THE THUNDER GOD HATH ENEMIES A'PLENTY!
MY TASK HERE IS DONE! NOW MUST I RETURN FORTHWITH TO THE COURT OF IMPERIAL ODIN!

FOR THE FINAL TIME I SHALL REQUEST MY REGAL FATHER'S PERMISSION TO MARRY JANE FOSTER!
AND, IF I BE DENIED, I SHALL RENOUNCE MY HERITAGE! I'LL BE GOD OF THUNDER NO MORE!
2

AT LAST! THE ENCHANTMENT BEGINS! THE WIND OF THE WORLDS DOTH ENGULF ME!
BLOW, YE POUNDING GALES! UNLEASH THE FURY OF THY AWESOME POWER! THE THUNDER GOD COMMANDS!

THEN, FASTER THAN THE EYE CAN FOLLOW, OR THE MIND CAN COMPREHEND--THE MIGHTY THOR IS GONE--!
SHOOOSH!

BUT, WHAT OF THE LOVELY MORTAL WHOM THE ASGARDIAN AVENGER DESIRES MORE THAN LIFE ITSELF? FOR THE ANSWER, LET US TURN OUR ATTENTION TO A CROSS-COUNTRY BUS, AS IT SPEEDS FROM THE BUSTLING CITY...
I DON'T WANT TO LEAVE NEW YORK! WHAT WILL HAPPEN WHEN THOR RETURNS AND FINDS ME GONE?
AND YET--I CANNOT STOP MYSELF! SOMETHING IS FORCING ME TO GO ON!

IT'S BECAUSE OF TANA NILE! WHEN SHE ANSWERED MY AD, TO BE MY ROOMMATE, I NEVER DREAMT SHE POSSESSED A STRANGE, UNDEFINABLE POWER...
IT WAS SHE WHO WILLED ME TO LEAVE--AND I CANNOT DEFY HER WISH!
BUT, WHY DID SHE DO IT? IF ONLY I KNEW! WHY? WHY?
YOU'VE BEEN SO QUIET, MY DEAR! WHERE IS YOUR DESTINATION?

I DO NOT KNOW! ALL I KNOW IS-- IT MUST BE VERY, VERY FAR AWAY!
THAT IS THE COMMAND I HAVE BEEN GIVEN--AND I MAY NOT DISOBEY--I CANNOT DISOBEY--THE ORDER OF TANA NILE!
TANA NILE--?

TANA NILE! THE STRANGE, INSCRUTABLE FEMALE WHOSE STARTLING, STAGGERING SECRET WE ARE NOW ABOUT TO LEARN...
THE NEED FOR HUMILIATING DISGUISE IS ENDED!
LET THERE THEN BE AN END TO MY MYTHICAL HUMAN FORM...

I HAVE LEARNED ALL I NEED KNOW ABOUT CONDITIONS ON THIS PRIMITIVE PLANET CALLED *EARTH*--

THUS, I HAVE DUTIFULLY FULFILLED THE FIRST BASIC TASK OF EVERY *SPACE COLONIZER!*

AND NOW, THE TIME HAS COME TO *COLONIZE* THIS UNSUSPECTING WORLD-- AND TO RULE IT AS *MY OWN!*

THE *OTHER* COLONIZERS HAVE *IGNORED* EARTH BECAUSE OF ITS SMALL SIZE AND RELATIVE UNIMPORTANCE!
BUT, IT WILL BE A PERFECT STEPPING-STONE FOR *ME!* THUS, I MUST CONTACT THE *COMMAND PLANET* AT THE CONSTELLATION *RIGEL*--

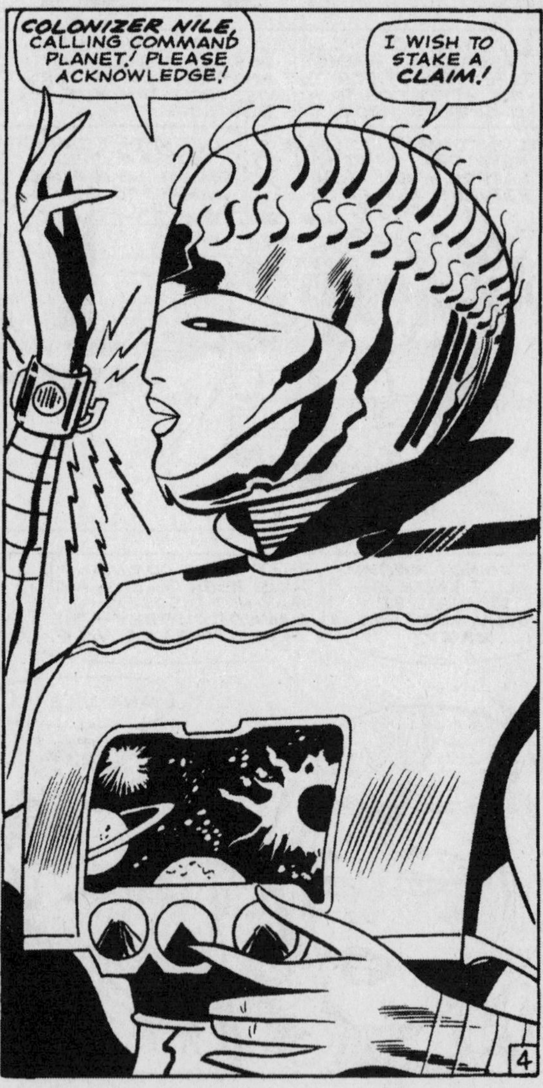
COLONIZER NILE, CALLING COMMAND PLANET! PLEASE ACKNOWLEDGE!
I WISH TO STAKE A *CLAIM!*

AT THAT MOMENT, ON A PLANET SO LARGE, IN A GALAXY SO DISTANT THAT IT BEGGARS OUR POOR, MORTAL POWER OF DESCRIPTION, AN INTERCOSMIC COMMUNICATIONS SYSTEM IS AUTOMATICALLY ACTIVATED...

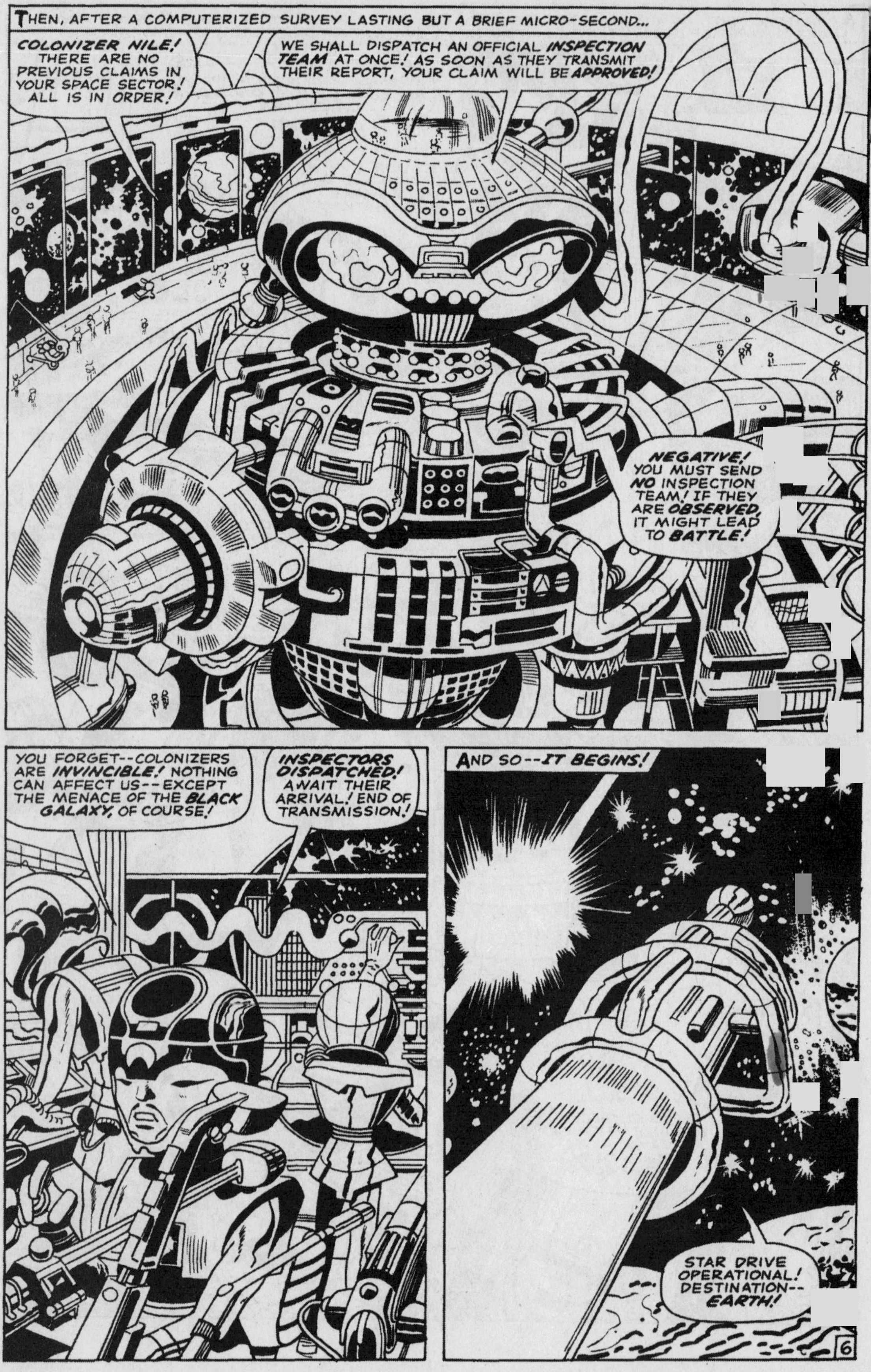

THEN, AFTER A COMPUTERIZED SURVEY LASTING BUT A BRIEF MICRO-SECOND...

COLONIZER NILE! THERE ARE NO PREVIOUS CLAIMS IN YOUR SPACE SECTOR! ALL IS IN ORDER!

WE SHALL DISPATCH AN OFFICIAL INSPECTION TEAM AT ONCE! AS SOON AS THEY TRANSMIT THEIR REPORT, YOUR CLAIM WILL BE APPROVED!

NEGATIVE! YOU MUST SEND NO INSPECTION TEAM! IF THEY ARE OBSERVED, IT MIGHT LEAD TO BATTLE!

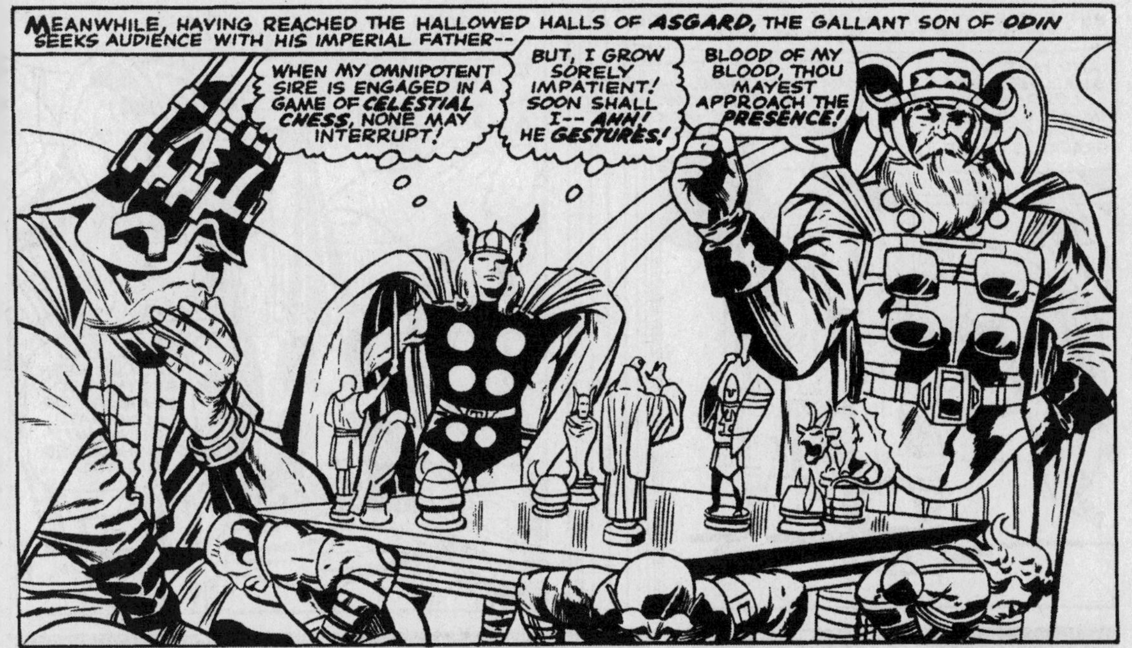
MEANWHILE, HAVING REACHED THE HALLOWED HALLS OF ASGARD, THE GALLANT SON OF ODIN SEEKS AUDIENCE WITH HIS IMPERIAL FATHER--
WHEN MY OMNIPOTENT SIRE IS ENGAGED IN A GAME OF CELESTIAL CHESS, NONE MAY INTERRUPT!
BUT, I GROW SORELY IMPATIENT! SOON SHALL I-- AHH! HE GESTURES!
BLOOD OF MY BLOOD, THOU MAYEST APPROACH THE PRESENCE!

REGAL LORD, I CRAVE ONE BOON! IT CONCERNS THE MORTAL GIRL--
HOLD! MY MIND DOTH PERCEIVE A MASTER STROKE! LET THERE BE SILENCE!
IS MY SUIT OF SO LITTLE IMPORTANCE? AM I TO BE DENIED ONCE MORE?

HAH! THE GAME IS MINE! SO BE IT!
FATHER, IF THINE ANSWER BE NO, THEN AS SURELY AS NIGHT DOTH FOLLOW DAY--
STILL THY TONGUE, THUNDER GOD!

THY LOVE FOR JANE FOSTER HATH ENDURED FOR LO, THESE MANY MONTHS!
IT HATH OVERCOME EVERY OBSTACLE-- I SHALL DENY IT NO LONGER!
MY LORD! YOU MEAN--YOU GIVE US LEAVE--TO BE WED?!!
IF THAT BE THY WISH, MY SON!

THEN--I NEED NOT RENOUNCE MY HERITAGE!
GOD OF THUNDER SHALL I REMAIN--NOW AND FOREVER!
AND HE WHO SAYETH NAY SHALL FEEL THE WRATH OF ODIN!

BUT, FORGET YE NOT, MY SON--THERE BE STILL CONDITIONS THAT MUST BE MET--
AND MET THEY SHALL BE, MY LORD! NOW IMPERIAL ONE, BY THY MOST GRACIOUS LEAVE--
AWAY WITH THEE, THOR! 'TIS A TIME FOR REJOICING--NOT THE MAKING OF SPEECHES!

HE HASTENS TO CONVEY THE JOYOUS TIDINGS TO HIS BELOVED, SIRE!
AY! THE GLADNESS IN HIS HEART DOTH MAKE MINE OWN REGAL SOUL REJOICE!
TOO LONG HATH HE BEEN BROTHER TO SORROW! TOO LONG HATH GRIM DUTY O'ERSHADOWED HIS DAYS!

YET, A FEELING OF UNEASE LIES WITHIN MY HEART! I FEAR THAT HAPPINESS MAY STILL BE DENIED TO THE SO-RICHLY-DESERVING, MOST NOBLE THOR!

AND, WHEN THE ALL-WISE ODIN HAS A PREMONITION, IT IS SOMETHING TO BE CONJURED WITH, AS WE--AND MIGHTY THOR--ARE NOW ABOUT TO LEARN--
WITHIN SECONDS I SHALL FEAST MY HUNGRY EYES ONCE AGAIN UPON THE LOVELY, THE FAITHFUL JANE FOSTER!
AND THEN, AT LONG LAST, WE SHALL REJOICE AT THE HAPPY TIDINGS--TOGETHER!

BUT, NO SOONER DOES THE EAGER THUNDER GOD REACH THE MORTAL GIRL'S WINDOW LEDGE, WHEN--
A BOLT OF EXTRA-TERRESTRIAL FORCE!
THERE IS SOMETHING SORELY AMISS WITHIN THE APARTMENT OF MY BELOVED!
8

FOOL! YOUR ILL-CONSIDERED BLAST HURLED THE GOD OF THUNDER FROM THE WINDOW LEDGE!
NO MATTER! EVEN HE DOES NOT POSSESS THE POWER TO INTERFERE WITH THE WORK OF A COLONIZER INSPECTION TEAM!
NOW WE CAN CONCEAL OUR PRESENCE FROM HIM NO LONGER!
DO NOT BE TOO CERTAIN! IN ALL THIS GALAXY--HIS STRENGTH HAS BEEN SUPREME!

CRRASH!
GET YOU BACK! THE WALL CRUMBLES BEFORE US!

I AM THOR! EXPLAIN THY PRESENCE HERE! BRING THE GIRL, JANE FOSTER, SAFELY FORTH!
ELSE, SHALL YOU TASTE VENGEANCE --MOST TERRIBLE-- MOST EVER-LASTING!

YOU KNOW NOT TO WHOM YOU SPEAK, GOD OF THUNDER!
YOU KNEW ME ONCE, IN DIFFERENT GUISE! YOU KNEW ME AS-- TANA NILE!
THE GIRL WITH WHOM JANE FOSTER ROOMED! I SENSED THOU WERT NOT WHAT THOU SEEMED TO BE!
BUT, NO MATTER! THE GIRL! BRING FORTH THE GIRL!

NAY, THUNDER GOD! SHE IS NO LONGER OF ANY CONSEQUENCE!
I HAD SENT HER AWAY--HOPING TO CAUSE YOU TO WASTE PRECIOUS HOURS SEARCHING FOR HER--UNTIL MY TASK WAS COMPLETED!
FOR I AM--A COLONIZER! AND I HEREBY CLAIM THE PLANET EARTH --AS MY OWN!
IT IS MADNESS! YOU HAVE NOT THE POWER!

SEE THE POWER OF A COLONIZER! BOW, GOD OF THUNDER--BOW DOWN BEFORE YOUR MASTER!
I CANNOT CONTROL MY LIMBS! I MUST OBEY HER COMMAND!
SEE HOW A SIMPLE MIND-THRUST CAN HUMBLE THE MIGHTIEST ASGARDIAN OF ALL!
9

NO LONGER SHALL YOU KNOW ME MERELY AS TANA NILE!
WHEN NEXT YOU ADDRESS ME, IT SHALL BE AS TANA THE FIRST, COLONIAL EMPRESS OF THE CAPTIVE PLANET EARTH!

"ONCE THE INSPECTION TEAM HAS APPROVED MY CLAIM, I SHALL ANNOUNCE MANKIND'S FATE TO THEIR SPOKESMEN AT YOUR SO-CALLED UNITED NATIONS!"
HENCEFORTH, ALL HUMAN LAWS--ALL HUMAN CODES OF CONDUCT SHALL BE ABOLISHED!
YOU SHALL BE GOVERNED SOLELY BY THE SUPREME WILL OF YOUR EMPRESS! THUS SPEAKS TANA THE FIRST!

"NATURALLY, IT IS TO BE EXPECTED THAT THERE WILL BE A MEASURE OF RESISTANCE FROM SOME WHO DO NOT FULLY COMPREHEND THE POWER OF A COLONIZER! FOR SUCH AS THEY, I POSSESS A CERTAIN REMEDY--"
THOSE OF YOU WHO DO NOT BELIEVE SHALL SOON WITNESS THE AWESOME EVIDENCE OF MY COMPLETE SUPREMACY!

"THEN IT IS THAT I SHALL UNLEASH ONE OF THE MOST SPECTACULAR DEVICES IN OUR ARSENAL-- THE UNBREAKABLE SPACE LOCK!"

"BY MEANS OF THAT IRRESISTIBLE RAY, I CAN EFFORTLESSLY REMOVE A PLANET FROM ITS NATURAL ORBIT, TAKING EARTH COMPLETELY OUT OF THE SOLAR SYSTEM ITSELF, IF I SO DESIRE!"
"THUS, AT MY MEREST WHIM, I CAN CAUSE THIS PLANET TO ENDURE THE HEAT OF THE 24TH QUADRANT--"

"--OR, I CAN PLACE THE EARTH BEYOND THE FAINTEST RAYS OF ANY SUN--CAUSING THE START OF A NEW ICE AGE--SHOULD I SO DESIRE!"
"BUT, I HAVE SPOKEN ENOUGH! NOW IT IS TIME TO ACT--"

IT CANNOT BE--IT MUST NOT BE! I SHALL FIGHT THEE--I SHALL STOP THEE!
MY POWER--MY LIMBS--MY VERY LIFE SHALL I GIVE IN THE CAUSE OF HUMANITY!
IT IS AS I FEARED--!
HIS WILL IS DAUNTLESS! HE MUST BE--DESTROYED!

BEHOLD! HE BEGINS TO RISE! HE THREATENS TO BREAK THE MIND THRUST!
NEVER--SINCE TIME'S FIRST DAWNING--HAS ANY LIVING BEING DISPLAYED SUCH POWER!
IN THE NAME OF IMPERIAL ODIN--!

REMOVE YOUR MIND THRUST, COLONIZER NILE!
NAUGHT BUT A PROTON COAGULANT RAY--FIRED AT MAXIMUM INTENSITY--CAN OVERCOME SUCH UNIMAGINABLE STRENGTH!
AN UNSHATTERABLE CAGE OF PROTON PARTICLES--FORMING ABOUT ME! I MUST SAVE MY STRENGTH--I SHALL NOT ATTEMPT TO SHATTER IT--YET!
FOR, THESE PROTONS SERVE TWO PURPOSES! THOUGH I AM THUS RESTRAINED--I AM ALSO SHIELDED FROM ANY FURTHER ATTACK!
AND, I MUST LEARN MORE--FAR MORE--ABOUT THEY WHO ARE KNOWN AS COLONIZERS!

IT IS WELL! HE IS SECURED!
NOW HE MUST BE TAKEN TO THE CONSTELLATION RIGEL, FOR FURTHER STUDY!
WE HAVE NO OTHER CHOICE! THE ONLY OTHER CREATURE ABLE TO RESIST A MIND THRUST LIVES IN THE DREADED BLACK GALAXY--WHICH EVEN WE FEAR TO ENTER!
YOU HAVE INSPECTED THIS PLANET! WHAT IS YOUR DECISION?

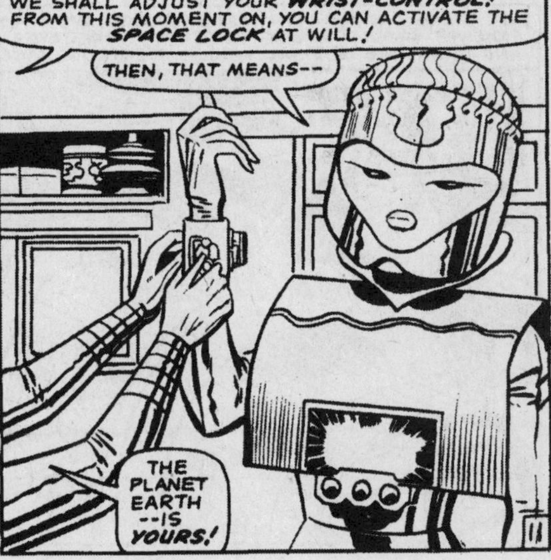
WE SHALL ADJUST YOUR WRIST-CONTROL! FROM THIS MOMENT ON, YOU CAN ACTIVATE THE SPACE LOCK AT WILL!
THEN, THAT MEANS--
THE PLANET EARTH--IS YOURS!
11

MOMENTS LATER, A SOMEWHAT UNUSUAL PROCESSION LEAVES THE APARTMENT ONCE OCCUPIED BY THE NOW-MISSING JANE FOSTER--
USE YOUR GRAVITY NULLIFIER TO TRANSPORT THE PROTON CAGE, INSPECTOR!
I AM SO DOING, INSPECTOR!
I'M SO GLAD I MOVED INTO THIS APARTMENT BUILDING--
--EVEN THOUGH IT'S TERRIBLY EXPENSIVE, ONE MEETS SUCH A NICE CLASS OF PEOPLE HERE!

STAND ASIDE, HUMAN CREATURE! NONE MAY IMPEDE THE PROGRESS OF ACCREDITED INSPECTORS!
I-I BEG YOUR PARDON! WHAT DID YOU SAY?

THERE IS NO NEED FOR REPETITION! WITHIN FIVE EARTH-TIME SECONDS, THIS MEMORY WILL HAVE FADED FROM YOUR BRAIN!
OH DEAR! CAN THIS BE ONE OF THOSE AVANT-GARDE NEW YORK HAPPENINGS THAT I SOMETIMES READ ABOUT?
WORDS! WORDS! WORDS! DO EARTHLINGS NEVER TIRE OF THEM?

THEN, FINALLY...
WE HAVE REACHED OUR DESTINATION! ACTIVATE THE VISI-ROD, SO THAT OUR SPACE CRAFT MAY BE REVEALED!
VISI-ROD OPERATIONAL! ALL CIRCUITS FUNCTIONING! STAND BACK, INSPECTOR!

FOR THOSE OF YOU WITH HOME WORKSHOPS WHO MIGHT LIKE TO PUTTER ABOUT WITH YOUR OWN VISI-ROD, WE SHOULD ADVISE YOU THAT IT OPERATES BY REMOVING, AND THEN RESTORING, ANY OBJECT TO AND FROM THE NORMAL VISUAL SPECTRUM RANGE! AND NOW, BACK TO OUR ROOFTOP---
PLACE THE PROTON CAGE WITHIN THE SHIP, INSPECTOR! THE HOUR GROWS LATE!
SINCE WE RECEIVE NO ADDITIONAL COMPENSATION FOR OVERTIME INSPECTING, YOU MAY BE ASSURED I SHALL NOT WASTE A SINGLE GALACTO-MOMENT!
12

CAREFUL OF THE PRISONER, INSPECTOR!
SINCE HE POSSESSES THE POWER TO RESIST A MIND THRUST, PERHAPS BY STUDYING HIM, OUR TECHNICIANS WILL BE ABLE TO FIND A WAY TO DEFEAT THE ONE WHO LURKS WITHIN THE BLACK GALAXY!
THE MERE MENTION OF THAT DREADED WORLD FILLS MY SOUL WITH NAMELESS FEAR! LET US SPEAK OF IT NO MORE!

AGREED! AND NOW, SET HOMEWARD COURSE ON ROBOT CONTROL!
COURSE CALCULATED AND SET! ALL SYSTEMS READIED FOR LIFT-OFF! FIRE ALL ROCKETS!

AND SO, SEALED WITHIN A SEEMINGLY IMPREGNABLE PROTON CAGE, THE MIGHTY GOD OF THUNDER BEGINS A JOURNEY TO THE CONSTELLATION RIGEL--HOME OF THE MYSTERIOUS COLONIZERS--!
CONDITION BLUE! TRAJECTORY ASSURED! ALL SYSTEMS OPERATING AT PRESCRIBED VELOCITY!

BUT, EVEN AS THE TWO INSPECTORS SETTLE BACK TO RELAX, KNOWING THAT THEIR SHIP'S AUTOMATIC CONTROLS ARE OPERATING PERFECTLY, THE MIGHTY THOR BEGINS TO FLEX HIS MASSIVE, MATCHLESS MUSCLES...
I HAVE SEEN AND HEARD ENOUGH!
THE TIME FOR OBSERVATION IS PAST! THE MOMENT FOR BATTLE HATH ARRIVED!

KRAKK!
PROTON LOCK INDEED! NO SUCH ARTIFICIAL DEVICE CAN LONG RESTRAIN THE SON OF ODIN!

AT THAT SELFSAME INSTANT, COUNTLESS LIGHT YEARS AWAY, A MAMMOTH CELESTIAL ***SPACE LOCK*** SOARS INTO ATTACK POSITION, ON BLINDING, BLAZING BLASTS OF ASTRAL ENERGY! AND THEN...

ATTAINING ITS PRESCRIBED ORBIT, A SILENT CIRCUIT IS ACTIVATED, HURLING A GIGANTIC RAY ACROSS THE ENDLESS REACHES OF SPACE...

--UNTIL IT UNERRINGLY REACHES ITS TARGET-- LOCKING THE PLANET EARTH IN THE INVISIBLE GRIP OF A RIGEL SPACE LOCK!

AND NOW, BACK TO THE INSPECTORS' SPACE SHIP ONCE AGAIN...
OUR CAPTIVE! HE HAS BROKEN FREE OF THE PROTON CAGE!
I AM CAPTIVE NO MORE! NOW YOU FACE--AN AVENGER!
QUICKLY, INSPECTOR! MAKE DENSITY ADJUSTMENT!

YOU WERE TOO LATE, THUNDER GOD! WE CAN MENTALLY CHANGE OUR PHYSICAL DENSITY WITH THE ACTUAL SPEED OF THOUGHT!
THUS, YOU NOW STRIKE TWO RIGELIANS WHOSE BODIES CAN RESIST ANY PHYSICAL FORCE!
UNNHHH--

PUT DOWN YOUR HAMMER, THUNDER GOD! IT CAN AVAIL YOU NAUGHT! YOU MUST SURRENDER!
NEVER!
STILL DO I LIVE--THUS, STILL DO I FIGHT!

FIGHT? HOW CAN YOU FIGHT THE POWER OF UNLIMITED DENSITY?
AT MAXIMUM DENSITY, A BLOW FROM AN INSPECTOR IS EQUAL TO THE FORCE OF A COSMIC TORNADO!

NEXT ISSUE: "RIGEL!"

TALES OF ASGARD, HOME OF THE MIGHTY NORSE GODS
THE ASGARD WARRIORS DO BATTLE WITHOUT THEIR LEADER-- THE PRINCELY THOR!
LET US ATTACK THEM NOW--ERE THE THUNDER GOD RETURNS!
THEY MUST BE TAKEN ALIVE! NO HARM IS TO BEFALL THEM!
"THE WARLOCK'S EYE!"
IS HAROKIN BEREFT OF HIS SENSES? NEVER BEFORE HAS HE ORDERED AN ENEMY SPARED!
HAVING DEFEATED HAROKIN IN FAIR BATTLE, MIGHTY THOR IMPERSONATES THE BARBARIAN CHIEFTAIN, THUS HOPING TO GAIN POSSESSION OF THE ENCHANTED WARLOCK'S EYE FROM HAROKIN'S GUARDS--
LEE WROTE IT! KIRBY DREW IT! COLLETTA INKED IT! SIMEK LETTERED IT!
NO WONDER IT'S ANOTHER MAGNIFICENT MARVEL MASTERWORK!

REMEMBER--THEY ARE THE PICKED WARRIORS OF ODIN HIMSELF! THEY ACKNOWLEDGE NO DEFEAT WHILE BREATH REMAINS WITHIN THEIR BREASTS!
ONLY WITH THE WARLOCK'S EYE CAN WE INSURE CERTAIN VICTORY FOR OURSELVES!
THEREFORE, LET TWO OF MY MOST LOYAL GUARDS HIE THEMSELVES TO WHERE THE EYE IS HIDDEN, AND FETCH IT TO HAROKIN FORTHWITH!
NOW, IF FORTUNE BE MINE, I SHALL HAVE THE ENCHANTED EYE BEFORE ANY CAN DISCOVER THAT IT IS THOR THEY DO SERVE --AND NOT THE FALLEN HAROKIN!
TO THE HIDING PLACE OF THE WARLOCK'S EYE-- QUICKLY!
HAROKIN HATH SO COMMANDED!
ONCE HE HOLDS THE ENCHANTED EYE, NOT ALL THE POWER OF ODIN CAN SAVE ASGARD FROM CERTAIN DEFEAT!
HAH! TWO BARBARIANS OFF UPON SOME SINISTER QUEST!!
BUT, THEY HAVE RECKONED WITHOUT THE MIND-STAGGERING POWER OF MIGHTY VOLSTAGG BEING HURLED AGAINST THEM!
NOW SHALL I LEAP FROM MY PLACE OF CONCEALMENT, AND--UNHHHH--
KRAK!
FIE UPON IT! THERE IS TOO LITTLE DIGNITY IN LEAPING! A DEEP BREATH WILL SERVE AS WELL!
AHH! AT LAST, THE EAGLE VISION OF VOLSTAGG HAS FOUND THE HIDING PLACE OF THE FATEFUL EYE!
NOW MUST I ATTACK WITH THE SPEED OF A BLAZING COMET!
HAVE A CARE!! IF WE DROP IT, WE ARE DOOMED!
CRR-EAK!
IF IT DROPS, WE ARE DOOMED!
PERHAPS IT WERE BETTER THAT VOLSTAGG EMPLOY THE CAUTION OF THE TURTLE!

BUT, BEFORE THE BARBARIANS CAN TAKE ANOTHER STEP, THE ENORMOUS VOLSTAGG TURNS TO FACE THEM--WITH THE WARLOCK'S EYE HELD FIRMLY IN HIS HANDS--AND THEN--

NEXT, THE BEARDED BEHEMOTH TURNS TOWARDS THE STAIRWAY, WITH THE ENCHANTED OBJECT IN HIS HANDS SWEEPING EVERYTHING BEFORE IT WITH ITS IRRESISTIBLE STUN BLASTS--!

THE WARLOCK'S EYE HAS FALLEN TO THE ENEMY!! WE ARE UNDONE!! ALL IS LOST!

BUT THEN, SUDDENLY, THE SON OF ODIN, WITH ONE PROUD GESTURE, WHIPS OPEN HIS CAPE, REVEALING HIS TRUE IDENTITY--
VOLSTAGG!! PUT DOWN THE EYE!! 'TIS THE THUNDER GOD HIMSELF THOU DOTH FACE!
BEHOLD!! THE PRINCE OF ASGARD!! WE HAVE BEEN DECEIVED!!

THE EYE-- QUICKLY!! THERE IS JUST TIME TO SEIZE IT BEFORE HAROKIN'S LEGIONS RECOVER FROM THEIR SHOCK!
OF WHAT USE IS SUCH AN OBJECT WHEN THE STRONG ARM OF VOLSTAGG THE ENORMOUS IS AT THY SIDE?
DO ARMADAS NOT TREMBLE AT THE SOUND OF MY NAME?
NO! STAND THEE BACK! HE HATH TAKEN THE EYE!
THUNDER GOD!! YIELD--OR DIE!

LAY YOU DOWN YOUR ARMS! THE BATTLE IS ENDED! THE WARLOCK'S EYE IS MINE!
FANDRAL! HOGUN! COLLECT YOU THEIR WEAPONS!
NONE WILL DARE RAISE SWORD AGAINST HIM WHO HOLDS THE WARLOCK'S EYE!
5

THE CAUSE NOW IS WON!
BUT--WHAT NOW BECOMES OF-- HAROKIN?
NEXT ISSUE:
"THE DARK HORSE OF DEATH!"

THE MIGHTY THOR
APPROVED BY THE COMICS CODE AUTHORITY
IND.
MARVEL COMICS GROUP
12¢
132
SEPT
"WHERE GODS MAY FEAR TO TREAD!"

THE MIGHTY THOR!
RIGEL
"WHERE GODS MAY FEAR TO TREAD!"
I HAVE OVER-POWERED THE TWO ALIEN BEINGS WITHIN THIS SHIP... BUT NOW WE APPROACH THEIR HOME WORLD...THE MYSTERIOUS RIGEL!
ATTENTION! THIS IS SKY-STATION 14-R! YOU ARE ORDERED TO IDENTIFY YOURSELF AND YOUR SPACECRAFT!
A VOICE!! FROM THE STRANGE OBJECT FLOATING BEFORE ME!
IT IS LIKE AN EARTHLY TOLL BOOTH... GUARDING THE ROUTE TO RIGEL!
BUT I MUST REACH RIGEL...TO DESTROY THE SPACE LOCK WHICH IS NOW MENACING ALL OF MANKIND!
ASTONISHING SCRIPT: STAN LEE
AWESOME ARTWORK: JACK KIRBY
ARTFUL DELINEATION: VINCE COLLETTA
AMAZING LETTERING: SAM ROSEN
ALIEN TRANSLATIONS: IRVING FORBUSH

WE CAN OBSERVE THAT YOU ARE NOT ONE OF OUR COLONIZERS! THEREFORE, YOU MUST BE AN ENEMY!
NEITHER FRIEND NOR FOE AM I! MY NAME IS THOR... MY RANK... PRINCE OF ASGARD... MY HERITAGE... GOD OF THUNDER!

I COMMAND THEE TO REMOVE YON SPACE LOCK FROM THE PLANET EARTH... OR SUFFER MY BOUNDLESS WRATH!
THUS SPEAKS THE SON OF ODIN!

NONE THREATEN THE COLONIZERS OF RIGEL!
A SHIP LEAVES THE SKY STATION -- HEADED DIRECTLY TOWARDS ME!

WE SHALL GAIN ENTRANCE TO THE INVADER'S SHIP VIA A BRIDGE OF ION-PACKED ATOMS!
BEHOLD! THE INVADER APPROACHES US!
QUICKLY! STOP HIM WITH A MIND THRUST!
STAND YE BACK... ALL! THE PATIENCE OF THOR HATH TRULY REACHED ITS END!
IT IS TO NO AVAIL! HIS POWER IS FAR GREATER THAN OURS!

HE MUST BE STOPPED! BRING FORTH THE ANTI-PERSONNEL BLASTERS..!
STILL THOU DAREST DEFY ME?!!
THEN LET THE FURY OF MY URU HAMMER TEACH THEE THE FOLLY OF SUCH A COURSE!

BUT, BEFORE THE ENCHANTED MALLET CAN STRIKE, A CALM, CLEAR COMMAND IS GIVEN...
FORM A GROUP MIND DEFENSE!! COMBINE MIND THRUSTS.. NOW!
IT IS SO DONE!

THE HAMMER HAS BEEN STOPPED! NOW, INTENSIFY FORCE TO CREMATION LEVEL...!
THOUGH WE HALTED ITS FLIGHT... WE CANNOT DESTROY IT... EVEN AT PEAK INTENSITY!

IT RESISTS OUR FORCE... IT BREAKS AWAY... AT EVER-INCREASING SPEED!
LOOK OUT! THE HAMMER IS TRULY BEWITCHED!

KNOW THEE NOW, MEN OF RIGEL...
'TIS THE SON OF IMPERIAL ODIN WHO STANDS THUS BEFORE THEE!
MY HAMMER DOTH SHATTER A SUN EASILY AS A STONE! IN ALL THE WORLD, MY POWER IS UNMATCHED!
BUT, THIS IS A DIFFERENT WORLD IN WHICH YOU FIND YOURSELF!

NO MATTER! I NOW TAKE COMMAND OF THY SHIP AND ALL ITS EFFECTS!
NOW GO WE FORTHWITH TO THE PLANET RIGEL...
..AND TO THE SPACE LOCK WHICH THREATENS THOSE WHO DWELL UPON EARTH!
3.

MEANWHILE, BACK UPON THE IMPERILED PLANET WHICH WE MARVELITES CALL HOME, THE FEMALE COLONIZER WHO HAD BEEN KNOWN AS TANA NILE NOW DARINGLY APPEARS IN PUBLIC...
SINCE I HAVE CLAIMED THIS WORLD FOR MY OWN, I MUST ALLOW MY SUBJECTS TO RECOGNIZE THEIR NEW MASTER!
POOR, PITIFUL HUMANS! SO MYSTIFIED.. SO HELPLESS!

MY CONTROL OF EARTH IS NOW ABSOLUTE! ACCORDING TO MY WRIST COMPUTOSCOPE, THE SPACE LOCK BEAM HAS COMPLETELY ENCIRCLED THIS PLANET!
THEREFORE, THE TIME IS COME TO TAKE OVER THE REINS OF GOVERNMENT FROM THE SUBJECT HUMANS!
WHAT IN THE NAME OF J. EDGAR HOOVER IS THAT??!

BEGGIN' YOUR PARDON, LADY... IF THAT'S WHAT YOU ARE... ARE YOU, EH, LOOKIN' FOR SOMETHING?
YOU MAY ADDRESS ME AS EMPRESS... FOR, I AM YOUR NEW SOVEREIGN ... TANA THE FIRST!
WHY DO I GET ALL THE KOOKS AND ODDBALLS ON MY BEAT??!
GLAD TO MEETCHA, EMPRESS!
NATURALLY!

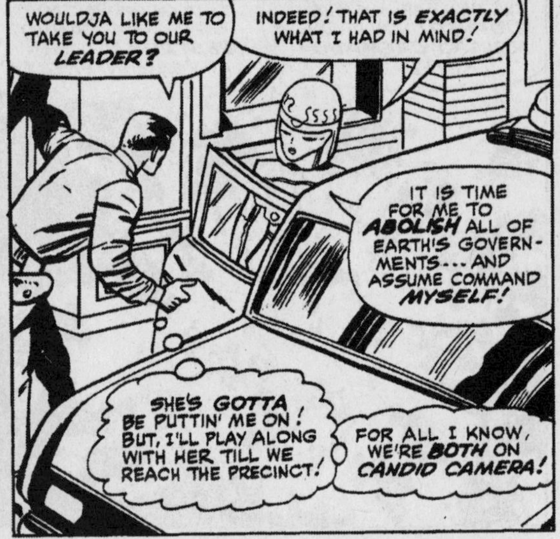
WOULDJA LIKE ME TO TAKE YOU TO OUR LEADER?
INDEED! THAT IS EXACTLY WHAT I HAD IN MIND!
IT IS TIME FOR ME TO ABOLISH ALL OF EARTH'S GOVERNMENTS... AND ASSUME COMMAND MYSELF!
SHE'S GOTTA BE PUTTIN' ME ON! BUT, I'LL PLAY ALONG WITH HER TILL WE REACH THE PRECINCT!
FOR ALL I KNOW, WE'RE BOTH ON CANDID CAMERA!

TAKE ME DIRECTLY TO THE UNITED NATIONS! WHEN I'M DONE, I SHALL APPOINT YOU IMPERIAL CHAUFFEUR TO THE COLONIAL EMPRESS!
MOST OF 'EM JUST THINK THEY'RE NAPOLEON... BUT THIS ONE'S GOT UPMANSHIP!
OF COURSE, SOME MAY NOT BELIEVE THAT EARTH IS NOW IN MY CONTROL...
YEAH, EMPRESS... THAT'S A REAL DISTINCT POSSIBILITY!

BUT, THEY WILL NOT DOUBT ME FOR LONG!
FOR, EVEN AS WE SPEAK, MY UNBREAKABLE SPACE LOCK IS SLOWLY PULLING EARTH OUT OF ITS NATURAL ORBIT... AND ONLY I CAN BRING IT BACK AGAIN!
HOOO BOY! WHAT MAKES YOU THINK ANYONE'LL DOUBT A NICE, SENSIBLE STORY LIKE THAT?
4.

AND, AN INCALCULABLE NUMBER OF LIGHT YEARS AWAY, THE COLONIZERS... KNOWING OF THOR'S INVASION OF THEIR REALM... SEND AN INDESTRUCTIBLE TO DEAL WITH THE MIGHTY THUNDER GOD...
OUR INDESTRUCTIBLE SHALL REACH THE INVADER WITHIN SECONDS!
NOTHING CAN WITHSTAND HIS MECHANICAL MIGHT! HE HAS HIS ORDERS!
I-MUST-DESTROY-THE-CREATURE-FROM-THE-DISTANT-SOLAR-SYSTEM! ALL-OTHER-COMMANDS-HAVE-BEEN-ERASED!
MY-SOLE-PURPOSE-IS-TO-SERVE-THE-COLONIZERS! THE-STRANGER-FROM-SPACE-MUST-BE-SLAIN!
SHOOOM!

SOME TYPE OF HUMANOID, STREAKING SKYWARD IN FRONT OF MY SHIP! I MUST LEARN HIS MISSION!

BUT, NO SOONER DOES THE NOBLE THUNDER GOD BRING HIS SPACECRAFT TO A HALT, WHEN...
HE FIRES SOME SORT OF RAY AT ME!
IT DISPERSES THE VERY MOLECULES OF THE SHIP IN WHICH I RIDE!

THEN, BEFORE THE STARTLED EYES OF THE SON OF ODIN, THE SPACECRAFT'S WALL SEEMS TO DISSOLVE INTO NOTHINGNESS AS A NULLIFIED-MOLECULAR-VACUUM IS CREATED... ALLOWING THE INDESTRUCTIBLE TO PASS RIGHT THROUGH...!
THE-INTRUDER-MUST-DIE!

PREPARE-TO-MEET-YOUR-FATE!
AN INDESTRUCTIBLE! YOU ARE DOOMED, THUNDER GOD! NOTHING CAN SURVIVE HIS MERCILESS ATTACK!
BE THOU SILENT! THOR SHALL SURVIVE!
5.

I-WAS-CREATED-TO-DEFEND-THE-WORLD-OF-RIGEL! MY-POWER-IS-SUPREME!
STRUGGLE-NOT! YOUR-END-SHALL-BE-SWIFT-AND-PAINLESS!
HIS GRIP IS STRONGER THAN ANY I HAVE EVER FELT!

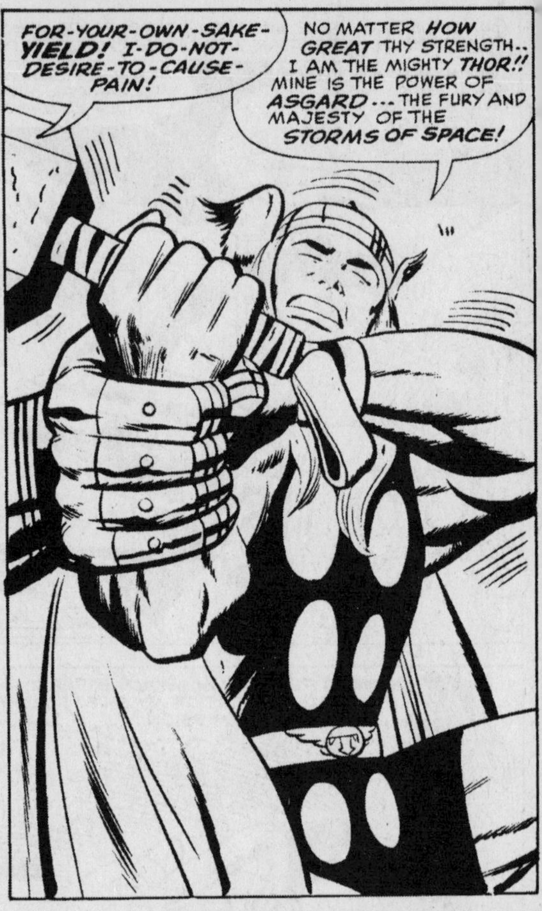
FOR-YOUR-OWN-SAKE-YIELD! I-DO-NOT-DESIRE-TO-CAUSE-PAIN!
NO MATTER HOW GREAT THY STRENGTH.. I AM THE MIGHTY THOR!! MINE IS THE POWER OF ASGARD... THE FURY AND MAJESTY OF THE STORMS OF SPACE!

BY THE BRISTLING BEARD OF ODIN... NONE MAY CONQUER THOR!

THEN, AS THE INDESTRUCTIBLE SHRUGS OFF THE STAGGERING BLOW, AND LUMBERS FORWARD AGAIN, THE THUNDER GOD WHIRLS HIS ENCHANTED HAMMER SO FAST THAT IT BEGINS TO HEAT ITS OWN ATOMS...
BACK, THOU UNSPEAKABLE MOCKERY OF ALL THAT BE MORTAL!
YOU-ARE-TOO-POWERFUL...TO-LIVE!
6.

THOUGH-YOUR-HAMMER-HAS-BECOME-AN-ATOMIC-FLARE... STILL-AM-I-UNHARMED! STILL-AM-I-INDESTRUCTIBLE!
NOW-STAND-READY-FOR-YOUR-DOOM!

HE WITHSTANDS A PLANET-SHAKING ATOMIC STORM AS THOUGH IT BE A MILD SUMMER RAIN!
TRULY, HE HATH BEEN NAMED INDESTRUCTIBLE FOR GOOD AND PROPER REASON!

AND-NOW--- MY-ULTIMATE-WEAPON!
A-GAMMA-POWERED-IMMOBILIZER-BEAM---SO-IRRESISTIBLE-THAT-EVEN-I-CANNOT-WITHSTAND-ITS-TOUCH!
A PITY THY SPEED IS NOT THE EQUAL OF THY POWER!

NO MATTER HOW INFALLIBLE ... HOW DEADLY THY RAY MAY BE ---
... UNLESS IT DOTH STRIKE THY VICTIM, IT IS AS NAUGHT!
THOK!

SLOWLY, AGONIZINGLY, THE MIGHTY THUNDER GOD FORCES THE INDE-STRUCTIBLE'S ARM BACK ---AND BACK.. AND BACK--- UNTIL---

--THE AWESOME CREATURE SLUMPS TO THE FLOOR.. MOTIONLESS--- HAVING BEEN FELLED BY THE IMPACT OF ITS OWN ULTIMATE WEAPON!
IT IS DONE!
NEVER BEFORE HAS AN INDESTRUCTIBLE SUFFERED SUCH DEFEAT!
NEVER HATH ONE FOUGHT THE GOD OF THUNDER!
7.

AND NOW, ON TO THE SPACE LOCK!! NO POWER IN THE UNIVERSE SHALL STOP ME FROM RENDING IT ASUNDER!
SO LONG AS THOR ENDURES, EARTH SHALL NEVER BE HOSTAGE TO THE LIKES OF THEE!
WE MUST OBEY! HIS POWER IS BEYOND ALL COMPREHENSION!
ONLY THE BLACK GALAXY ITSELF CAN SO FILL MY HEART WITH FEAR!
AND, EVEN AS THE DISHEARTENED COLONIZERS MENTION THE MYSTERIOUS BLACK GALAXY--- AT THAT VERY INSTANT... ACROSS THE VASTNESS OF SPACE... A GIGANTIC, HEAVILY-ARMED RIGEL SPACE CRUISER IS ATTACKED AND DESTROYED BY A DEADLY BEAM FROM THE FORBIDDEN GALAXY--!
BWEEOK!

WHILE, IN THE RIGEL CONTROL CENTRAL, A WEARY, BROODING MAN WATCHES THE SCENE OF DISASTER ON HIS ELECTRONIC VISO-SCANNERS! FOR LONG, SILENT SECONDS HE SITS, STARING THOUGHTFULLY AT THE COMPLEX RADARSCOPIC SYMBOLS, UNTIL AN EXCITED VOICE SHATTERS THE STILLNESS...
OBSERVER 3B-Y REPORTING, EXCELLENCY!
IT HAS JUST BEEN LEARNED THAT THE BEING FROM EARTH HAS DEFEATED THE INDESTRUCTIBLE!
EVEN NOW, THE FEARSOME INVADER SPEEDS TOWARDS OUR SPACE LOCK SECTOR!
BEGONE! YOU TELL ME NOTHING I DO NOT ALREADY KNOW!
NEVER HAS THE WORLD OF RIGEL BEEN FACED WITH SUCH CALAMITY! NEVER HAS THE FUTURE SEEMED SO GRAVE!
I NEVER DESIRED TO BE GRAND COMMISSIONER OF RIGEL! THE BURDENS OF MY SUPREME OFFICE ARE TOO MUCH FOR ANY ONE MAN!
BUT, SINCE MY I.Q. RATING IS HIGHEST IN ALL THIS SECTOR, IT HAS BEEN MY DUTY TO SERVE!
YET NOW, AFTER ALL THESE DECADES... WE ARE THREATENED WITH... DISASTER!
EACH DAY, THE DANGER FROM THE BLACK GALAXY GROWS GREATER! AND NOW, A POWERFUL INVADER FROM THE SOLAR SYSTEM DARES TO ATTACK US!
THOUGH THEY ARE TWO SEPARATE PROBLEMS... EVEN NOW MY BRAIN IS FORMULATING A PLAN... A PLAN WHEREIN I MAY SOLVE THEM BOTH.. WITH BUT ONE STROKE!
ATTENDANT!! ACTIVATE THE OFFICIAL MATTER TRANSMITTER!
I MUST SPEED TO OUR POWER PLANETOID AT ONCE!
AS YOUR EXCELLENCY COMMANDS!
9.

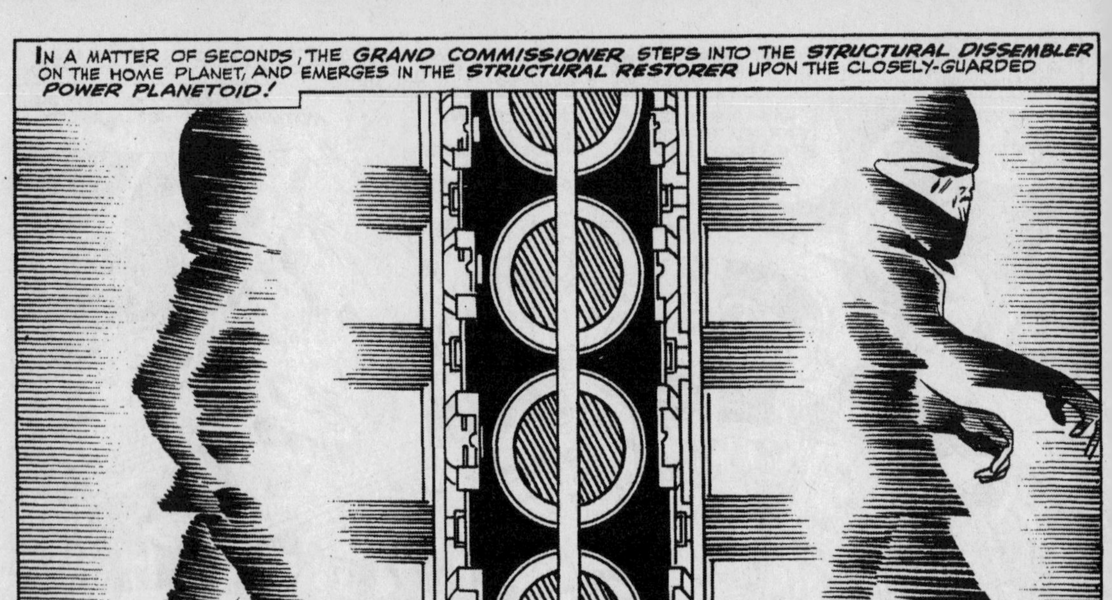
IN A MATTER OF SECONDS, THE GRAND COMMISSIONER STEPS INTO THE STRUCTURAL DISSEMBLER ON THE HOME PLANET, AND EMERGES IN THE STRUCTURAL RESTORER UPON THE CLOSELY-GUARDED POWER PLANETOID!

YOUR EXCELLENCY! HAD WE KNOWN OF YOUR ARRIVAL, WE WOULD HAVE MUSTERED THE HONOR GUARD!
NO TIME FOR THAT NOW!
ARE YOUR OBSERVO-LENSES STILL TRACKING THE INVADER'S APPROACH? IS HE STILL HEADED THIS WAY?
YES, EXCELLENCY!
THEN IT IS AS I FEARED!
HE COMES TO ATTACK OUR SPACE LOCK, TO FREE THE DISTANT PLANET EARTH!
IT IS THE FAULT OF COLONIZER TANA NILE! IF SHE HAD REPORTED THAT EARTH HAD SO MIGHTY A DEFENDER, WE WOULD NOT HAVE GIVEN PERMISSION TO ATTEMPT COLONIZATION!
BUT THE SPACE LOCK MUST BE PROTECTED AT ALL COSTS!

AND, AS FATE WOULD HAVE IT, AT THAT SELF-SAME INSTANT...
I SEE THE SPACE LOCK NOW!
DRAW CLOSER TO IT, AND TO THE PLANETOID OVER WHICH IT ORBITS!

NOW, HOLD THY COURSE, AS I SHATTER YON EVIL DEVICE WITH BUT ONE BLOW OF MY URU HAMMER!

BUT, BEFORE THE THUNDER GOD CAN HURL HIS ENCHANTED MALLET, AN INVISIBLE TRACTOR FORCE ZEROES IN ON HIS MAJESTIC FIGURE, DRAWING HIM IRRESISTIBLY TOWARDS THE PLANETOID BELOW...
WE'VE GOT HIM!
BY THE GOLDEN SPIRES OF ASGARD... WHAT WITCHERY IS THIS?!!
AN UNSEEN FORCE... DRAWING ME DOWN... TO WHERE YON COLONIZERS WAIT TO ATTACK ME BELOW!
BUT, THEY SHALL LEARN... TO THEIR ETERNAL DISMAY.. IT IS THOR WHO ATTACKS!! IT IS THOR WHO WIELDS THE POWER!
BACK, YE SCURRILOUS KNAVES!! THOUGH YE BE MANY AS THE SANDS ON THE SHORE... NONE MAY STAY MY HAMMER'S VENGEANCE!
BACK, THEN, BEFORE THE FURY OF A GOD!! MY WRATH SHALL BE UNABATED SO LONG AS YONDER SPACE LOCK ENDURES!
SKAK!
EARTH IS NO UNPROTECTED WASTELAND, TO BE CONQUERED AND PILLAGED BY SUCH AS THEE!

LET HIM WHO WOULD DEFY ME STAND FORTH!! ELSE SURRENDER ALL... WHILE YET YE MAY!
THUS SPEAKS THOR..PRINCE OF ASGARD... SON OF LORDLY ODIN!
WHOOOOOOSHHH

AS EASILY AS I SHATTER YON MACHINE BEFORE ME...JUST SO EASILY SHALL I DESTROY THINE INFERNAL SPACE LOCK!
THRAK!

TO ME, FAITHFUL HAMMER! THY MOST IMPORTANT TASK IS NOW BEFORE US!

AND NOW... IN THE NAME OF EARTH... I STRIKE..!
HOLD!! THROW NOT THAT HAMMER!!
WHAT?? WHO NOW DARES RAISE VOICE AGAINST THOR'S WILL??
STAND THOU FORTH...AND BE COUNTED!

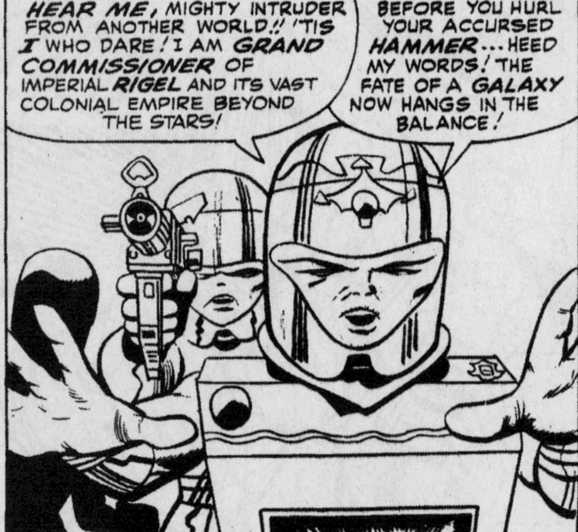
HEAR ME, MIGHTY INTRUDER FROM ANOTHER WORLD!! 'TIS I WHO DARE! I AM GRAND COMMISSIONER OF IMPERIAL RIGEL AND ITS VAST COLONIAL EMPIRE BEYOND THE STARS!
BEFORE YOU HURL YOUR ACCURSED HAMMER...HEED MY WORDS! THE FATE OF A GALAXY NOW HANGS IN THE BALANCE!

DESTROYING OUR SPACE LOCK WILL NOT SAVE THE PEOPLE OF EARTH!
THERE IS A FAR GREATER DANGER WITH WHICH THEY ARE SOON DESTINED TO BE CONFRONTED!
NO PATIENCE HAVE I FOR IDLE TALK! WHAT PROOF CANST THOU OFFER?
YOU SHALL HAVE YOUR PROOF!
12.

I SHALL DESCRIBE THE MENACE... BECAUSE MY CALCULATIONS INDICATE THAT ONLY YOU HAVE THE POWER TO OVERCOME IT! ONLY YOU CAN SAVE THE EARTH... AND PERHAPS... THE UNIVERSE ITSELF!
IDLE TALK, STILL! WHERE IS THY PROOF?
FOLLOW ME... TO THE TOWER OF TELESCOPES!

AND, AS THE TWO FIGURES ENTER THE COMPLEX, EVER-REVOLVING STRUCTURE...
FOR, THE PLANETS OF YOUR SOLAR SYSTEM ARE SO SMALL.. SO DISTANT.. THAT THEY ARE OF NO TRUE IMPORTANCE TO RIGEL!
ACCOMPLISH THE MISSION I SHALL DESCRIBE TO YOU, AND EARTH WILL BE FREED OF OUR SPACE LOCK!
LET ME HEAR MORE! THE VERY THOUGHT OF A CHALLENGE DOTH INFLAME MY BLOOD!

AND THEN, AT LAST, THE GALLANT THUNDER GOD FINALLY IS SHOWN... ON AN ELLIPTICAL PROJECTION OF THE RIGELIAN SECTOR OF THE UNIVERSE... THE MOST DRAMATIC, THE MOST MYSTERIOUS, THE MOST DREADED GALAXY OF ALL...
THE BLACK GALAXY!
THEN THAT IS WHAT YE RIGELIANS SO DESPERATELY FEAR!
INDEED, THUNDER GOD... YOU BEHOLD THE BLACK GALAXY!
THOUGH WE ARE ABLE TO ACCURATELY CHART IT FROM THE OUTSIDE, NO RIGELIAN HAS EVEN SEEN THE INSIDE... AND LIVED TO TELL OF IT!
IN TRUTH, IT IS THE MOST MYSTERIOUS, THE MOST DEADLY AREA IN ALL THE KNOWN UNIVERSE!

THY WORDS ARE FRAUGHT WITH DRAMA--- BUT, IN WHAT MANNER IS EARTH ENDANGERED BY YON GALAXY?
DO YOU NOT SEE? THE GREATEST MENACE OF ALL TIME IS CONCEALED WITHIN THAT FORBIDDEN WORLD...!!
EACH DAY IT GROWS MORE POWERFUL... MORE THREATENING! SOON, IT WILL BREAK OUT OF ITS SHADOWY CONFINES!

AND, WHEN IT DOES, NOTHING THAT LIVES... NOTHING IN THE UNIVERSE... INCLUDING EARTH... WILL BE SAFE!
ENOUGH TALK! I SHALL ENTER THE BLACK GALAXY!
SO SPEAKS THOR!
YOU SHALL LEAVE IMMEDIATELY... ACCOMPANIED BY A RECORDER, TO RECORD WHATEVER YOU LEARN... IN CASE... YOU NEVER RETURN!
13.

BUT, BACK ON EARTH ONCE AGAIN, ANOTHER JOURNEY IS ALSO IN PROGRESS ...
IT'S SO DESOLATE DOWN THERE.. SO LONELY...
I WANT TO RETURN...TO GO BACK, AND SEE THE MAN I LOVE ONCE AGAIN...TO FEEL THE STRONG ARMS OF THOR AROUND ME...BUT...I CANNOT..!
PARDON ME, MISS! THE WAY YOU'VE BEEN STARING OUT OF THAT WINDOW.. FOR HOURS.. SO SILENTLY...IS..IS ANYTHING WRONG?
I..I DON'T KNOW! I HAD TO TAKE THIS PLANE... SOMETHING COMPELLED ME!
I HAD TO GET AWAY... ALTHOUGH I'M NOT SURE WHY...!
STRANGE..I, TOO, HAD NO OTHER CHOICE!
TANA NILE TOLD ME TO LEAVE...AND, I CANNOT DISOBEY HER! I MUST KEEP TRAVELLING... TRAVELLING..!
AND SO, ONCE AGAIN WE TAKE OUR LEAVE OF LOVELY JANE FOSTER, WHILE HER INQUISITIVE FELLOW PASSENGER STUDIES HER THOUGHT-FULLY.. APPRAISINGLY.. AS THE GIANT JET ROARS ON INTO THE GATHERING DUSK...
AND, MANY GALAXIES AWAY, THE GOD OF THUNDER LEARNS THAT HE, TOO, HAS A STRANGE TRAVELLING COMPANION... A NON-CELLULAR HUMANOID RECORDER... CREATED IN THE IMAGE OF MAN... AN IMMORTAL THINKING MACHINE... INCAPABLE OF FEELING EMOTION...!
PREPARE TO ENTER THE BLACK GALAXY IN EXACTLY THREE AND ONE HALF SOLAR SYSTEM MINUTES!

ALREADY THE STYGIAN DARKNESS LOOMS AHEAD... BLOTTING OUT THE COMFORTING GLOW OF A THOUSAND STARS..!

MY MEMORY BANKS INFORM ME THAT WE ARE THE FIRST BEINGS TO ENTER THE BLACK GALAXY WITHOUT BEING ATTACKED BY BLAST RAYS!
PERHAPS THOSE WHO DWELL WITHIN ARE AWARE THAT WE ARE NOT COLONIZERS!

WE HAVE LEFT THE KNOWN UNIVERSE BEHIND!! WE ARE COMPLETELY WITHIN THE DARKNESS-SHROUDED BLACK GALAXY! WE MUST NOT RELAX OUR VIGILANCE FOR AN INSTANT!
I AM EVER VIGILANT! I HAVE BEEN PROGRAMMED TO REQUIRE NO REST--NO SLEEP!

LOOK! STRANGE, UNSTABLE, WRITHING SHAPES... SOME AS LARGE AS FIERY STARS... STREAKING THROUGH THE DARKNESS... ACROSS THE VAST, ENDLESS IMMENSITY..

I COMPUTE THAT WE ARE WITHIN AN INCREDIBLE UNIVERSE, COMPOSED OF LIVING, BIOLOGICAL MATTER!
NO!! IT IS NOT A UNIVERSE! IT IS FAR MORE FANTASTIC! IT IS ACTUALLY A BIO-VERSE!
A BIO-VERSE?!!

BUT, BEFORE THE HUMANOID HAS A CHANCE TO EXPLAIN...
OUT THERE! THAT IS THE OBJECTIVE WE SEEK... THE MENACE WHICH MAKES EVEN COLONIZERS TREMBLE..!
15

I HAVE BEEN **WAITING** FOR YOU!

I AM **EGO!**

NEXT ISSUE: THE LIVING PLANET!

TALES OF ASGARD, HOME OF THE MIGHTY NORSE GODS
"THE DARK HORSE OF DEATH!"
NOW THAT WE HAVE DEFEATED THE HORDES OF HAROKIN, IT IS TIME FOR US TO REST, WARRIORS OF ASGARD!
EVEN NOW, THE BARBARIAN CHIEFTAIN LIES A'BED, NURSING HIS BATTLE WOUNDS!
'TWAS A ZESTFUL SKIRMISH! A PITY IT MUST NEEDS COME TO SO UNTIMELY AN END!
REST? THAT IS FOR LESSER BEINGS! THE VIGILANT VOLSTAGG SHALL REMAIN EVER ALERT!
HAIL TO ASGARD! MAY ITS GLORY ENDURE FORE'ER!
I HEREBY DECLARE THE LAND OF MUSPELHEIM LIBERATED! THUS SPEAKS THOR, SON OF IMPERIAL ODIN!
SCRIPT WRITING: STAN LEE
PICTURE DRAWING: JACK KIRBY
PANEL INKING: VINCE COLLETTA
WORD LETTERING: SAM ROSEN
ARMOR POLISHING: IRVING FORBUSH

THEN, AS VOLSTAGG THE VAINGLORIOUS, HOGUN THE GRIM, AND FANDRAL THE DASHING REPORT TO THEIR VALIANT WARLORD, THE IMMORTAL WARRIORS PREPARE TO ATTEND THEIR BATTLE WOUNDS AND REFRESH THEMSELVES AT THE WATERS OF THE BATH...

DIDST THOU SEE HOW BRAVE MEN TREMBLED WHEN THEY BEHELD THE FIERCE VISAGE OF THE VALOROUS VOLSTAGG!

TREMBLED INDEED! METHINKS THEY DID BUT ROAR WITH LAUGHTER AT THY GIRTH!

IT MATTERS NOT... SO LONG AS THE VICTORY BE OURS!

TRULY, HOGUN, THOUGH THOU BE A MASTER IN BATTLE, THOU ART BUT A FLEDGLING IN MATTERS OF HUMOR!

THOOM!
WHAT FOUL INFAMY IS THIS?? DO THEY DARE SUMMON THEIR FORCES AGAINST US ONCE MORE ?
NAY, VOLSTAGG! 'TIS THE DRUM-BEAT OF MOURNING THOU DOST HEAR ... NOT THE CLARION CALL TO COMBAT!

WELL DO I KNOW THAT OMINOUS DRUMBEAT!
IT SUMMONS THE GREAT BLACK STALLION OF DOOM!
IT MEANS THE DEATH OF A MIGHTY WARRIOR IS NEAR AT HAND!

AND, FROM THE FURTHERMOST OUTPOST, THE DREAD CRY IS SOUNDED ...
IT COMES! IT COMES!
TRAGEDY AWAITS US! BEHOLD THE STALLION OF DOOM!

THE GATES OF MUSPELHEIM SWING OPEN WIDE ... FOR NONE DARE OPPOSE THE FEARSOME BEAST AS IT SPEEDS UPON ITS GRIM, UNALTERABLE MISSION ...
ITS UNBLINKING EYES GLOW LIKE TWIN DEMONS!
CLOP!
CLOP!
CLOP!

THE FEARFUL FLEE BEFORE THE MIGHTY EBONY STALLION... WHILE THOSE OF STOUTER HEART STAND FAST! YET, EACH MAN KNOWS THAT THE BEAST WILL STOP BEFORE *ONE WARRIOR*... THE ONE WHO IS FATED TO *DIE!*

HE HATH PASSED ME BY! THE GODS BE PRAISED!

I MUST *FLEE!* I CANNOT PEER INTO THOSE BLAZING EYES!

FLIGHT IS *USELESS!* WHAT IS TO BE... IS TO BE!

THOUGH WE JOUSTED WITH GREAT VIGOR, I DID NOT THINK I HAD INJURED THEE THUS SEVERELY!
'TWAS NOT THY DOING ALONE, SON OF ODIN! I HAVE WAGED MANY BATTLES... IN MANY LANDS... AND WITH EACH, A NEW WOUND DID I SUSTAIN!
I, WHO HAVE LIVED FOR WAR... WHO HAVE SAVORED THE NECTAR OF CONQUEST.. MUST NOW PAY THE FINAL PRICE!
BUT I SHALL ACQUIT MYSELF AS BEFITS A BARBARIAN BORN!

THY PROWESS IN BATTLE IS PROCLAIMED FAR AND WIDE! THOU SHALT LIVE TO FIGHT AGAIN... THOUGH NOT AGAINST THE FORCES OF ASGARD!
THOUGH THOU BE GOD OF THUNDER... IN THIS MATTER, MY WISDOM EXCEEDS THINE OWN!
DIDST THOU NOT HEAR THE RUMBLE OF DRUMS? DIDST THOU NOT SEE THE DARK HORSE OF DOOM?
VERILY, HAROKIN HATH FOUGHT HIS FINAL BATTLE!

BEHOLD THE FACE OF THE BARBARIAN'S HEALER, THUNDER GOD! HAROKIN DOTH SPEAK THE TRUTH! EVEN HE DOTH KNOW THE END IS NEAR!
'TIS FOR HAROKIN THE STALLION HATH COME! AND 'TIS THE WAY HE WOULD TRULY WISH TO DEPART!

THY WORDS ARE TRUE, GRIM HOGUN! FOR THE MIGHTY STEED DOTH STAND... OUTSIDE THIS CHAMBER!
THOUGH WE MET AS FOES UPON THE FIELD OF BATTLE, MY HEART IS HEAVY WITHIN ME! WHEN SO HONORABLE A LIFE BE LOST... WE DO EACH BECOME THE POORER FOR IT!
NEXT ISSUE... "The PHANTOMS OF VALHALLA!"
5.

THOR SPECIAL
KING-SIZE SPECIAL!
APPROVED BY THE COMICS CODE AUTHORITY
MORE PAGES! MORE THRILLS!
THE MIGHTY THOR
SEPT.
#2 1966
25¢
MARVEL COMICS GROUP
WHO DARES DEFY... THE DESTROYER?
ALL NEW!
EXTRA!! RE PRESENTING: THE VERY FIRST APPEARANCES OF THE VICEROYS OF VILLAINY...
THE ENCHANTRESS AND THE EXECUTIONER!
THE MAD MERLIN!

STAN LEE PRESENTS: THE MIGHTY THOR!™
"IF ASGARD FALLS.."
HEAR ME, HEROES OF THE REALM!
THE TOURNAMENT OF TITANS WILL SOON BEGIN! TO THE WINNER OF EACH EVENT WILL BE GIVEN A SUIT OF GOLDEN ARMOR... PROCLAIMING HIM A CHAMPION OF ASGARD!
LET THE NEWS ISSUE FORTH... I HEREBY SUMMON EVERY WARRIOR, FROM EVERY LAND! ODIN HATH SPOKEN! SO BE IT!
FEATURING: THE ALMOST UNSPEAKABLE MENACE OF...
THE INDESTRUCTIBLE DESTROYER!
SCRIPTED in SOLEMN SPLENDOR By: STAN LEE
ILLUSTRATED in IDEALISTIC IMAGERY By: JACK KIRBY
DELINEATED in DELICIOUS DELICACY By: VINCE COLLETTA
LETTERED in LIVING LUMINESCENCE By: SAM ROSEN
UNAFFECTED BY THE UNABASHED UTTERANCES of: IRVING FORBUSH

LET THE *TORCH-BEARERS* STEP FORWARD!

THE TIME IS COME TO LIGHT THE FLAMES! *STAND YE STEADY!*

THE BEACON IS LIT!
ITS GLOW SHALL BE SEEN IN EVERY CORNER OF THE COSMOS!
THUS DO WE PROCLAIM FOREVER THE GLORY THAT IS ASGARD!

IT IS DONE! NOW SHALL WE AWAIT THE COMING OF THE MIGHTIEST WARRIORS IN ALL OF CREATION!

AND SO IT BEGINS! IN FAR OFF GYMIRSGARD, THE FIRST CRY IS GIVEN...
A FIERY BOLT FROM HALLOWED ASGARD!
THE WORD MUST BE SPREAD... THE TIME OF TRIAL IS COME!

EVEN AT THE OPPOSITE END OF THE INFINITE VOID, IN THE NAMELESS LAND OF THE WIND GIANTS, THE FLAMING BOLT OF ODIN IS VIEWED WITH MARROW-CHILLING AWE..!
A SUMMONS FROM THE ALL-WISE!
'TIS A CALL TO BATTLE... FOR THE GREATEST STAKES OF ALL!

AND, DRIFTING AIMLESSLY, ETERNALLY, IN A REGION OF NEVER-CHANGING NON-SPACE... BEYOND THE FARTHEST BOUNDARY OF HUMAN THOUGHT... WHERE THEY HAD BEEN SENTENCED BY IMPERIAL **ODIN** FOR THE MOST HEINOUS CRIMES AGAINST THE REALM... WE FIND HIM WHO HAD BEEN KNOWN AS THE **ABSORBING MAN**... AND THE EVIL, EVER-VENGEFUL STEP-SON OF ODIN... **LOKI**, PRINCE OF VILEST VILLAINY...

A **FIERY BOLT**... HERALDING THE START OF THE GREATEST **BATTLE TOURNAMENT** SINCE THE DAWN OF TIME!!

AND HERE DRIFTS **LOKI**, THE CRAFTIEST CHAMPION OF ALL... HELPLESS AND FORGOTTEN!

LOKI! THAT BLINDING, SHOOTING **FLAME!!** WHAT DOES IT **MEAN?**

YET... **ONE POWER** DO I STILL POSSESS!! ONE POWER WHICH **STILL** MAY BRING ME THE FINAL **VICTORY!** THE POWER OF... **THOUGHT!**

SILENCE, THOU WORTHLESS NON-ENTITY! TOO MANY TIMES HAST THOU **FAILED** ME! THE PRINCE OF EVIL HATH CONCEIVED A MISSION FOR ONE FAR MORE **POWERFUL** THAN THEE!

YET, WELL DO I REMEMBER THOSE HALLOWED DAYS OF YORE ... WHEN THE BLUDGEONING BLADE OF ODIN DID STRIKE WITH THE FURY OF A THOUSAND STORMS! 'TWAS THEN THE SUMMER OF MY LIFE ... WHEN TALL AND STRAIGHT AS AN OAK STOOD ODIN!
SSSSSSSSTT!
SOMEONE SEEKS TO GAIN THE NOTICE OF THOR..!
AHH ... WELL MIGHT I HAVE GUESSED WHO 'TWOULD BE!

'TIS A TIME FOR RIOTOUS REVELING, THUNDER GOD! WE AWAIT THY PRESENCE!
THERE IS MUCH BRAWLING AND CAREFREE CAROUSING TO BE DONE 'ERE THE TOURNAMENT BEGINS!
FANDRAL... CEASE THY WIGGLING, OR VOLSTAGG SHALL SHAKE THEE LIKE A FLEA!
SILENCE, ENORMOUS ONE! THY BOOMING TONES MAY REACH THE EARS OF ODIN, HIMSELF!

AND NOW, THOUGH MINSTRELS STILL SING OF ODIN'S FEATS ... WHILE CAMPFIRES FLICKER ... THY FATHER HATH REACHED THE TWILIGHT OF HIS YEARS ...
'TIS FOR THE YOUNG TO SEIZE THE TORCH OF GALLANTRY, AND HOLD IT HIGH! THUS HAS IT EVER BEEN! THUS SHALL IT EVER BE! EVEN THE AGING LION MUST ONE DAY ALLOW THE EAGER CUB TO LEAD THE HUNT!
NOT YET!! AWAY... GET THEE AWAY! MY LIEGE HATH NOT DISMISSED ME!
WHAT IS THIS? THE ATTENTION OF THE THUNDER GOD DOTH SEEM TO FALTER!

AHHH, SON OF MY HEART... I HAVE DETAINED THEE TOO LONG
FULL WELL DOTH ODIN REMEMBER THE RIOTOUS CELEBRATION IN WHICH THE WARRIORS PARTAKE ON THE EVE OF BATTLE!
GET THEE HENCE, VALIANT THOR! I'LL SEE THEE ANON!
THEN, BY YOUR LEAVE, MOST NOBLE MONARCH!

AND, AS THE GOD OF THUNDER EAGERLY JOINS HIS COLORFUL COMPANIONS...
EVEN I... OMNIPOTENT LORD OF ALL I SURVEY... MUST SUFFER THE PANGS OF BITTER DESPAIR!
FOR, THOUGH MIGHTY THOR DOTH TRULY GLADDEN ODIN'S HEART.. STILL AM I FATHER TO ANOTHER... THE EVIL LOKI!
A TOAST THEN, TO THE SONS OF ODIN!
MAY THE FRUITS OF VICTORY BE EVER HARVESTED BY THE GALLANT THOR!
FOR HE, ABOVE ALL, ART TRULY A GOD AMONGST GODS!
AND, MAY THE SHAME OF LOKI PROCLAIM TO THE WORLD THAT EVEN ODIN HATH TASTED OF THE CUP OF SORROW... AND DISMAL FAILURE!
BUT, ENOUGH OF SUCH SORDID SOLILOQUIZING! WE HAVE A GLORY-DRENCHED TALE TO TELL... THE LIKE OF WHICH YOUR MORTAL EYES HAVE NEVER BEFORE BEHELD... AND TELL IT NOW WE SHALL...!
FROM GALAXIES WITHOUT END WARRIORS DO POUR INTO ETERNAL ASGARD... HOPING TO WIN THE COVETED SUITS OF GOLDEN ARMOR!
AY! THIS SHALL TRULY BE THE MOST MAGNIFICENT TOURNEY OF ALL!
TO HOGUN THE GRIM, ONE TOURNEY IS LIKE ANOTHER!
NOT SO WITH VALOROUS VOLSTAGG! THIS SHALL BE MY HOUR OF SUPREME TRIUMPH! AT LAST I SHALL PROVE THAT I AM EVERY BIT AS POWERFUL AS I AM UNDENIABLY HANDSOME!
IF HIS POWER WERE THE EQUAL OF HIS GIRTH, VOLSTAGG WOULD BE FEARED BY ODIN HIMSELF!

KAROOM!

WHAT IS THIS?!! KNOW THEY NOT THAT BRAWLING IS FORBIDDEN ERE THE GAMES HAVE STARTED?

BUT, IF BRAWL THEY MUST.. LET IT BE WITH US! THE BLADE OF FANDRAL FAIR CRIES OUT TO BE DRAWN!

BASE YARLET!! YOU DARE OPPOSE THE WILL OF BROK, THE CRUSHER!!

STAND YE BACK, ALL!! BROK BODES NO INTERFERENCE WHEN HE HAS HIS SPORT!

SPORT?? TO FLAY UPON SMALLER FOES?? THOR CALLS IT COWARDICE!

AND FANDRAL THE DASHING ECHOES THE WORDS OF THE THUNDER GOD!

HAH! NOW SHALT THOU PAY FOR THINE UN-WARRANTED ATTACK!

FIE!! THE BONE-CRUSHING BROK FEARS NO PUNY SCIONS OF ASGARD! DRAGONS DO FLEE AT MY APPROACH!
DRAGONS PERHAPS... BUT NOT SO THE SON OF ODIN!
NOR HOGUN THE GRIM!
NOR FANDRAL... WHO CLAIMS THEE FIRST!

BRAGGART, CHOOSE THY WEAPON! THE BLADE OF FANDRAL SHALL HEW THEE DOWN TO SIZE WITH THE SPEED OF A STRIKING COBRA!
THOUGH, 'TIS POOR PAYMENT, INDEED, FOR ONE WHO SHALL AFFORD ME SUCH PRICE-LESS AMUSE-MENT!

IF THY WEAPON BE THE SWORD, THEN I SHALL STRIKE FOR BROK!
FOR I BE TYR, OF THE BLINDING BLADE...MOST DEADLY SWORDSMAN IN THE THOUSAND GALAXIES!
UNSPEAKABLE KNAVE!! THOUGH THOU WERT TWICE AS GOOD AS THY BOAST, STILL WOULDST THOU BE BUT HALF A MATCH FOR FANDRAL!

FOPPISH FOOL! I'LL QUARTER THEE LIKE A SACK OF GRAIN!
LET ME STILL HIS MOUTH WITH MY POUND-ING MACE!
AH NO, GRIM ONE! THIS SPORT IS TOO DELICIOUS! THE BUMPKIN DOTH POSSESS SOME SKILL...THOUGH IT PALES BESIDE THE WIZARDRY OF FANDRAL!
SSSSSSSSWIT

HOGUN THE GRIM!! I HAVE HEARD OF THEE AND THY PUNY MACE! 'TIS I THOU SHALT BATTLE --- NOT MY BROTHER TYR!
FOR MEN CALL ME GALP... OF THE STEEL ARM!
KNOW THEN, GALP... THERE ARE ARMS MORE MIGHTY THAN THOSE OF STEEL!
WHAT? THOU DOTH FORCE ME BACK? FOR THAT, THE PAYMENT MUST BE THY LIFE!
NOTHING DO I HOLD MORE CHEAP... BUT NOTHING SHALL COST THEE SO DEAR!
HAVE AT THEE THEN... DOOMED ONE!
THOOM!

AGREED! I SHALL CHOOSE YON GRINNING FOP TO BE MY VICTIM!
THE BLADE OF TYR SHALL WRITE FINIS TO HIS POMPOUS SWASH-BUCKLING!
AND I SELECT HOGUN! AFTER TESTING THE STRENGTH OF GALP, HE SHALL HAVE REASON INDEED TO BE SO GRIM!
NONE BUT THOR SHALL DO FOR BROK! I SHALL CRUSH THE SON OF ODIN WITH A SINGLE BLOW!
WHAT?!! ALL THE FOES HAVE THUS BEEN CHOSEN? HOW MONUMENTAL IS THE DISAPPOINTMENT OF VALOROUS VOLSTAGG!
THOU COULDST HAVE SPARED THYSELF SUCH DISAPPOINTMENT BY NOT WATCHING FROM A SAFE DISTANCE, THOU OVERSTUFFED CABBAGE!
ONCE AGAIN THE LION-HEARTED VOLSTAGG HATH BEEN WRONGED BY A FRIEND!
BUT THERE IS YET NO FOE FOR DROM!! EVEN A TROLL MAY LUST FOR BATTLE!

MEANWHILE, AN UNMENTIONABLE, INDESCRIBABLE DISTANCE AWAY, THE BODILESS, INVISIBLE THOUGHT-IMAGE OF EVIL LOKI HURTLES TOWARDS THE PLANET EARTH AT A SPEED WHICH SURPASSES HUMAN COMPREHENSION...
THOUGH MY BODY IS THE PRISONER OF A LIMITLESS LIMBO... MY THOUGHTS ARE FREE TO ROAM TO THE ENDS OF INFINITY!
THERE IS MY GOAL! THERE... IN A HIDDEN JUNGLE IN THE VERY HEART OF MYSTERIOUS ASIA...!
FOR, WITHIN THAT JUNGLE, LIES THE UNDISCOVERED, MOUNTAINOUS RUINS OF A LONG-FORGOTTEN TEMPLE...
...BENEATH WHICH IS BURIED THE MOST POWERFUL, SINGLE ENTITY IN ALL THE UNIVERSE!
BUT...HE SHALL REMAIN BURIED... NO LONGER!!

AT THAT MOMENT, AMONG THE FORBIDDING RUINS, A BAND OF MOUNTAIN MARAUDERS CAUTIOUSLY PROWL...
THERE IS LOOT ENOUGH TO BE STOLEN FROM PASSING TRAVELLERS WHO HAVE LOST THEIR WAY!
WHY THEN DO WE SET FOOT IN THIS PLACE WHERE DEMONS DWELL??
IT IS WHISPERED THAT A TREASURE LIES BURIED HERE... AND HE WHO FINDS IT SHALL FIND POWER GREATER THAN ANY MAN HAS EVER KNOWN!

BUT, BEFORE ANOTHER WORD CAN BE UTTERED...
BAKA-ROOOOM!
THE VERY EARTH TRIES TO SWALLOW US FOR OUR TRESPASS!
WHAT WONDER IS THIS?? THE MOUNTAIN IS SPLITTING ASUNDER?!

HOW COULD ANY MERE MORTAL SURMISE THE TRUTH?? WHO COULD IMAGINE THAT THE THOUGHT-IMAGE OF LOKI HAS BREATHED ONE SILENT COMMAND TO HIM WHO LIES BENEATH THE RUINS...
...AND, AT THAT SELF-SAME INSTANT, A CURRENT OF UNIMAGINABLE FORCE GUSHES UPWARDS FROM THE RUBBLE BELOW... HURLING GIANT BOULDERS INTO THE AIR WITH THE FURY OF AN EXPLODING NOVA...!

...UNTIL, ONE FEARSOME FIGURE STANDS FORTH FROM THE RUBBLE... THE FIGURE OF--THE DESTROYER!!
FOR LONG, BREATHLESS SECONDS HE STANDS MOTIONLESS... SILENT.. UNTIL, AT LAST...

...THE VOICE OF THE DESTROYER THUNDERS FORTH... AS THE VERY MOUNTAINS TREMBLE...
I LIVE AGAIN!!
HEAR ME, ODIN!! THE STAKES OF THY TOURNAMENT HAVE BEEN RAISED!
NOW IT IS THINE OWN LIFE ITSELF WHICH IS THE PRIZE!
AND, AS THE INDESTRUCTIBLE DESTROYER GLANCES HEAVENWARD, THE VERY ATMOSPHERE AROUND HIM BEGINS TO CRACKLE WITH SHIMMERING BOLTS OF LETHAL, UNCONTROLLABLE ENERGY... ENOUGH RAW, LIVING POWER TO SHATTER A PLANET!!

WHILE, A UNIVERSE AWAY, THE SOARING FLIGHT OF EAGLES AND GOLDEN FALCONS HERALDS THE START OF THE TOURNAMENT OF CHAMPIONS... A TOURNEY SUCH AS MORTAL MAN HAS NEVER WITNESSED... SUCH AS MORTAL MIND CAN SCARCELY CONCEIVE...!
THE TIME IS COME FOR THE WARRIORS' CHARGE... THE MOST AWESOME DISPLAY OF FIGHTING POWER EVER WITNESSED IN ONE ARENA!
THOUGH THIS DAY HATH BEEN PROCLAIMED A TIME OF GLORY, THERE IS A COLD CHILL O'ER YON PROCEEDINGS...
I SENSE IT, TOO! LIKE SOME DARK, DREAD OMEN OF IMPENDING EVIL... SOON TO BE UNLEASHED UPON US ALL!
THE COMBATANTS ASSEMBLE IN TWO GROUPS, EACH POSSESSING A SYMBOLIC PENNANT! THE FIRST PENNANT TO FALL SIGNIFIES THAT GROUP'S DEFEAT!
LET THY LIPS BE SILENT! IMPERIAL ODIN HATH NODDED HIS HEAD!
HO! LET THE CHAMPIONS OF EACH CONTENDING GROUP NOW APPROACH THE PRESENCE!

WARRIORS ALL! THE BLESSING OF THY LIEGE UPON THEE!

TO THE BRAVEST SHALL GO THE PRIZE!

AND NOW, FOR THE GREATER GLORY OF THE ETERNAL REALM... LET THE BATTLE BEGIN!

I HAVE SPOKEN!

SO BE IT!

BUT THEN, AS THE BATTLE RAGES, A STARTLING HAPPENSTANCE BEFALLS...

FOR EACH FOE I UNHORSE, TWO *OTHERS* APPEAR... SEEMINGLY FROM THE *AIR* ITSELF... TO TAKE HIS PLACE!

HATH SOME *ENCHANTMENT* BEEN PLACED UPON YON FIELD OF BATTLE? OR, IS A NEW, SINISTER FORCE HERE AT WORK?

WOK!

KRAK!

HORSEMAN AFTER HORSEMAN DOES THE GRIM-VISAGED IMMORTAL BATTER INTO HELPLESSNESS, UNTIL AT LAST... THE IRON-NERVED HOGUN IS BESET FROM ALL SIDES AT ONCE...
BY THE THREE-HEADED SERPENT OF THRACE!! A LUCKY BLOW HATH TORN MY SADDLE FROM BENEATH ME..!!
FTOK!

HOGUN SHALL TROUBLE US NO LONGER...TILL THE TOURNEY BE WON!
BUT, LOOK YE ALL!! THE DASHING FANDRAL DOTH MAKE A MOCKERY OF OUR FINEST BLADES-MEN!
AFTER HIM!! EVEN HIS DAZZLING SWORD CANNOT BE EVERY-WHERE!

SPANG!
HAVE AT THEE, CRAVEN CHURLS!! TO LIVE IS TO FIGHT... AND FANDRAL YIELDS TO NONE!

HAH! NOT EVEN THE PRINCE OF DUELISTS CAN POSSESS VISION IN BACK OF HIS HEAD!
THY SWORD SHALL NOW BE STILLED, TILL THE BATTLE DOTH END!
CHOK!

WHILE, DIRECTLY BEHIND THE SCENE OF CRASHING COMBAT, WE FIND...

YONDER IS THE PENNANT WE SEEK... BORNE BY THE OAFISH VOLSTAGG!!

OUR BROTHER DROM, THE SPIRIT WEAVER, HATH WOVEN A SPELL ROUND MIGHTY THOR, CAUSING HIM TO STRIKE AT WARRIORS WHO MULTIPLY BEFORE HIS VERY EYES!

...THUS ALLOWING US TO BREAK THROUGH TO THE REAR... AND SEIZE YON PENNANT!

THE ENORMOUS ONE SHALL NEVER KNOW WHAT HATH HIT HIM!

BEHIND THEE, VOLSTAGG!! LOOK YOU TO THE REAR!!

THE HOOF-BEATS DROWN OUT OUR WARNING!

VOLSTAGG!! POOR VOLSTAGG!

I SEEM TO HEAR MEN CRY MY NAME! SMALL WONDER, INDEED! FOR, IS VOLSTAGG NOT THE MOST ADMIRED OF ALL?!!

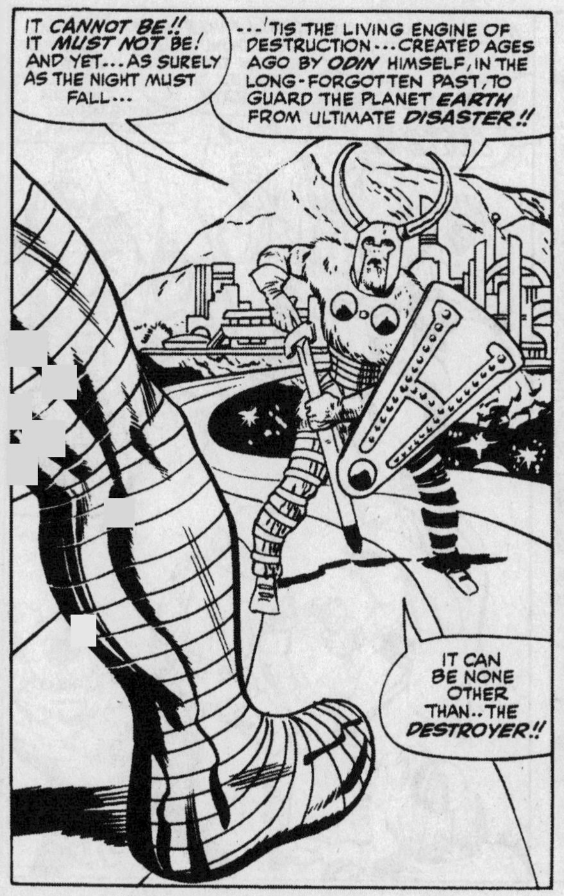
IT CANNOT BE!! IT MUST NOT BE! AND YET... AS SURELY AS THE NIGHT MUST FALL...
...'TIS THE LIVING ENGINE OF DESTRUCTION... CREATED AGES AGO BY ODIN HIMSELF, IN THE LONG-FORGOTTEN PAST, TO GUARD THE PLANET EARTH FROM ULTIMATE DISASTER!!
IT CAN BE NONE OTHER THAN.. THE DESTROYER!!

VALIANTLY, FEARLESSLY, THE GALLANT GUARDIAN OF THE GATES OF ASGARD STANDS HIS GROUND... BUT, THOUGH HE POSSESSES THE POWER TO TURN ASIDE AN ARMADA... HE NOW FACES THE MOST DESTRUCTIVE FORCE EVER CREATED BY OMNIPOTENT ODIN...
WHILE HEIMDALL STANDS, THOU SHALT NOT... UNHHH!
THEN NO LONGER SHALL YOU STAND!
I HAVE BUT ONE MISSION.. BUT ONE PURPOSE.. ODIN MUST BE SLAIN!!

THUS, FALL THEE, HEIMDALL!!
FOR NONE CAN WITHSTAND A SOLID BOLT OF ELEMENTAL FORCE... WHICH ONLY THE DESTROYER POSSESSES!

AND NOW, THE TIME IS COME!!
ERE THIS FATEFUL DAY BE ENDED, IMPERIAL ODIN SHALL BE NO MORE!
THE DESTROYER SHALL RULE THE UNIVERSE!
AND LOKI SHALL RULE THE DESTROYER!

MEANWHILE, AT THE ARENA, MIGHTY THOR REJOINS HIS FALLEN LIEUTENANTS...
O BASEST OF INFAMY! TO THINK THAT EVER-ALERT VOLSTAGG COULD HAVE BEEN TAKEN BY SURPRISE!
A FAR GREATER WRONG THAN THAT WAS HERE COMMITTED..!
AY, FANDRAL! OUR FOES HAVE EMPLOYED THE USE OF SPELLS TO CONFUSE US... ALTHOUGH THEY BE FORBIDDEN BY THE RULES!
BUT DEARLY SHALL THEY PAY FOR SUCH DECEPTION!

HOLD, VILLAINS! THE BATTLE IS NOT YET ENDED!
WE STILL MAY REGAIN YON PENNANT BY RIGHT OF PERSONAL CHALLENGE!!
CHALLENGE AWAY THEN, THUNDER GOD! SURELY THOU ART DOOMED TO DEFEAT!
SINGLY, EACH OF US IS THE SUPERIOR OF OUR ASGARDIAN COUNTERPART!
THE CHALLENGE HAS BEEN MET!
HA!! LET THE COMBAT BEGIN!

DIDST THOU THINK THY SIZE ALONE COULD TRIUMPH OVER THOR?
THOU HAST MUCH TO LEARN ABOUT SUCH MATTERS, YE WHO CALL THYSELF THE CRUSHER!
WHAT? A SINGLE BLADE AGAINST THE WIZARDRY OF FANDRAL? SURELY THOU DOST JEST!
BOM!
NOW, GALP, THERE ARE NONE TO SAVE THEE!
DROM! GET THEE TO MY SIDE!

BUT, DROM, THE SPIRIT WEAVER, NEEDS HIS ENCHANTMENT FOR HIMSELF... AS THE MOUNTAINOUS VOLSTAGG LUMBERS TOWARDS HIM WITH THE GRACE AND AGILITY OF AN EARTHQUAKE...
IN ALL THE UNIVERSE, ONLY ONE THING EXCEEDS THE FABLED STRENGTH OF VOLSTAGG... AND THAT IS THE FURY OF MY FEARSOME ANGER!
THOU ART BRAVE AS THE LION AGAINST ONE SINGLE TROLL...
BUT, LET US TEST THY COURAGE AGAINST THE IMAGERY I SHALL WEAVE FROM THE MOLECULES OF INFINITY..!

THIS IS WHY I AM CALLED WEAVER OF SPIRITS!
THOUGH THOU SELECTED THE SMALLEST BROTHER TO BE THY FOE... THOU DIDST ALSO SELECT THE MOST TRULY POWERFUL!
JUST AS V-VALIANT VOLSTAGG INTENDED!
THEN WHY QUAKEST THOU IN FEAR?
FEAR?? THE VERY WORD IS A STRANGER TO VOLSTAGG!
I DO BUT TREMBLE WITH SHEER EAGER-NESS..!!

TURN THEN, EAGER ONE! 'TIS BUT DROM HIMSELF WHO STANDS BEHIND THEE!
THE MONSTER IS THERE NO MORE..?
O, GRAVE INJUSTICE!! JUST WHEN I WAS READY TO SPIN ABOUT AND VANQUISH HIM!

ART THOU CERTAIN HE HATH FLED?
HOW DIS-APPOINTMENT DOTH FILL MY HEART!
BUT, 'TIS THE PRICE I MUST PAY.. THE PRICE OF UNIVERSAL FAME!
FOR, WHO WOULD DARE FACE THE MIGHT OF VOLSTAGG... WHEN MY NAME HATH BECOME A SYMBOL FOR ENDURING COURAGE!!
WHAT'S THIS?? EVEN AS I SPEAK, THE SPIRIT WEAVER FLEES BEFORE ME!

COME YE BACK, VILLAINOUS DROM! VOLSTAGG HATH NOT YET DONE WITH THEE!
I SHALL PURSUE THEE WITH THE SPEED OF THE SHOOTING STAR... THE SILENCE OF THE EVENING BREEZE ... THE GRACE OF A VERITABLE WATER NYMPH..
THUMP! THUMP!
BUT, THE GELATINOUS, WADDLING WARRIOR DOES NOT YET REALIZE THAT HIS FEARFUL FOE IS NOT FLEEING FROM VOLSTAGG, BUT RATHER FROM A FAR MORE TERRIFYING SIGHT...

...THE STULTIFYING SIGHT OF... THE DESTROYER!!
ANOTHER SPIRIT IMAGE! BUT, WILY VOLSTAGG SHALL NOT BE FOOLED AGAIN!
I SHALL TRAMPLE THEE LIKE A TOAD-STOOL!!

FTOOM!
ODD'S BLOOD! I KNOW WHO THOU ART.!!
LET THE TOURNEY CEASE!!! LET THE WARRIORS ASSEMBLE!! THE DESTROYER LIVES!!!
THE ALARM!! SOUND THE ALARM!!
SUDDENLY, ALL THOUGHT OF COMPETITION VANISHES, AS GLADIATORS FROM BOTH SIDES OF THE LISTS HURL THEMSELVES AT THE GREATEST SINGLE MENACE EVER TO ENTER THE HALLOWED GATES OF ASGARD...!
DEATH TO THE DESTROYER!
HE HATH THE POWER TO REDUCE ALL THE REALM TO RUBBLE!
FOOLS!! WHAT ODIN HATH CREATED, NO OTHERS CAN DEFEAT!
KRAKK!
THEN, EFFORTLESSLY, CONTEMPTUOUSLY, WITH ONE SINGLE SWEEP OF HIS MAILED FIST, THE DEADLY DESTROYER SHATTERS EVERY SWORD WITHIN REACH AS THOUGH THEY ARE NAUGHT BUT TWIGS!

HE DOTH MOVE DIRECTLY TOWARDS LORD ODIN!! AND ALL OUR MIGHT IS POWERLESS TO STOP HIM!
WE ARE LIKE UNTO HELPLESS GNATS... BUZZING ABOUT A BEHEMOTH!
YET... STOP HIM WE MUST!
'TIS FUTILE FOLLY! ASGARD IS DOOMED!

THE DESTROYER'S BODY GLOWS... VERITABLE SHOCK WAVES POUR FORTH... WHICH NO LIVING BEING CAN ENDURE!
BEGONE, HELPLESS ONES! SUCH AS THEE ARE BENEATH MY NOTICE!
'TIS ODIN ALONE I MUST DESTROY!

MOST NOBLE LORD! HOW CAN ONE WHOM THOU THYSELF CREATED HAVE THE POWER TO VANQUISH THEE?
HE WAS DESIGNED TO SERVE ASGARD ...TO BE THE WEAPON SUPREME AN HOUR OF NEED!
HENCE, IT DID PLEASE ME TO MAKE HIM INDESTRUCTIBLE!

BUT HE DOTH POSSESS NO WILL OF HIS OWN! ONLY ANOTHER CAN PROVIDE THE NECESSARY LIFE FORCE TO GUIDE MY CREATION!
AND HIM WHO GUIDES THE DESTROYER NOW MUST SURELY BE AN IMMORTAL... FOR WHO ELSE COULD FIND AND CROSS THE FABLED RAINBOW BRIDGE?
AND, OF ALL THE IMMORTALS OF THE REALM, ONLY LOKI WOULD DARE SUCH A DEADLY CHALLENGE TO MY POWER... TO MY VERY LIFE!

MEANWHILE, EVEN AS A SORELY TROUBLED ODIN SPEAKS...
THE DESTROYER!
NOW MUST WE CEASE THIS PETTY AMUSEMENT THAT WE MAY DEFEND OUR LIEGE!
SHOULD THE DESTROYER PREVAIL, THEN ASGARD MUST SURELY FALL!
ASGARD FALL?? NEVER... WHILST ONE OF US LIVES! ALL TOGETHER THEN...
BUT, HOLD! ONE FACE HAVE I SOUGHT IN VAIN! THE VISAGE OF BALDER!
I, TOO, HAVE PONDERED YON MYSTERY!
IN OUR HOUR OF TRIAL, WHAT OF HIM WHO HATH BEEN MORE THAN BROTHER TO US ALL??
WHAT OF BALDER?
BUT, AT THE SIGHT OF THE DESTROYER, MIGHTY THOR CAN THINK OF NOTHING SAVE THE DANGER THAT CONFRONTS HIS REGAL FATHER...
FOR ODIN!
FOR ASGARD!
THE THUNDER GOD STRIKES!
DEATH TO HIM WHO THREATENS THE PRESENCE ROYAL!
WHROOOM
BACK, THOU BESTIAL, BLOODLESS THING OF EVIL! BACK, BEFORE THE POWER OF THOR!

HE TOTTERS! HE REELS BACK!
THE ADVANTAGE MUST BE PRESSED, ERE HE DOTH RECOVER!

THOU SHALT NEVER REACH ODIN WHILST THE GOD OF THUNDER ENDURES!
BLANG!

AGAIN... AND AGAIN.. AND AGAIN.. MUST I STRIKE...!
FTOK!

...UNTIL MY LORD ODIN HATH FOUND A MEANS TO VANQUISH THIS MOST MONSTROUS MENACE OF ALL!

THEN, WITH ONE INDESCRIBABLE BLOW, THE MIGHTY THOR DOES WHAT NONE HAVE EVER DONE BEFORE -- HE DOWNS THE DREAD DESTROYER --!
ASGARD BE PRAISED! I HAVE ACHIEVED THE IMPOSSIBLE!
SKRAK!
THUD!

BUT, THOUGH MOMENTARILY HURLED OFF-BALANCE, THE DEADLY DESTROYER... CREATED BY OMNIPOTENT ODIN HIMSELF... HAS BEEN CREATED TOO WELL...
NO HAMMERING ATTACK... NO HUMILIATING FALL... CAN EVER LESSEN THE DEVASTATING LETHAL POWER OF THE DESTROYER!
ZAK!
VERILY HE SPEAKS THE TRUTH!

SZZZZK!
HE WHOM ALL-WISE ODIN HATH CREATED.. NO OTHER FORCE CAN REND ASUNDER!

BUT, IF THE THUNDER GOD SHOULD FALL... THEN WHAT BECOMES OF...?
UNNHHH..!!!
FTAK!

SLOWLY, EFFORTLESSLY, THE STEEL-SINEWED DESTROYER RISES TO HIS FEET ONCE MORE... HIS FINGERS FLAMING WITH THE HEAT OF SURTUR, THE FIRE DEMON... HEAT MORE POTENT THAN A DOZEN FLAMING SUNS...!
THE MOMENT IS NOW!
THE MOMENT WHEN... ODIN MUST PERISH!

NO RESCUER CAN PIERCE THESE WALLS OF FLAME! NOTHING CAN KEEP ME FROM THEE, DOOMED ONE!
THOU DAREST CALL ODIN... THY CREATOR... DOOMED?!!
VERILY... I DARE!
THEN, HEAR THIS, MERCILESS ONE! I KNOW 'TIS LOKI'S SPIRIT WHICH HATH RETURNED THEE TO LIFE!
WHAT MATTERS THAT NOW? ONLY BY FINDING THE BODY OF LOKI CANST THOU STOP ME.!
AND, BY THINE OWN COMMAND, THE PRINCE OF EVIL HATH BEEN LOST IN A NAMELESS LIMBO, WHERE EVEN THY POWERS CANNOT FIND HIM IN TIME!
AND NOW, A LIVING AGE DOTH COME TO AN END! THE REIGN OF ALL-MIGHTY ODIN SHALL GIVE WAY TO THE AGE OF LOKI... AND THE DESTROYER!
THEREFORE, BEHOLD... AS I LOWER MY VISOR...
LIKE A LIVING THING, THE DEADLY CREATURE'S VISOR GLOWS BRIGHTER AND BRIGHTER, GATHERING ONTO ITSELF ENOUGH ELEMENTAL ENERGY TO ANNIHILATE HIM WHO IS SURELY THE MIGHTIEST BEING OF ALL...
PREPARE THEE, THEN, FOR THE FINAL ADVENTURE... THE SLEEP WHICH HATH NO ENDING!!
EVIL ONE, HEAR ME! THOU CANST NOT! THOU MUST NOT!
SUCH MONUMENTAL INFAMY WILL MAKE THE HEAVENS THEMSELVES CRUMBLE AND TURN ASHEN IN AN AGONY OF SHAME!
TAKE THOU THE LIFE OF A THUNDER GOD...
..BUT SPARE HIM WHO IS SOVEREIGN OF US ALL!

BUT, THEN..
A FLYING ASTRAL FIGURE... SPEEDING TO MY LIEGE!
WHAT UNSEEMLY ENCHANTMENT IS THIS??!
MOST NOBLE ODIN... I HAVE RETURNED!

HOW WELL I KNEW THOU WOULDST NOT FAIL ME, LOYAL ONE!
THE ONE THOU SEEKEST HATH BEEN FOUND! A TRILLION THOUGHT-YEARS TO THE NORTHERNMOST PERIMETER OF NON-SPACE... THERE DRIFTS LOKI!
RETURN THEN TO THY PHYSICAL FORM! THOU HAST SERVED ME WELL... BRAVE BALDER!

BUT, SIRE... WHAT IF THE DESTROYER STRIKES ERE THOU CANST FELL THE INFAMOUS LOKI FROM SUCH AN UNTHINKABLE DISTANCE?!!
BANISH THY FEARS! AM I NOT ETERNAL ODIN?!!

THOUGH THE DESTROYER BE READY TO HURL HIS BOLT OF DEATH... 'TIS I WHO POSSESS THE POWER TO TEAR THE VERY FABRIC OF ETERNITY!
THUS, AT MY COMMAND.. LET TIME STAND STILL!

NOW, BY THE POWER OF THE LIVING COSMOS... I SEND A BEAM OF FORGETFUL-NESS ACROSS THE INFINITE VOID...

AND, AT THE FURTHEST REACH OF THE LIMITLESS UNIVERSE, THE PRINCE OF EVIL IS DEFEATED ONCE MORE ...

...AS THE ALL-ENCOMPASSING BEAM CLOSES LOKI'S MIND TO ALL THOUGHT... TO ALL MEMORY...!

THEN, SUDDENLY BEREFT OF MENTAL GUIDANCE, THE DESTROYER BECOMES A HOLLOW, HELPLESS SHELL ... WHICH CAN DO NO MORE THAN CRUMBLE BROKENLY TO THE GROUND ...

'TIS ENDED! THE DANGER IS PAST... THE VICTORY WON!

HAIL, MIGHTY ODIN! IN THINE INFINITE WISDOM, THOU HAST SAVED THE REALM!
TRULY, THE TRIUMPH IS THINE!
I SAY THEE NAY, SON OF MY HEART!
IN THIS HOUR OF REJOICING, THE GLORY SHALL BE SHARED BY ALL!

IN ASGARD'S HOUR OF NEED, THINE EVERY SWORD WAS RAISED IN OUR BEHALF!
THOU ART HEROES ALL! THOU ART VERILY THE PRIDE, THE NOBLE FRUIT OF ASGARD!

EACH YEAR, AT THIS VERY INSTANT, THINE ARMOR WILL GLOW AS BRIGHTEST GOLD FOR ONE FULL DAY!
THUS, SO LONG AS TIME ENDURES... NONE SHALL FORGET THE GLORY WE HAVE SHARED TOGETHER!
I HAVE SPOKEN!

HAIL, NOBLE ODIN! THY NAME BE PRAISED!
ODIN HATH SPOKEN! SO BE IT!
ASGARD FOREVER!

BUT, 'MIDST ALL THE FANFARE, POMP, AND PAGEANTRY... ONE FIGURE FINDS HIMSELF AMONG THE MISSING...
O MOST PERFIDIOUS FATE!
TO THINK THAT VOLSTAGG, MIGHTIEST OF ALL... SHOULD BE SO IGNOMINIOUSLY TRAPPED BY HIS OWN NOBLE BULK!
WHAT STARK TRAGEDY THAT MY DAUNTLESS ARM WAS NOT RAISED IN BATTLE!

HOW I WOULD HAVE LEPT TO THE ATTACK LIKE A TIGER.. HAD I BEEN ABLE TO DISLODGE MYSELF!
EVEN NOW, I SLIP AND FALL BACK--- AS HARDLY BEFITS THE GREATEST OF WARRIORS!
SKLUPP!

FIE UPON IT! I SHALL WAIT FOR RESCUE!
AND, I PRAY IT MAY BE A LONG TIME COMING --- FOR THERE ARE MANY MEMORIES TO SAVOR ... MEMORIES OF THE GLORY OF ASGARD, THAT SHALL LIVE FOREVER IN THE HEARTS OF MEN!
VERILY, WE HAVE SPOKEN!

THE MIGHTY
THOR
APPROVED BY THE COMICS CODE AUTHORITY
MARVEL COMICS GROUP
12¢ IND.
133 OCT
BEHOLD..
"THE LIVING PLANET!"

THE MIGHTY THOR!
"BEHOLD... THE LIVING PLANET!"
CAN IT BE TRUE? WE GAZED AT A PLANET--AND SAW IT BECOME A LIVING FACE!! WE HEARD IT SPEAK TO US!!
I CANNOT TESTIFY TO THE TRUTH OF A MATTER! I AM BUT A RECORDER--FASHIONED IN HUMAN FORM!
I MUST NOW ACTIVATE MY DERMA-CIRCUITS FOR MAXIMUM AND CONTINUOUS OPERATION! MY ENTIRE BODY--SKIN, FEATURES, LIMBS, AND ELECTRONIC BRAIN WILL ACCURATELY RECORD WHATSOEVER TRANSPIRES--
ACCOMPANIED BY A HUMANOID RECORDER, THE MIGHTY THOR LEAVES THE WORLD OF THE COLONIZERS, TO ENTER THE DREADED, TOTALLY MYSTERIOUS BLACK GALAXY, FROM WHENCE NO LIVING BEING HAS EVER RETURNED!
AND NOW, PREPARE FOR WONDERMENT BEYOND MEASURE ON THE INCREDIBLE PAGES THAT FOLLOW--
STAR-STUDDED SCRIPT: STAN LEE
PLANET-POUNDING PENCILLING: JACK KIRBY
REAL RIGELLIAN RENDERING: VINCE COLLETTA
LOTS OF LITTLE LETTERING: ARTIE SIMEK
POSSIBLY THE MOST DARINGLY IMAGINATIVE SAGA YOU HAVE EVER MARVELLED AT!!
1

STEPPING FROM THEIR RIGELLIAN SPACE SHIP, THE GOD OF THUNDER AND HIS EMOTIONLESS COMPANION FIND THEMSELVES IN A GALAXY TOTALLY BEYOND OUR MEAGER POWERS OF DESCRIPTION! IT IS TRULY A WORLD WHICH IS NOT A WORLD--EXISTING IN A TIME WHICH IS MORE THAN TIME...!
MY VERY SENSES REEL BEFORE THE SIGHT WHICH DOTH CONFRONT US! OF ALL THE GALAXIES, KNOWN TO MAN OR IMMORTAL, THIS IS SURELY THE MOST INCOMPREHENSIBLE!
WE ARE IN THE CENTER OF THE BLACK GALAXY! MY SENSITIZERS DETECT THE PRESENCE OF--EGO! CLASSIFICATION: MULTIPLE VIRUS LIVING MATTER! SIZE: PLANETARY RANGE! LOCATION: EXISTING NOT IN PHYSICAL UNIVERSE, BUT IN FLUID BIO-VERSE!
2

CONCLUSION: THE PLANET UPON WHICH WE STAND IS NOT MERELY A RECEPTACLE UPON WHICH LIFE DWELLS-- IT IS TRULY LIFE ITSELF! HERE, WITHIN THE ONLY KNOWN BIO-VERSE IN ALL OF CREATION, WE ARE IN THE PRESENCE OF EGO, THE LIVING PLANET!!
3

THE HUMANOID'S WORDS ARE *TRUE!*

I AM *EGO*, THE LARGEST, MOST POWERFUL INTELLIGENCE IN ALL OF *INFINITY!* YOU ARE LIKE *DUST* UNTO MY FEET!

POSSESSING *POWERS WITHOUT END*, I HAVE FASHIONED MYSELF A *FACE*, IN THE MANNER OF THOSE *BEYOND* THE BLACK GALAXY!

THUS, WE MAY *ADDRESS* EACH OTHER WITH COMPARATIVE *EASE!*

HAVE A *CARE*, THOU WHO ART A LIVING *WORLD!* NO MATTER THY SIZE--'TIS *THOR* WHO FACES THEE!

SO *CONFIDENT* IS HE--SO CONVINCED OF HIS TOTAL *SUPREMACY*--THAT HE HATH *IGNORED* MY IRATE WORDS!

BUT *HOLD!* HE PREPARES TO SPEAK *AGAIN*--!

IN ORDER THAT WE MAY CONVERSE MORE COMFORTABLY, I HAVE GIVEN MYSELF A MORE CONVENIENT SIZE--AND FORM!
NOW, MOUNT THESE BEASTS WHICH I HAVE CREATED FROM IMPRESSIONS WITHIN YOUR OWN BRAIN--AND WE SHALL RIDE TO THE NEW ASGARD WHICH AWAITS YOU!
OBSERVATION: BEING ABLE TO RE-FORM BIO-VERSAL MOLECULES, THE ENTITY KNOWN AS EGO CAN RESHAPE MATTER INTO ANY SEMBLANCE HE DESIRES!
BUT, FOR WHAT PURPOSE?? WHY DOTH HE TOY WITH US IN SUCH FASHION?
IT IS NOT FOR ME TO SAY! I MAY ONLY OBSERVE--AND RECORD!
MY PURPOSE MAY NOT BE FATHOMED BY SUCH AS YOU! IT SHALL BE REVEALED--IN DUE TIME!
ALL THIS HAVE I CREATED FROM YOUR OWN MEMORY! BUT, IT GIVES EVIDENCE OF MERELY THE SLIGHTEST FRACTION OF MY TRUE AND TOTAL POWER!
OBSERVATION: IN ALL THE KNOWN COSMOS, THERE EXISTS NO SCALE OF VALUE WHICH CAN EVEN MEASURE THE ACTUAL POWER OF EGO!
THE LARGEST--AND POSSIBLY THE MOST DANGEROUS LIVING ENTITY OF ALL TIME--AMUSING HIMSELF WITH GAUDY DEMON-STRATIONS OF HIS SKILL! WHAT MOTIVE CAN THERE BE TO SUCH SEEMING MADNESS???
BUT HOLD!! HE SPEAKS AGAIN! I MUST ATTEND HIS EVERY WORD UNTIL HIS AWESOME SECRET BE DIVULGED!
I HAVE AWAITED YOUR COMING FOR COUNTLESS MILLENNIUMS! TOO LONG HAVE I BEEN CONFINED WITHIN THE BLACK GALAXY--'TIS TIME FOR EGO TO CONQUER ALL OF SPACE!
5

MEANWHILE, AT THAT VERY MOMENT--BACK UPON THE MORE FAMILIAR PLANET EARTH, WE FIND JANE FOSTER, THE THUNDER GOD'S TRULY BELOVED, DINING IN A MOUNTAIN VILLAGE SOMEWHERE IN EUROPE--
IT WAS GOOD OF YOU TO ACCEPT MY OFFER OF DINNER, MISS FOSTER!
I MUST ADMIT YOU AROUSED MY FEMALE CURIOSITY BY THE STORY YOU TOLD, MR. PORGIA!
YOU SAID YOU HAD BEEN SEARCHING THE ENTIRE EARTH FOR SOMEONE--

AH, YES! I--AND MY FRIEND, TAGAR--SEEK ONE PERSON--POSSESSING TRUE COURAGE, ENTHUSIASM, AND A SPIRIT OF DEDICATION!
THERE MUST BE MANY WITH SUCH QUALIFICATIONS! I DON'T SEE WHY YOU'RE HAVING SUCH DIFFICULTY!
BUT, YOU HAVEN'T YET TOLD ME THE MOST IMPORTANT PART--WHY DO YOU NEED SUCH A PERSON? WHAT IS YOUR BUSINESS?
YOU SHALL LEARN THAT SOON--WHEN TAGAR HIMSELF ARRIVES!

I AM HERE! IS SHE THE ONE? HAVE YOU FOUND HER AT LAST, PORGIA?
TAGAR!! NO, SHE HAS NOT YET CONSENTED! I WAS AWAITING YOUR ARRIVAL BEFORE I DARED REVEAL OUR GREAT MISSION!
WHAT HAVE I STUMBLED INTO? THERE IS FAR MORE TO THIS THAN PORGIA HAS IMPLIED! PORGIA--AND TAGAR--WHO ARE THEY--REALLY??

STAND ASIDE, PORGIA! IF SHE POSSESSES THE QUALIFICATIONS, I SHALL PERSONALLY SPEAK TO HER!
ONCE WE FIND THE TEACHER WE SEEK, WE SHALL BE ON THE THRESHHOLD OF SOLVING THE ETERNAL SECRET OF LIFE ITSELF!! YOU CANNOT REFUSE US!
CAREFUL, TAGAR! YOU MUST NOT FRIGHTEN HER!
THE SECRET OF LIFE!! CAN THEY BE--MAD??
BUT, I'M NOT A TEACHER! I'M A NURSE!

A NURSE, YOU SAY? AHHH--GOOD! SO MUCH THE BETTER!
A KNOWLEDGE OF MEDICINE WOULD ACTUALLY DOUBLE YOUR VALUE!
I'M SORRY! I'M AFRAID IT'S OUT OF THE QUESTION--!

YOU DO NOT REALIZE WHAT YOU'RE SAYING!
BY THE GENETIC TABLE OF THE HIGH EVOLUTIONARY, WE MUST HAVE YOUR SERVICES!!
AND--HAVE THEM WE SHALL!

BUT ALAS, WE CAN REMAIN WITH LOVELY, MYSTIFIED *JANE FOSTER* NO LONGER, FOR DRAMATIC NEW DEVELOPMENTS AWAIT OUR STARTLED GAZE ONCE MORE, DEEP WITHIN THE UNCANNY, UNTHINKABLE *BLACK GALAXY*--

I HAVE CREATED A *CASTLE,* SUCH AS YOU HAVE KNOWN BEFORE--GUIDED BY THE THOUGHTS WITHIN YOUR BRAIN!

AND NOW, IT IS TIME FOR US TO *TALK!*

FOR AGES I HAVE TESTED THE SMALLEST PORTION OF MY POWER BY DESTROYING ANY *COLONIZER SHIP* FROM RIGEL WHICH VENTURED TOO CLOSE TO ME!

BUT, ALTHOUGH I SOON REALIZED THAT THE *COLONIZERS* WERE HELPLESS TO DEFY ME, I KNEW THERE WERE *OTHERS* IN YOUR UNIVERSE--OTHERS FAR *STRONGER* THAN THEY!

I *KNEW* THAT ONE DAY THERE WOULD COME ONE SUCH AS *YOU*--AND THEN, IT WOULD BE TIME FOR MY *ULTIMATE TEST!*

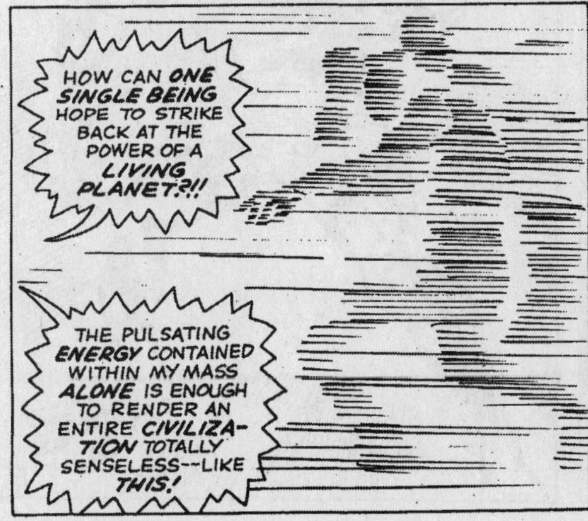

I SHALL USE YOU YOURSELF AS A MOLECULAR MODEL IN ORDER TO CREATE AN ENDLESS ARMY OF BIO-VERSAL CREATURES!
SEE HOW EASILY I CAN CAUSE A PHYSIOLOGICAL INTER-CHANGE, ENABLING ME TO CREATE A HUMANOID FORM OF LIFE OUT OF AN ANTI-BODY ORGANISM!
LET YOUR VERY SENSES REEL AT THE MIRACLE WHICH OCCURS BEFORE YOUR EYES!
HE THINKS TO CONFOUND ME WITH SCIENTIFIC PARLANCE! HE KNOWS NOT THAT I AM A LEARNED PHYSICIAN IN MY MORTAL FORM, AND COMPREHEND ALL THAT OCCURS!
MY SENSES REEL NOT! THOUGH THOU POSSESS THE POWER OF A LIVING PLANET--
KNOW YOU THAT MY REGAL FATHER POSSESSES THE POWER OF AN ETERNAL GALAXY!
OBSERVATION: THE MOLECULES WHIRL AND SHIFT AS THE ANTI-BODY BEGINS TO ASSUME THE FORM OF A HUMANOID!
THERE! THE PROCESS IS COMPLETE! YOU BEHOLD THE PROTOTYPE OF BILLIONS OF SUCH ANTI-BODIES WHICH SHALL MAKE EGO MASTER OF ALL CREATION!
8

I HAVE RECORDED ALL THAT HAS COME TO PASS!
NOW, I MUST RECHARGE MY POWER CIRCUITS! LET THE HUMANOID AND THE IMMORTAL STAND BACK!

NEVER HAVE EVENTS OF SUCH SCOPE, SUCH IMPORT BEEN PRESERVED FOR FUTURE STUDY!
NEVER HAS A RECORDER WITNESSED WONDERMENT THE EQUAL OF THIS!

WITH SUCH AS THESE, THE ENTITY KNOWN AS EGO INTENDS TO CONQUER A UNIVERSE?
THEN, LET THE GOD OF THUNDER DEMONSTRATE THE FATAL FOLLY OF SUCH ASPIRATIONS!

OBSERVATION: A BATTLE BETWEEN GOD AND BIO-VERSAL ENTITY IS ABOUT TO ENSUE!
NOTHING THAT LIVES-- NO POWER THAT THREATENS INNOCENT MASSES--CAN DEFEAT THE HAMMER OF THOR!

YOU ARE TOO LATE! THE ANTI-BODY HAS VANISHED! EGO CAN CREATE COUNTLESS OTHERS, IN THE SPACE OF A HEARTBEAT!
OBSERVATION: THOUGH YOU ARE GOD OF THUNDER, YOU CANNOT COMBAT A LIVING PLANET, FOR WHAT EGO SO WILLS--MUST THEN COME TO PASS!
LET THY VOICE BE STILLED! THE SON OF ODIN SHALL EVER BE A STRANGER TO FECKLESS SURRENDER!

YOU ARE OF NO FURTHER INTEREST TO ME!
HAVING SERVED AS MY MOLECULAR MODEL, YOU HAVE ENABLED ME TO CREATE AN ENDLESS NUMBER OF ANTI-BODIES!
AND SO-- FAREWELL!
NONE MAY DISMISS THE THUNDER GOD IN SUCH CAVALIER FASHION!
OBSERVATION: YOU CANNOT THREATEN ONE WHO IS AN ENTIRE WORLD UNTO HIMSELF!

THERE IS MUCH WISDOM IN THY PRONOUNCEMENT!
BEFORE OUR VERY EYES HATH EGO VANISHED!
SINCE MEMORY DAWNED, NEVER HAVE I FOUGHT IN SO STRANGE, SO ALIEN A LAND!
HERE, WITHIN THIS WONDROUS BIO-VERSE, THE LAND, THE SEAS, THE VERY AIR ABOUT US ARE ALL... ALIVE!

EVERY PART OF THIS PLANET UPON WHICH WE STAND IS VERILY A PART OF EGO! HE IS EVERYWHERE--HE IS EVERYTHING! HE IS A LIVING WORLD!
THAT NOISE! LIKE THE ONRUSHING TORRENT OF A BOTTOMLESS SEA!
IT IS THERE--!

OBSERVATION: NOTHING OCCURS UPON THIS PLANET UNLESS EGO WILLS IT! THEREFORE, IT IS BY HIS WILL THAT A VERITABLE OCEAN AT FLOOD-TIDE NOW ENGULFS US--!
AN OPENING-- JUST AHEAD! TO MY SIDE, RECORDER! WE SHALL YET PLUCK VICTORY FROM THE SEEMINGLY CERTAIN WHIRLPOOL OF DISMAL DEFEAT!

SINCE THOU ART NOT A BEING OF FLESH AND BLOOD, THOU SHALT NOT SUFFER INJURY!
AND AN IMMORTAL OF ASGARD WILL DARE ALL FOR A CAUSE!
SO I SAY-- FOLLOW ME-- NO MATTER WHERE THE PLUNGE DOTH LEAD!
I MAY DO NAUGHT ELSE! I MUST ATTEND-- AND RECORD!
10

A VALVE HATH CLOSED ABOVE US--KEEPING THE WATERS FROM RUSHING IN!
OBSERVATION: WE HAVE ENTERED THE INTERIOR OF THE PLANET--THRU AN OPENING WHICH, IN A HUMAN BEING, WOULD BE CALLED A SKIN PORE!
ALL ABOUT US--LIFE! LIFE, THE NATURE OF WHICH NO MAN HATH EVER DREAMED!
OBSERVATION: HERE WITHIN THE PLANET'S CORE, WE ARE NEW FOREIGN BODIES--AS GERMS WOULD BE IN THE BLOOD STREAM OF A HUMAN!
THEREFORE--
I KNOW WHEREOF THOU SPEAKEST!
SOON, THE PLANET SHALL SEND FORTH ANTI-BODIES TO GIVE US BATTLE!
AND THEN, AS THOUGH TO LEND AWESOME EMPHASIS TO THE THUNDER GOD'S WORDS--
OBSERVATION! OUR DEDUCTION WAS COMPLETELY WITHOUT ERROR! THE ATTACK HAS BEGUN!
THOUGH THEIR NUMBERS BE LIMITLESS, THE VICTORY SHALL BE OURS!
BY THE TOWERING SPIRES OF ETERNAL ASGARD, EVEN A PLANET SHALL FALL THIS DAY!
THOP

THUS BEGINS THE STRANGEST BATTLE IN RECORDED COSMIC HISTORY! ANTI-BODIES WITHOUT END, CREATED ON THE SPOT BY AN OMNIPOTENT EGO, ATTACK THE THUNDER GOD AND HIS HUMANOID COMPANION IN EVER-INCREASING NUMBER!
BEGONE, THINGS OF EVIL! NOT ALL THY MASSES SHALL TOPPLE MIGHTY THOR!
OBSERVATION: IT SHALL TAKE MORE THAN PLATITUDES TO STEM THIS DEADLY TIDE!
SPECIAL MARVEL MESSAGE: SINCE CAMERAS ARE EXPRESSLY FORBIDDEN ANYWHERE IN EGO'S BIO-VERSE, KING KIRBY WAS FORCED TO DRAW THIS INIMITABLE ILLUSTRATION ENTIRELY FROM MEMORY! HENCE, IF ANY SLIGHT INACCURACIES SHOULD BE NOTICED, WE BEG YOUR KIND INDULGENCE! —YE OLDE BENIGN BULLPEN.
12

CONTINUED AFTER NEXT PAGE

MEANWHILE, COUNTLESS LIGHT-YEARS AWAY, THE INVISIBLE BEAM OF THE COLONIZERS' SPACE-LOCK DRAWS THE PLANET EARTH SLOWLY, SILENTLY, SECRETLY OUT OF ORBIT--!
AS THE FLEDGLING COLONIZER KNOWN AS TANA NILE IMPERIOUSLY ENTERS A LOCAL POLICE PRECINCT--
TAKE ME TO THE RULER OF YOUR PLANET EARTH!
-ULP!- SORRY, LADY--HE'S OUT HAVIN' A CUP OF JAVA NOW!
TAKE WARNING! DO NOT SPEAK LIGHTLY TO THE NEW COLONIZER OF THIS PRIMITIVE WORLD!
HOW'S ABOUT VISITIN' OUR PRISON PSYCHOLOGIST, INSTEAD?
HENCEFORTH, I AM TO BE ADDRESSED AS EMPRESS TANA, THE FIRST!
YOU'RE THE FIRST, ALL RIGHT! I NEVER SAW ANOTHER ONE LIKE YA!

LOOK--HOW'S ABOUT TAKIN' OFF THAT NUTTY FACE MASK AND CLEARIN' OUT OF HERE? GO PLAY JUNIOR SPACEMAN IN SOMEONE ELSE'S BACK YARD, HUH?
SO! YOU ARE STILL AN UNBELIEVER!
BUT I HAVE WAYS TO CONVINCE SCOFFING PRIMITIVES SUCH AS YOURSELF!
ALL I NEED DO IS CONTACT MY HOME WORLD VIA DIRECT SOLAR BEAM!

YOU WILL SING A DIFFERENT TUNE WHEN I ORDER THE SPACE-LOCK TO INCREASE VELOCITY, THUS PULLING EARTH OUT OF ORBIT AT STILL GREATER SPEED!
COLONIZER NILE, CALLING COMMAND PLANET! REQUEST INCREASE IN SPEED OF SPACE-LOCK! PLEASE ACKNOWLEDGE!

AND, IN THE WORLD CALLED RIGEL--AT AN INTER-COSMIC SWITCHBOARD--
REQUEST DENIED! PLANET EARTH TO BE FREED OF SPACE-LOCK--BY DIRECT ORDER OF GRAND COMMISSIONER!

YOU ARE ORDERED TO END COLONIZATION AND RETURN TO RIGEL!
NO! NO! IT WAS MY FIRST CONQUEST! WHAT WENT WRONG? YOU MUST TELL ME! YOU MUST--!
TRANS-GALACTIC TRANSMISSION
TRANSMISSION IS CLOSED!
CLICK!
14

BUT, IF TANA NILE THINKS SHE HAS PROBLEMS, LET'S RETURN TO OUR SORELY HARASSED HERO--!
I HAVE MANAGED TO GAIN A HAND-HOLD--BUT, THE RECORDER IS BEING SWEPT AWAY!!
WHOOM
OBSERVATION: EVERY ROCK, STONE, AND PEBBLE OF THIS PLANET IS LIKE THE CELL OF A LIVING BODY--BUT, EVEN MORE--EACH POSSESSES THE WILL OF EGO--AND THE URGE TO DESTROY!
SOON, MY MEMORY BANKS WILL BE SHATTERED--THEN I SHALL RECORD NO MORE!
MY VISION IS OBSCURED BY IMMOVABLE DEBRIS! I AM GROWING INOPERATIVE! MY SERVICE HAS COME TO AN END--!
JUST AHEAD--I SEE THEE! BE OF STOUT HEART!
THE STRENGTH OF MY LIMBS SHALL FREE THEE BEFORE IT BE TOO LATE!
WRRAK
NO! SAVE YOURSELF! ABANDON ME! I AM BUT A MACHINE!
THOU WERT A FAITHFUL AND TRUE COMPANION--AND THOR SHALT NOT DESERT THEE!
OBSERVATION: FOR THE FIRST TIME--A RECORDER FEELS--THE EMOTION OF--GRATITUDE!
EGO HATH RAISED HIS BODY TEMPERATURE--BUT IT IS TO NO AVAIL! SUCH HEAT CANNOT AFFECT THE GOD OF THUNDER!
NOR CAN IT DAMAGE MY INSULATED MEMORY BANKS!
BUT NOW, 'TIS TIME TO BREAK FREE OF THIS PLANET--TO LEAVE YON BIO-VERSE FOREVER BEHIND! AND BREAK FREE WE SHALL--BY THE POWER OF THOR--!

IN THE NAME OF MIGHTY ODIN-- BY THE FURY OF THE THUNDER-- LET THE WINDS WHICH FILL THE COSMOS-- --TEAR THIS EVIL WORLD ASUNDER!!
LET THE LIGHTNING AND THE GALE-- PIERCE THIS PLANET TO THE CORE-- LET THE STORM NOW HUMBLE EGO-- THUS COMMANDS THE MIGHTY THOR!!

IT IS DONE!! WE ARE FREE OF THE DEADLY EGO!
NOT EVEN A LIVING PLANET COULD EQUAL THE POWER OF A THUNDER GOD TO CAUSE THE ELEMENTS THEMSELVES TO COMBINE IN A UNIVERSE--SHAKING THERMO-BLAST!

FOR THE FIRST TIME IN COUNTLESS MILLENNIA I HAVE BEEN BESTED! NEVER AGAIN SHALL I SUFFER SUCH HUMILIATION!!
HENCEFORTH, MY BIO-VERSE SHALL BE SEALED OFF FROM EACH AND ANY KNOWN UNIVERSE!
NEVER AGAIN SHALL I ATTACK RIGEL! NEVER AGAIN SHALL I SEEK TO INVADE OTHER GALAXIES! I SHALL EVER BE A WORLD APART-- TILL ETERNITY CRUMBLES!

THE QUEST IS ENDED! NEVER-MORE SHALL THE BLACK GALAXY MENACE THE ETERNAL COSMOS! NOW, BACK TO RIGEL, AND THENCE TO EARTH!
YET, SOMEHOW I FEEL THE GREATEST DANGER OF ALL AWAITS ME-- IN THE WORLD WHERE MORTALS DWELL!
NEXT ISSUE:
THE PEOPLE BREEDERS!

TALES OF ASGARD, HOME OF THE MIGHTY NORSE GODS
"VALHALLA!"
HAROKIN, VALIANT LEADER OF THE BARBARIAN HORDES, HAS BEEN DEFEATED IN BATTLE BY THE MIGHTY LEGIONS OF THOR AND NOW, THE FATALLY WOUNDED CHIEFTAIN PREPARES FOR HIS FINAL JOURNEY...
THE BLACK STALLION OF DOOM AWAITS THEE, MASTER!
ALL IS IN READINESS FOR THY LAST ADVENTURE!
A STAN LEE-JACK KIRBY PRODUCTION
INKED BY: VINCE COLLETTA
LETTERED BY: SAM ROSEN
(MAY THEIR ARMOR NEVER TARNISH!)

STAND YE BACK, ALL!
LET NO MAN APPROACH THE MIGHTY HAROKIN!
PLACE ME THEN UPON THE STALLION!
IN THE FURY OF A THOUSAND BATTLES, I GAVE NO QUARTER! NOW, IN MY LAST MORTAL HOUR, I ASK FOR NONE!
THOOM! THOOM!

MUFFLE YE THY DRUMS!
ALL HONOR TO HIM WHO HATH FALLEN WITH VALOR!
HE FOUGHT WITHOUT FAULT---AND FELL WITHOUT FEAR!
THOUGH HE WERE BARBARIAN BORN... HIS COURAGE DOTH CREDIT TO ETERNAL ASGARD!
VOLSTAGG! TO THY FEET, MOUNTAINOUS ONE! WHY CRINGEST THOU THUS?
DOST THOU NOT SEE..?

AT HELA'S COMMAND.. LET ALL LIVING FACES BE TURNED ASIDE...
LET EVERY EYE BE THUS AVERTED!
'TIS NOT FOR THE LIVING TO BEHOLD THAT WHICH SHALL NOW BEFALL!
HAROKIN HATH PASSED THIS WAY BUT ONCE! HIS LIKE SHALL NOT SOON BE SEEN AGAIN!

CONTINUED AFTER NEXT PAGE

SLOWLY, THE VAPORS PART, REVEALING A GLISTENING, GOLDEN BRIDGE WHICH GLITTERS WITH A BRILLIANCE BEYOND MORTAL KEN ...
THEN, THE SILENCE IS BROKEN BY THE CLATTER OF RUNNING FEET --- AND THE MUFFLED THUNDER OF UNSHOD HOOVES...

...AS THE TOWERING HILLS OF VALHALLA COME INTO VIEW... VALHALLA, WHERE THE BRAVEST AND MOST GALLANT OF ALL ARE MAJESTICALLY MARSHALLED IN ENDLESS ARRAY!
BEHOLD!! ANOTHER HERO COME TO GLORY!

HERE WILT THOU FIND THE HERALDRY, THE BATTLE, THE ADVENTURE THY SPIRIT CRAVES --- HERE, 'MIDST PAGEANTRY EVERLASTING!
KNOW THOU, HAROKIN, THAT DEATH IS MORE THAN AN ENDING... 'TIS THE GREATEST BEGINNING OF ALL!
TO OUR SIDE THEN, WARRIOR! WE AWAIT THEE IN OUR SERRIED RANKS!

THE WEARINESS DOTH LEAVE MY LIMBS!! I FEEL NEW STRENGTH WITHIN ME --- VIGOR, SUCH AS I HAVE NEVER KNOWN!
THE SOUND OF BATTLE...THE CLANG OF ARMOR.. THE MOST JOYOUS MUSIC EVER HEARD!
4.

NEXT:
"WHEN SPEAKS THE DRAGON!"

THE MIGHTY THOR
APPROVED BY THE COMICS CODE AUTHORITY
MARVEL COMICS GROUP
12¢ IND.
134 NOV
"THE PEOPLE BREEDERS!"
GUEST STARRING: QUICKSILVER and THE SCARLET WITCH! (IN POSSIBLY THE BRIEFEST, MOST UNNECESSARY GUEST APPEARANCE YOU'VE EVER SEEN!)

THE MIGHTY THOR!
"The PEOPLE-BREEDERS!"
AS LAST ISSUE REVEALED TO ALL TRUE BELIEVERS, THE GOD OF THUNDER FOUGHT EGO, THE LIVING PLANET, TO A STANDSTILL WITHIN THE MYSTERIOUS BLACK GALAXY! NOW, MIGHTY THOR, AND THE HUMAN-FORM RECORDER, WHOM HE HAS RESCUED, RETURN TO RIGEL...
EGO HAS VOWED NEVER TO ATTACK ANY FOE BEYOND THE BLACK GALAXY! THEREFORE, MY QUEST HAS BEEN SUCCESSFUL!
OBSERVATION: SINCE YOU HAVE SAVED THIS WORLD FROM INVASION, RIGEL MUST FULFILL ITS PROMISE TO YOU!
THEY SHALL ABANDON ALL ATTEMPTS TO CONQUER EARTH!
A STAN LEE * JACK KIRBY FANTASTI-CLASSIC!
INKED BY: VINCE COLLETTA
LETTERED BY: SAM ROSEN
WE HAVE SPOKEN!

SUDDENLY, AS THE TWO FLYING FIGURES APPROACH THE PERIPHERY OF RIGEL, A PREVIOUSLY-PROGRAMMED COLONIZER SENTRY SHIP FIRES A STRANGE MESA BEAM AT THEM...!
OBSERVATION: WE ARE TO REMAIN MOTIONLESS! THIS BEAM, COMPOSED OF CONTRACTING MESONS, WILL DRAW US SAFELY INSIDE THE SHIP!
THOR TAKES YOU AT YOUR WORD, RECORDER.
I SHALL NOT RESIST!

YOU HAVE DONE THE IMPOSSIBLE, THUNDER GOD!
OUR LEGENDS SHALL EXTOLL YOUR GREATNESS TILL THE END OF TIME!
WHEN YOU DECLARE THE SOLAR SYSTEM OFF-LIMITS TO YOUR COLONIZERS, I SHALL HAVE BEEN AMPLY REPAID!
THE ORDER HAS ALREADY BEEN GIVEN!
OBSERVATION: I SENSE THE PRESENCE OF APPROACHING POWER!
THE RECORDER SPEAKS TRUE! A BRIGHT MASS OF ENERGY IS STREAKING THIS WAY!

WE HAVE BEEN TRACKING THAT MYSTERIOUS OBJECT WHILE WAITING FOR YOU!
IT HAS LEAPED ACROSS COUNTLESS LIGHT YEARS OF SPACE WITH UNBELIEVABLE SPEED!
WHAT MANNER OF ENTITY CAN IT BE?

AT FIRST WE THOUGHT IT WAS A GIGANTIC STAR, WHOSE LIGHT BLAZES WITH SUCH INTENSITY IT CAN SPAN VAST GALAXIES!
ON EARTH, MEN REFER TO SUCH CELESTIAL BODIES AS QUASARS!
BUT, OUR SPECTRO-SCANNER REVEALS IT IS SMALLER THAN A STAR... THOUGH WITH EVEN GREATER ENERGY!

OBSERVATION: SO GREAT IS ITS SPEED, THAT IT IS ALREADY ALMOST UPON US!
ALTHOUGH I SENSE IT IS NOT CONCERNED WITH THIS SHIP, NOR WITH ITS OCCUPANTS!
NO MATTER! IT'S ON COLLISION COURSE!
EFFECT TIME-WARP ESCAPE DRIVE... MACH THRUST!
WITHIN SECONDS WE'LL BE GONE... AND WE MAY NEVER KNOW WHO... OR WHAT... THAT OBJECT WAS!

THUS DOES AN ENIGMATIC FATE PLAY INCOMPREHENSIBLE TRICKS UPON US ALL! HOW COULD MIGHTY THOR HAVE SUSPECTED THAT HE WAS ALMOST WITHIN HAMMER-THROWING DISTANCE OF THE MOST AWESOME LIVING ENTITY IN THE COSMOS? SLOWLY, MAJESTICALLY, THE INDESCRIBABLE FIGURE OF GALACTUS RISES FROM HIS GIANT STAR-SHIP AS HE AIMS AN INFALLIBLE QUADRANT ANALYZER AT THE BLACK GALAXY WHICH SWIRLS IN THE INFINITE EMPTINESS BEFORE HIM...!*
MY QUADRANT ANALYZER REGISTERS AN ABUNDANCE OF LIFE ENERGY EMANATING FROM WITHIN THE SHADOWY GALAXY BEFORE ME!
SINCE I AM DESTINED TO ROAM THE ENDLESS SKYWAYS, EVER SEEKING NEW SOURCES OF ENERGY UPON WHICH TO FEED, I HAVE BUT ONE CHOICE...
I MUST ENTER THE BLACK GALAXY AND DESTROY WHATEVER LIFE MAY THEREIN EXIST!
I DO SO...NOT OUT OF GREED..NOT OUT OF HATE..NOT OUT OF AMBITION... FOR THOSE ARE EMOTIONS OF LESSER BEINGS! I DO SO BECAUSE I MUST...BECAUSE I AM...GALACTUS!!
*AS ALL MARVELDOM KNOWS, GALACTUS FIRST APPEARED IN FANTASTIC FOUR #48, 49, AND 50...AND IT IS NOT UNLIKELY THAT WE SHALL MEET HIM AGAIN AT SOME FUTURE TIME...WHEN WE, AND MANKIND, LEAST EXPECT IT! ...STENTORIAN STAN.

BUT, SINCE THIS EPIC EXTRAVAGANZA IS CONCERNED WITH OTHER MATTERS, WE MUST TAKE OUR LEAVE OF GALACTUS FOR NOW, AS WE VISIT A NEW YORK POLICE PRECINCT BACK ON MOTHER EARTH...
OUR ORDERS ARE FINAL...AND IRREVOCABLE, COLONIZER NILE! WE HAVE REMOVED THE SPACE LOCK FROM THE PLANET EARTH!
BUT...YOU CAN'T! I TOOK POSSESSION --BY RIGHT OF CONQUEST!
IT WAS MY FIRST COLONIZATION! WHAT DID I DO WRONG?
NOTHING, COLONIZER NILE! EVENTS FAR GREATER THAN YOU CAN COMPREHEND HAVE CAUSED OUR DECISION!
BUT, YOU SHALL NOT GO UNREWARDED! AT THIS VERY INSTANT, YOU WILL BE BROUGHT BACK TO RIGEL, FOR YOUR GREATEST ASSIGNMENT!
COLONIZER NILE! WE HAVE COME FOR YOU!
DO NOT FEAR! WE HAVE ESCORTED THE GOD OF THUNDER TO THIS GALAXY, AND SHALL ESCORT YOU BACK TO RIGEL!
YOUR REIGN OVER EARTH IS ENDED, TANA NILE! ENDED FOREVER!
THOR!! THEN... THIS IS YOUR DOING!
THEY...WALKED PAST US...LIKE WE WEREN'T HERE!
KNOW SOME-THIN', JIM? I WISH WE WEREN'T!
IF YOU GUYS SEE 'EM, TOO--THEN.. I AIN'T DREAMIN'!!
I BEAR YOU NO MALICE! YOU DID WHAT YOU HAD BEEN TRAINED TO DO! BUT, ONE THING I MUST KNOW...
THE GIRL...JANE FOSTER...WHAT HAVE YOU DONE WITH HER?
SHE IS UNHARMED! I MERELY SENT HER AWAY, HOPING YOU WOULD WASTE TIME SEARCHING FOR HER!
I DO NOT KNOW HER PRESENT WHEREABOUTS!
SHE MAY SPEAK NO MORE, THUNDER GOD!
BY MEANS OF THIS RIGELLIAN COMPELLOR BEAM, I HEREBY PLACE EX-COLONIZER TANA NILE IN CUSTODY!
YOU WILL ENTER THE SHIP WHICH AWAITS US UPON THE ROOF!
YOU SHALL FIND THE ONE YOU SEEK! THIS PSYCHE-SEARCH GAUGE WILL LEAD YOU TO THE GIRL BY LOCATING HER LIFE FORCE AURA!
YOU HAVE EARNED THE GRATITUDE OF THOR!
WAIT A MINUTE! WHERE ARE THEY TAKIN' HER??
4

THEY'RE HEADING FOR THE ROOF, CAPTAIN!
I CAN'T THINK OF ANY LEGAL REASON TO STOP THEM... NOT THAT I'M SURE WE COULD, EVEN IF WE WANTED TO!
BY MY AUTHORITY AS AN AVENGER, I SAY STAND BACK! SHE SHALL BE PROPERLY DEALT WITH UPON HER OWN PLANET!, UNDER THE LAWS OF RIGEL!
HE REALLY MEANS IT! HE THINKS THEY ARE TAKIN' HER TO ANOTHER PLANET!
Y'KNOW SOMETHIN', CHARLIE? WE MAY ALL BE CANDIDATES FOR A PADDED CELL!

NOW THAT YOU ARE ENTERING OUR SHIP, I MAY TELL YOU OF YOUR NEW ASSIGNMENT, TANA NILE!
WHAT DOES IT MATTER? WHAT FUTURE CAN THERE BE... FOR A FAILURE?
A FAILURE?? THEN... YOU HAVEN'T HEARD..?

SINCE RIGEL IS SAFE FOREVER FROM THE BLACK GALAXY, YOU ARE TO RECEIVE THE HIGHEST REWARD FOR HAVING A PART IN OUR GOOD FORTUNE!
YOU HAD YEARNED TO RULE A PLANET... BUT NOW, YOU SHALL RULE A GALAXY!
THE HIGH COMMISSIONER HAS CHOSEN YOU.. FOR HIS WIFE!
THE HIGH COMMISSIONER... WHOM I HAVE LOVED FROM AFAR FOR YEARS!
THEN... ON TO RIEGEL.. WHERE WAITS MY HEART'S DESIRE!

IT'S OVER! THEY'RE GONE! BUT... HOW CAN WE EVER TALK ABOUT THIS?? WHO'S GONNA BELIEVE US?
BELIEVE WHAT, SAM? SO FAR AS I'M CONCERNED, IT NEVER HAPPENED!
THEY CALLED THIS A PSYCHE-SEARCH GAUGE! CAN IT TRULY LOCATE THE ONE I LOVE?

FOR, UNLESS I FIND JANE FOSTER, I... WAIT!!
NO SOONER DID I THINK HER NAME, THAN A LIGHT APPEARED UPON THE GAUGE... LIKE A LIVING BEACON, POINTING THE WAY TO MY BELOVED!
I MUST GO TO HER... THOUGH ALL THE POWER IN THE COSMOS ATTEMPTS TO BAR MY WAY!

BUT, THE MAGIC OF THE PRINTED PAGE IS EVEN GREATER THAN THAT OF THOR... THUS, WE ARE ABLE TO FIND JANE FOSTER FIRST! OUR SCENE IS THE VILLAGE SQUARE IN A SMALL EUROPEAN PRINCIPALITY..
SEE! IT IS THE VEHICLE OF COUNT TAGAR! WE MUST WARN HIM!
AY! HE MUST NOT TAKE THE ROAD TO WUNDAGORE!
COUNT TAGAR!! YOU HAVE BEEN AWAY TOO LONG! THE SURROUNDING HILLS ARE FILLED WITH ARMED BANDITS!
THEY HAVE HEARD OF THE WEALTH OF WUNDAGORE! THEY BRAG THAT ONCE THEY HAVE CAPTURED YOU, THAT WEALTH WILL BE THEIRS!
I HAVE NOTHING TO FEAR! THE INVINCIBLE KNIGHTS OF WUNDAGORE WILL PROTECT US!
DRIVE ON, PORGA!
THE WEALTH OF WUNDAGORE! ARMED BANDITS! INVINCIBLE KNIGHTS! WHY DID I ACCEPT HIS JOB OFFER? WHAT AM I GETTING INTO?
IF BANDITS HAVE HEARD OF WUNDAGORE, THEN OUR SECRET MUST BE LEAKING TO THE OUTSIDE WORLD!
SECRET?
WE NEED NOT BE CONCERNED! NOTHING CAN HARM US! NOTHING CAN STOP US... NOW!
THE HIGH EVOLUTIONARY HAS PLANNED TOO WELL! WUNDAGORE IS GREATER THAN ANYONE CAN EVER IMAGINE!
IT IS THEM!
QUICK! RADIO AHEAD! TELL THEM THAT COUNT TAGAR IS APPROACHING!
THEY WILL KNOW WHAT TO DO!
CODE THREE! VICTIM APPROACHING..!!
BUH-ROOM!
MINES!! WE ARE BEING ATTACKED! IT IS THE BANDITS!
STOP THE CAR! DO NOT FEAR!
IT IS THEY WHO ARE IN DANGER!
THEY'RE GETTING OUT OF THE CAR!!
GRAB THEM! THEY MUSTN'T ESCAPE! SURROUND THEM!
THE OTHERS ARE NOT IMPORTANT! SEIZE COUNT TAGER! HE WILL LEAD US TO THE TREASURES OF WUNDAGORE!
6.

ARRRHHHH! HE FIGHTS... LIKE A WILD BEAST!!
BACK! BACK, YOU CRAVEN CARRION! YOU DO NOT DREAM WHOM YOU ARE ATTACKING!!
THRAPT!
STAY BACK, TAGAR! DON'T COME ANY CLOSER!! I'M WARNING YOU..!

HE'S TOO DANGEROUS!! THEY CAN'T HOLD HIM! HE MUSTN'T REACH US!! FIRE!
FTHOK!

WHIRRIZZZ
A BOLA!! THROWN FROM... THE SKY! LOOK OUT!! ABOVE US... NOOO!
ZZZZZ

SPLANG!
I CAN'T MOVE!! A METAL LANCE IS PINIONING ME AGAINST THE CLIFF!

OUR WEAPONS DON'T STOP THEM!
RUN!! THEY'RE ATTACKING FROM THE SKY! THEY'LL KILL US ALL!! RUN!!
KRAK!

AND, AT THAT MOMENT, ABOVE THE LONELY ROAD TO WUNDAGORE...
THE LIGHT ON THE GAUGE GLOWS BRIGHTER! I MUST BE NEARING JANE FOSTER!
THERE ... IN THE SKY!! IT IS THE MIGHTY THOR!
EVEN HE WILL NOT GAIN ENTRANCE TO THE FORBIDDEN WUNDAGORE!

MEN LIMPING WEAKLY TOWARDS THE VILLAGE! WHAT CATASTROPHE CAN HAVE BEFALLEN THEM?
I MUST NOW DESCEND! PERHAPS THEY HAVE SEEN THE ONE I SEEK!

HOLD, FLEEING MORTALS! 'TIS THE THUNDER GOD WHO SPEAKS!
RUN! IT MUST BE ANOTHER OF THOSE THINGS FROM ABOVE!
RUN?? AFTER THE DRUBBING WE TOOK? I COULDN'T RUN...FOR ANYTHING!

I DO NOT FATHOM YOUR WORDS! WHAT THINGS FROM ABOVE HAVE ATTACKED YOU?
THEY... CALLED THEMSELVES... SOMETHING LIKE KNIGHTS OF WUNDAGORE!! I SAW ONE OF THEM ... WHEN HIS HELMET SHOOK LOOSE!! IT..IT ISN'T POSSIBLE!!
YOU SPEAK IN RIDDLES! WHAT IS NOT POSSIBLE??
NO! I CAN'T EVEN SAY IT! I CAN'T! I CAN'T!!

THERE IS NO MORE TO BE GAINED BY INTERROGATING SUCH COWARDLY CREATURES AS THEY!
AND YET... WHAT MADE THEM AS THEY ARE? IT IS AS THOUGH THEIR EYES BEHELD A SIGHT WHICH THEIR MINDS COULD NOT COMPREHEND!

YONDER MOUNTAINS MUST SURELY HOLD THE SECRET!
AND SO, 'TIS THERE THE THUNDER GOD MUST FLY!!
8.

WHAT NOW IS *THIS???*

WE HAVE APPREHENDED A *KNIGHT* WHO FLIES WITHOUT USE OF AN *ATOMIC STEED!*

LET US BIND HIM *SECURELY!*

HE MUST THEN BE TAKEN TO THE *HIGH EVOLUTIONARY!*

WHAT MANNER OF *MADNESS* HAVE I SO SOON ENCOUNTERED?

CONTINUED AFTER NEXT PAGE

I SHALL NOT RESIST... FOR, EVERY INSTINCT TELLS ME THAT ONLY IN THE PLACE KNOWN AS WUNDAGORE WILL I FIND JANE FOSTER!
HERE, AT THE VERY SUMMIT OF THE MOUNTAIN, A STRUCTURE SUCH AS NONE I HAVE EVER SEEN BEFORE... WITH STRANGELY OMINOUS RAYS CONSTANTLY ISSUING FORTH!!
I KNOW NOT WHAT I HAVE STUMBLED UPON... BUT I AM TRULY THANKFUL TO POSSESS THE POWER OF MIGHTY THOR AT SUCH A MOMENT!
FINALLY, AFTER LANDING ATOP A BARREN PLATFORM, THE THUNDER GOD SPEAKS --- AS A SILENT, IRIS-TYPE ENTRANCE OPENS MENACINGLY BEHIND HIM --!
SINCE I HAVE WILLINGLY ACCOMPANIED YOU THUS FAR, I DESIRE TO HAVE THESE BONDS REMOVED FROM MY WRISTS!
THE SON OF ODIN MAY NOT BE KEPT PRISONER ANYWHERE... OR ANY TIME!
NO MORE THAN ONCE DOES THE GOD OF THUNDER MAKE A REQUEST! IF YOU CHOOSE NOT TO OBEY, THEN UPON YOUR OWN HEADS SHALL EVER BE THE CONSEQUENCES!
SILENCE! YOU APPROACH THE COURT OF THE HIGH EVOLUTIONARY!
YOU ARE ARMED, WHILE HE IS ALONE AND DEFENSELESS!! SILENCE HIM!!
10.

UHHHH!
SIR OSSILOT! SIR LIYAN! TO MY SIDE! THE ENEMY MUST BE SMASHED!
I HAVE NO WISH TO JOUST WITH WEAKER BEINGS! BUT, IF I AM THUS COMPELLED..!
HE SPINS SIR LEPARD ABOUT AS THOUGH HE WERE BUT A TOY!

ENOUGH, GOD OF THUNDER! THE TIME HAS COME FOR US TO SPEAK!
SPEAK, THEN!! THOR SHALL LEND AN EAR!

ALL OF YOU...BEATEN BY ONE INTRUDER! THE HIGH EVOLUTIONARY SHALL HEAR OF THIS!
ON YOUR FEET!! THERE ARE MANY QUESTIONS...BUT TOO FEW ANSWERS!
YOU MUST REMEMBER.. HE IS NO MERE HUMAN!

I SHALL REMOVE YOUR BONDS! YOU ARE WORTHY OF A FAR MORE DIGNIFIED ENTRANCE TO THE LAND OF WUNDAGORE..!
IF THE FIGHTING IS ENDED, REMOVE THEN YOUR HELMETS!
I DESIRE TO SEE THE FACES OF MY FOES!

SEE OUR FACES?? THEN, DID YOU NOT KNOW? WE ARE NOT WHAT YOU EXPECT! WE ARE NEW-MEN!
YOUR FACE!! BY THE BRISTLING BEARD OF ODIN.. WHAT ARE NEW-MEN??

FEAR NOT, FRANTIC ONE! WE SHALL HAVE THE ANSWER TO THOR'S QUESTION IN DUE TIME! BUT FIRST, LET'S VISIT A VALLEY JUST BELOW THE MACABRE MOUNTAIN, WHERE WE FIND...
IF YOU OUTRUN MY LAMBORGHINI 330 GT, PIETRO, I'LL NEVER TALK TO YOU AGAIN!
DON'T WORRY, WANDA! I'LL PROMISE TO RUN ONLY AT HALF-SPEED!

IT IS IMPOSSIBLE! I CANNOT HOLD MYSELF BACK ENOUGH TO LET MY SISTER KEEP UP WITH ME!
BUT, I KNOW SHE IS AS JOYFUL AS I THAT WE HAVE BOTH REGAINED OUR POWERS SO COMPLETELY!*
QUICKSILVER.. WAIT! YOU'RE LIABLE TO LOSE ME!
* IF YOU'RE WONDERING WHO THESE TWO NEWCOMERS ARE, IT PROVES YOU HAVEN'T READ THE AVENGERS, OR THE EARLIER ISSUES OF X-MEN! SHAME ON YOU! ANYWAY, THEY'RE MEMBERS OF THE AVENGERS WHO RETURNED TO EUROPE HOPING TO REGAIN THEIR WANING MUTANT POWERS! --SUCCINCT STAN!

THEN, A FEW MOMENTS LATER...
I THOUGHT I'D NEVER CATCH YOU! IT'S TOO BAD YOU'RE NOT EQUIPPED WITH DISC BRAKES!
WANDA.. LOOK.. ATOP THE MOUNTAIN BEFORE US...
THAT STRANGELY FLICKERING LIGHT!
I CANNOT TAKE MY EYES OFF IT!

REMEMBER THE LEGENDS, WANDA? WE WERE TOLD THAT SUCH A LIGHT FLASHED ABOVE THE MOUNTAINS ON THE NIGHT WE WERE BORN!
YES, PIETRO... YES! IT WAS SAID THAT ITS BRILLIANCE SEEMED TO LIGHT UP THE ENTIRE SKY!

DO YOU THINK..?
CAN IT BE POSSIBLE THAT OUR OWN MUTANT-TYPE POWERS ARE IN SOME WAY RELATED TO...THAT??
I DO NOT KNOW, WANDA! AND YET...A NAME ECHOES IN MY BRAIN...
I HAVE HEARD STRANGE TALES OF THE MIRACLE LAND OF...WUNDAGORE! NOW, I WONDER..?

BUT WE NEED WONDER NO LONGER! SURELY YOU HAVE ALREADY GUESSED THAT THE HIGH EVOLUTIONARY IS CREATING ANOTHER SEEMING MIRACLE IN HIS MOUNTAINTOP LABORATORY...
THE SHIFTING GENE PATTERN FALLS INTO PLACE PERFECTLY..!
IT IS TIME TO BEGIN ANOTHER TRANSFORMATION.. ..TO CREATE ANOTHER NEW-MAN!
12

CONTINUED AFTER NEXT PAGE

THIS INTRUSION IS UNFORGIVEABLE!! WHO ARE YOU? WHY ARE YOU HERE? SPEAK... WHILE YOU STILL MAY!
HE REFERS TO HIMSELF AS THOR, GOD OF THUNDER... SON OF ODIN, MASTER!
HIS POWER IS GREATER THAN ANY WE HAVE EVER BEHELD... SAVE FOR YOURS, MASTER!
HE CLAIMS HE SEEKS THE FEMALE -- SHE WHO IS CALLED JANE FOSTER!
IF SHE BE HERE, NO POWER ON EARTH SHALL KEEP ME FROM HER SIDE!

JANE! I HAVE FOUND YOU!
BUT, WHAT..?!!
'TIS THE SEMBLANCE OF A CLASSROOM! BUT ONE SUCH AS THE BRAIN CAN BARELY COMPREHEND!
AND YOU... UNLESS MINE EYES DO FAITHLESSLY DECEIVE ME... YOU ARE INSTRUCTRESS... TO STUDENTS WHO CAN EXIST IN NONE BUT THE MOST FANTASTIC NIGHTMARE!
IS THAT A NEW PUPIL WHO INTERRUPTS OUR CLASS SO SUDDENLY?
WE SHALL SOON FIND OUT!
THOR! MY DARLING..!

HIS EVOLUTION WILL BE SPEEDED UP FURTHER THAN I WOULD EVER DARE TO GO! NO ONE CAN SAY WHAT THE DREAD RESULT WILL BE!
CAN YOU NOT HALT THE MACHINE?
NO! IT IS... TOO LATE!

SHOULD MY BESTIAL SUBJECT SURVIVE, HE WILL BE FAR MORE THAN A NEW-MAN--- FAR MORE THAN A WOLF WHOSE EVOLUTIONARY PROCESS WAS SPEEDED UP!!
IN POINT OF FACT, HE WILL BE THE ULTIMATE END OF EVOLUTION --- A COMBINATION OF THE SUPREME MAN --- COUPLED WITH THE SUPREME BEAST!!
HIS POWER WILL BE TOO AWESOME TO IMAGINE!! AND, IF HE SHOULD BE EVIL --!

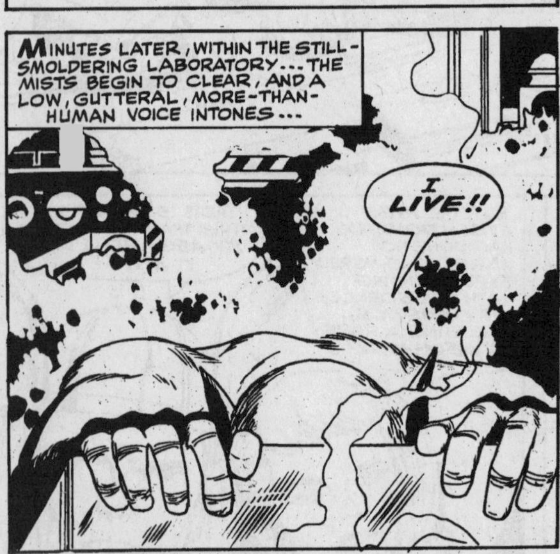
MINUTES LATER, WITHIN THE STILL-SMOLDERING LABORATORY... THE MISTS BEGIN TO CLEAR, AND A LOW, GUTTERAL, MORE-THAN-HUMAN VOICE INTONES...
I LIVE!!

I FEEL!!
AND MORE...
I HATE!!

AUTOMATICALLY, WITHOUT CONSCIOUS THOUGHT, THE BROODING MAN-BEAST ALLOWS HIS MIND TO PROBE RIGHT THROUGH THE CONCRETE WALL ---
I SENSE LIFE NEARBY!!

AND WHATEVER LIVES, MUST BE MY ENEMY... MUST BE DESTROYED!
FOLLOW ME! I SHALL LEAD YOU FROM THIS PLACE... WHILE THERE IS TIME!
BUT THEN THE FLEEING DUO REALIZE...

..THEIR TIME HAS FINALLY... RUN OUT!!
WE'RE BEING WATCHED! I CAN FEEL IT!
IT IS TOO LATE FOR FLIGHT! THE DANGER IS UPON US!
NEXT: THE FUTURE MAN-BEAST!
16

TALES OF ASGARD, HOME OF THE MIGHTY NORSE GODS
"WHEN SPEAKS THE DRAGON!"
AT THE FARTHEST REACHES OF ASGARD, LIES THE FORBIDDEN DOMAIN KNOWN AS NASTROND... A LAND WHERE NOTHING LIVES--NOT A TREE--NOT A SINGLE BLADE OF GRASS--NOT THE HUMBLEST INSECT! IT IS HERE, TO NASTROND, THAT MIGHTY THOR AND HIS COMPANIONS RIDE--
IN THIS LAND ONCE LIVED AN EVIL RACE WHO DARED DEFY REGAL ODIN HIMSELF!
SO MONUMENTAL WAS ODIN'S WRATH, THAT HE LAID WASTE THE COUNTRY-SIDE, SO THAT NOTHING HERE COULD LIVE!
NOW, THESE LONG YEARS AFTER, HE BIDS US INSPECT THIS LAND AND SURVEY HIS AWESOME HANDIWORK!
SO COME YE--FANDRAL, THE DASHING--HOGUN, THE GRIM--AND VORACIOUS VOLSTAGG--
LET US COMPLETE YON MISSION AND THEN BEGONE!
A STAN LEE • JACK KIRBY PICTORIAL PRESENTATION
DELINEATED BY: VINCENT COLLETTA
LETTERED BY: ARTIE SIMEK
1

METHINKS 'TIS PASSING STRANGE TO FIND A MIRROR ON THE GROUND BENEATH US!
THAT IS NO MERE MIRROR, ENORMOUS ONE!
IN TRUTH, T'WAS ONCE A MIGHTY RIVER, WHOSE TRIBUTARIES DID FEED THE WHOLE OF THIS PARCHED LAND!
AY! UNTIL ODIN, IN HIS KINGLY WRATH, DID SEAR THE WATERS--FUSING THEM INTO THE DRY, CRACKED CRYSTAL WE SEE BELOW!
TRULY, THERE IS NO LIMIT TO THE POWER OF MY REGAL FATHER!

VOLLLLLLSTAG! HEAR ME, VOLSTAGG! MAKE THOU NO NOISE--NO SOUND!
MY NAME! I AM BEING SUMMONED!
BUT, BY WHOM ??
IN THIS LAND OF DEATH, AND DESOLATION-- WHO CAN IT BE??

AH HA! I HAVE CAUGHT YOU!
NONE CAN ESCAPE THE WATCHFUL EYE OF VOLSTAGG WHEN HE DEVOTES HIS FEARSOME TALENTS TO GUARD DUTY!
TRUE, MIGHTY WARRIOR-- TRUE! BUT, WAS IT NOT I WHO AWOKE THEE?
DIDST THOU THINK I SLEPT? KNOW THEE NOT T'WAS BUT A RUSE, TO ENTRAP THEE!
BE THAT AS IT MAY-- I HAVE AN OFFER TO MAKE THEE!
FAUGHH! WHAT CAN SUCH AS THOU OFFER THE WELL-FAMED VOLSTAGG?
ATTEND MY WORDS, MOUNTAINOUS ONE--AND THOU SHALT LEARN--!

CONTINUED AFTER NEXT PAGE

THAT GIGANTIC CAVERN BEFORE US--METHINKS WE HAVE *FOUND* OUR DESTINATION!

IN TRUTH, 'TWAS THE LAST REFUGE OF THE *RULER* OF THIS LAND--BEFORE A VENGEFUL *ODIN* BANISHED ALL AND SUNDRY!

ONE QUESTION YET PERPLEXES ME! IF *ALL* WERE BANISHED--AND NO LIFE HERE ENDURES --FROM WHENCE IS IT THAT *THOU* HAST COME??

BUT, HE WAS TO LEARN THAT THEY WERE *NOT* DEADLY!!

INSTEAD, LONG YEARS OF *EXPOSURE* CHANGED THE *FORM* OF THE ANCIENT RULER--AND BESTOWED UPON HIM A MATCHLESS *POWER*--

THE POWER TO PROJECT THE IMAGE OF AN *AGED MAN*!!

'TIS A *TRAP*! TRUSTING VOLSTAGG HATH BEEN SHAMEFULLY *BETRAYED*!

YES, THE *RADIANT POOL* BROUGHT A GREAT *CHANGE* TO THE ANCIENT KING'S *BODY*!! IT TRANSFORMED HIM INTO A CREATURE POWERFUL ENOUGH TO *SURVIVE* IN THIS DEADLY LAND!

WHAT *MADNESS* IS THIS?? A MONSTROUS *HAND*--LARGER BY FAR THAN *ALL* OF VOLSTAGG!!

BEHOLD FAFNIR, THOU SNIVELLING, QUAKING JELLY-FISH OF A WARRIOR!!
I AM HE THAT WAS THE ANCIENT KING!
I AM HE WHOM ODIN-- ACCURSED BE HIS NAME-- STRIPPED OF HIS POWER, HIS SUBJECTS, HIS REALM!
FOR UNTOLD AGES HAVE I WAITED HERE--GATHERING NEW STRENGTH, NEW POWER WITH EACH PASSING DAY--
AND, ALWAYS WAITING-- HOPING--FOR A VISITATION FROM THE SONS OF ASGARD!
BUT, MY FORTUNE IS GREATER THAN EVER I DARED TO HOPE!
FOR THOR HIMSELF, SON OF ODIN, NOW STRIDES MY LAND--AND I POSSESS A PERFECT HOSTAGE WITH WHICH TO ENTRAP HIM!
NEXT: FAFNIR STRIKES!
5

THE MIGHTY
THOR
APPROVED BY THE COMICS CODE AUTHORITY
MARVEL COMICS GROUP
12¢ IND.
135 DEC
"THE MADDENING MENACE OF
THE SUPER-BEAST!"

THE MIGHTY THOR!
"THE MADDENING MENACE OF THE MAN-BEAST!"
I, WHO WAS ONCE A MERE WOLF-- HAVE BEEN TRANSFORMED!
I AM THE ULTIMATE END OF EVOLUTION --A SUPREME BEAST-- COMBINED WITH A SUPREME MAN!
IN THE HIDDEN KINGDOM OF WUNDAGORE, MIGHTY THOR HAS FOUND HIS BELOVED JANE FOSTER SERVING AS A TEACHER! BUT, NEVER BEFORE HAS MORTAL WOMAN TAUGHT SUCH A CLASS!--A CLASS COMPOSED OF ANIMALS WHOSE EVOLUTION HAS BEEN SPEEDED UP BY THE MYSTERIOUS HIGH EVOLUTIONARY! AND NOW, DUE TO A DISASTROUS ACCIDENT, ONE SUCH BEAST HAS BECOME VIRTUALLY ALL-POWERFUL--!
I SENSE LIFE NEARBY! AND WHATEVER LIVES-- MUST BE DESTROYED!
THOR! WHAT IS IT? WHAT'S HAPPENING?
A FIGURE BEGINS TO EMERGE-- THRU THE WALL ITSELF-- BY TRANSPOSING THE MOLECULES THEREIN!
WHATEVER IT MAY BE-- IT POSSESSES POWER BEYOND MORTAL KEN!
A STAN LEE • JACK KIRBY FEATURE FANTASY!
DELINEATION BY: VINCENT COLLETTA
LETTERING BY: ARTIE SIMEK
1

IT LOOKS LIKE SOME IMPOSSIBLE CROSS BETWEEN MAN AND WOLF!
BUT, HOW CAN IT DARE CHALLENGE THOR??
I POSSESS THE BRAIN OF MAN-- AS IT WILL BE A MILLION YEARS HENCE!
PLUS, THE POWER OF WOLF --AS HE WILL BE A MILLION YEARS HENCE!
THY WORDS HAVE THE FEARFUL RING OF TRUTH!
THEREFORE, HOW EASY IT IS FOR ME TO MENTALLY SENSE THE PRESSURE POINTS IN YOUR BODY WHICH ARE THE MOST VULNERABLE!

MY KNOWLEDGE OF EVERY FORM OF COMBAT IS A MILLION YEARS MORE ADVANCED THAN YOURS!
A DEADLY KARATE CHOP--YET, ONE THE LIKE OF WHICH I HAVE NEVER SEEN-- NEVER DREAMED!
TTAM!

THOUGH YOU SURVIVED MY OTHER BLOW, THIS WILL FINISH YOU FOREVER!
BY EMPLOYING A SCIENCE WHICH WILL NOT BE DISCOVERED FOR FIFTY THOUSAND YEARS, I DESTROY YOUR TIME SENSE-- LEAVING YOU ETERNALLY UNABLE TO MOVE!

AND NOW TO ANNIHILATE EVERY OTHER FORM OF LIFE I CAN FIND!
MY INTELLECT MAKES ME SUPREME--AND MY SAVAGE WOLF ANCESTRY MAKES ME THE MOST DEADLY BEING ALIVE!

EVIL ONE! 'TIS NO ORDINARY MORTAL THOU HAST ATTACKED-- BUT THE MIGHTY GOD OF THUNDER!
POK!
IN NATURAL STRENGTH AND FIGHTING PROWESS THOR YIELDS TO NONE!

AT THAT VERY MOMENT, HE WHO CALLS HIMSELF THE HIGH EVOLUTIONARY APPEARS ON THE SCENE, FLANKED BY HIS NEW-MEN--AN ARMY OF KNIGHTS, HALF-BEAST, HALF-HUMAN--
STAND BACK--ALL OF YOU!
I CREATED THAT MURDEROUS ABOMINATION--AND I SHALL DESTROY HIM!
THOUGH HE IS COUNTLESS YEARS MORE ADVANCED THAN WE--STILL HE HAS THE BLOOD OF HIS CANINE ANCESTORS!
NOW, IN THE NAME OF THE LAND OF WUNDAGORE--HE SHALL DIE!
THE MASTER USES THE SUB-SONIC DISCORDION!
THIS ACTS LIKE A SUPER-POWERED DOG WHISTLE--PRODUCING SOUNDS FAR BEYOND THE RANGE OF HUMAN EARS!
BUT, SOUNDS WHICH ARE SCALED TO BRING INSTANT DEATH TO ANY WOLF!
IT CANNOT BE! HE IS EVEN STRONGER THAN I GUESSED! THOUGH THE SOUNDS ARE PAINFUL TO HIM, HE DOES NOT CRUMBLE INTO A LIFELESS HEAP!
PAIN!! DEEP IN MY SKULL--SUCH AS I HAVE NEVER KNOWN!
THE WORLD WILL PAY DEARLY FOR THIS! I'LL HAVE MY REVENGE ON ALL MANKIND!
SURRENDER, WOLF WHO ART MAN--WHILE THOU HAST THE CHANCE!
3

HE FLEES--TO ESCAPE THE PUNISHMENT OF THE DISCORDION! ONCE OUT OF RANGE, NOTHING CAN STOP HIM!
HE SHALL NOT ESCAPE-- WHILE THOR IS STILL MASTER OF THE URU HAMMER!!

HIS SPEED IS BEYOND BELIEF! YET, STILL SHALL MY AVENGING MALLET OVERTAKE HIM!

IT IS AS I FEARED, THUNDER GOD!
ONCE OUT OF RANGE OF MY DISCORDION, HIS POWER HAS RETURNED!
EVEN YOUR ENCHANTED HAMMER CANNOT PENETRATE HIS FIELD OF BASIC MENTAL REPULSION!
SPOK!

IT IS GOOD THAT MY VICTIMS VAINLY ATTEMPT TO SAVE THEMSELVES FROM ME!
THEIR FEEBLE STRUGGLES WILL MAKE MY TRIUMPH ALL THE MORE ENJOYABLE!
NOW I WILL GO--TO CREATE A PLAN FOR OVERWHELMING ALL OF WUNDAGORE-- AND, AFTER THAT--THE WORLD!

NO MERE DOOR CAN RESIST THE THUNDER OF MY HAMMER!
WHEREVER THOU GOEST-- THE SON OF ODIN SHALL OVERTAKE THEE!
THOR HAS SPOKEN!

STOP, THUNDER GOD! EVEN YOU DO NOT YET COMPREHEND THE POWER OF THE MAN-BEAST!
WITH A SINGLE THOUGHT, HE CAN HURL A BARRIER AROUND THE ENTIRE WALL THAT FACES YOU!
A BARRIER! OF WHAT CONCERN CAN THAT BE TO THOR?

DON'T YOU SEE? WE ARE NOT MERELY MENACED BY SOME MIGHTY, SAVAGE CREATURE!
THE MAN-BEAST HAS ATTAINED A COMBINATION OF THE POWER BOTH MAN AND WOLF WILL HAVE--A MILLION YEARS IN THE FUTURE!
HIS INDESCRIBABLE STRENGTH-- HIS KNOWLEDGE OF SCIENCE-- MAKE HIM MORE THAN THE MASTER OF ANY FOE!
NONE IS THE MASTER OF MIGHTY THOR!
YOU THINK NOT? THEN WATCH--AS I THROW THIS SIMPLE OBJECT TOWARDS THE WALL--!
'TIS THE WALL BEHIND WHICH THE MAN-BEAST HIDES!
THOU SPAKE THE TRUTH!
VERILY, HE HATH CREATED AN UNSEEN ANTI-MATTER BARRIER WHICH NO POSITIVE ATOMS CAN HOPE TO PENETRATE!
SSZZT!
HAD YOU ADVANCED TOWARD THAT WALL--THERE IS NO TELLING WHAT FATE MIGHT HAVE BEFALLEN YOU!
BUT, THE WORST IS YET TO BE!
BEHIND THAT WALL IS MY GENETIC LABORATORY--WHICH CONTAINS THE ALL-POWERFUL EVOLUTIONARY RAY! IF HE SHOULD GAIN CONTROL OF THAT RAY--!
HE COULD CREATE HIS OWN RACE OF NEW-MEN--EACH AS SUPREMELY POWERFUL --AS COMPLETELY EVIL-- AS HE HIMSELF!
SUCH AN UNSPEAKABLE ACT MUST NEVER COME TO PASS!
BUT--EVEN NOW--IT MAY BE TOO LATE TO STOP HIM!
IT IS I WHO AM TO BLAME--AND I ALONE!
I TRIED TO TAMPER WITH NATURAL EVOLUTION--TO CREATE A NEW RACE OF SUPER-BEINGS--MY NEW-MEN, AS I CALLED THEM! I WANTED IT TO BE THE BEST OF ALL POSSIBLE WORLDS!
BUT, WITH THE WOLF-- I FAILED!
AND, THAT ONE MONUMENTAL FAILURE THREATENS TO BE THE DEATH KNELL OF THE ENTIRE HUMAN RACE!
THOR! IS IT-- REALLY THAT SERIOUS?
A FORCE HAS BEEN UNLEASHED THIS DAY-- LIKE NONE THE WORLD HAS EVER KNOWN!
5

MEANWHILE, IN THE CELESTIAL REALM OF ASGARD, THE MONARCH OF ALL HE SURVEYS WITNESSES A SPORTING JOUST WITH LESS THAN FEVERISH ENTHUSIASM...
BALDER THE BRAVE DOTH WIELD HIS TRUNCHEON LIKE A WARRIOR BORN, MY LORD!
YOU DO NOT DEIGN TO ANSWER, SIRE! IS SOMETHING AMISS?
NAY! ALL GOES WELL IN THE UNIVERSE ABOUT US!
AND TRULY, BALDER INDEED DOTH BATTLE WITH A SKILL SECOND TO NONE!
STILL, THE HEART OF ODIN IS HEAVY-- AND MY SPIRIT TROUBLED!

I GROW WEARY OF THIS CONTEST! PUT THOU AN END TO IT, NOBLE BALDER!
SKLAN!
AS THOU COMMAND, OMNIPOTENCE!

YON VICTOR AWAITS THY APPROBATION, SIRE!
SIRE? WILT THOU NOT SIGNAL BALDER TO BE AT HIS EASE?
HMMM... WHAT SAYEST THOU?

AHHH, YES-- OF COURSE!
I SALUTE THEE, FRUIT OF ASGARD! THY COURAGE FINDS FAVOR IN THE EYES OF ODIN!
YOU DO ME GREAT HONOR, MY LORD!
IF ONLY MIGHTY THOR WERE HERE! THEN THOU WOULDST SEE A JOUST MOST WORTHY IMPERIAL PRESENCE!

THOR! 'TIS HE DOTH OCCUPY MY THOUGHTS!
I FEEL WITHIN ME A HAUNTING PREMONITION--A FEELING OF DIRE DISASTER WHICH BIDS FAIR TO THREATEN THE GOD OF THUNDER!
6

AND, EVEN AS THE TROUBLED ODIN BROODS DARKLY IN FABLED ASGARD, THE NEW-MEN KNIGHTS OF WUNDAGORE PATROL THEIR MYSTIC MOUNTAIN ON ATOMIC-POWERED STEEDS--

STAND YE BACK, ALL!
NO MATTER WHAT THE RISK, THE GOD OF THUNDER SHALL DESTROY YON MONSTER WHO LURKS WITHIN!
WHATEVER YOU DO, MY DARLING-- TAKE ME WITH YOU! WHETHER YOU FIND TRIUMPH OR TRAGEDY, LET US SHARE IT TOGETHER!
WAIT! THERE IS NO NEED FOR YOU TO GO AFTER HIM--!
I HAVE A BETTER WAY--!

THIS INDUCTION DEVICE CLAMPED MAGNETICALLY TO THE WALL, WILL BRING HIM OUT INTO THE OPEN-- WHERE YOUR HAMMER CAN STRIKE ONCE MORE!
THIS WILL SEND A VIBRA-BEAM THRU THE ENTIRE CASTLE--A BEAM POWERFUL ENOUGH TO CAUSE THE MAN-BEAST TO LEAVE HIS ANTI-MATTER BARRIER AND RACE HERE TO DESTROY IT!
BUT, YOU MUST BE EQUAL TO THE TASK, THUNDER GOD--FOR HE WILL COME TO DESTROY US, AS WELL!

THERE! I'VE DONE NOTHING CAN KEEP HIM FROM US NOW!
JANE! GET THEE TO A PLACE OF SAFETY--A PLACE OF CONCEALMENT!
THOR CANNOT BATTLE SUCCESSFULLY IF HE FEARS FOR THY LIFE!
GO, MY BELOVED--AND REMEMBER--MY HAMMER STRIKES FOR THEE!
THERE! I'VE DONE IT! NOTHING CAN KEEP HIM FROM US NOW!
TSSST

THE FEMALE HAS GONE! NOW YOU ARE FREE TO CONCENTRATE UPON THE COMING ATTACK!
THE MAN-BEAST MAY STRIKE AT ANY TIME--FROM ANYWHERE!!
NO MATTER! THOUGH HE APPEAR FROM ALL DIRECTIONS AT ONCE, STILL SHALL HE FIND THOR AT THE READY!
HARK! FOOTFALLS-- GETTING CLOSER! STAND FAST! OUR TIME IS COME!

WE WERE **TOO LATE!** HE HAS ALREADY **CREATED** AN ARMY OF EVIL **NEW-MEN!**
I HEAR NO **COMMANDS!** HE MUST BE CONTROLLING THEM **MENTALLY**-- FROM AFAR!
WE ARE **LOST,** THUNDER GOD! THE GAME IS **ENDED!**
SAY **NOT** SO! FOR **THOR,** 'TIS JUST **BEGINNING!**
NO MATTER THE ODDS-- NO MATTER THE COST-- **THOR** SHALL FIGHT **ON!**

CONTINUED AFTER NEXT PAGE

MEANWHILE, IN STILL ANOTHER PART OF THE CASTLE--
ATTENTION, KNIGHTS OF WUNDAGORE! BACK INTO THE CASTLE! THE BATTLE IS HERE! WE SHALL FIGHT-- IN THE NAME OF THE HIGH EVOLUTIONARY!
TAGAR! WHAT SHALL I DO? I WAS NOT BRED FOR BATTLE!
NO MATTER, PORGA! THERE ARE ENOUGH OF US WHO WERE!
WAIT, TAGAR! YOU WERE NOT TRAINED FOR COMBAT! YOU HAVE BEEN THE HIGH EVOLUTIONARY'S AMBASSADOR!
I NEED NO TRAINING! MY ANCESTORS LIVED FOR BATTLE! NOW, THE TIME HAS COME FOR ME TO REVERT TO TYPE!

I SHALL DON THE CATHODE GLOVES WHICH WERE GIVEN TO ME WHEN I EMERGED FROM THE GENETIC RAY!
AND NOW-- THE ARMY OF NEW-MEN SHALL STRIKE--FOR THE DEFENSE OF WUNDAGORE!

KNIGHTS OF THE REALM--TO MY SIDE! THE CRISIS IS AT HAND!
THE MAN-BEAST HAS CREATED AN ARMY OF EVIL NEW-MEN! WE MUST CRUSH THEM--OR DIE IN THE ATTEMPT!

THUS, ONE OF THE MOST FANTASTIC BATTLES OF ALL TIME IS BEGUN--BETWEEN TWO OPPOSING FORCES OF UNCANNY NEW-MEN--
FOR THE GLORY OF WUNDAGORE-- ATTACK!!

WITH A DEAFENING DIN THAT SEEMS TO REND THE VERY AIR ABOUT THEM, THE TWO MIGHTY FORCES MEET HEAD-ON IN A CATACLYSMIC CONFRONTATION SUCH AS NO MORTAL EYES HAVE EVER WITNESSED SINCE THE DAWN OF TIME--
THE MAN-BEAST HAS REACHED THE HIGH EVOLUTIONARY!
ONWARD!! TO THE MASTER'S SIDE-- BEFORE IT IS TOO LATE!
11

NONE CAN REACH THE FOE AS QUICKLY AS MIGHTY THOR!
HAH! AND NONE CAN PERISH AS QUICKLY BENEATH THE POWER OF THE MAN-BEAST!

I AM THE CULMINATION OF A MILLION YEARS OF EVOLUTION! I AM TOTALLY SUPREME!
YOU CHALLENGED ME ONCE BEFORE!! YOU SHALL NOT LIVE TO DO SO AGAIN!

YOUR HAMMER WILL NEVER STRIKE ME!
I AM ABOUT TO DISINTEGRATE IT-- WITH ONE SIMPLE, ELEMENTARY MIND BLAST--!

THOUGH YOU SURELY POSSESS THE AWESOME POWERS OF THE DISTANT FUTURE--
THE GOD OF THUNDER DOTH POSSESS THE POWERS OF ALL ETERNITY!

STILL ART THOU NO MORE THAN MORTAL--!
AND STILL AM I SON OF ODIN, PRINCE OF ETERNAL ASGARD!
12

CONTINUED AFTER NEXT PAGE

SECONDS LATER, THE STAR CHAMBER IS ROCKETTED INTO THE VAST ABYSS OF ENDLESS SPACE--
SHOOOM!

THEY WERE NOT TO BLAME FOR WHAT MY MACHINE HAD MADE THEM!
HENCE, IT IS NOT PUNISHMENT THEY NOW RECEIVE--BUT A NEW LEASE ON LIFE!
THEY GO TO A FAR DISTANT GALAXY--WHERE THEY MAY FORM A SOCIETY OF THEIR OWN!
AY! UNINHABITED DROMISANA SHALL MAKE A PERFECT HOME FOR A STRANGE NEW RACE!

AND NOW, I SHALL HAVE NO FURTHER NEED FOR MY PROTECTIVE HELMET!
FOR, I--AND MY KNIGHTS OF WUNDAGORE--MUST SOON DEPART, AS WELL!
THOR! EVERYTHING HAPPENED SO QUICKLY! IS IT--IS IT REALLY OVER?
IT IS ENDED! BUT, STILL THERE IS MUCH TO LEARN!

SHORN OF THY HELMET, THOU ART A NORMAL HUMAN!
YES--I WAS A HUMBLE RESEARCH SCIENTIST--THOSE LONG YEARS AGO--BEFORE IT ALL BEGAN--!

WHILE WORKING IN MY CHOSEN FIELD--THE SCIENCE OF GENETICS--I CREATED THE WORLD'S FIRST GENETIC ACCELERATOR! BUT--MY COLLEAGUES MERELY SCOFFED AT ME--!
IMPOSSIBLE! RIDICULOUS! IT CAN NEVER WORK!
IT'S AN UGLY MOCKERY! NO MAN HAS THE RIGHT TO TAMPER WITH EVOLUTION!

"DETERMINED TO PROVE MY REVOLUTIONARY THEORIES, I SUBJECTED MY PET DALMATION TO THE RAYS OF MY MACHINE--AND THE RESULT WAS A SUCCESS--A TRAGIC SUCCESS--!"
WE THOUGHT IT WAS SOME SORT OF WILD BEAST!
YOU SHOT HIM--YOU FOOLS!
I MUST FIND A PLACE TO WORK--WHERE MY SUBJECTS WILL BE SAFE FROM UNTHINKING BUMBLERS!
14

"WHILE SEARCHING FOR A PROPER SPOT, FATE BESTOWED HER BLESSING UPON ME--I DISCOVERED A LODE OF **URANIUM**, MAKING ME WEALTHY BEYOND MY WILDEST DREAMS--WEALTHY ENOUGH TO CREATE THE PLACE CALLED **WUNDAGORE**!"

"HERE I CREATED MY **NEW-MEN**, MODELING THEM AFTER THE KNIGHTS OF OLD--STRIVING TO TEACH THEM A CODE OF HONOR, AND CHIVALRY!"

"TWO OF MY FIRST--MY MOST TRUSTED **NEW-MEN** WERE **TAGAR**, AND **PORGA**, WHO ACTED AS MY AGENTS, TRAVELLING THE WORLD TO BRING ME INFORMATION AND VITAL SUPPLIES!"

WE NEED ONE TO **TEACH** OUR EVER-INCREASING BAND OF KNIGHT ERRANTS!

YOU WILL SEEK OUT SUCH AN INSTRUCTOR--AND YOU MUST NOT **FAIL**!

OUR **NEW-MEN** MUST BE TAUGHT LANGUAGE, SCIENCE, BIOLOGY, HISTORY--EVEN AS **I** HAVE TAUGHT **YOU**!

IT SHALL BE DONE, MASTER!

'TIS AS I BUT *SUSPECTED!*
ALL OF *WUNDAGORE* WAS NAUGHT BUT A GIANT *SPACE-SHIP* HIDDEN WITHIN AN ALL-CONCEALING PEAK--!
IT'S *TAKING OFF!* BUT-- BUT *WHERE?* WHERE CAN THEY BE *GOING?*
BUHROOOM

NEXT: JANE BECOMES AN IMMORTAL!

TALES OF ASGARD, HOME OF THE MIGHTY NORSE GODS
"THE FIERY BREATH OF FAFNIR!"
VOLSTAGG WAS TO HAVE STOOD GUARD THIS NIGHT... BUT NOW, THE ENORMOUS ONE HAS VANISHED!
THIS DOTH SURELY MEAN THAT THE FORBIDDEN LAND OF NASTROND IS NOT YET FREE OF EVIL! SOMEWHERE A DEADLY DANGER LURKS!
'TIS SURELY WHY IMPERIOUS ODIN HATH DISPATCHED US HENCE! HE DID SURMISE THIS ACCURSED REALM HATH NOT YET BEEN CLEANSED OF EVERY LAST VESTIGE OF LIFE!
NO MATTER! THY HAMMER, HOGUN'S MACE, AND MY OWN FLASHING SWORD SHALL SOON ENOW PUT ALL TO RIGHTS!
EVEN ODIN DID NOT SUSPECT THAT KING FAFNIR WOULD SURVIVE HIS PUNISHMENT... BY BATHING IN THE RAYS OF THE RADIANT POOL!
RAYS WHICH TRANSFORMED ME INTO THE SHAPE OF A DRAGON--- STRONG ENOUGH TO EXACT THE DIRE REVENGE WHICH MUST BE MINE!
PROUDLY PRODUCED BY STAN LEE and JACK KIRBY
DELINEATION: VINCE COLLETTA
LETTERING: SAM ROSEN
AND NOW, PREPARE FOR SPECTACLE BEYOND MORTAL WORDS...

AT LAST!! THE TIME IS COME FOR FAFNIR TO SLAY THE GOLDEN-HAIRED SON OF THE UNSPEAKABLE ODIN!
TO ARMS! A MONSTER STANDS BELOW!
'TWAS HE WHO CAPTURED VOLSTAGG!! 'TIS HE WHO SHALL PAY FOR SO SORRY A DEED!
FAFNIR!! THE ONCE-KING OF NASTROND!! MOST HEARTLESS OF ALL TO WEAR A CROWN
BY SOME STRANGE, EVIL ALCHEMY, HE LIVES... IN THE FORM OF A TOWERING DRAGON!

AND, WHEN THE ENCHANTED MALLET OF THOR FINDS ITS MARK, THE VERY MOUNTAINS OF NASTROND QUAKE FROM THE AWESOME IMPACT..!
THOOM!
EVIL ONE! NO HAND MAY IMPRISON THOR... NO MATTER WHAT ITS SIZE!
NOW, SPEAK YOU... BEFORE MY HAMMER STRIKES AGAIN! WHERE IS VOLSTAGG TO BE FOUND?
WHERE YOU SHALL NEVER FIND HIM!!
THOUGH YOU FREED YOURSELF FROM MY GRASP... STILL DOES CERTAIN DOOM AWAIT YOU!
FOR COUNTLESS CENTURIES HAVE I WAITED... ALONE IN THIS BARREN LAND... WAITED FOR A KIN OF ODIN TO BE MY VICTIM!
TOO LONG HAVE I DREAMED OF THIS MOMENT!! NOW SHALL FAFNIR CLAIM HIS VENGEANCE!
DO THY WORST, KING OF VILLAINY! STILL SHALL THOR DEFY THEE!
HE EXPELS HIS FIERY BREATH... LIKE A LIVING WALL OF FLAME!
WHROOSH!
CONTINUED AFTER NEXT PAGE
3.

HAH! NEVER WAS SUCH A BLOW DELIVERED! THE LEGENDS SHALL TELL HOW ONE SINGLE THRUST LIFTED FAFNIR OFF HIS FEET!

BUT, WHY FROWN YOU NOW, MIGHTY THOR?

'TIS NOT ENOUGH, FANDRAL! THOUGH MY MALLET DOTH RETURN TO ME, FAFNIR IS NOT YET BESTED!... THE BATTLE NOT YET WON!

AND, IN THE GREAT HALL OF THE ROYAL COURT, IN THE IMPERIAL CASTLE OF ODIN, THE MAJESTIC MONARCH OF ALL HE SURVEYS OBSERVES THE FATEFUL BATTLE IN HIS SHIMMERING UNIVERSAL MIRROR...

JUST AS THOU PREDICTED, SIRE! THE FEARSOME FAFNIR STILL LIVES.. IN AN IMPREGNABLE BODY, FASHIONED IN THE SHAPE OF A FIRE-BREATHING DRAGON!

SO BE IT!

NO MATTER WHAT MAY NOW BEFALL... THE FLESH OF MY FLESH SHALL FACE IT AS ONE TO THE MANNER BORN...AS ONLY THE THUNDER GOD CAN!

THE MIGHTY

THOR

APPROVED BY THE COMICS CODE AUTHORITY

MARVEL COMICS GROUP

12¢ IND.

136 JAN

"TO BECOME AN IMMORTAL!"

FEATURING THE UNCANNY MENACE OF HIM... WHO IS UNKNOWN!

THE MIGHTY THOR!
"TO BECOME AN IMMORTAL!"
THE TIME IS COME, BELOVED!
I MUST TAKE THEE--TO ASGARD!
THERE, THOU SHALT STAND BEFORE MY FATHER--THE OMNIPOTENT ODIN--WHO HATH PLEDGED THAT WE MAY BE WED!
WITH YOU BESIDE ME, MY DARLING--I FEAR NOTHING!
--NOT EVEN THE INCREDIBLE PROSPECT OF SEEING--THE HOME OF THE GODS!
ATOP A TOWERING MOUNTAIN PEAK SOMEWHERE IN EUROPE, THE MIGHTY THOR AND LOVELY JANE FOSTER, THE MORTAL WHO HAS WON HIS HEART, PREPARE FOR WHAT IS DESTINED TO BE THE MOST FATEFUL JOURNEY THEY HAVE EVER TAKEN--
A PROUD PHANTASMAGORIA OF PAGEANTRY, PRESENTED BY:
STAN LEE and JACK KIRBY
DELINEATED BY VINCE COLLETTA
LETTERED BY ARTIE SIMEK
AND NOW, BE THOU PREPARED FOR THRILLS AND WONDERMENT BEYOND MORTAL KEN--
1

NEVER AGAIN, MY LOVE, SHALT THOU HAVE CAUSE FOR FEAR!
NEVER AGAIN SHALL THE GOD OF THUNDER FORSAKE THEE!
MY LIFE SHALL BE THINE-- FOREVERMORE!

AND NOW-- PLACE THINE ARMS AROUND ME --SO!
BY THE POWER OF MY ENCHANTED MALLET, WE NOW DEPART THIS MORTAL SPHERE!

LET THINE EYELIDS BE CLOSED, BELOVED--

FOR, WHEN NEXT THEY ARE OPENED--

THEY SHALL BEHOLD THE SIGHT OF ALL SIGHTS--
NOW, JANE FOSTER! NOW SHALT THOU LOOK--
THE COLORS-- THE BRIGHTNESS THE SHEER BEAUTY --IT'S ALMOST UNBEARABLE!

'TIS BUT THE SHIMMERING SPLENDOR OF THE FABLED RAINBOW BRIDGE, UPON WHICH WE DO STAND!
THOR! THAT NOISE! THOSE MEN--!

HAIL TO THEE, MOST NOBLE PRINCE!
HAIL TO THE MIGHTY GOD OF THUNDER!
'TIS BUT THE LOYAL CAVALRY OF ASGARD!
BUT, UPON WHAT MISSION DO THEY RIDE?
WE RIDE INTO BATTLE, O SON OF ODIN!
THE POWERFUL AND SINISTER KINGDOM OF THE TROLLS HATH RISEN AGAINST US!
EVEN NOW THEY DO CHALLENGE THE ROYAL RULE OF THY FATHER-- THE ALL-WISE!
ONWARD-- FOR IMMORTAL ASGARD!
MAKE WAY! WE HAVE CAPTURED A PRISONER--FOR INTERROGATION!
HOW MONSTROUS! THAT UNSPEAKABLE CREATURE-- IS HE-- A TROLL?
DO NOT AVERT THINE EYES, BELOVED!
THOU MUST BECOME ACCUSTOMED TO SUCH SIGHTS--
FOR, WITHIN THIS FABLED REALM, THE FORCE OF EVIL HATH MANY FACES!

SOMEHOW I-- I NEVER THOUGHT IT WOULD BE-- LIKE THIS--!
I GREET THEE, HEIMDALL!
BY RIGHT OF BIRTH DO I CLAIM THY LEAVE TO PASS!

LEAVE GRANTED-- FOR THEE AND THY COMPANION, MIGHTY ONE!
WHA--?!! THAT MAN! THAT SWORD! THAT HORNED HELMET--!

TREMBLE THOU NOT! 'TWAS ONLY HEIMDALL-- MATCHLESS, GRIZZLED GUARDIAN OF BIFROST, THE RAINBOW BRIDGE!
FORGIVE ME, DARLING! IT'S ALL SO NEW-- SO TERRIBLY STARTLING TO ME--!
FORGIVE THEE? ANYTHING THOU WOULDST DO REQUIRES NO FORGIVING, BELOVED!
COULDST I ASK FORGIVENESS OR MY HEART--MY VERY SOUL?

BUT, THE TIME IS COME TO PREPARE THYSELF--
FOR, THE GLORY AND THE GRANDEUR OF ASGARD NOW AWAIT THEE!

EHOLD THE WAR COUNCIL OF REGAL ODIN, WITHIN HIS ROYAL PALACE--!
WE HAVE CHARTED THE TROLL BATTLE-GROUND FOR THY ROYAL OBSERVATION, SIRE!
OUR WARRIORS AWAIT THY SUPREME COMMAND!
ASSEMBLE YE MY LEGIONS AT THE FAR PERIMETER! 'TIS THERE THE FOE IS WEAKEST!
A THOUSAND PARDONS, SIRE!
THE ROYAL DOOR DOTH OPEN BEHIND THEE!
WHO DARES BREACH THE PRIVACY OF IMPERIAL ODIN?!!

HAIL TO THEE, SOVEREIGN MOST SUPREME! HAIL, LORDLY MONARCH OF THE REALM!
THY SON MOST DUTIFUL HATH RETURNED-- TO PRESENT TO THEE --HIS BELOVED!
THOU MAYEST ENTER THE PRESENCE, THUNDER GOD!

ADVANCE, AND BE RECOGNIZED! I WOULDST FAIN SPEAK WITH YON MORTAL FEMALE!

ON EARTH, MY LORD, SHE DOTH POSSESS THE NAME JANE FOSTER!
I--CAN'T BELIEVE IT! I'M ACTUALLY --FACE-TO-FACE--WITH ODIN--THE ALL-FATHER!
FORGIVE ME, SIR--I-I'M AT A LOSS FOR WORDS--!

THOU MUST NOT TREMBLE, MY CHILD!
GIVE ME THY HAND-- THAT I MAY PLACE IT ON MINE!
MAYHAP THOU WILT DRAW CONFIDENCE, AND SERENITY, FROM THE STRENGTH WHICH IS MINE OWN!

MANY DAYS AGO, HONORED FATHER, THOU DIDST AFFIRM THAT WE MIGHT BE WED!
THE WORD OF ODIN IS A BOND ETERNAL!
MORTAL FEMALE --STAND FORTH! I SHALL MAKE THEE RAIMENT FIT FOR A GODDESS!
FOR GODDESS SHALT THOU BE!

SO BE IT!
WHAT-- WHAT HAS HAPPENED TO ME?

'TIS THE MOMENT WE HAVE LONG AWAITED! MY FATHER PREPARES TO MAKE THEE--AN IMMORTAL!
FOR, NONE BUT A TRUE GODDESS MAY WED A GOD!
I HAVE A GIFT TO BESTOW! STAND THEE BACK, FLESH OF MY FLESH!

I GRANT THEE A GIFT WORTHY OF A THUNDER GOD'S BRIDE...
THE ENCHANTED GIFT OF UNLIMITED FLIGHT!
NO LONGER ART THOU EARTHBOUND, JANE FOSTER! THUS SPEAKS ODIN!
I-I'M SOARING --INTO THE SKY!
MERELY THINK OF A DESTINATION --AND THOU SHALT FLY THERE FORTHWITH!
6

AS A CHILD, I OFTEN DAY-DREAMED--THOUGHT HOW WONDERFUL IT WOULD BE TO FLY LIKE A BIRD!
BUT, I NEVER DREAMT IT COULD BE SO TERRIFYING--SUCH AN ALIEN, UNNATURAL SENSATION!
SUDDENLY, THE TENSE, STARTLED GIRL GROWS PANICKY--OVERWHELMED BY HER NEW POWER--UNABLE TO ADJUST TO IT IN TIME--
IT-IT ISN'T POSSIBLE...TO FLY--BY THOUGHT ALONE! WHAT IF SOMETHING GOES WRONG?
WHAT IF--THE POWER VANISHES--?
OHHH!
SHE FALLS! SHE WAS NOT YET READY FOR SUCH A GIFT!

FATHER--BY THY LEAVE--I MUST FLY TO HER SIDE!

MY BREAST IS SORELY TROUBLED!
DOTH MY TRULY BELOVED HAVE SO LITTLE FAITH?
DID SHE DEIGN TO DOUBT THE WORD OF ODIN--THE PLEDGE OF THOR?

MY DARLING! THANK HEAVEN YOU REACHED ME IN TIME!
THOU MUST PUT ASIDE THINE EARTHLY FEARS!
THOU MUST LEARN THE UNQUESTIONING COURAGE OF AN IMMORTAL BORN!
7

SIRE, THE EARTH FEMALE SEEMS TO HAVE LITTLE TASTE FOR IMMORTALITY!
YET, SHE MUST LEARN TO AQUIT HERSELF LIKE A GODDESS! THERE IS NO OTHER WAY!
I SHALL AFFORD HER THE OPPORTUNITY TO MAKE AMENDS FOR WHAT HAS GONE BEFORE--!
SUMMON YE-- THE UNKNOWN!

SIRE! HAST THOU CONSIDERED THE AWESOME CONSEQUENCES?
THE UNKNOWN IS TOO FEAR-SOME--TOO POWERFUL FOR ANY SAVE THEE!
TRUE! BUT GODHOOD IS NOT LIGHTLY WON! LET THE TEST CONTINUE!
BRING THEE FORTH THE UNKNOWN! I HAVE SPOKEN!

SO TOTALLY FEARED-- SO UNIVERSALLY DREADED IS THE UNKNOWN, THAT NONE SAVE ODIN KNOW THE FULL EXTENT OF HIS POWER--
AND, IT HATH BEEN WHISPERED THAT EVEN THE ALL-WISE KNOWETH NOT FROM WHENCE THE MONSTER COMES!

ONLY A SOUND CAN SUMMON THE UNKNOWN!
A SOUND SUCH AS THE ONE WHICH WILL OCCUR WHEN I STRIKE YON ENCHANTED TUNING FORK--!

IT IS DONE!
THYONNNG

THE PULSATING ECHOES FILL MY VERY SOUL WITH DREAD!
I MUST FLEE THIS ACCURSED CHAMBER BEFORE IT IS TOO LATE--BEFORE THE UNKNOWN APPEARS!
8

BY YOUR LEAVE, SIRE --THINE EMISSARY IS TRULY NUMB WITH FEAR! MAY I BRING HIM TO THE CHAMBER OF SILENT REPOSE?
AY! HE HATH FAITHFULLY FULFILLED HIS MACABRE MISSION! AWAY WITH HIM!
NOW, 'TIS TIME FOR THE BELOVED OF THOR TO PROVE WORTHY OF THAT WHICH IS TO BE!
HAVE COURAGE, MY LOVE! WHATEVER BEFALLS THEE, THOU MUST FACE IT LIKE ONE TO THE MANNER BORN!

FACE IT? FACE WHAT??
THOR! DON'T LEAVE ME! I-I'M AFRAID--!
I SHALL NOT BE FAR FROM THEE, BELOVED!
REMEMBER--THY NEWLY-GRANTED POWERS MAY AID THEE IN WHAT IS TO COME!
HAVE THEE FAITH, MY LOVE! THE PRIZE IS WORTH THE RISK!

THE DOOR IS CLOSED BEHIND ME! I'M ALONE-- BUT WHERE? WAIT-- MY EYES ARE ROWING ACCUSTOMED TO THE GLOOM--!
THERE IS-- SOMEONE ELSE HERE! A PRESENCE I CANNOT CLEARLY SEE--BUT, I CAN SENSE ITS MONSTROUS FORM!

IT'S DRAWING CLOSER--CLOSER-- I CAN HEAR IT BREATHING--HEAR ITS HEAVY LUMBERING FOOTFALLS--!

AND THEN, THE DESPERATE EARTH GIRL SEES--
A HAND-- FROM OUT OF SOME UNSPEAKABLE NIGHTMARE--!

IN HER PANIC--HER NAMELESS, INDESCRIBABLE FEAR--THE HAPLESS GIRL FORGETS HER POWER OF FLIGHT --FORGETS HER PURPOSE IN THE GRIM RITUAL--FORGETS ALL, SAVE THE NAME OF--
THOR! THOR-- HELP ME, MY DARLING-- THOR!
9

BUT THEN, BEFORE ANOTHER WORD CAN BE UTTERED--BEFORE ANOTHER MOVE CAN BE MADE--THE MYSTERIOUS, INDESCRIBABLE UNKNOWN STRIKES--!

HE IS GONE! THE FURY OF MY MALLET HATH DRIVEN HIM BEYOND THIS IMMORTAL SPHERE!
I MUST GET OUT! I MUST LEAVE--RUN AWAY--ESCAPE THIS WORLD OF FEAR AND MADNESS!
I CAN STAND NO MORE! IF I STAY --I'LL GO MAD!

OMNIPOTENT ONE! WITH ALL DUE RESPECT, ART THOU NOT CAUSING JANE FOSTER TO UNDERGO MORE THAN MORTAL FEMALE CAN ENDURE?
I SAY THEE NAY! IF THOU WOULDST HAVE HER A GODDESS BE, THEN A GODDESS' HEART MUST SHE POSSESS!

HAST THOU SO SOON FORGOTTEN?
ON FEAR DOTH THE UNKNOWN FEED! IT IS FOR THAT REASON HE HATH NEVER INVADED THE GOLDEN REALM--
FOR THE GODS OF ASGARD KNOW NOT THE MEANING OF FEAR!

BUT--HEAR ME, FATHER! SHE IS NO WARRIOR! SHE IS NO VALKYRIE BORN! SHE IS BUT MY BELOVED--GENTLE--AND KIND--AND TRUE!
IS THERE NO PLACE FOR ONE SUCH AS SHE IN THE HOME OF THE GODS??
NO! DON'T ASK HIM! I DON'T WANT IT! I WON'T BE A GODDESS I WON'T STAY IN ASGARD!
IT'S TOO HORRIBLE! TOO UNENDURABLE! DON'T YOU REALIZE HOW MAD IT IS?!!

SHE HATH MORE WISDOM THAN THEE, MY SON! THOUGH ASGARD BE HEAVEN ENOW--HER PLACE IS ON EARTH--BELOW!
NO, FATHER--
NO!

I HAVE SPOKEN!

'TIS CLEAR TO ME NOW! THOU DIDST PLAN THE ENTIRE THING!
IT WAS NEVER INTENDED THAT JANE FOSTER SHOULD BECOME AN IMMORTAL!
STAND THEE BACK, THUNDER GOD! NONE MAY APPROACH THE PRESENCE IN ANGER!
LET HIM BE! MY SON HATH THE RIGHT!
MOST NOBLE THOR-- I UNDERSTAND THY RAGE, THY DISAPPOINTMENT --BUT, 'TIS NOT AS THOU HAST STATED!

MY HEART DOTH GRIEVE FOR THEE! BUT, THOU MUST ENDURE THIS HAPPENSTANCE IN GODLY MANNER!
I SHALL ENDURE NOTHING! I SHALL FOLLOW HER--!
WHAT?!! YOU DARE DISPUTE THE WILL OF ODIN!

THOUGH MY MERCY BE WITHOUT PEER--KNOW YOU MY WRATH IS ALL-CONSUMING!

THOU BE THE SON OF MY HEART--THE FLESH OF MY FLESH!
THOU ART BRAVEST --MOST FAITHFUL-- MOST HEROIC IN ALL THE COSMOS!
BUT STILL AM I LORD ODIN! STILL IS MY WORD SUPREME-- MY WILL UNQUESTIONED!

NOW RISE, GOD OF THUNDER! IN THY HEART OF HEARTS THOU KNOWEST GODHOOD WAS NOT FOR ONE SUCH AS SHE!
STILL DO I LOVE HER, MY FATHER! THOUGH SHE BE FRAIL, AND WEAK--HAVE I NOT STRENGTH ENOW FOR THE TWO?

MY POWER IS BEYOND ALL MEASURE--BEYOND ALL COMPREHENSION--AND YET, I CANNOT ALTER AN EMOTION OF THE HEART!
BUT, WE SHALL SPEAK OF THIS NO MORE!
SINCE THE UNKNOWN IS NOW AT LARGE, I ORDER THEE TO GUNDERSHELM, TO GUARD THE GLADE OF CRYSTALS FROM HIS ATTACK!
'TIS JUST AS WELL! IF FORTUNE LOOKS UPON ME WITH FAVOR, MAYHAP I SHALL FALL IN BATTLE!

WONDROUS IS THE POWER OF ODIN! NO SOONER DO I RAISE MY HEAD, THAN I AM IN THE LAND OF GUNDERSHELM--
ONLY HERE, AT THE EDGE OF THE GLADE OF CRYSTALS, CAN THE UNKNOWN ENTER ASGARD!
I MUST DEVOTE MYSELF TO MY TASK WITH A MIGHTY VENGEANCE--!
FOR, IF I SHOULD DWELL UPON WHAT HATH BEFALLEN, THEN SURELY SHALL I LOSE THE VERY WILL TO LIVE!

NO! THERE IS ONLY ONE REMEDY! ONLY ONE BALM FOR MY ACHING HEART!
I MUST HURL MYSELF INTO BATTLE--FIGHT AS NEVER-BEFORE--FIGHT AS ONLY THE GOD OF THUNDER CAN!
TLANNNG!
THAT SOUND! THE CRYSTALS RING! 'TIS THE OMINOUS NOTE WHICH HATH THE POWER TO SUMMON--THE OUTSIDER!

AN EVIL TROLL! 'TIS THOU WHO HAST DARED GIVE THE FORBIDDEN SIGNAL!
TLANNG
IT IS DONE! NOT EVEN THE HAMMER OF THOR CAN STOP HIM NOW!

AND, EVEN AS MIGHTY THOR HEARS THE THUNDEROUS APPROACH OF THE UNKNOWN, A MYSTIFIED JANE FOSTER FINDS HERSELF IN A BUSTLING HOSPITAL CORRIDOR, SOMEWHERE ON THE WEST COAST--
STRANGE--I SEEM TO HAVE FORGOTTEN WHY I CAME HERE!
AND YET, I KNOW THAT THIS IS WHERE I BELONG! I FEEL AS THOUGH FATE IS GUIDING MY FOOTSTEPS!
YOUNG LADY--!

ARE YOU THE NEW RESIDENT NURSE WHO WAS DUE TO ARRIVE TODAY?
ALL OF A SUDDEN IT'S CRYSTAL CLEAR TO ME! HOW FOOLISH I WAS TO HAVE FORGOTTEN!
WHY YES, I AM! MY NAME IS JANE FOSTER! I HOPE I'M NOT TOO LATE!
NO--YOU'RE RIGHT ON TIME, MY DEAR!

DR. BENEDICT, THIS IS NURSE FOSTER--OUR NEW RESIDENT!
THANK YOU, NURSE PARKWELL!
I FEEL SO--SECURE! AS IF--I'VE COME HOME--AT LAST!
PLEASE COME IN, YOUNG LADY!

I'M DR. KINCAID! IT'S MY CUSTOM TO WELCOME THE NEW NURSES AND EXPLAIN THEIR DUTIES TO THEM!
HE'S SO--HANDSOME! I FEEL AS THOUGH I'VE--KNOWN HIM--BEFORE!
OR--IS IT JUST THAT I'VE SEEN HIM SO OFTEN--IN MY DREAMS?
I HOPE YOU WILL BE HAPPY HERE WITH US, NURSE FOSTER!
OH, I WILL, DOCTOR! I JUST KNOW I WILL!

THUS, WE BID ADIEU TO LOVELY JANE FOSTER, THE MORTAL GIRL WHOM ODIN, IN HIS INFINITE WISDOM, HAS GIVEN A SECOND CHANCE AT LIFE--AND LOVE--AND ULTIMATE HAPPINESS!
BUT, WHAT OF THE HEART-SICK THUNDER GOD? LET US RETURN TO THE BATTLING THOR, AS HE WHEELS ABOUT TO CHALLENGE--THE UNKNOWN--!
BACK, THOU NAMELESS SOULLESS THING OF EVIL! BACK, TO THE STYGIAN NOWHERE FROM WHENCE THOU CAME!

BUT, THE UNKNOWN HAS STRENGTH BEYOND MEASURE IN HIS MANY GRAPPLING ARMS--
--AND, THE GOD OF THUNDER, WITH A SOUL TURNED TO ASHES, FIGHTS LIKE A MAN IN A TRANCE--
HE TURNS ASIDE MY BLOWS AS THOUGH THEY BE WEIGHTLESS!

BUT, HE DOTH STRIKE AT ME WITH A FORCE BEYOND COMPREHENSION--
STAM!

HE FEELS DEFEAT IS COME! HE GIRDS HIMSELF --FOR THE FINAL KILL!
IF THIS THEN IS THE END WHICH FATE HATH ORDAINED FOR THE LUCKLESS THOR--SO BE IT!

SUDDENLY, AS THE GOLDEN-HAIRED GLADIATOR--SEEMINGLY LACKING THE WILL TO FIGHT ON--WATCHES HIS FOE WITH HYPNOTIC FASCINATION, ANOTHER ARM IS RAISED AGAINST THE UNKNOWN--
RISE AND FIGHT, THUNDER GOD!
CLLANNG!

FIGHT, SON OF ODIN! FIGHT, AS YOU HAVE FOUGHT SO GALLANTLY IN DAYS OF YORE!
FOR, IF YOU SHOULD FAIL NOW--THEN MY LIFE, TOO, IS SURELY FORFEIT!
I SAY THEE NAY! NONE OTHER SHALL PERISH THRU FAULT OF THOR!

THEN, WITH A BLOOD-CURDLING BATTLE CRY RINGING FROM HIS LIPS, THE MIGHTIEST WARRIOR OF ALL TIME ONCE AGAIN ENTERS THE FRAY-- HIS SMASHING HAMMER DRIVING THE UNKNOWN BACK AS DAYLIGHT SHATTERS THE GLOOM OF NIGHT--!
THOOM!
CLANG!

FINALLY, WHEN THE HAZE OF WHITE-HOT FURY CLEARS FROM THE TORTURED BRAIN OF THE IMMORTAL AVENGER, HIS STEELY-BLUE EYES BLINK IN ASTONISHMENT--FOR, THE UNKNOWN IS--GONE!
HE HATH BEEN VANQUISHED!
THOUGH I HAVE HEARD OF YOUR PROWESS SINCE MY BIRTH--NEVER HAVE I BEHELD SO MAGNIFICENT A SIGHT AS--THOR IN BATTLE!
BUT, WHAT OF MY NEW-FOUND ALLY?
LET ME NOW BEHOLD THE ONE WHOSE BLADE HATH BEEN UNSHEATHED IN THOR'S BEHALF!

BY THE BRISTLING BEARD OF ODIN--'TIS A FEMALE! --SO BEAUTEOUS AS TO STAGGER EVEN A GOD!
ART THOU TRULY REAL--OR MERELY A VISION OF LOVELINESS, CONJURED IN DESPERATION BY THE AGONY OF A BREAKING HEART?
YOU KNEW ME ONCE, MANY YEARS AGO!
--AS TODAY YOU KNOW MY BROTHER--THE EVER-FAITHFUL HEIMDALL!
CAN IT BE--? THOU ART SIF! THE RAVEN-TRESSED CHILD WHOM ONCE I DANGLED UPON MY KNEE!
BUT, BY MY MALLET--THOU ART CHILD NO LONGER!

AS A YOUNG GIRL--SILENTLY WATCHING YOU GALLOP INTO BATTLE, I HAVE LOVED YOU, SON OF ODIN! I HAVE LOVED YOUR SPIRIT, YOUR STRENGTH--YOUR MATCHLESS COURAGE--AS ONLY A CHILD CAN LOVE!
BUT, NOW YOU HAVE CHANGED! AN AURA OF SORROW PERVADES YOUR MANNER--!
AY! EVEN A GOD MAY KNOW THE PANGS OF DESPAIR!

SIF, TOO, HAS BEEN NO STRANGER TO HEART-BREAK! EVER SINCE CHILDHOOD HAVE I SUFFERED THE ACHE OF LOVE UNREQUITED!
--A HOPELESS LOVE--FOR ONE WHO EVER HAD EYES FOR ANOTHER--ONE TO WHOM SIF WAS NAUGHT BUT A FORGOTTEN MEMORY!
MINE EARS HEAR THY WORDS--BUT MY HEART CANNOT BELIEVE THAT ANY COULDST FORGET ONE SUCH AS THEE!

THOU ART FAIR BEYOND MEASURE --VALIANT AS ONLY A GODDESS CAN BE--AND I, LOVELY SIF, HAVE BEEN BLINDEST OF ALL WHO DWELL IN THE GOLDEN REALM!
VERILY, THOU HAST RESTORED THE LUST FOR LIFE TO THE SMOLDERING SOUL OF AN ERRANT THUNDER GOD!
AND YOU, MY LORD, HAVE REKINDLED AN EMOTION I FEARED HAD BEEN LOST TO ME FOREVER!
16
THEN, AS MIGHTY THOR AND THE STUNNING SIF TURN AND WALK INTO THE GATHERING TWILIGHT...
IN THINE INFINITE WISDOM, SIRE, THOU HAST THIS DAY PERFORMED A SEEMING MIRACLE!
NAY, NOT SO! I DID BUT PROVIDE THE TIME--THE SETTING--

BUT, ONLY IN THE HEART CAN BE FOUND THE FINAL, ENCHANTED INGREDIENT--MEN CALL LOVE!
AND SO SAY WE ALL!

TALES OF ASGARD, HOME OF THE MIGHTY NORSE GODS
"THERE SHALL COME A MIRACLE!"
AT THE ROYAL COURT OF ASGARD, ETERNAL DOMAIN OF HIM WHO IS THE POWER... WHO IS THE JUDGEMENT... HIM WHO IS NOW AND EVERMORE ODIN, THE ALL-WISE... THE MOST AWESOMELY HEEDED VOICE IN ALL THE COSMOS SHATTERS THE SILENCE, AND ANOTHER TALE BEGINS...
EVIL FAFNIR, DEPOSED KING OF NASTROND, WHOM I SENTENCED TO DEATH AGES AGO, STILL LIVES--- IN THE FORM OF YONDER DRAGON!
BUT, EVEN WHILST WE WATCH, THE TRUE SON OF MY HEART... MIGHTY THOR... AND HIS MOST NOBLE COMPANIONS, SHALL VANQUISH FAFNIR FORE'ER!
SUCH IS THE PRONOUNCEMENT OF ODIN, THY RIGHTFUL LIEGE O. ALL THE REALM!
GARNISHED WITH GLORY IN THE MARVEL TRADITION BY:
STAN LEE and JACK KIRBY
DELINEATED BY: Vince COLLETTA • LETTERED BY: Sam ROSEN

AND, EVEN AS THE STAGGERING TABLEAU UNFOLDS UPON THE ETERNA-SCREEN OF THE CASTLE ROYAL...

SKRAK!

NOW AT LAST MY VENGEANCE IS AT HAND! NOW AT LAST THE SON OF ODIN DIES!

HE DOTH TEAR ASUNDER THE MOUNTAINS BEFORE HIM WITH A STRENGTH UNSURPASSED BY ANY WHO LIVE!

FANDRAL! HOGUN! STAND YE BACK!
CERTAIN DEATH AWAITS US IF THE VILE FAFNIR BE NOT SPEEDILY DESTROYED!
ONLY THE POUNDING POWER OF MY ENCHANTED HAMMER MAY YET PREVAIL....!

LET THE GROUND BELOW ME SHATTER!! LET THE SKIES ABOVE BE RENT ASUNDER!!
LET THE FURY OF THE STORM, THE DEADLY STING OF LIGHTNING, STRIKE..AS COMMANDS THE GOD OF THUNDER!
FTOOOM!

NEVER WITHIN MEMORY OF MAN OR IMMORTAL HAS SUCH A STORM BEEN UNLEASHED WITHIN THE KNOWN COSMOS! FROM EVERY PART OF THE SKY ABOVE, POTENT FINGERS OF FLASHING LIGHTNING LASH OUT AT THE STARTLED, UNCOMPREHENDING FAFNIR...
ZZZT!

UNTIL, AT LAST, AS THOUGH THE GROUND ITSELF CAN NO LONGER BEAR THE AWESOME ASSAULT, A GIGANTIC CHASM YAWNS BENEATH THE HELPLESS FEET OF THE DRAGON...THE DRAGON WHICH ONCE HAD BEEN---A MAN!
CRAKKK!
3.

THE DRAGON IS VANQUISHED!!
BUT, WHAT OF THE MISSING VOLSTAGG?
WITHIN THE MOUNTAIN CAVE YONDER... A BELLOW ISSUES FORTH... AS FROM A BRAYING MULE IN DIREST PAIN!
NAY! NO MERE BEAST OF BURDEN WAS EVER CURSED WITH SUCH A VOICE!
IF THEN HE BE NOT BEAST, ONE ANSWER... AND ONE ALONE DOTH REMAIN...

...'TIS THE VOLUMINOUS VOLSTAGG... VERITABLY IMPRISONED WITHIN A CAGE OF ROUGH-HEWN STONE...!
THOR! HOGUN! FANDRAL! BE OF STOUT HEART, ONE AND ALL!
THE UNMATCHED STRENGTH OF VOLSTAGG SOON SHALL SHATTER YON IGNOBLE CAGE, AND I SHALL RESCUE THEE FORTHWITH!

THINE INTENTIONS WARM THE VERY COCKLES OF OUR HEARTS, MOST VOLUBLE ONE...
STILL, SINCE TIME BE OF THE ESSENCE...
I SHALL AID THEE IN THY NOBLE ENDEAVOR!
HOW NOW?!! TO SPEAK SO OF GIVING AID TO VOLSTAGG IS AKIN TO GIVING THE PEA-COCK AN EXTRA FEATHER... THE PORCUPINE AN EXTRA QUILL!

SHIELD THY FACE AND CLOSE THY MOUTH, MOUNTAINOUS FRIEND...
THOUGH, FOR THEE, THE LATTER MAY BE WELL NIGH IMPOSSIBLE!
BTOW!
4

WITHIN A MATTER OF FLEET SECONDS, THE FABLED QUARTET, MOUNTED ONCE MORE, GALLOPS BEYOND THE BORDERS OF THE LAND OF NASTROND... A LAND STILL WRACKED BY STORM AND SEARED BY FLASHING FLAME..!
OUR TASK IS ENDED! NOW, NAUGHT BUT THE PROMISED MIRACLE REMAINS!
OF WHAT MANNER OF MIRACLE HAST THOU BEEN FORETOLD?
I KNOW NOT ITS NATURE... BUT THE SACRED WORD OF ODIN HATH BEEN SO PLEDGED!

'TIS DONE, MY LORD!
YET, MINE EYES DO NOT PERCEIVE THE MIRACLE OF WHICH THOU HAST SPOKEN!
THINE EYES ARE WITNESS TO IT EVEN NOW!
'TIS THE VERY SIGHT THOU DOEST GAZE UPON!

NEVER BEFORE HATH A BLESSED BLANKET OF RAIN SO CARESSED THE BARREN WASTELAND OF NASTROND!
RAIN... WHICH IS TRULY THE HARBINGER OF LIFE... THE PROMISE OF THE NEW DAY WHICH IS YET TO BE!

AND, IN TIME TO COME, THE SOIL SHALL TURN GREEN ONCE MORE... THE GRASS SHALL GROW, AND PLANTS SHALL SPROUT ABOVE THE PLACE WHERE FAFNIR FELL! FOR, SUCH IS THE WAY OF LIFE... LIFE UNIVERSAL... WHICH CAN NEVER VANISH WHILST FAITH ENDURES!
NEXT ISSUE:
"A GRIM SECRET HATH HOGUN!"